Rendering for Beginners

Image synthesis using RenderMan

Saty Raghavachary

AMSTERDAM • BOSTON • HEIDELBERG • LONDON • NEW YORK • OXFORD
PARIS • SAN DIEGO • SAN FRANCISCO • SINGAPORE • SYDNEY • TOKYO

Focal Press is an imprint of Elsevier

Focal Press
An imprint of Elsevier
Linacre House, Jordan Hill, Oxford OX2 8DP
30 Corporate Drive, Burlington MA 01803

First published 2005

British Library Cataloguing in Publication Data
A catalogue record for this book is available from the British Library

Library of Congress Cataloguing in Publication Data
A catalogue record for this book is available from the Library of Congress

ISBN   0 240 51935 3

For information on all Focal Press publications visit our website at:
www.focalpress.com

Printed and bound in Italy

Contents

Preface v

Acknowledgments xi

1 Rendering 1
   1.1 Artistic rendering 1
   1.2 Computer graphical image synthesis 2
   1.3 Representational styles 5
   1.4 How a renderer works 14
   1.5 Origins of 3D graphics, future directions 23

2 RenderMan 25
   2.1 History, origins 25
   2.2 Interface, implementations 27
   2.3 How PRMan works 32

3 RIB syntax 39
   3.1 Standards, interfaces and protocols 39
   3.2 Formats for graphics description 39
   3.3 RIB structure 53

4 Geometric primitives 73
   4.1 Surfaces 73
   4.2 Points 73
   4.3 Curves 76
   4.4 Polygons 88
   4.5 Polygonal meshes 94
   4.6 Subdivision surfaces 100
   4.7 Patches 105
   4.8 Spheres 127
   4.9 Cylinders 128
   4.10 Cones 129
   4.11 Tori 129
   4.12 Hyperboloids 130
   4.13 Paraboloids 131
   4.14 Disks 133
   4.15 Blobbies 133
   4.16 Constructive Solid Geometry (CSG) 138
   4.17 Procedurals 143
   4.18 Instancing 146
   4.19 Reference geometry 148
   4.20 Handedness, sides 150

5 Transformations 157
   5.1 Coordinate systems 157
   5.2 Translation 158
   5.3 Scale 161
   5.4 Rotation 164
   5.5 Perspective 167

5.6   Skew   168
5.7   Rotation, scale   171
5.8   Translation, scale   174
5.9   Rotation, translation   177
5.10   Rotation, scale, translation   183
5.11   Concatenating transforms   187
5.12   Transformation hierarchies   190
5.13   Custom spaces   198

6   Camera, output   201
6.1   Proxy viewpoints   201
6.2   Camera angles, moves   202
6.3   Camera artifacts   210
6.4   Output: frame   218
6.5   Output: channels   224
6.6   Fun with cameras   234

7   Controls   239
7.1   Tradeoffs in rendering   239
7.2   Image-related controls   239
7.3   Object-related controls   249
7.4   REYES-related controls   254
7.5   Miscellaneous controls   258

8   Shading   261
8.1   Introduction   261
8.2   Using light shaders   264
8.3   Using other shaders   273
8.4   The RenderMan Shading Language (RSL)   280
8.5   Surface shaders   285
8.6   Displacement shaders   315
8.7   Light shaders   320
8.8   Volume shaders   329
8.9   Imager shaders   333
8.10   Global illumination   336
8.11   Non-photoreal rendering   344
8.12   Wrapup   352

9   What's next?   355
9.1   Next steps for you   355
9.2   PRMan advances   356
9.3   Future directions for rendering   356

10   Resources   361
10.1   Books and papers   361
10.2   Courses   362
10.3   Web sites   363
10.4   Forums   363
10.5   Software documentation   364
10.6   Miscellaneous   364

Index   365

Preface

This is an introductory-level book on RenderMan, which since its inception in the 1980s has continued to set the standard for the creation of high quality 3D graphics imagery.

Structure and organization of contents

The book explores various facets of RenderMan, using small self-contained RIB (scene-description) files and associated programs called "shaders".

There are three threads interwoven throughout the book. First, 3D graphics rendering concepts are thoroughly explained and illustrated, for the sake of readers new to the field. Second, rendering using RenderMan is explored via RIB files and shaders. This is the main focus of the book, so nearly every chapter is filled with short examples which you can reproduce on your own, tinker with and learn from. Third, several of the examples present unusual applications of RenderMan, taken from the areas of recreational mathematics (a favorite hobby of mine), non-photoreal rendering, image-processing, etc. Take a quick look at the images in the book to see what I mean. I also use these examples to provide short digressions on unusual geometric shapes, pretty patterns and optical phenomena.

Here is how the book is organized:

- Part I consists of chapters 1, 2 and 3 that talk about the 3D graphics pipeline, RenderMan and RenderMan's scene description format called RIB (RenderMan Interface Bytestream).

- Part II is made up of chapters 4 and 5. Here we cover RenderMan's geometry generation features and transformations.

- Part III comprises chapters 6, 7 and 8. Chapter 6 covers the basics of manipulating cameras and obtaining output. Chapter 7 explains ways in which you can control RenderMan's execution. Chapter 8 is about coloring, lighting and texturing, topics collectively referred to as "shading".

- Part IV (chapters 9 and 10) wraps things up by offering you suggestions on what to do next with RenderMan and listing resources to explore.

A different way to present the materials in this book might have been to classify them along the lines of Hollywood's "lights/camera/action/script". Chapter 9, "What's next?", lists an alternate table of contents based on such an organization.

Who the book is for

You'd find the book useful if you are one or more of the following:

- new to computer graphics, wanting to get started on 3D graphics image synthesis ("rendering") and RenderMan in particular

- a student enrolled in a course on rendering/RenderMan

- a Technical Director (TD) in a CG production studio, interested in shader writing. Note however that this book does not discuss third-party scene translators (e.g. MTOR or MayaMan for Maya) that automatically generate RIB output and shaders from 3D animation packages – instead it uses self-contained example RIB files and shaders that are independent of 3D modeling/animation programs.

- a 2D artist working with Photoshop, Flame etc. and want to make the transition to 3D rendering

- a computer artist interested in procedural art creation and painterly rendering

- a recreational mathematician looking for ways to generate high quality imagery of shapes and patterns

- a hobbyist animator looking to create high quality animations from 3D scene descriptions

- a software developer interested in shape/pattern/shading synthesis

- someone who wants a comprehensive non-technical coverage of the RenderMan feature set (e.g. a supervisor or production assistant in a graphics/animation studio)

- interested in RenderMan for its own sake (a "RenderManiac")

Software requirements

The following are PC-centric requirements, but you should be able to find equivalents for other machines.

Pixar's RenderMan (PRMan) is predominantly used to illustrate the concepts in the book, so ideally you would have access to a copy of it. If not, you can still run many of the book's examples on alternate RenderMan implementations, including freeware/shareware ones. Please see the book's "RfB" website (**http://www.smartcg.com/tech/cg/books/RfB**) for up-to-date links to such alternate RenderMan implementations.

The RfB site contains all the scene files (RIB files), associated programs (shaders) and images (textures, etc.) required for you to recreate the examples in each chapter. Feel free to download, study, modify and thus learn from them. A text editor (such as Notepad or WordPad) is required to make changes to RIB files and to create/edit shader files. A programmers' editor such as "emacs" or "vi" is even better if you are familiar with their usage.

While it is possible to get by with a Windows Explorer type of file navigation program to organize and locate materials downloaded from the RfB site, it is tedious to use the Explorer interface to execute commands related to RenderMan. So I highly recommend that you download and install "cygwin" (see the RfB site for link and set up help) which comes with "bash", a very useful command-line shell which makes it easier to move around your file-system and to run RenderMan-related and other commands.

How to use the book

Depending on your focus, there are several ways you can go through this book:

- if you want an executive summary of RenderMan, just read the opening paragraphs of the chapters

- for a more detailed introduction read the whole book, preferably sequentially

- browse through selected chapters (e.g. on shader writing or cameras) that contain specific information you want

- simply browse through the images to get ideas for creating your own

While you could do any of the above, if you are a beginner, you will derive maximum benefit from this book if you methodically work through it from start to end. As mentioned earlier, all the RIB files, shaders and associated files you would need to recreate the examples in the chapters are available at the RfB site. The site layout mirrors the way chapters are presented in the book so you should be able to quickly locate the materials you want.

Download the files, examine and modify them, re-render and study the images to learn what the modifications do. This coupled with the descriptions of the syntax that the book provides is a good way to learn how RenderMan "works".

Here is a quick example. The "teapot" RIB listing below produces Figure P.1. RIB consists of a series of commands which collectively describe a scene. Looking at the listing, you can infer that we are describing a surface (a teapot) in terms of primitives such as cylinders. The description uses RIB syntax (explained in detail throughout the book). RenderMan accepts such a RIB description to produce (render) the image in Figure P.1.

```
# The following describes a simple "scene". The overall idea is
# to encode a scene using RIB and then hand it to RenderMan to
# create an image using it.

teapot.rib
# Author: Scott Iverson <jsiverso@midway.uchicago.edu>
# Date: 6/7/95
#

Display "teapot.tiff" "framebuffer" "rgb"
Format 900 600 1
Projection "perspective" "fov" 30

Translate 0 0 25
Rotate -22 1 0 0
Rotate 19 0 1 0
Translate 0 -3 0

WorldBegin

LightSource "ambientlight" 1 "intensity" .4
LightSource "distantlight" 2 "intensity" .6 "from" [-4 6 -7] "to" [0
0 0]  "lightcolor" [1.0 0.4 1.0]
LightSource "distantlight" 3 "intensity" .36 "from" [14 6 7] "to" [0
-2 0] "lightcolor" [0.0 1.0 1.0]

Surface "plastic"
Color [1 .6 1]

# spout
AttributeBegin
    Sides 2
    Translate 3 1.3 0
    Rotate 30 0 0 1
    Rotate 90 0 1 0
    Hyperboloid  1.2 0 0 .4 0 5.7  360
AttributeEnd
```

```
# handle
AttributeBegin
    Translate -4.3 4.2 0
    TransformBegin
        Rotate 180 0 0 1
        Torus 2.9 .26 0 360 90
    TransformEnd
    TransformBegin
        Translate -2.38 0 0
        Rotate 90 0 0 1
        Torus 0.52 .26 0 360 90
    TransformEnd
    Translate -2.38 0.52 0
    Rotate 90 0 1 0
    Cylinder .26 0 3.3 360
AttributeEnd

# body
AttributeBegin
    Rotate -90 1 0 0
    TransformBegin
        Translate 0 0 1.7
        Scale 1 1 1.05468457
        Sphere 5 0 3.12897569 360
    TransformEnd
    TransformBegin
        Translate 0 0 1.7
        Scale 1 1 0.463713017
        Sphere 5 -3.66606055 0 360
    TransformEnd
AttributeEnd

# top
AttributeBegin
    Rotate -90 1 0 0
    Translate 0 0 5
    AttributeBegin
        Scale 1 1 0.2051282
        Sphere 3.9 0 3.9 360
    AttributeEnd
    Translate 0 0 .8
    AttributeBegin
        Orientation "rh"
        Sides 2
        Torus 0.75 0.45 90 180 360
    AttributeEnd
    Translate 0 0 0.675
    Torus 0.75 0.225 -90 90 360
    Disk 0.225 0.75 360
AttributeEnd

WorldEnd
```

Figure P.1 *Rendered teapot, with a narrow field of view to frame the object*

Now what happens when we change the Projection command (near the top of the listing) from

```
Projection "perspective" "fov" 30
```

to

```
Projection "perspective" "fov" 60
```

and re-render? The new result is shown in Figure P.2. What we did was to increase the field-of-view (which is what the "fov" stands for) from 30 to 60 degrees, and you can see that the image framing did "widen". The descriptive names of several other commands (e.g. Color, Translate) in the RIB stream encourage similar experimentation with their values. This book contains numerous RIB and shader examples in chapters 4 through 8, and you are invited to download, study and modify them as you follow along with the text. Doing so will give you a first-hand feel for how RenderMan renders images.

Figure P.2 *Same teapot as before but rendered with a wider field of view*

As mentioned before, the RfB site also has detailed instructions on how to get set up with "bash" to help you get the most use of RIB files and shaders. In addition there is also help on rendering RIB files using a few different implementations of RenderMan available to you. If you need more information on any of this you can feel free to email me at **saty@smartcg.com**.

About the image on the front cover

The cover shows a rendered image of the classic "tri-bar impossible object". As you can see such an arrangement of cubes would be impossible to construct in the real world – the tri-bar is just an optical illusion. Figure P.3 shows how the illusion is put together. The cubes are laid out along three line segments that are perpendicular. One of the cubes has parts of two faces cut away to make it look like the three line segments form a triangle backbone when viewed from one specific orientation. Viewing from any other orientation gives the illusion away. The RIB files for the figure on the cover as well as for Figure P.3 are online, so you too can render them yourself. I chose the illusory image of an impossible tri-bar for the cover to underscore the fact that all rendering is ultimately an illusion. You can find a variety of such optical illusions in a book by Bruno Ernst called *Adventures with Impossible Objects*.

Figure P.3 *Illusion exposed! Notice the "trick" cube along the column on the right*

Acknowledgments

Several people were instrumental in making this book come together. The editorial team at Focal Press did a stellar job of guiding the whole production. Thanks to Marie Hooper for getting the effort started. Throughout the writing process, Georgia Kennedy was there to help, with patient encouragement and words of advice. Thanks also to Christina Donaldson and Margaret Denley for top notch assistance towards the end.

I am grateful to Prof. John Finnegan for his technical feedback. His comments were extremely valuable in improving the accuracy of the material and making it read better. If there are errors that remain in the text, I take sole responsibility for them.

Thanks to my wife Sharon for her love, patience and encouragement. Writing a book is sometimes compared to giving birth. Sharon recently did it for real, bringing our delightful twins Becky and Josh into the world. Caring for two infants takes a lot of time and effort, but she managed to regularly free up time for me to work on the book. Our nanny Priscilla Balladares also deserves thanks for helping out with this.

My parents and in-laws Peg, Dennis, Marlene and Dennie helped by being there for moral support and asking "Is it done yet?" every time we spoke on the phone.

I would also specifically like to acknowledge the support of my close friend and colleague of over ten years, Gigi Yates. Gigi has been aware since 1994 that I have been wanting to put together a book such as this. Thanks for all your encouragement and advice and being there for me, Gigi. I am also grateful to Valerie Lettera and several other colleagues at DreamWorks Feature Animation for technical advice and discussions. I feel lucky to work with extremely nice and talented people who make DreamWorks a special place.

Christina Eddington is a long-time dear friend who offered encouragement as the book was being written, as did Bill Kuehl and Ingall Bull. Thanks also to Tami and Lupe who did likewise. Our friendly neighbors Richard and Kathy, Dan and Susan helped by becoming interested in the contents and wanting periodic updates. Having the support of family, friends and colleagues makes all the difference – book-writing feels less tedious and more fun as a result.

A big thanks to my alma mater IIT-Madras for providing me a lifetime's worth of solid technical foundation. The same goes for Ohio State, my graduate school. Go Buckeyes! I feel very privileged to have studied computer graphics with Wayne Carlson and Rick Parent. They have instilled in me a lifelong passion and wonder for graphics.

I am indebted to Gnomon School of Visual Effects for providing me an opportunity to teach RenderMan on a part-time basis. I have been teaching at Gnomon for about four years, and this book is a synthesis of a lot of material presented there. I have had the pleasure of teaching some very brilliant students, who through their questions and stimulating discussions have indirectly helped shape this book.

Thanks also to the RenderMan community for maintaining excellent sites on the Web. People like Tal Lancaster, Simon Bunker, Rudy Cortes, ZJ and others selflessly devote a lot of their time putting up high-quality material on their pages, out of sheer love of RenderMan.

Finally, thanks to the great folks at Pixar (the current team as well as people no longer there) for coming up with RenderMan in the first place, and for continuing to add to its feature set.

Specifically, the recent addition of global illumination enables taking rendered imagery to the next level. It is hard to imagine the world of graphics and visual effects without RenderMan.

Dedication

To Becky and Josh, our brand new stochastic supersamples
and future RenderMan enthusiasts

1
Rendering

Renderers synthesize images from descriptions of scenes involving geometry, lights, materials and cameras. This chapter explores the image synthesis process, making comparisons with artistic rendering and with real-world cameras.

1.1 Artistic rendering

Using images to communicate is a notion as old as humankind itself. Ancient cave paintings portray scenes of hunts. Religious paintings depict scenes relating to gods, demons and others. Renaissance artists are credited with inventing perspective, which makes it possible to faithfully represent scene elements with geometric realism. Several modern art movements have succeeded in taking apart and reconfiguring traditional notions of form, light and space to create new types of imagery. Computer graphics, a comparatively new medium, significantly extends image creation capabilities by offering very flexible, powerful tools.

We live in a three-dimensional (3D) world, consisting of 3D space, light and 3D objects. Yet the images of such a 3D world that are created inside our eyes are distinctly two-dimensional (2D). Our brains of course are responsible for interpreting the images (from both eyes) and recreating the three-dimensionality for us. A film camera or movie camera does something similar, which is to form 2D images of a 3D world. Artists often use the term "rendering" to mean the representation of objects or scenes on a flat surface such as a canvas or a sheet of paper.

Figure 1.1 shows images of a torus (donut shape) rendered with sketch pencil (a), colored pencils (b), watercolor (c) and acrylic (d).

Each medium has its own techniques (e.g. the pencil rendering is done with stippling, the color pencil drawing uses cross-hatch strokes while the watercolor render uses overlapping washes) but in all cases the result is the same – a 3D object is represented on a 2D picture plane. Artists have an enormous flexibility with media, processes, design, composition, perspective, color and value choices, etc. in rendering their scenes. Indeed, many artists eventually develop their own signature rendering style by experimenting with portraying their subject matter in a variety of media using different techniques. A computer graphical renderer is really one more tool/medium, with its own vocabulary of techniques for representing 3D worlds ("scenes") as 2D digital imagery.

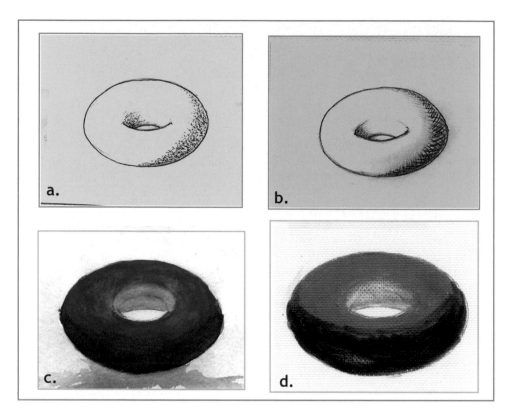

Figure 1.1 *Different "renderings" of a torus (donut shape)*

1.2 Computer graphical image synthesis

Computers can be used to create digital static and moving imagery in a variety of ways. For instance, scanners, digital still and video cameras serve to capture real-world images and scenes. We can also use drawing and painting software to create imagery from scratch, or to manipulate existing images. Video editing software can be used for trimming and sequencing digital movie clips and for overlaying titles and audio. Clips or individual images can be layered over real-world or synthetic backgrounds, elements from one image can be inserted into another, etc. Digital images can indeed be combined in seemingly endless ways to create new visual content.

There is yet another way to create digital imagery, which will be our focus in this book. I am of course referring to computer graphics (CG) rendering, where descriptions of 3D worlds get converted to images. A couple of comparisons will help make this more concrete. Figure 1.2 illustrates this discussion.

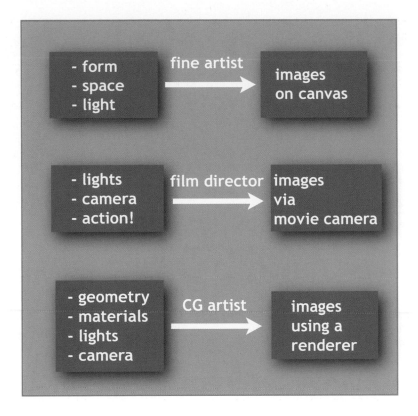

Figure 1.2 *Three routes to image synthesis*

Think of how you as an artist would render a scene in front of you. Imagine that you would like to paint a pretty landscape, using oil on canvas. You intuitively form a scene description of the things that you are looking at, and use creativity, judgment and technique to paint what you want to portray onto the flat surface. You are the renderer that takes the scene description and eventually turns it into an image. Depending on your style, you might make a fairly photorealistic portrait which might make viewers feel as if they are there with you looking at the landscape. At the other extreme you might produce a very abstract image, using elements from the landscape merely as a guide to create your own shapes, colors and placement on canvas. Sorry if I make the artistic process seem mechanical – it does help serve as an analogy to a CG renderer.

A photographer likewise uses a camera to create flat imagery. The camera acts as the renderer, and the photographer creates a scene description for it by choosing composition, lighting and viewpoint.

On a movie set, the classic "Lights, camera, action!" call gets the movie camera to start recording a scene, set up in accordance with a shooting script. The script is interpreted by the movie's Director, who dictates the choice and placement of lights, camera(s) and actors/props in the scene. As the actors "animate" while delivering dialog, the movie camera renders the resulting scene to motion picture film or digital output media. The Director sets up the scene description and the camera renders it.

In all these cases, scene descriptions get turned into imagery. This is just what a CG renderer does. The scene is purely synthetic, in the sense that it exists only inside the machine. The renderer's output (rendered image) is equally synthetic, being a collection of colored pixels which the renderer calculates for us. We look at the rendered result and are able to reconstruct the synthetic 3D scene in our minds. This in itself is nothing short of wonderful – we can get a machine to synthesize images for us, which is a bigger deal than merely having it record or process them.

Let us look at this idea of scene description a bit closer. Take a look at Figure 1.3. and imagine creating a file by typing up the description shown using a simple text editor. We would like the renderer to create us a picture of a red sphere sitting on a blue ground plane. We create this file which serves as our scene description, and pass it on to our renderer to synthesize an image corresponding to the description of our very simple scene.

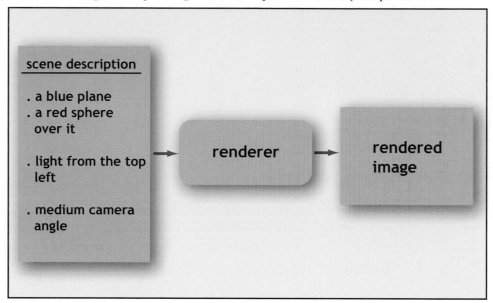

Figure 1.3 *A renderer being fed a scene description*

The renderer parses (reads, in layperson's terms) the scene file, carries out the instructions it contains, and produces an image as a result. So this is the one-line summary of the CG rendering process – 3D scene descriptions get turned into images.

That is how RenderMan, the renderer we are exploring in this book, works. It takes scene description files called **RIB** files (much more on this in subsequent chapters 3 to 8) and creates imagery out of them. **RIB** stands for RenderMan Interface Bytestream. For our purposes in this book, it can be thought of as a language for describing scenes to RenderMan. Figure 1.4 shows the **RIB** version of our simple red sphere/blue plane scene, which RenderMan accepts in order to produce output image shown on the right.

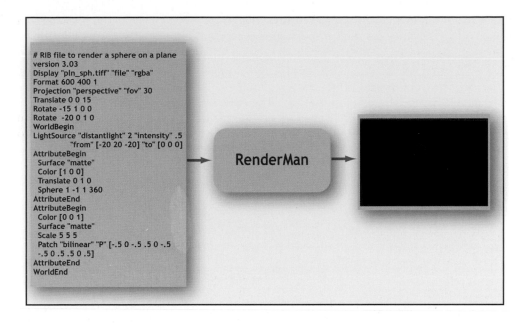

```
# RIB file to render a sphere on a plane
version 3.03
Display "pln_sph.tiff" "file" "rgba"
Format 600 400 1
Projection "perspective" "fov" 30
Translate 0 0 15
Rotate -15 1 0 0
Rotate  -20 0 1 0
WorldBegin
LightSource "distantlight" 2 "intensity" .5
        "from" [-20 20 -20] "to" [0 0 0]
AttributeBegin
  Surface "matte"
  Color [1 0 0]
  Translate 0 1 0
  Sphere 1 -1 1 360
AttributeEnd
AttributeBegin
  Color [0 0 1]
  Surface "matte"
  Scale 5 5 5
  Patch "bilinear" "P" [-.5 0 -.5 .5 0 -.5
  -.5 0 .5 .5 0 .5]
AttributeEnd
WorldEnd
```

RenderMan

Figure 1.4 *RenderMan converts RIB inputs into images*

You can see that the RIB file contains concrete specifications for what we want RenderMan to do. For example "Color [1 0 0]" specifies red color for the sphere (in RGB color space). The RIB file shown produces the image shown. If we made derivative versions of RIB files from the one above (e.g. by changing the "Translate 0 0 15" to "Translate 0 0 18", then to "Translate 0 0 21" and so on, which would pull the camera back from the scene each step, and by changing the "pln_sph.tiff" to "pln_sph2.tiff", then to "pln_sph3.tiff", etc. to specify a new image file name each time), RenderMan will be able to read each RIB file and convert it to an image named in that RIB file. When we play back the images rapidly, we will see an animation of the scene where the light and two objects are static, and the camera is being pulled back (as in a dolly move – see Chapter 6, "Camera, output"). The point is that a movie camera takes near-continuous snapshots (at 24 frames-per-second, 30 frames-per-second, etc.) of the continuous scene it views, while a CG renderer is presented scene snapshots in the form of a scene description file, one file per frame of rendered animation. Persistence of vision in our brains is what causes the illusion of movement in both cases, when we play back the movie camera's output as well as a CG renderer's output.

1.3 Representational styles

With the eye/camera/CG renderer analogy in mind, it is time to look at the different ways that renderers can render scene descriptions for us.

For the most part, we humans visually interpret the physical world in front of us fairly identically. The same is generally true for cameras, aside from differences in lenses and film/sensor type. Their inputs come from the real world, get processed through optical elements based on physical and geometric laws, leading to image formation on physical media. But this is not how CG renderers work. As you know by now, their inputs are scene descriptions. They turn these scene descriptions into imagery, via calculations embodied in rendering algorithms (recipes or procedures) for image synthesis. The output images are really grids of numbers that represent colors. Of course we eventually have to view the outputs on physical devices such as monitors, printers and film-recorders.

Because rendered images are calculated, depending on the calculations, the same input scene description can result in a variety of output representations from the renderer. Each has its use. We will now take a look at several of the most common rendering styles in use. Each shows a different way to represent a 3D surface. By 3D we do not mean stereo-viewing, rather we mean that such a surface would exist as an object in the real world, something you can hold in your hands, walk around, see it be obscured by other objects.

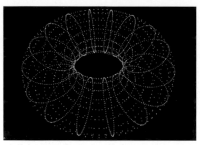

Figure 1.5 *Point-cloud representation of a 3D surface*

Figure 1.5 shows a point-cloud representation of a torus. Here, the image is made up of just the vertices of the polygonal mesh that makes up the torus (or of the control vertices, in the case of a patch-based torus). We will explore polygonal meshes and patch surfaces in detail, in Chapter 4. The idea here is that we infer the shape of a 3D object by mentally connecting the dots in its point cloud image. Our brains create in our mind's eye, the surfaces on which the dots lie. In terms of Gestalt theories, the law of continuation (where objects arranged in straight lines or curves are perceived as a unit) and the principle of closure (where groups of objects complete a pattern) are at work during the mental image formation process.

Next is a wireframe representation, shown in Figure 1.6. As the name implies, this type of image shows the scaffolding wires that might be used to fashion an object while creating a sculpture of it. While the torus is easy to make out (due to its simplicity of shape and sparseness of the wires), note that the eagle mesh is too complex for a small image in wireframe mode. Wireframe images are rather easy for the renderer to create, in comparison with the richer representations that follow. In wireframe mode the renderer is able to keep up with scene changes in real time, if the CG camera moves around an object or if the object is translated/rotated/scaled. The wireframe style is hence a common preview mode when a scene is being set up for full-blown (more complex) rendering later.

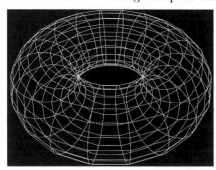 

Figure 1.6 *Wireframe view*

A hidden line representation (Figure 1.7) is an improvement over a wireframe view, since the renderer now hides those wires in the wireframe that would not be visible as if they were obscured by parts of the surface near to the viewer. In other words, if black opaque material were to be used over the scaffolding to form a surface, the front parts of that surface would hide the wires and the back parts behind it. The result is a clearer view of the surface, although it is still in scaffolding-only form.

A step up is a hidden line view combined with depth cueing, shown in Figure 1.8. The idea is to fade away the visible lines that are farther away, while keeping the nearer lines in contrast. The resulting image imparts more information (about relative depths) compared to a standard hidden line render. Depth cueing can be likened to atmospheric perspective, a technique used by artists to indicate far away objects in a landscape, where desaturation is combined with a shift towards blue/purple hues to fade away details in the distance.

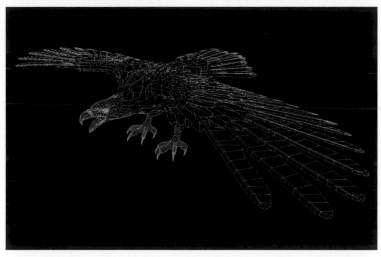

Figure 1.7 *Hidden-line view – note the apparent reduction in mesh density*

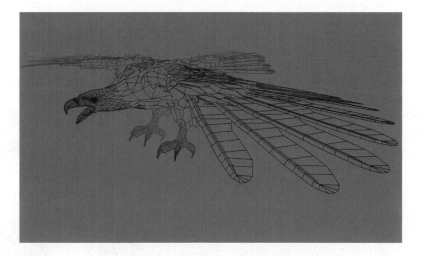

Figure 1.8 *Hidden line with depth cue*

A bounding box view (Figure 1.9, right image) of an object indirectly represents it by depicting the smallest cuboidal box that will just enclose it. Such a simplified view might be useful in previewing composition in a scene that has a lot of very complex objects, since bounding boxes are even easier for the renderer to draw than wireframes. Note that an alternative to a bounding box is a bounding sphere, but that is rarely used in renderers to convey extents of objects (it is more useful in performing calculations to decide if objects inter-penetrate).

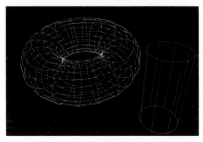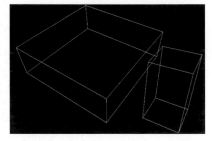

Figure 1.9 *Bounding box view of objects*

We have so far looked at views that impart information about a surface but do not really show all of it. Views presented from here on show the surfaces themselves. Figure 1.10 is a flat shaded view of a torus. The torus is made up of rectangular polygons, and in this view, each polygon is shown rendered with a single color that stretches across its area. The shading for each polygon is derived with reference to a light source and the polygon's orientation relative to it (more on this in the next section). The faceted result serves to indicate how the 3D polygonal object is put together (for instance we notice that the polygons get smaller in size as we move from the outer rim towards the inner surface of the torus). As with depth-cueing discussed earlier, the choice of representational style determines the type of information that can be gleaned about the surface.

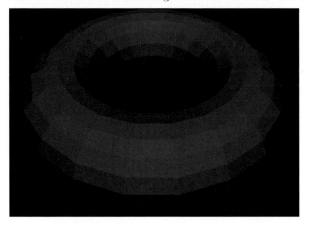

Figure 1.10 *Flat shaded view of a torus*

Smooth shading is an improvement over the flat look in Figure 1.10. It is illustrated in Figure 1.11, where the torus polygonal mesh now looks visually smoother, thanks to a better shading technique. There are actually two smooth shading techniques for polygonal meshes, called Gouraud shading and Phong shading. Of these two, Gouraud shading is easier for a renderer to calculate, but Phong shading produces a smoother look, especially where the surface displays a highlight (also known as a hot spot or specular reflection). We will discuss the notion of shading in more detail later, in Chapter 8. For a sneak preview, look at Figure 8.33 which compares flat, Gouraud and Phong shading. On a historic note, Henri Gouraud invented the Gouraud shading technique in 1971, and Bui Tui Phong came up with Phong shading a few years later, in 1975. Both were affiliated with the computer science department at the University of Utah, a powerhouse of early CG research.

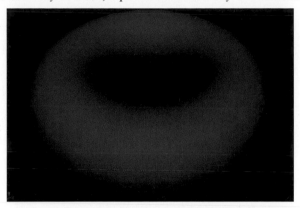

Figure 1.11 *Smooth shaded view*

A hybrid representational style of a wireframe superimposed over a shaded surface is shown in Figure 1.12. This is a nice view if you want to see the shaded form of an object as well as its skeletal/structural detail at the same time.

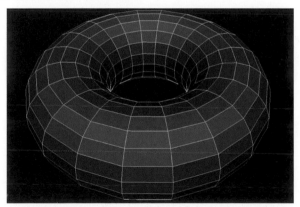

Figure 1.12 *Wireframe over smooth shading*

Also popular is an x-ray render view where the object is rendered as if it were partly transparent, allowing us to see through the front surfaces at what is behind (Figure 1.13). By the way, the teapot shown in the figure is the famous "Utah Teapot", a classic icon of 3D graphics. It was first created by Martin Newell at the University of Utah. You will encounter this teapot at several places throughout the book.

Until now we have not said anything about materials that make up our surfaces. We have only rendered dull (non-reflective, matte) surfaces using generic, gray shades. Look around you at the variety of surfaces that make up real-world objects. Objects have very many properties (e.g. mass, conductivity, toughness) but for rendering purposes, we concentrate on how they interact with light. Chapter 8 goes into great detail about this, but for now we will just note that CG surfaces get associated with materials which specify optical properties for them, such as their inherent color and opacity, how much diffuse light they scatter, how reflective they are, etc. When a renderer calculates an image of an object, it usually takes these optical properties into account while calculating its color and transparency (this is the shading part of the rendering computation – see the next section for more details).

Figure 1.13 *An x-ray view of the famous Utah teapot*

Figure 1.14 shows a lit view of the teapot meant to be made of a shiny material such as metal or plastic. The image is rendered as if there were two light sources shining on the surface, one behind each side of the camera. You can deduce this by noticing where the shiny highlights are. Inferring locations and types of light sources by looking at highlights and shaded/shadowed regions in any image is an extremely useful skill to develop in CG rendering. It will help you light CG scenes realistically (if that is the goal) and to match real-world lights in filmed footage, when you are asked to render CG elements (characters/props) for seamless integration into the footage.

Figure 1.14 *Teapot in "lit" mode*

Figure 1.15 shows the teapot in a lit, textured view. The object, which appears to be made of marble, is illuminated using a light source placed at the top left. The renderer can generate the marble pattern on the surface in a few different ways. We could photograph flat marble slabs and instruct the renderer to wrap the flat images over the curved surface during shading calculations, in a process known as texture mapping. Alternately we could use a 3D paint program (in contrast to the usual 2D ones such as Photoshop) where we can directly paint the texture pattern over the surface, and have the renderer use that while shading. Or we could write a small shader program which will mathematically compute the marble pattern at each piece of the teapot, associate that shader program with the teapot surface, and instruct the renderer to use the program while shading the teapot. The last approach is called procedural shading, where we calculate (synthesize) patterns over a surface. This is the approach I took to generate the figure you see. RenderMan is famous for providing a flexible, powerful, fun shading language which can be used by artists/software developers to create a plethora of appearances. Chapter 8 is devoted exclusively to shading and shader-writing.

Figure 1.15 *Teapot shown lit and with a marble texture*

Are we done with cataloging rendering representations? Not quite. Here are some more. Figure 1.16 is a cutout view of the eagle we encountered before, totally devoid of shading. The outline tells us it is an eagle in flight, but we are unable to make out any surface detail such as texture, how the surfaces curve, etc. An image like this can be turned into a matte channel (or alpha channel), which along with a corresponding lit, shaded view can be used for example to insert the eagle into a photograph of a mountain and skies.

Figure 1.16 *Cutout view showing a silhouette of the object*

Since a renderer calculates its output image, it can turn non-visual information into images, just as well as it can do physically accurate shading calculations using materials and light sources. For instance, Figure 1.17 depicts a z-depth image where the distance of each visible surface point from the camera location has been encoded as a black to white scale. Points farthest from the camera (e.g. the teapot's handle) are dark, and the closest parts (the spout) are brighter. People would find it very difficult to interpret the world in terms of such depth images, but for a renderer, it is rather routine, since everything is calculated instead of being presented merely for recording. Depth images are crucial for a class of shadow calculations, as we will see in Chapter 8 ("Shading").

Figure 1.17 *A z-depth view of our teapot*

Moving along, Figure 1.18 shows a toon style of rendering a torus. Cartoons, whether in comic book (static images) or animated form, have been a very popular artistic rendering style for many decades. A relatively new development is to use 3D renderers to toon-render scenes. The obvious advantage in animation is that the artist is spared the tedium of having to painstakingly draw and paint each individual image – once the 3D scene is set up with character animation, lights, props, effects and camera motion, the renderer can render the collection of frames in toon style, eliminating the drawing and painting process altogether. In practice this has advantages as well as drawbacks. Currently the biggest drawback seems to be that the toon lines do not have a lively quality that is present in the frame-by-frame hand-generated results – they are a bit too perfect and come across as being mechanical, dull and hence lifeless. Note that the toon style of rendering is the 3D equivalent of posterization, a staple in 2D graphic design. Posterization depicts elements using relatively few, flat tones in favor of more colors that depict continuous, smooth shading. In both toon rendering and posterization, form is suggested using a well-chosen, small palette of tones which fill bold, simple shapes.

Improving toon rendered imagery is an area of ongoing research that is part of an even bigger umbrella of graphics research called non-photoreal rendering. Non-photoreal rendering (NPR for short) aims to move CG rendering away from its traditional roots (see Section 1.5) and steer it towards visually diverse, artistic representational styles (as opposed to photoreal ones).

Figure 1.18 *Non-photoreal "toon" style rendering*

Here is our final sample of representations. Figure 1.19 shows the teapot again, this time with a process called displacement mapping. The surface appears made out of hammered sheet metal.

What gives it the hammered look? The imperfections on the surface do. The knob on the lid and the rim of the body in particular show that the surface is indeed deformed. But what is interesting is that the same Utah teapot used in previous illustrations was the one used here also. In other words, the object surface itself was not remodeled with imperfections, prior to rendering. What causes the realistic displacements is a displacement shader (a small piece of software), which together with a another surface shader for the metallic appearance was associated with the teapot surface and was input to RenderMan via a RIB file. RenderMan carried out the local surface modifications (displacements) by consulting the associated shader program, during rendering. Letting the user specify surface modifications during rendering is a significant capability of RenderMan which we will further explore in Chapter 8, "Shading".

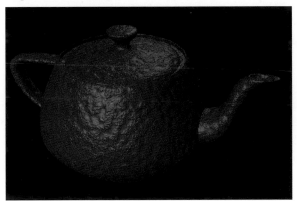

Figure 1.19 *Displacement mapped teapot*

We surveyed many ways a renderer can represent surfaces for us. But the list is not exhaustive. For instance none of the images had objects casting shadows with either hard or soft edges (e.g. as if the teapot were sitting on a plane and lit by a directional light source or maybe a more diffused light). There were no partially transparent objects (the x-ray view was a mere approximation) showing refraction (light-bending) effects. Surfaces did not show other objects reflecting on them, nor did they bleed color on to neighboring surfaces. The point is that real-world surfaces do all these and even more. Many of the things just mentioned were faked in most renderers for years because the renderers were incapable of calculating them in a physically accurate manner, the way a camera would simply record such effects on film. Modern renderers (including version 11 of Pixar's RenderMan, the latest release at the time of this writing) are increasingly capable of rendering these effects without user-set up cheats, getting ever closer to the ideal of a CG renderer producing photoreal images of almost any scene description fed to them. Note that by definition, photoreal images are meant to be indistinguishable from camera-derived images of the real world. Speaking of photorealism, we know that cameras invariably introduce artifacts into the images they record. These artifacts stem from their physical/mechanical/electronic subsystems interfering with the image recording process. For instance, lens distortions and flares, chromatic aberrations, motion blur, etc. are camera-derived artifacts not present in images we see with our naked eyes. It is interesting that CG renderers are outfitted with additional capabilities that let users synthetically add such imperfections to the otherwise perfect images they render, in order to make those images look that much more photoreal. These imperfections are part of our subconscious cues that make recorded/rendered images appear real to us.

1.4 How a renderer works

Now we take a brief look at how a renderer accomplishes the task of converting a 3D scene description into an image.

As I have been pointing out, the entire process is synthetic, calculation-driven as opposed to what cameras and eyes do naturally. The CG renderer does not "look at" anything in the physical or biological sense. Instead it starts with a scene description, carries out a well-defined set of subtasks collectively referred to as the 3D graphics pipeline or the rendering pipeline, and ends with the generation of an image faithful to the scene described to it.

What follows is an extremely simplified version of what really goes on (renderers are very complex pieces of software where a lot of heavy-duty calculations and book-keeping goes on during the rendering process). In other books you might come across descriptions where some of the presented steps differ (this is especially true for the first part of the pipeline) but the following description will give you a feel for what goes on "under the hood" during rendering.

Figure 1.20 shows the pipeline as a block diagram where data flows from top to bottom. In other words the scene description enters at the top (this is the input), and the rendered image is produced in the bottom as the output.

The scene description consists of surfaces made of materials spatially composed, lit by light sources. The virtual camera is also placed somewhere in the scene, for the renderer to look through, to create a render of the scene from that specific viewpoint. Optionally the atmosphere (the space in which the scene is set) itself might contribute to the final image (e.g. think of looking at an object across a smoke-filled room) but we ignore this to keep our discussion simple. The renderer must now convert such a scene description into a rendered image.

The first few steps in the pipeline are space transformations. What we mean is this. Figure 1.21 shows two images, those of a cube and a cylinder. Each object is shown modeled in its own, native object space. For a cube, this space consists of the origin in the middle of the volume, and the mutually-perpendicular X, Y and Z axes are parallel to the edges of the cube. Cubes can be modeled/specified using alternate axes (e.g. one where the origin is in one corner and the Z axis is along the volume diagonal) but what is shown above is the most common specification. The cylinder is usually modeled with respect to an origin in its center, with the Z axis pointing along the length or height. The surface description consists of parameters that describe the shape in relation to the axes. For our polygonal cube for instance, a description would consist of the spatial (x, y, z) locations of its eight vertices (e.g. -0.5, -0.5, -0.5 for one corner and 0.5, 0.5, 0.5 for the opposite corner) and vertex indices that make up the six faces (e.g. "1 2 3 4" making up a face). Loosely speaking, edges are the wireframe lines that make up our surfaces, vertices are the corners where edges meet and faces are the flat areas bounded by edges and vertices. Similar to our cube and cylinder, character body parts, props, abstract shapes and other modeled objects carry with them their own object or model axes, and their surfaces are described in relation to those axes.

When objects are introduced into a scene, they are placed in the scene relative to a common origin and set of axes called the world coordinate system. Figure 1.22 shows our cube and cylinder together in a little scene, where they are placed next to each other interpenetrating (to better illustrate some of the following steps).

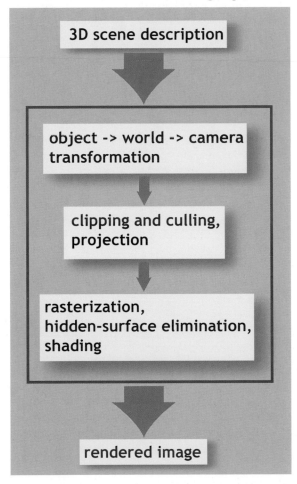

Figure 1.20 *Stages in a classical rendering pipeline*

What is important is that an object placed into a world coordinate system will in general undergo any combination of translation, rotation or scale in order to be placed in its location. In other words, it is as if our cube and cylinder were placed at the world origin, with their model axes and the world axes initially coincident. From there, each object undergoes its own translation/rotation/scaling (chosen by the user setting up the scene) to end up where it is. This placement process is called object to world transformation. Note from the figure that the scene also contains a camera, which is itself another object which underwent its own translation/rotation/scaling to end up where it is, which in our case is in front of the cube and cylinder.

Since we will be viewing the scene through this camera which is near our objects, the next transformation is to relocate the world origin smack in the middle of the camera and point an axis (usually Z) along the camera's viewing direction. This is called the camera or eye coordinate system. The positions, orientations and sizes of the elements in the rest of the scene, which include both objects and light sources, can now be described in terms of this new coordinate system. The scene elements are said to undergo a world to camera space transformation when they are being described this way in terms of the new set of axes.

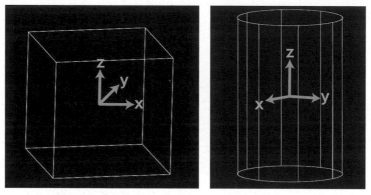

Figure 1.21 *Object space views of a cube and cylinder*

The view of the scene through our scene camera is shown in Figure 1.23. More accurately, what the camera sees is what is inside the rectangular frame, which is the image area. The reason is that just like animal eyes and physical cameras, CG cameras too have a finite field of view, meaning that their view is restricted to what is in front of them, extending out to the sides by a specified amount (called the view angle or field of view or FOV).

Take a look at Figure 1.22 again which shows the placement of the camera in the world. You see a square pyramid originating from the camera. This is called the view volume, which is the space that the camera can see. The view volume is not unbounded, meaning the camera cannot see things arbitrarily far away. A plane called the far clipping plane which is parallel to the image plane (not tilted with respect to it) defines this farther extent. Similarly, CG cameras will not be able to process surfaces placed very close to them either. So a near clipping plane is placed a short distance away from the camera, to bound the viewing volume from the near side. The result is a view volume in the shape of a truncated pyramid (where the pyramid's apex or tip is cut off by the near clipping plane). This volume is also known as the camera's view frustum.

Now that we have made the camera the center of the scene (since the new world origin is located there) and situated objects relative to it, we need to start processing the scene elements to eventually end up with computed images of them. In the diagram shown in Figure 1.20, this is the middle set of operations, namely clipping, culling, projection.

Figure 1.24 illustrates the result of the clipping operation, where the six planes of our viewing frustum (near and far clipping planes, and the top, bottom, left and right pyramid planes) are used to bound scene elements meant for further processing. Objects completely lying within the volume are left untouched. Objects lying completely outside are totally discarded, since the camera is not supposed to be able to see them. Objects that partially lie inside (and intersect the bounding planes) are clipped, meaning they are subdivided into smaller primitives for the purposes of retaining what is inside and discarding what falls outside. In Figure 1.24, the cylinder's top part is clipped away. Likewise, the cube intersects two bounding planes (the near clipping plane and a side plane) and is therefore clipped against each of them. What is left inside the view frustum can be processed further.

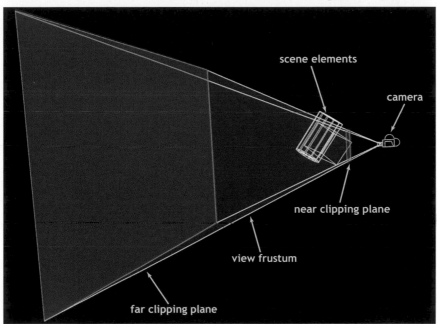

Figure 1.22 *World space representation*

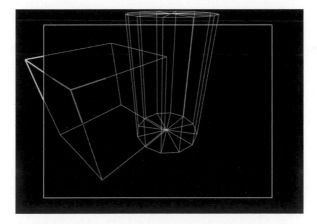

Figure 1.23 *Camera view of the scene*

The renderer further simplifies surfaces by discarding the flip sides of surfaces hidden by camera-facing front ones, in a step known as back face culling (Figure 1.25). The idea is that each surface has an outside and an inside, and only the outside is supposed to be visible to the camera. So if a surface faces the same general direction that the camera does, its inside surface is the one visible to the renderer, and this is what gets culled when another front-facing surface obscures it. Most renderers permit surfaces to be specified as being two-sided, in which case the renderer will skip the culling step and render all surfaces in the view volume.

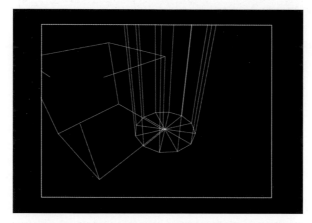

Figure 1.24 *Results of the clipping operation*

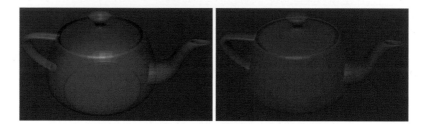

Figure 1.25 *Back face culling - before and after*

The step that follows is projection, where the remaining 3D surfaces are flattened (projected) on to the image plane. Perspective projection is the most common type of projection employed (there are several other types) to create a sense of realism. We see the effects of perspective around us literally all the time, e.g. when we see the two sides of a straight road converge to a single vanishing point far ahead, look up to see the straight rooflines of buildings slope down to vanishing points, etc. Figure 1.26 shows our cube and cylinder perspective-projected on to the CG camera image plane. Note the three edges shown in yellow converge to a vanishing point (off the image) on the right. Square faces of the cube now appear distorted in the image plane. Similarly the vertical rules on the cylinder appear sloped so as to converge to a point under the image.

Once the surfaces are projected on the image plane, they become 2D entities that no longer retain their 3D shape (although the 2D entities do contain associated details about their unprojected counterparts, to be used in downstream shading calculations). Note that this projection step is where the geometric part of the 3D to 2D conversion occurs – the resulting 2D surfaces will subsequently be rasterized and shaded to complete the rendering process.

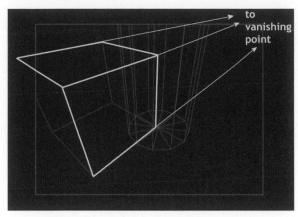

Figure 1.26 *The projection operation*

Before we leave the projection step in the pipeline, I would like to point out that using perspective is not the only way to project surfaces on to image planes. For instance, Figure 1.27 shows an isometric projection, where the cube and cylinder have been tilted towards the camera (from their original object space vertical orientation) and projected in such a way that their XYZ axes make a 120 degree angle on the projection plane (this is particularly evident in the cube). As a result the opposite edges of the cube retain their parallelism after projection, as do the walls of the cylinder. This type of projection is commonly used in engineering drawings of machine parts and in architectural drawings to show buildings, where retaining the parallel lines and planes helps to better visualize the structures (the sloping lines from perspective projection get in the way of our comprehension of shapes and angles).

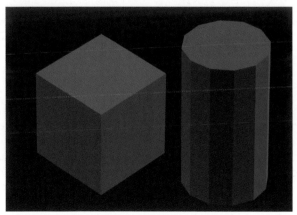

Figure 1.27 *An isometric (non perspective) projection*

We are now at the last stage of our pipeline. Hidden surface elimination, rasterization and shading are steps performed almost simultaneously, but for illustration purposes we will discuss each in sequence. Hidden surface elimination is shown in Figure 1.28. When we are done projecting our surfaces on the image plane, we need to process them in such a way that surfaces that were in front of other surfaces correspondingly end up in front on the image plane as well. There is more than one technique to ensure this, and we will focus on the most common, successful technique that uses a portion of computer memory called a z-buffer (the "z" stands for the z-axis which points away from the camera and so is the axis along which relative depths of objects in the scene will be measured).

Figure 1.28 *Hidden surface elimination*

Think of a z-buffer as a block of memory laid out like a grid (in other words, a rectangular array of slots) for the renderer to store some intermediate computational results. How many slots? As many pixels as there will be in our final image (pixel count or "resolution" will be one of the inputs to the renderer, specified by the user as part of the scene description). What calculations will the renderer store in the z-buffer? Depth-based comparisons. Before anything is stored in the z-buffer by the renderer, the z-buffer set up process will initialize (fill with values during creation time) each slot to a huge number that signifies an infinite depth from the camera. The renderer then starts overwriting these slots with more realistic (closer) depth values each time it comes across a closer surface which lines up with that slot. So when the cylinder surfaces get processed (we have not processed the cube yet), they all end up in the z-buffer slots, as they are all closer compared to the "very far away from the camera" initial values. After being done with the cylinder, the renderer starts processing the cube surfaces. In doing so it discovers (through depth comparisons) that parts of the cube are closer than parts of the cylinder (where the two overlap), so it overwrites the cylinder surfaces' depth values with those of the cube's parts, in those shared z-buffer slots.

When this depth-sorting calculation is done for all the surfaces that are on the image plane, the z-buffer will contain an accurate record of what obscures what. In other words, surfaces that are hidden have become eliminated. Note that the renderer can process these projected surfaces in any arbitrary order and still end up with the same correct result. z-buffer depth sorting serves two inter-related purposes. The renderer does not need to shade (calculate color and opacity for) surface fragments that get obscured by others. In addition, it is important to get this spatial ordering right so the image looks physically correct. Note that the z-buffering just described is for opaque surfaces being hidden by other opaque surfaces, as is the case for the two objects we are considering. The overall idea is still the same for transparent objects but there is more book-keeping to be done, to accurately render such surfaces.

Together with the z-buffer, the renderer also deals with another rectangular array, called the raster (these arrays are all in memory when the renderer performs its tasks). The raster array is what will soon get written out as a collection of pixels that make up our final rendered result. In other words, doing 3D rendering is yet another way to create a collection of pixels making up a digital image, other ways being using a drawing or paint program, scanning or digitally photographing/filming real-world objects, etc.

Figure 1.29 shows a magnified view of the raster, zoomed in on the cube–cylinder intersection. The rasterization step is where the projected surfaces become "discretized" into collections of pixels. In the figure you can see the individual pixels that go to make up a cube edge, a cylinder edge and the intersection curve between the objects. There is no colorization yet, just some indication of shading based on our light sources in the scene.

Figure 1.29 *Rasterization of surface fragments*

All that is left to do is shading, which is the step where the pixels in the raster are colorized by the renderer. Each pixel can contain surface fragments from zero or one or more surfaces in the scene. Figure 1.30 shows the shaded versions of the pixels in the previous figure. The pixels in the top left are black, a default color used by many renderers to indicate that there are no surfaces there to shade. The cylinder and cube show their yellow and blue edges, and at the intersection, each pixel contains a color that is a blend between the cube and cylinder colors.

Where do these colors come from? As mentioned before, objects in a scene as associated with materials, which are property bundles with information on how those surfaces will react to light. In our example, the cube and cylinder have been set up to be matte (non-glossy) surfaces, with light blue and light yellow-orange body colors respectively. The renderer uses this information, together with locations, colors and intensities of light sources in the scene, to arrive at a color (and transparency or opacity) value for each surface fragment in each pixel. As you might imagine, these have the potential to be lengthy calculations that might result in long rendering times (our very simple example renders in no time at all).

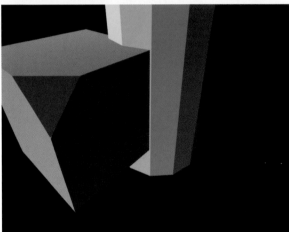

Figure 1.30 *The shading step, and our final result*

Once shading calculations are done, the renderer sends the pixel data (the final result of all the steps we discussed) to the screen for immediate viewing or creates an image file on disk with the data. The choice of destination for the calculated result is inferred by the renderer from the input scene description. Such a rendered result of our basic cube/cylinder scene is shown at the bottom of Figure 1.30.

The pipeline just described is that of a scanline z-buffer renderer, a staple workhorse in modern rendering implementations. While it is good for shading situations where the scene description calls for localized light interactions, it is unsuitable for cases that require global illumination. Chapter 8 ("Shading") has more on global illumination – here I will just say that the term serves as an umbrella for a variety of rendering algorithms that all aim to capture more realistic interactions between surfaces and lights. For instance, our pipeline does not address reflections, refractions, color bleeding from one surface to another, transparent shadows (possibly colored), more complex light/surface interactions (e.g. subsurface scattering), certain focussed-light patterns called caustics, etc.

1.5 Origins of 3D graphics, future directions

The beginnings of 3D rendering parallel the evolution of computer graphics itself. Early uses focussed on scientific and technical areas. 3D models of machine parts and architecture helped with design aspects, and later with analysis. Flight simulators were early examples of 3D CG rendered in real time, under user control as they steered. Of course this required very powerful graphics machines, built by companies such as Evans and Sutherland.

The 1970s and 1980s saw an explosion of research in the field, leading to a whole slew of algorithms that are commonly employed today. These include techniques for hidden surface elimination, clipping, texture and reflection mapping, shadow generation, light/surface interaction calculations, ray tracing, radiosity, etc.

In 1981, Silicon Graphics was founded by James Clark, with the goal of creating powerful graphics computers. They were totally successful in their endeavor and launched a new era of visual computing. Their machines featured custom graphics chips called Geometry Engines which accelerated steps in rendering pipelines similar to those described in the previous section. Such hardware acceleration was accessible to programmers via SGI's GL programming library (a set of prebuilt modules). Many common tasks for which computers are used require the machine to mostly pattern match, count, sort and search. These operations do not involve floating point (involving decimals) calculations which are processor intensive. Graphics programs, particularly renderers, do. This rationale for off-loading such heavy calculations to custom-built hardware was recognized early on, so custom-built graphics machines have been part of 3D graphics from the early days.

GL later gave way to OpenGL, a platform independent version of these programming building blocks. Several vendors began manufacturing OpenGL cards that plugged into PCs, for accelerating graphics intensive applications such as video games.

Today we have game platforms such as PlayStation and Xbox which feature incredibly powerful graphics hardware to keep up with the demands of modern game environments.

The evolution of software renderers has its origins in academia. Researchers from the University of Utah pooled their expertise at Pixar to create RenderMan, which has been publicly available since the late 1980s. CG production companies such as Cranston-Csuri, Digital Productions, Omnibus, Abel & Associates, MetroLight Studios, PDI, RezN8 and Rhythm & Hues were formed during the 80s, to generate visual effects for movies and in television, to create commercials, station logos, interstitials, visuals for upcoming programs and other broadcast graphics. In-house software developers in these production companies had to create their own proprietary renderers, since none were available for purchase. Recognizing this need for production quality rendering (and other CG) software, several companies were launched to fill the void. These include Wavefront, Alias, TDI, Softimage, Side Effects, etc. Early versions of RenderMan had been around at Pixar since the mid-80s, and began to be commercially offered as a product in 1989 (much more on RenderMan in the following chapter). Thanks to its stellar image quality, RenderMan quickly found its way into the production pipelines of visual effects houses. Integration of RenderMan with existing software was done by in-house programmers, who wrote custom software to create RIB files out of scene descriptions originating from home-grown modeling and animation software as well as from third-party packages such as Alias.

These days native renderers are built into programs such as Maya, Softimage XSI, Houdini, LightWave, 3D Studio Max, etc. These programs offer integrated modeling, animation, rendering and in some cases, post-production capabilities. Alternatively, renderers such as RenderMan and mental ray are "standalone" in the sense that their scene descriptions come from external sources. Bridging these two extremes are plugins that create on-the-fly scene descriptions out of Maya etc. for consumption by RenderMan, mental ray and other standalones. For instance, MTOR (Maya To RenderMan) and MayaMan are plugins that generate RenderMan RIB descriptions of Maya scenes. Three-dimensional rendering is also increasingly popular on the Internet, e.g. in the form of "talking head" character animation and visually browsable environments (called worlds) built using a specification called VRML (Virtual Reality Modeling Language) and its descendants such as X3D. MPEG-4, another modern specification for video streaming, even has provision for some limited rendering to occur in handheld devices (e.g. for rendering talking head "avatars" or game characters on your cell phone). By the way, MPEG stands for Motion Picture Experts Group and is a standards body responsible for some video formats widely in use today, such as MPEG and DVD-quality MPEG-2. It seems like 3D rendering has escaped its academic and industrial roots, evolving through visual effects CG production into somewhat of a commodity, available in a variety of affordable hardware and software products.

Rendering is an ongoing active graphics research area where advances are constantly being made both in software as well as hardware. Global illumination, which enhances the realism of rendered images by better simulating interactions between surfaces and lights, is one such area of intensive research. Since photorealism is just one target representation of 3D scenes, how about using techniques and styles from the art world for alternate ways to render scenes? Another burgeoning field called painterly rendering or non-photoreal rendering explores this idea in detail. This will open up the possibility of rendering the same input scene in a multitude of styles. On the hardware front, effort is underway to accelerate RenderMan-quality image generation using custom graphics chips. The goal is nothing short of rendering full motion cinematic imagery in real time, on personal computers. This should do wonders for entertainment, education, communication and commerce in the coming years.

2
RenderMan

We begin this chapter by exploring the origins of RenderMan and its continuing contribution to the world of high-end visual effects. We then move on to discussing the various components of the RenderMan system from a user's perspective, and conclude with a behind-the-scenes look at how Pixar's RenderMan implementation works.

2.1 History, origins

During the 1970s, the computer science department at The University of Utah was a computer graphics hotbed which gave rise to a host of innovations widely used in the industry today. Its alumni list reads like a CG who-is-who, including pioneers such as Jim Blinn, Lance Williams, Ed Catmull, John Warnock, Jim Clark, Frank Crow, Fred Parke, Martin Newell and many others. Catmull's work there covered texture mapping, hidden surface elimination and the rendering of curved surfaces.

The scene shifted to New York Institute of Technology (NYIT) after that, where Catmull and numerous others did ground-breaking work spanning almost every area of CG, both 2D and 3D. It does not do justice to list just a few of those names here. Please see the RfB site for links to pages documenting the contributions of these pioneers. They set out to make a full length movie called *The Works*, written and pitched by Lance Williams. Although they had the technical know-how and creative talent to make it happen, the movie never came to fruition due to the lack of production management skills. The experience they gained was not wasted as it would come in handy later at Pixar.

In 1979 George Lucas established a CG department in his Lucasfilm company with the specific intent of creating imagery for motion pictures. Ed Catmull, Alvy Ray Smith, Tom Duff, Ralph Guggenheim and David DiFrancesco were the first people in the new division, to be joined by many others in the years following. This group of incredibly talented people laid the ground work for what would eventually become RenderMan.

The researchers had the explicit goal of being able to create complex, high quality photorealistic imagery, virtually indistinguishable by definition, from filmed live action images. They began to create a renderer to help them achieve this audacious goal. The renderer had an innovative architecture, designed from scratch and at the same time incorporated technical knowledge gained from past research both at Utah and NYIT. Loren Carpenter implemented core pieces of the rendering system, and Rob Cook implemented the shading subsystem with Pat Hanrahan as the lead architect for the project. The rendering algorithm was termed "Reyes", a name with dual origins. It was inspired by Point Reyes, a picturesque spot on the California coastline which Carpenter loved to visit. To the rendering team the name was also an acronym for "Render Everything You Ever Saw", a convenient phrase to sum up their ambitious undertaking.

At the 1987 SIGGRAPH conference, Cook, Carpenter and Catmull presented a paper called "The Reyes Rendering Architecture" which explained how the renderer functioned. Later at the SIGGRAPH in 1990, the shading language was presented in a paper titled "A Language for Shading and Lighting Calculations" by Hanrahan and Jim Lawson. In 1989 the software came to be known as RenderMan and began to be licensed to CG visual effects and animation companies. Also, the CG division of Lucasfilm was spun off into its own company, Pixar in 1983 and was purchased by Steve Jobs in 1986.

Even though the public offering of RenderMan was not until 1989, the software was used internally at Lucasfilm/Pixar way before that, to create movie visual effects, animation shorts and television commercials.

In 1982, the Genesis Effect in the movie *Star Trek II: The Wrath of Khan* was created using an early version of RenderMan, as was the stained glass knight in the movie *Young Sherlock Holmes* released in 1985.

Between 1989 and 1994, Pixar created over 50 commercials using RenderMan, including those for high-profile products such as Tropicana, Listerine and Lifesavers.

Right from the beginning, a Lucasfilm/Pixar tradition has been to create short films that serve as a medium for technical experimentation and showcasing and provide an opportunity for story-telling as well (usually involving humor). Starting with *The Adventures of Andre and Wally B.* in 1984, there have been nine shorts to date (Figure 2.1). They are lovely visual treats which chronicle the increasingly sophisticated capabilities of Pixar's RenderMan through the years. You can view them online at the Pixar web site.

In 1995 Pixar/Disney released *Toy Story*. Being a fully computer-animated movie, it represented a milestone in CG. Other movies from Pixar (again, all-CG) include *A Bug's Life* (1998), *Toy Story 2* (1999), *Monsters, Inc.* (2001) and *Finding Nemo* (2003). Two others scheduled for future release are *The Incredibles* (2004) and *Cars* (2005).

All of these creations serve as a testimonial of the power of RenderMan. You can freeze-frame these movies/shorts/commercials to see RenderMan in action for yourself.

Pixar's short films

- **The Adventures of Andre and Wally B. (1984)**
- **Luxo Jr. (1986)**
- **Red's Dream (1987)**
- **Tin Toy (1988)**
- **Knickknack (1989)**
- **Geri's Game (1997)**
- **For the Birds (2000)**
- **Mike's New Car (2002)**
- **Boundin' (2004)**

Figure 2.1 *Pixar's short animations*

In addition to being used internally at Pixar, RenderMan has become an unofficial gold standard for visual effects in live action and hybrid 2D/3D animated movies. Figure 2.2 shows a nearly-complete alphabetical list of movies that have used RenderMan to date. You can see every blockbuster movie for the past 15 years appear in that list. The Academy of Motion Picture Arts and Sciences has honored the RenderMan team not once but twice with "Oscars" (a Scientific and Engineering Academy Award in 1993 and an Academy

Award of Merit in 2001) to recognize this contribution to motion pictures. In addition, Pixar's shorts, commercials and movies have won numerous awards/nominations over the years (too many to list here), including "Best Animated Short" Oscars for *Tin Toy* and *For The Birds.*

RenderMan today has widespread adoption in the CG industry, even though it has contenders such as Mental Ray and Brazil. It has reached critical mass in terms of the number of visual effects and movies in which it has been used. It enjoys a large user base, and RenderMan knowledge is available in the form of books, online sites, SIGGRAPH course notes, etc. See the online RfB page for links to these, and Chapter 10 ("Resources") for additional notes on some of these learning materials.

In their 1987 Reyes paper, Cook, Carpenter and Catmull stated that they wanted their architecture to handle visually rich scenes with complex models, a variety of geometric primitives and be flexible enough to accommodate new rendering techniques. Over the years, the evolution of Pixar's RenderMan has been in conformance with these expectations. Modern scenes contain primitives many orders of magnitude more than what was possible in the early days. Also, newer primitives have been added, e.g. subdivision surfaces, metaballs (isosurfaces or "blobbies"), curves and particles.

Pixar's latest Photorealistic RenderMan release (R11) offers global illumination features in the form of a well-crafted set of additions to the core Reyes implementation, which permit synthesis of images with unprecedented levels of realism. You can see these new features in action, in the recent animated films *Finding Nemo* (Pixar) and *Shark Tale* (DreamWorks).

It helps that the moviemaking division of Pixar is PRMan's internal client. Newer PRMan features are typically developed first for use in Pixar's movies and are subsequently offered to the external customer base. It is my personal hope that the innovations will continue, maintaining RenderMan's lead in the world of rendering for years to come.

2.2 Interface, implementations

The term "RenderMan" actually stands for two things. First, it is the name of the standard interface (as defined by Pixar) through which modelers and renderers communicate. Second, it has also come to stand for Pixar's own rendering software which implements the standard interface.

Pixar's version of RenderMan is more accurately called Photorealistic RenderMan, or "PRMan" for short. The bulk of this book deals with PRMan, although we will occasionally use a non-Pixar version of RenderMan to generate an image to acknowledge the diversity of RenderMan implementations out there. You need to realize that to many people, the term RenderMan denotes the Pixar implementation of the interface. By being the leading vendor of an implementation and by owning the standard, Pixar has had its product become synonymous with the standard itself.

A Bug's Life	Outbreak
A.I.	Patch Adams
Aladdin	Pearl Harbor
Apollo 13	Pitch Black
Atlantis: The Lost Empire	Planet of the Apes
Babe: Pig in the City	Pocahontas
Balto	Shark Tale
Batman Forever	Sinbad: Legend of the Seven Seas
Batman Returns	Sleepy Hollow
Beauty and the Beast	Small Soldiers
Bicentennial Man	Space Cowboys
Black Hawk Down	Species
Casper	Speed
Cast Away	Spider Man
Cats & Dogs	Spirit: Stallion of the Cimarron
Chicken Run	Star Trek VI
Clear & Present Danger	Star Wars Episode I: The Phantom Menace
Cliffhanger	Star Wars Episode II: Attack of the Clones
Contact	StarQuest
Death Becomes Her	Starship Troopers
Demolition Man	Stuart Little
Dinosaur	Stuart Little 2
Evolution	Terminator II
Fight Club	The Abyss
Final Fantasy: The Spirits Within	The Adventures of Rocky & Bullwinkle
Finding Nemo	The Beach
Forrest Gump	The Incredibles
Free Willy	The Jungle Book
Gladiator	The Lion King
Harry Potter and the Chamber of Secrets	The Lord of the Rings: Return of the King
Harry Potter and the Sorcerer's Stone	The Lord of the Rings: The Fellowship of the Ring
Hollow Man	The Lord of the Rings: The Two Towers
How the Grinch Stole Christmas	The Mask
Indian in the Cupboard	The Matrix
Inspector Gadget	The Mummy
Interview with a Vampire	The Mummy Returns
Iron Giant	The Perfect Storm
Jetsons	The Prince of Egypt
Jumanji	The Road to El Dorado
Jurassic Park: The Lost World	The Scorpion King
Jurassic Park 2	The Time Machine
Jurassic Park 3	The World is Not Enough
Men in Black	Titanic
Men in Black II	Tomb Raider
Minority Report	Toy Story
Miracle on 34th Street	Toy Story 2
Mission to Mars	True Lies
Monsters, Inc.	Vanilla Sky
Moulin Rouge	What Dreams May Come
Nutty Professor II: The Klumps	Young Sherlock Holmes

Figure 2.2 *Movies containing RenderMan-generated imagery*

So how did RenderMan come to be a standard in the first place? When the folks at Pixar began working on their renderer, there was a dearth of movie quality photorealistic renderers. They realized that in the future, this void might be filled by several implementations of renderers other than their own. They came up with the RenderMan Interface (RI) specification with the expectation that it would become a true industry-wide standard to be acknowledged and accepted by graphics software/hardware vendors. When the specification was initially announced, leading graphics vendors of the time such as Sun, Apollo, Prime, NeXT, etc. did endorse it. The hope was that modeling and rendering programs would use RenderMan as a medium through which to inter-communicate (Figure 2.3). In practice this is a one-way communication from a modeler to a renderer, where the modeler conveys its scene description (possibly animating each frame) via RenderMan, to a RenderMan-compliant (by definition) renderer. Note that having such an intermediate communication protocol is far better than the alternatives. If each renderer came with its own unique protocol, then every modeling program would need to support every such protocol and would need upgrading each time a new renderer is announced. This would lead to a tangle of interdependencies between the two sets of programs. Or at the other extreme, every modeler would come bundled with its own renderer which is the only one expected to be used with that modeler, preventing users from being able to use the renderer of their choice with it. This would lead to tightly coupled, mutually incompatible products, thereby limiting choices for end users.

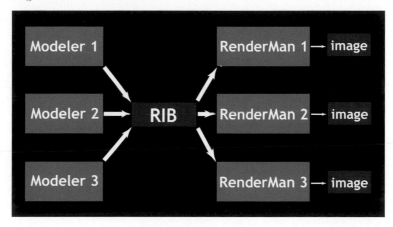

Figure 2.3 *RIB as an interface between modelers and renderers*

Pixar created PRMan as a reference implementation of the RenderMan interface and began publicly offering it as a commercial licensed product in 1989. That same year, Steve Upstill's *The RenderMan Companion* book was published, detailing the use of the programmatic aspects of the RI specification (the specification includes a "C" language interface, allowing programmers to write custom software which would output RIB, using "C"). The specification document, labeled "RenderMan Interface Specification, version 3.0" had been publicly released in 1988, a year prior to PRMan's debut. In 1989, version 3.1 of the specification was made available, its major feature being the introduction of the RIB protocol/format. The latest specification is contained in version 3.2, dated July 2000.

Unfortunately the specification never came to be a true industry-wide standard ratified by the graphics products community. For several years following its initial release, PRMan was the only commercial implementation of RenderMan, and the Blue Moon Ray Tracer (BMRT) by Larry Gritz was the only alternate version (available free for individuals, and at a nominal charge for a commercial site license). RenderMan today is a "de facto" standard that is owned by Pixar. In 2000 they updated the specification to version 3.2 in order to reflect the changes to PRMan they had made in the intervening decade.

Let us take a brief look at what is in the standard. The specification document ("RI Specification") is available at the Pixar website (www.pixar.com) if you want the complete treatment. Note that the specification should be considered the final word on RenderMan. It says that renderers aspiring to create movie quality visuals and adhering to the RenderMan Interface should provide these core capabilities:

- a complete hierarchical graphics state, meaning the ability to nest geometry (via transformations) and attribute specifications

- a set of geometric primitives useful in describing the large variety of shapes encountered in complex, non-trivial animation scenes

- perspective as well as orthographic camera projections; good image quality obtained through depth-based hidden surface elimination and pixel filtering

- ability to perform shading calculations through shaders written using the RenderMan Shading Language; a set of 15 shaders (which include light sources) capable of describing basic material/light interactions; ability to use "maps" (image-like files containing rectangular arrays of color values, depth, etc.)

- output images with arbitrary user-specified resolution (width and height in pixel units), containing any combination of RGB, A (alpha) and Z (depth) channels, with the RGB values gamma-corrected and dithered before being quantized

All of the above features are covered in detail in subsequent chapters, so it is not a concern if you currently do not quite understand what they mean.

The specification also lists the following capabilities as being "advanced", some or all of which implementations might offer in addition to the core, mandatory features:

- solid modeling, i.e. ability to specify shapes as the union, intersection, difference etc. (which are operations borrowed from set theory) of existing surfaces; ability to specify several "levels of detail" for a single shape

- additional camera projections, e.g. to create imagery as might be obtained through a fisheye lens; ability to simulate motion blur and depth of field which movie cameras inherently provide

- ability to do displacement mapping which creates rich surface detail through rendering, allowing modeled surfaces to remain simpler; global illumination, including ray-tracing and radiosity algorithms; area (extended) light sources; volumetric shading

- ability to calculate pixel values containing an arbitrary number of color channels, not just RGB

Again, several of these you will encounter in detail in forthcoming chapters.

The RI specification also covers the RenderMan Shading Language (RSL), a C-like programming language used to write shaders which are programs that describe materials, light sources etc. and used by RenderMan during the rendering process.

As mentioned earlier, for a few years PRMan and BMRT were the only two available implementations of the RenderMan standard. Today there are several more to choose from. Rick Lamont's RenderDotC is one of the more complete implementations available, as is Scott Iverson's AIR. For the sake of completeness, I also want to mention Entropy which was another implementation by Larry Gritz's company Exluna (Entropy is now off the market and Exluna has been acquired by NVIDIA Corporation). There are several other open source and freeware implementations as well, some of which are Aqsis, Angel and FreeMan. Please see the RfB web page for links to these. All these implementations tend to be platform-specific and mostly run on PCs. In contrast to these is jrMan which is an open source implementation using the Java programming language and can therefore run on multiple platforms.

Since rendering is hardware-intensive, almost from RenderMan's inception there have been attempts to run it directly on hardware, that is, to build RenderMan-specific computers. To this end Pixar created the Reyes Machine to execute the Reyes algorithm on custom graphics hardware. It was subsequently modified into another machine called RM-1. While RM-1 was never sold to the public, it was instrumental in the creation of the *Tin Toy* short. ART is a UK company which makes a rendering appliance called RenderDrive which can process RIB files using special-purpose hardware. Their latest offering targeted towards smaller outfits is called PURE which is a PCI card with onboard RenderMan hardware. Believe, Inc. was a company planning to offer the Believe Renderer, another hardware-accelerated RenderMan implementation. The product however never came to market due to financial difficulties.

Effort is underway by two leading graphics chipmakers NVIDIA and ATI, to create hardware which will accelerate shading calculations to the point of being able to generate photoreal renders in real time, at high resolution. These are not full-blown RenderMan implementations in hardware however. They accelerate the equivalents (translations) of RenderMan shaders, to provide real-time previews for quick turnarounds and experimentation in an animation production environment.

Figure 2.4 is a block diagram of the RenderMan system from an end user's (your) point of view. You need to input to RenderMan, at the very minimum, RIB files to be rendered. Usually you will also need to provide additional inputs in the form of shaders and maps. Shaders are external programs (small files on disk) that are used by RenderMan in conjunction with the RIB files in order to calculate shading for objects in your scene. Most shaders are self-contained, but there are some that need to access maps which are image-like data files containing information such as depth, color, etc. RenderMan takes these inputs (RIB files, and additionally, shaders and maps) and produces rendered images as outputs. Images used to illustrate concepts in subsequent chapters in the book were generated using such sets of RIB files, shaders and maps. At the online RfB page you will find links to download all these files so that you can recreate the images on your own machine, examine and modify the RIB files and shaders to gain hands-on knowledge of RenderMan.

Figure 2.4 *RenderMan block diagram*

So where do RIB files, shaders and maps come from? Let us look at sources for each. RIB files have multiple sources. The simplest ones can be just typed up using a text editor program (for this you need to know RIB "syntax" or structure, which the following chapter goes through in detail). Modeling/animation programs might have built-in RIB output capability (e.g. Houdini, Ayam, solidThinking and Blender are examples of programs that directly output RIB). Alternately, separate plugins might work in conjunction with the modeling application, helping to translate scene description to RIB. For example Maya has the MTOR and MayaMan plugins, Softimage XSI has RiO, LightWave has LightMan, 3D Studio Max has MaxMan and so on. In addition, RIB can output from running custom programs written in programming languages such as "C". The RenderMan specification lists C bindings (function calls) throughout the document, and these can be integrated into custom applications to output RIB. For example, terrains, foliage, mathematical shapes etc. could be output as RIB through custom programs that encode the logic to synthesize these shapes as well to output them as RIB. Even though the RI specification only lists C language bindings, you can find bindings on the web for other popular programming languages such as Tcl, Perl, Python, Java, etc. What this means is that you can write your software in one of the languages and use the bindings to convert your output into RIB. Finally, RIB translators exist, which are programs that create RIB from other scene description formats such as Mental Ray's format. What about shaders? In the early days, the only way to create shaders was to create them by hand, i.e. write a small piece of software using a text editor and then have it converted (compiled) into a form RenderMan can use. These days there are other alternatives, although writing them from scratch is still an invaluable skill (we will address shader writing in detail, in Chapter 8, "Shading"). One modern alternative is to use the facilities provided by a RenderMan plugin attached to a host modeling/animation program. For example Maya's translator plugin is MTOR, whose shader component is called Slim. Using Slim you can visually hook up primitive building blocks to create complex, non-trivial, layered appearances (materials). In addition there are standalone programs that specialize in shader construction. Best among them is ShadeTree which is commercial software. Shrimp is an open source alternative that also lets you interactively create shaders. Finally we consider map sources. Maps come in a variety of forms, e.g. texture maps, shadow maps and reflection maps. We will deal with them in more detail in Chapter 8, and for now it is sufficient to mention that maps can originate from regular digital imagery (photos, scanned art, hand-painted images, etc.) or from rendered and other computer-generated sources. If they come from RenderMan itself, they could be viewed as intermediate sources which help with the ultimate end product which would be the final rendered image.

2.3 How PRMan works

In order to get the most out of PRMan, it is helpful to know how the underlying Reyes algorithm works, and that is the topic of this concluding section. I am leaving out details and am presenting just the overall idea behind each step in the algorithm. Figure 2.5 shows the pipeline. As you know by now, the input is a RIB file (along with associated shaders and maps), and the output, a rendered image.

The discussion is very similar to section 1.4 in the previous chapter on how a renderer works, except here we are specifically talking about PRMan.

The very first thing that happens is that the RIB file gets "parsed", that is, scanned, interpreted and understood. This is similar to how you would read a sentence and make sense of it through the words that make up that sentence.

Parsing breaks down a RIB file into components, of which surface primitives (the geometry that makes up your scene elements) are of chief interest here. Each primitive is first bound (using bounding box estimates) to see if it fully or partially lies inside the camera frustum. If it does not, it can be discarded and no more processing of it is necessary since the camera cannot see it.

Primitives that are visible are usually too large to start shading, so they are usually split into spatially smaller subprimitives (Figure 2.6). This is done iteratively, meaning that each split primitive is examined to see if it is too big, and if so, split again. Eventually the primitives pass a threshold when they are no longer too big, and so can continue down the pipeline.

When is a primitive too big to shade? To answer that, you need to know a central fact about the Reyes algorithm. Each small-enough primitive, regardless of its user-level type, is broken down (diced) into a rectangular grid of small, flat shapes called micropolygons (Figure 2.7).

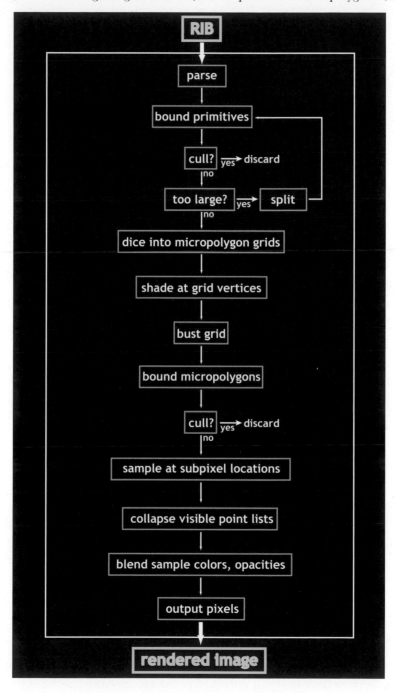

Figure 2.5 *The Reyes rendering pipeline*

It is these micropolygons that get shaded, and those shaded results eventually contribute to final pixel colors and opacities. By breaking every high level primitive (polygons, spline surfaces, blobbies, curves, particles etc.) into micropolygons, a certain uniformity is achieved in processing them downstream. This also future-proofs the algorithm when it comes to including new geometry types. The Reyes algorithm is in essence a micropolygon-centered algorithm.

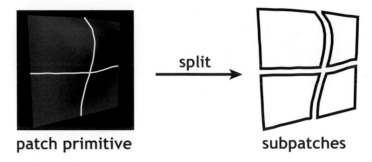

patch primitive   **subpatches**

Figure 2.6 *Splitting a primitive into subprimitives*

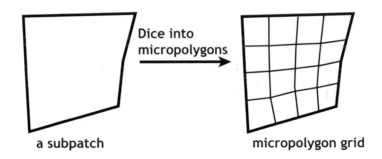

a subpatch   **micropolygon grid**

Figure 2.7 *Dicing a primitive into a micropolygon grid*

Micropolygons are approximately pixel-sized. The user controls their size, through a ShadingRate specification in the RIB file (Chapter 7, "Controls", has more to say on this). Usually several micropolygons (4 for example) might fit inside one pixel. The user can also specify a grid size, that is, the number of subdivisions into which our primitive should be diced. This is therefore a way to specify micropolygon count for our primitive. If the grid size is 8, for example, we are specifying that our primitive should be split into 8x8, i.e. 64 micropolygons. Grid size is specified via a RIB specification appropriately named "gridsize" (again, Chapter 7 has more about this).

So if a primitive were to be diced into a collection of micropolygons specified by gridsize, then each micropolygon's size (area) will be the total primitive size (area) divided by the micropolygon count derived from gridsize. What if the calculated micropolygon area were to turn out larger than what we specified through the ShadingRate attribute? It simply means that our primitive is too large, and needs to be split further into smaller primitives. The idea is to continue splitting so that primitives eventually become small enough for Reyes to dice them into micropolygons which meet both our count (via gridsize) and size specification (via ShadingRate).

Once such a micropolygon grid is generated from a split primitive, the algorithm proceeds to the shading stage. Shading calculations (using external shader programs we talked about earlier) happen at each vertex of the micropolygon grid, yielding a color and opacity value at the grid vertices (Figure 2.8).

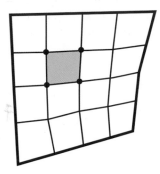

Figure 2.8 *A micropolygon and its four corners (vertices)*

After shading is completed, the grid of micropolygons is broken up (busted) into individual micropolygons (each with four corners, each corner with its own color and opacity) and passed down the pipeline (Figure 2.9). Every micropolygon is first tested for bounds, that is, to see if it is still visible. If not, it can be discarded. Why test again? Because the shading step, specifically, displacement shading calculations, might have spatially moved our micropolygon to outside the camera limits.

Our final goal is to derive pixel colors and opacities from these micropolygon corner colors and opacities. This is done in two stages. In the first stage, each micropolygon is sampled at pre-determined subpixel locations, at the pixel (or pixels) containing the micropolygon.

Figure 2.10 illustrates the situation, where there are four subpixel samples (black filled circles) inside the central square which denotes a pixel.

A subpixel location might lie enclosed within a micropolygon, in which case the four corner colors and opacities of the micropolygon are blended (interpolated) at the subpixel location to yield a weighted color/opacity value at the location. The color/opacity value is stored at the location, along with the micropolygon's z-depth (from the camera) to form a visible-point list for the location. On the other hand if the subpixel location is not covered by the micropolygon at all, that micropolygon does not contribute towards the color/opacity at that location. Once all the micropolygons that cover a pixel are accounted for and visible point lists generated at subpixel locations, each such list can be collapsed (colors and opacities blended using the associated z values) to yield a single color and opacity at each subpixel sample (Figure 2.11).

In Figure 2.10, you can see that the two sample locations (black dots) on the right are each covered by two micropolygons, and the two sample locations on the left are each covered by a single micropolygon (where both the micropolygons are part of the same grid). Figure 2.11 shows the collapsing of the sample points from Figure 2.10. On the right illustration in Figure 2.11, sampled values from the micropolygons at each location are blended to yield colors C3 and C4 (opacities follow similar calculations). The left side samples do not have values from multiple micropolygons to blend, and the individual micropolygons covering those samples yield interpolated values C1 and C2.

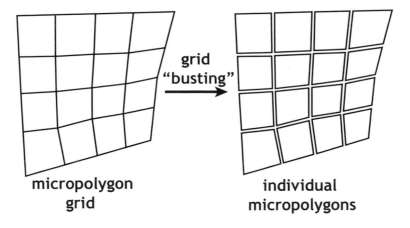

Figure 2.9 *Grid "busting"*

The last stage (Figure 2.12) involves spatially blending these subpixel color/opacity values to yield a final, single value for the entire pixel (after all, the output image can have just one color value and one opacity value at each pixel, since a pixel by definition is the smallest indivisible unit in a digital image). This blending operation is also known as filtering, involving a classic speed/quality tradeoff which is under user control (see Chapter 7, "Controls").

After this last blending step, each pixel has a color and opacity (alpha channel) value, and the entire pixel array is output to its destination (file or screen or other) as the PRMan-rendered final image.

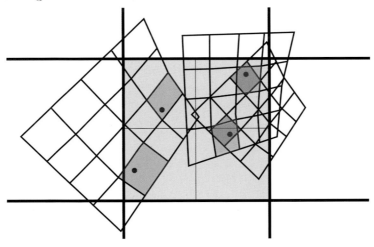

Figure 2.10 *Sampling micropolygons at subpixel locations*

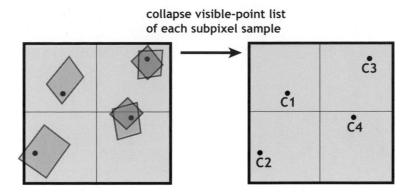

Figure 2.11 *Collapsing visible-point sample lists*

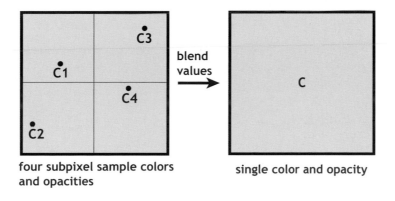

Figure 2.12 *Blending (filtering) subpixel values to produce final pixel result*

The above description does leave out an important memory-related enhancement to the Reyes algorithm, called bucketing. Without bucketing, Reyes would need prohibitive amounts of memory to keep track of subpixel visible-point lists for all pixels in the image. The one line explanation of bucketing is that the image is rendered in small pixel blocks (tiles) called buckets and not all at once. Again, Chapter 7 talks about how you can specify the bucket size for your renders and why/how it matters.

Note that hidden surface elimination is performed as a combination of visible-point list collapsing and subsequent subpixel sample blending. Visible-point subpixel lists are needed in the first place, to handle semi-transparent surface primitives that all happen to cover the same pixels. If micropolygons from fully opaque surfaces are found to cover a set of pixels, subsequent primitives that lie entirely behind the opaque grids can be discarded without further processing, since they are obscured by the existing micropolygons (primitives that happen to lie in front still need to be processed however). This optimization, called occlusion culling, is another enhancement made to the basic Reyes algorithm.

Also, another unique feature of the Reyes algorithm is that primitives are hidden after they are shaded, not before. This permits displacement mapping in a straightforward way, where a displacement shader can move micropolygons around in space without worrying about them obscuring others (hiding occurs only after the micropolygons are all shaded and possibly displaced during shading). On the flip side, this strategy does lead to shading calculations being wasted on micropolygons that get hidden (and hence discarded) in subsequent steps. High quality displacement creation is one of RenderMan's strong features and is considered worthy enough to offset inefficiencies resulting from wastage of shading calculations.

3
RIB syntax

This chapter explores the organization and syntax of RIB files. A lot of how RenderMan (and 3D graphics) works can be learned by "tinkering" with RIB files. The knowledge you gain by doing so will help you in putting your own RIB files together, modifying existing ones and debugging ones which do not quite produce the images you want. It will also help you understand RIB file fragments that are used throughout the rest of the book for illustrating rendering concepts.

3.1 Standards, interfaces and protocols

Take a look around you to get a sense for how standards are essential in today's world. Items relating to food, clothing, shelter and day-to-day living (e.g. milk cartons, shoes, door frames, batteries, bulbs) come in standard quantities such as length, weight, volume, voltage, etc. Standards promote interoperability through precise specifications, thereby letting us mix and match compatible things. For instance, phones and electrical appliances come with standard connectors that let us simply plug them into our wall sockets. Related to the notion of standards are protocols, which provide well-defined interfaces for systems to communicate with each other. For example, telephones, modems and cable boxes each have their preset communication protocols. And in the world of computers, protocols abound. TCP/IP is the message protocol that forms the basis of all Internet communications. On personal computers it is common to see interfaces (with their associated protocols) such as RS232 (serial port), USB and IEEE 1394 (FireWire). Such interfaces permit a diverse set of devices which implement the protocol to interoperate. MIDI is a very popular interface that lets digital musical instruments interact with each other to exchange data and/or control signals. In a similar sense, RIB (RenderMan Interface Bytestream) serves as a protocol for modelers to communicate with RenderMan-compliant renderers. The internals of the modelers are hidden from the renderers and vice-versa. The modelers output RIB which the renderers consume. The communication between them occurs solely through the RIB interface. Note however that RIB is not a true bi-directional protocol, since the renderer hardly "talks back" to the modeler. The communication is essentially one-way, with RIB serving as the intermediary.

3.2 Formats for graphics description

Notations, symbols and diagramming schemes exist to describe content in a variety of domains, be it music, building construction, electronic circuitry or needlework embroidery. The structured content encoded in notation is transcribed into a product or result, by the person(s) processing ("parsing") the content. In a similar sense, digital files serve as a vehicle to create, store, transmit and consume content such as audio, video and still imagery. Associated with the notion of a file is that of a file format, a predetermined way to store information in the file. It is the format that provides structure (and hence, meaning) to the sequence of 1s and 0s that make up any digital file. For instance the wildly popular MP3 format for digital audio lets users create music files using one of many different "ripper" programs (which encode audio as MP3) and play the files back using their choice of hardware/software MP3 players (which read them and recreate audio from the stored data). File formats also exist to describe content/data created by programs in a variety of application areas including email, web browsing, audio/video, typesetting, finance, machine control, etc. In this section we will look at some file formats that specifically relate to graphics. This is to motivate the discussion of the RIB format in the following section.

3.2.1 PBM

The PBM file format is for storing 1-bit (black and white) images, and is shown here for its simplicity (it is not widely used in practice). Here is a simple image in the PBM format:

```
P1
8 8
0 1 1 1 1 1 0 0
0 0 0 0 0 0 0 1
0 0 0 0 0 0 0 0
0 0 1 1 1 1 1 0
0 0 0 0 0 0 0 0
0 1 0 0 0 0 0 1
1 0 0 0 0 0 1 0
1 1 0 0 1 1 0 0
```

As you can see, a white pixel is encoded by a "0" and a black pixel, by a "1". The first line is the PBM image header and the second line contains the image resolution (pixel count).

Figure 3.1 shows the corresponding 8x8 image, magnified 990% for illustration. If you were to save the above data in a file (e.g. simple.pbm) and use a program such as IrfanView (on a PC) to open and view the file, you would see the pictured result.

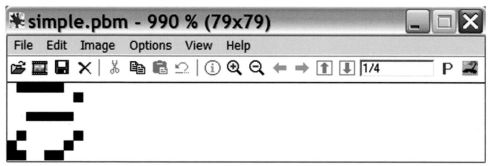

Figure 3.1 *An 8x8 PBM image*

The pixel data stored in the file is "rendered" by the viewer program to produce the resulting image. There are literally dozens of other pixel-based image formats in widespread use, some examples being TIFF, JPEG, PNG, WBMP and Cineon.

3.2.2 SVG

SVG (Scalable Vector Graphics) is a relatively new format approved by the World Wide Web Consortium (W3C) for representing vector data, typically for use in web browsers. It presents an alternative to proprietary formats such as Macromedia's .swf Flash format.

Here is the SVG code for a simple diagram:

```
<?xml version="1.0" encoding="ISO-8859-1" standalone="no"?>

<!DOCTYPE svg PUBLIC "-//W3C//DTD SVG 20010904//EN"
"http://www.w3.org/TR/2001/REC-SVG-0010904/DTD/svg10.dtd">

<svg xmlns="http://www.w3.org/2000/svg"
xmlns:xlink="http://www.w3.org/1999/xlink">

<rect
  x="0"
  y="0"
  width="300"
  height="300"
  style="fill:none; stroke:#AA0099; stroke-width:6;"/>

<rect x="100" y="100"
rx="5" ry="5"
width="120" height="120"
fill="red"/>

  <circle
   cx="0"
   cy="0"
   r="90"
   fill="yellow"
   stroke="blue"
   stroke-width="10"/>

<g style="stroke-width:4; stroke:black">
<path d="M 40 250 L  40 100 L 40 250 L 275 250 Z"/>
</g>

<text style="font-size:72; text-anchor:start"
x="100" y="80">
RfB
</text>

</svg>
```

As you can see, the code is very easy to read and is almost self-descriptive. SVG itself is a form of XML data. XML stands for "eXtensible Modeling Language" and provides a way for content in a variety of application domains (2D vector graphics in our case) to be represented using self-describing tags.

Figure 3.2 shows our SVG code running inside Adobe's free SVG viewer. In addition to SVG and the SWF format, several other vector formats exist, e.g. Adobe Illustrator .ai, PostScript (see the following subsection) and .DWG.

Figure 3.2 *SVG image*

3.2.3 PostScript

PostScript, which is really a programming language rather than just a file format, practically launched the desktop publishing revolution in the mid-1980s. More precisely, it is a page description language specifically designed for representing content for a printed piece of paper. In that sense it is a graphics format, the graphics being typeset text and illustrations on a 2D page.

Here is a piece of PostScript code which takes two strings of text ("RenderMan" and "for Beginners") and repeatedly rotates each of them.

```
%!
306 396 translate
0.2 setgray
/Helvetica-BoldOblique findfont 42 scalefont setfont
20 30  360 {
gsave
      rotate 0 0 moveto
      (    RenderMan) true charpath fill
grestore
} for
0.4 setgray
/Helvetica-BoldOblique findfont 26 scalefont setfont
16 rotate
20 30 360 {
gsave
```

```
        rotate 0 0 moveto
        (                for Beginners) true charpath fill
grestore
} for
showpage
```

If you create a file with this code and send it to a PostScript-capable printer, you would see what looks like Figure 3.3 printed on a page. Alternately you could use a PostScript viewer such as Ghostview to see the same result on your screen.

Figure 3.3 *PostScript output*

As mentioned above, PostScript is also a general purpose programming language and so can be used to compute arbitrary things. For instance, the following PostScript program computes the value of "pi" to over 1000 decimal places and formats the result for printing out.

```
%!PS-Adobe-2.0
%%Title: Calculate Pi in PostScript
%%Creator: Frank Martin Siegert [frank@this.net] -
http://www.this.net/
%%Date: 23. November 1996 02:23
% Updated 2. April 1998 23:40
```

```
%%BoundingBox: 0 0 592 792
%%DocumentNeededFonts: Courier Courier-Bold
%%EndComments

% Enter your desired number of digits here, min. 20, max. 262136
% Be prepared to wait a long time for anything > 1000

/ndigits 1000 def

% If your printer fails with a timeout error try to uncomment the
next line
% this will give you one hour extra time...

% statusdict begin 3600 setjobtimeout end

% Some defines for startup

/i 0 def
/str4 4 string def
/nblock ndigits 4 idiv 2 sub def
/t1 nblock 1 add array def
/t2 nblock 1 add array def
/t3 nblock 1 add array def
/tot nblock 1 add  array def
/base 10000 def
/resstr 4 string def
% Define the page sizes and margins
/pagemargin 60 def
/lineheight 12 def
/pageheight 792 lineheight sub pagemargin sub def
/pagewidth 592 pagemargin sub def
pagemargin pageheight moveto
/bigfont {
    /Courier-Bold findfont 36 scalefont setfont
} bind def
/smallfont {
    /Courier findfont 12 scalefont setfont
} bind def
/scratch 16 string def
% Define bigmath routines - still a bit suboptimal
% (direct ported from the C implementation by Roy Williams)
/bigadd { % increment result
    /result exch store
    /increment exch store
    0 1 nblock 1 sub {
        nblock exch sub /i exch store
        result i get
        increment i get
        add dup base ge {
            base sub
            result exch i exch put
            result dup i 1 sub get
            1 add i 1 sub exch put
        } {
            result exch i exch put
```

```
            } ifelse
        } for
    } bind def
    /bigsub { % decrement result
        /result exch store
        /decrement exch store
        0 1 nblock 1 sub {
            nblock exch sub /i exch store
            result i get
            decrement i get
            sub dup 0 lt {
                base add
                result exch i exch put
                result dup i 1 sub get
                1 sub i 1 sub exch put
            } {
                result exch i exch put
            } ifelse
        } for
    } bind def
    /bigmult { % factor result
        /carry 0 store
        /result exch store
        /factor exch store
        0 1 nblock {
            nblock exch sub /i exch store
            result i get factor mul
            carry add
            dup /carry exch base idiv store
            base mod
            result exch i exch put
        } for
    } bind def
    /bigdiv { % denom result
        /carry 0 store
        /result exch store
        /denom exch store
        0 1 nblock {
            /i exch store
            result i get carry base mul add
            dup denom mod /carry exch store
            denom idiv
            result exch i exch put
        } for
    } bind def
    /bigset { % rhs result
        /result exch store
        /rhs exch store
        0 1 nblock {
            result exch 0 put
        } for
        result 0 rhs put
    } bind def
    /bigzero { % result
        /result exch store 1
```

```
        0 1 nblock {
            result exch get 0 ne { pop 0 exit } if
        } for
    } bind def
    /bigcopy { % from result
        copy pop
    } bind def
    /bigprint { % result
        /result exch store
        bigfont result 0 get str4 cvs onpage smallfont (.) onpage
        1 1 nblock {
            result exch get str4 cvs resstr 0 (0000) putinterval resstr
            exch dup length 4 exch sub exch putinterval resstr onpage
        } for
    } bind def

    /bigatan { % onestep denom w2 w1 result
        /result2 exch store
        /w1 exch store
        /w2 exch store
        /denom exch store
        /denom2 denom denom mul store
        /onestep exch store
        /k 1 def
        1 result2 bigset
        denom result2 bigdiv
        result2 w1 bigcopy
        {
            onestep 0 ne {
                denom2 w1 bigdiv
            } {
                denom w1 bigdiv
                denom w1 bigdiv
            } ifelse
            w1 w2 bigcopy
            k 2 mul 1 add w2 bigdiv
            k 2 mod 0 ne {
                w2 result2 bigsub
            } {
                w2 result2 bigadd
            } ifelse
            /k k 1 add store
            w2 bigzero 1 eq { exit } if
        } loop
    } bind def
    % Define output routines
    /didpaint false def
    /onpage {
        /didpaint true store
        show
        currentpoint exch pagewidth ge {
            pagemargin exch lineheight sub moveto
            currentpoint exch pop pagemargin le {
                showpage
                    pagemargin pageheight moveto
```

```
        /didpaint false store
      } if
    } {  pop } ifelse
} bind def
% Using Machin's formula:  pi/4 = 4 arctan(1/5) - arctan(1/239)
1 5 t2 t1 tot bigatan 4 tot bigmult 2 239 t2 t1 t3 bigatan
t3 tot bigsub 4 tot bigmult tot bigprint
didpaint { showpage } if
%%EOF
```

If you were to print a file containing the above program on a PostScript printer, you would be making the processor in the printer carry out the computations! The output is shown in Figure 3.4.

An alternative page description language is HP-GL, used in HP's laser printers. Also, the PDF file format (which is related to PostScript and is more compact in terms of file size) has become the de facto standard for document handling, both on and offline. While we are on the subject of documents and printer page description, it is worth mentioning that formats exist to describe page composition and layout from a design point of view. For instance RTF (Rich Text Format) adds fonts, color handling, image support and rudimentary layout information to plain text files. SGML is a highly structured document description format used for very large documents. TeX (pronounced "Tech") is an expressive, powerful typesetting format very popular in academic circles.

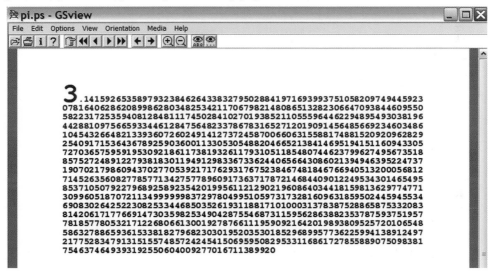

Figure 3.4 *PostScript output showing the computation of pi*

3.2.4 Wavefront .obj

Having seen some formats to describe 2D elements, we now turn to 3D. The .obj file format from Wavefront corporation is a way of representing polygonal meshes (and polylines). Here is what a dodecahedron looks like, in .obj format:

```
# Dodecahedron
# 20 vertices
v 0.469 0.469 0.469
```

```
v 0.290 0.000 0.759
v -0.759 -0.290 0.000
v 0.759 0.290 0.000
v -0.469 0.469 -0.469
v 0.000 -0.759 -0.290
v -0.759 0.290 0.000
v 0.469 -0.469 0.469
v -0.469 0.469 0.469
v -0.469 -0.469 0.469
v 0.469 -0.469 -0.469
v 0.290 0.000 -0.759
v -0.469 -0.469 -0.469
v 0.000 -0.759 0.290
v 0.000 0.759 -0.290
v -0.290 0.000 0.759
v 0.759 -0.290 0.000
v -0.290 0.000 -0.759
v 0.469 0.469 -0.469
v 0.000 0.759 0.290
# 12 pentagonal faces
f 10 14 8 2 16
f 7 5 15 20 9
f 13 6 14 10 3
f 7 3 13 18 5
f 17 11 12 19 4
f 20 9 16 2 1
f 17 8 2 1 4
f 6 13 18 12 11
f 19 15 5 18 12
f 17 11 6 14 8
f 3 7 9 16 10
f 20 1 4 19 15
```

The output, as rendered by the shareware "quick3D" viewer, is shown in Figure 3.5.

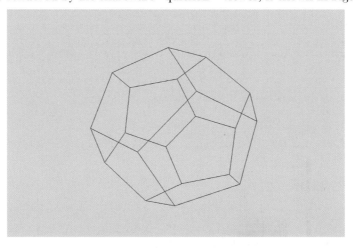

Figure 3.5 *Dodecahedron .obj*

Note that a .obj polymesh can be imported into a variety of 3D software such as Maya, LightWave etc. for inclusion in scenes. In addition it can also be converted into a multitude of other polymesh formats e.g. LWO, 3DS, etc., which store the same mesh data using alternate representations.

3.2.5 Maya .ma

3D graphics scenes created using programs such as Maya, Softimage XSI and Houdini are stored using proprietary formats. The data held in a scene file comes to life when opened by the application that created the file. Shown below is a Maya .ma file containing a torus and a light source.

```
//Maya ASCII 4.5 scene
//Name: torus_dirlt.ma
requires maya "4.5";

currentUnit -l centimeter -a degree -t film;
fileInfo "application" "maya";
fileInfo "product" "Maya Unlimited 4.5";
fileInfo "version" "4.5";
fileInfo "cutIdentifier" "200208160001";
fileInfo "osv" "Microsoft Windows XP Professional  (Build 2600)\n";

createNode transform -s -n "persp";
    setAttr ".v" no;
    setAttr ".t" -type "double3" 3.1745809971311574 4.553452528656317
3.6058736909890516 ;
    setAttr ".r" -type "double3" -40.538352729602479 38.19999999999991
-2.0236220545269295e-015 ;

createNode camera -s -n "perspShape" -p "persp";
    setAttr -k off ".v" no;
    setAttr ".fl" 34.999999999999993;
    setAttr ".coi" 6.6278017430569589;
    setAttr ".imn" -type "string" "persp";
    setAttr ".den" -type "string" "persp_depth";
    setAttr ".man" -type "string" "persp_mask";
    setAttr ".tp" -type "double3" -4.4408920985006262e-016 0 0 ;
    setAttr ".hc" -type "string" "viewSet -p %camera";

createNode transform -s -n "top";
    setAttr ".v" no;
    setAttr ".t" -type "double3" 0 100 0 ;
    setAttr ".r" -type "double3" -89.999999999999986 0 0 ;

createNode camera -s -n "topShape" -p "top";
    setAttr -k off ".v" no;
    setAttr ".rnd" no;
    setAttr ".coi" 100;
    setAttr ".ow" 30;
    setAttr ".imn" -type "string" "top";
    setAttr ".den" -type "string" "top_depth";
    setAttr ".man" -type "string" "top_mask";
    setAttr ".hc" -type "string" "viewSet -t %camera";
    setAttr ".o" yes;
```

```
createNode transform -s -n "front";
    setAttr ".v" no;
    setAttr ".t" -type "double3" 0 0 100 ;

createNode camera -s -n "frontShape" -p "front";
    setAttr -k off ".v" no;
    setAttr ".rnd" no;
    setAttr ".coi" 100;
    setAttr ".ow" 30;
    setAttr ".imn" -type "string" "front";
    setAttr ".den" -type "string" "front_depth";
    setAttr ".man" -type "string" "front_mask";
    setAttr ".hc" -type "string" "viewSet -f %camera";
    setAttr ".o" yes;

createNode transform -s -n "side";
    setAttr ".v" no;
    setAttr ".t" -type "double3" 100 0 0 ;
    setAttr ".r" -type "double3" 0 89.999999999999986 0 ;

createNode camera -s -n "sideShape" -p "side";
    setAttr -k off ".v" no;
    setAttr ".rnd" no;
    setAttr ".coi" 100;
    setAttr ".ow" 30;
    setAttr ".imn" -type "string" "side";
    setAttr ".den" -type "string" "side_depth";
    setAttr ".man" -type "string" "side_mask";
    setAttr ".hc" -type "string" "viewSet -s %camera";
    setAttr ".o" yes;

createNode transform -n "nurbsTorus1";
createNode nurbsSurface -n "nurbsTorusShape1" -p "nurbsTorus1";
    setAttr -k off ".v";
    setAttr ".vir" yes;
    setAttr ".vif" yes;
    setAttr ".tw" yes;
    setAttr ".dvu" 0;
    setAttr ".dvv" 0;
    setAttr ".cpr" 4;
    setAttr ".cps" 4;
    setAttr ".nufa" 4.5;
    setAttr ".nvfa" 4.5;

createNode transform -n "directionalLight1";
    setAttr ".t" -type "double3" -1.5375070753177869
1.5801823064849607 0.067431258236601899 ;
    setAttr ".r" -type "double3" -48.123063671300734 -
29.397848432889013 -2.4973563936518759 ;
    setAttr ".s" -type "double3" 0.46489882824435241
0.46489882824435241 0.46489882824435241 ;
createNode directionalLight -n "directionalLightShape1" -p
"directionalLight1";
    setAttr -k off ".v";
```

```
createNode lightLinker -n "lightLinker1";

createNode displayLayerManager -n "layerManager";
createNode displayLayer -n "defaultLayer";

createNode renderLayerManager -n "renderLayerManager";
createNode renderLayer -n "defaultRenderLayer";
createNode renderLayer -s -n "globalRender";

createNode brush -n "brush1";

createNode makeNurbTorus -n "makeNurbTorus1";
    setAttr ".ax" -type "double3" 0 1 0 ;
    setAttr ".nsp" 4;
    setAttr ".hr" 0.5;

createNode script -n "sceneConfigurationScriptNode";
    setAttr ".b" -type "string" "playbackOptions -min 1 -max 400 -ast
1 -aet 450 ";
    setAttr ".st" 6;
select -ne :time1;
    setAttr ".o" 1;
select -ne :renderPartition;
    setAttr -s 2 ".st";
select -ne :renderGlobalsList1;
select -ne :defaultShaderList1;
    setAttr -s 2 ".s";
select -ne :postProcessList1;
    setAttr -s 2 ".p";
select -ne :lightList1;
select -ne :initialShadingGroup;
    setAttr ".ro" yes;
select -ne :initialParticleSE;
    setAttr ".ro" yes;
select -ne :defaultLightSet;

connectAttr "makeNurbTorus1.os" "nurbsTorusShape1.cr";
connectAttr ":defaultLightSet.msg" "lightLinker1.lnk[0].llnk";
connectAttr ":initialShadingGroup.msg" "lightLinker1.lnk[0].olnk";
connectAttr ":defaultLightSet.msg" "lightLinker1.lnk[1].llnk";
connectAttr ":initialParticleSE.msg" "lightLinker1.lnk[1].olnk";
connectAttr "layerManager.dli[0]" "defaultLayer.id";
connectAttr "renderLayerManager.rlmi[0]" "defaultRenderLayer.rlid";
connectAttr "lightLinker1.msg" ":lightList1.ln" -na;
connectAttr "directionalLightShape1.ltd" ":lightList1.l" -na;
connectAttr "nurbsTorusShape1.iog" ":initialShadingGroup.dsm" -na;
connectAttr "directionalLight1.iog" ":defaultLightSet.dsm" -na;
// End of torus_dirlt.ma
```

Figure 3.6 shows a screen shot of the torus scene opened in Maya.

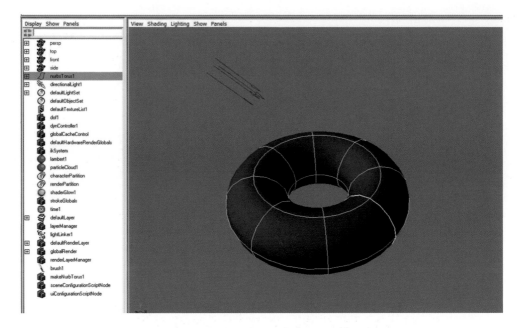

Figure 3.6 *Contents of a Maya scene file*

Every 3D animation package records data in its own format. For instance Softimage's scene databases are stored in the XSI file format, and Houdini generates .hip scene files. In addition to proprietary scene file formats, there are cross-platform open formats such VRML .wrl which can be used for encoding scene information. Renderers expect data in their own formats as well. For instance, just as RIB files represent scenes destined for RenderMan, Mental Ray scenes are described using the .mi file format.

3.2.6 HTML

Our final example illustrates HTML, which is the web page description format that ushered in the World Wide Web revolution, along with the HTTP server/browser protocol. Like SVG, HTML is also a tag-based format (and can also be regarded as a subset of XML just like SVG). Here is some HTML representing a simple web page:

```
<html>

<hr>

<center> <img src = "tribar_cubes.jpg"> </center>

<h1> <center> RenderMan for Beginners </center> </h1>


<h2> <center> Saty Raghavachary </center> </h2>

<h3> <center> Focal Press </center> </h3>

<hr>

</html>
```

Figure 3.7 shows the page viewed using the Opera browser.

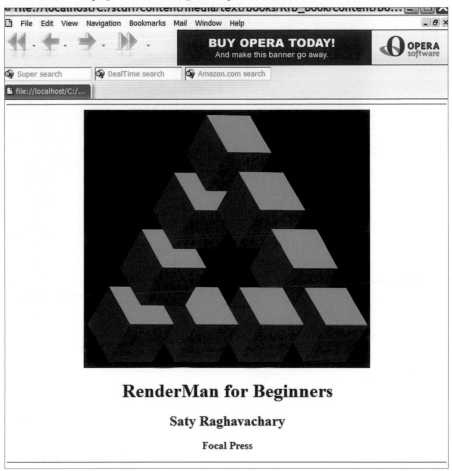

Figure 3.7 *HTML page viewed under Opera*

In addition to the formats mentioned above, there are several programmatic interfaces also available for describing graphics. One of the most widely used is OpenGL, which is an interface implemented in hardware by vendors who produce 3D graphics acceleration cards and chips. Programs wanting to take advantage of the hardware acceleration simply translate their graphics into appropriate OpenGL "calls", and the hardware (if available on the user's machine) does the rest. The common interface is what makes it possible for diverse programs (e.g. renderers, flight simulators, 3D games) to accelerate their graphics on compliant hardware manufactured by a variety of vendors.

3.3 RIB structure

Having examined several formats that represent graphics data, we now turn to the main topic of this chapter, namely the structure and syntax of RIB files. The RIB format is formally defined in the RenderMan specification document. Instead of presenting the format as a set of "dry" rules, we will use a couple of RIB files and short snippets to illustrate the salient features. You can always consult the RI Specification (see Chapter 10,

"Resources") for the full details. The commands in the snippets of code presented here will be explained in greater detail in later chapters. The informal discussion presented here will cover just the basics, to get you started with your own experimentation with RIB.

3.3.1 Overall idea

As has been mentioned several times so far, scene descriptions are encoded as RIB files which get rendered by RenderMan, resulting in output imagery. The inputs you provide to RenderMan in addition to the RIB files usually include shaders and associated map (processed image) files.

Production-quality RIB files are typically generated by scene translators that work in conjunction with 3D animation packages such as Maya and Houdini. RIB files can also be programmatically generated, in other words, by running software written to output RIB.

Small RIB files can be created "by hand" using text editing programs, for instructional purposes. You can use any plain-text (ASCII) editing program for this purpose (e.g. Notepad, Wordpad on PCs). Simply create and edit RIB files as you would any other text. Once you have a collection of RIBs you can create new ones by cutting and pasting sections from existing ones. Several RIB examples for this book were generated that way. For editing larger RIB files, programmers' text editors such as emacs, vi, CoolEdit, etc. are more suitable than general purpose text editors since they offer useful features such as syntax coloring (where key words in your RIB files will be highlighted using colors you choose, making it easier to spot them) and parenthesis matching (where the program will point out a parenthesis or brace that matches the one your cursor is currently on, by briefly "jumping" to it and back).

3.3.2 Syntax

Take a look at the listing below which contains RIB code to render the teapot which you encountered earlier in Figure 1.13.

```
# teapot.rib
# Author: Stephen H. Westin,
# Ford Motor Company Corporate Design
#   <swestin@ford.com>
# Date: 9/5/95
#
# This is the traditional Utah teapot from
# Martin Newell's breakfast table.
# I got it from a demo directory for
# Apollo's 3D Graphics Metafile Resource
# (GMR) on an Apollo DN10000. I translated it
# manually to RIB and set up
# the view and light sources.

Display "uteapot.tiff" "framebuffer" "rgb"
#Display "teapot" "framebuffer" "rgb"
Format 320 200 1.0
PixelSamples 2 2
# Correct for monitor gamma of 2.2
Exposure 1.0 2.2
Projection "perspective" "fov" 25
Translate 0 0 400
Rotate -115 1 0 0
```

```
Rotate 19 0 0 1
Translate -25 0 -50
WorldBegin
LightSource "ambientlight" 1 "intensity" .7 "lightcolor" [.4 0 1]
LightSource "distantlight" 2 "intensity" 1.0
            "from" [-50 300 200] "to" [0 0 0] "lightcolor" [1 .8
.7]
LightSource "distantlight" 2 "intensity" 0.6
            "from" [-50 -300 200] "to" [0 0 0]
LightSource "distantlight" 2 "intensity" 0.4
            "from" [50 -200 10] "to" [0 0 0] "lightcolor" [.4 .3 1]
Color [1 .5 .3]
Surface "plastic" "Ka" 0.1 "Kd" 0.05 "Ks" 1.0 "roughness" 0.1
"specularcolor" [1 .4 .1]
# xBodyBack
AttributeBegin
  Basis "bezier" 3 "bezier" 3
  Patch "bicubic" "P" [
    -80.0 0.0 30.0 -80.0 -44.8 30.0 -44.8 -80.0 30.0 0.0 -80.0 30.0
    -80.0 0.0 12.0 -80.0 -44.8 12.0 -44.8 -80.0 12.0 0.0 -80.0 12.0
    -60.0 0.0 3.0 -60.0 -33.6 3.0 -33.6 -60.0 3.0 0.0 -60.0 3.0
    -60.0 0.0 0.0 -60.0 -33.6 0.0 -33.6 -60.0 0.0 0.0 -60.0 0.0
  ]
  Patch "bicubic" "P" [
    0.0 -80.0 30.0 44.8 -80.0 30.0 80.0 -44.8 30.0 80.0 0.0 30.0
    0.0 -80.0 12.0 44.8 -80.0 12.0 80.0 -44.8 12.0 80.0 0.0 12.0
    0.0 -60.0 3.0 33.6 -60.0 3.0 60.0 -33.6 3.0 60.0 0.0 3.0
    0.0 -60.0 0.0 33.6 -60.0 0.0 60.0 -33.6 0.0 60.0 0.0 0.0
  ]
  Patch "bicubic" "P" [
    -60.0 0.0 90.0 -60.0 -33.6 90.0 -33.6 -60.0 90.0 0.0 -60.0 90.0
    -70.0 0.0 69.0 -70.0 -39.20 69.0 -39.20 -70.0 69.0 0.0 -70.0
69.0
    -80.0 0.0 48.0 -80.0 -44.8 48.0 -44.8 -80.0 48.0 0.0 -80.0 48.0
    -80.0 0.0 30.0 -80.0 -44.8 30.0 -44.8 -80.0 30.0 0.0 -80.0 30.0
  ]
  Patch "bicubic" "P" [
    0.0 -60.0 90.0 33.6 -60.0 90.0 60.0 -33.6 90.0 60.0 0.0 90.0
    0.0 -70.0 69.0 39.20 -70.0 69.0 70.0 -39.20 69.0 70.0 0.0 69.0
    0.0 -80.0 48.0 44.8 -80.0 48.0 80.0 -44.8 48.0 80.0 0.0 48.0
    0.0 -80.0 30.0 44.8 -80.0 30.0 80.0 -44.8 30.0 80.0 0.0 30.0
  ]
  Patch "bicubic" "P" [
    -56.0 0.0 90.0 -56.0 -31.36 90.0 -31.36 -56.0 90.0 0.0 -56.0
90.0
    -53.5 0.0 95.25 -53.5 -29.96 95.25 -29.96 -53.5 95.25 0.0 -53.5
95.25
    -57.5 0.0 95.25 -57.5 -32.20 95.25 -32.20 -57.5 95.25 0.0 -57.5
95.25
    -60.0 0.0 90.0 -60.0 -33.6 90.0 -33.6 -60.0 90.0 0.0 -60.0 90.0
  ]
  Patch "bicubic" "P" [
    0.0 -56.0 90.0 31.36 -56.0 90.0 56.0 -31.36 90.0 56.0 0.0 90.0
    0.0 -53.5 95.25 29.96 -53.5 95.25 53.5 -29.96 95.25 53.5 0.0
95.25
```

```
      0.0 -57.5 95.25 32.20 -57.5 95.25 57.5 -32.20 95.25 57.5 0.0
95.25
      0.0 -60.0 90.0 33.6 -60.0 90.0 60.0 -33.6 90.0 60.0 0.0 90.0
   ]
AttributeEnd
# xBody_Front
AttributeBegin
   Basis "bezier" 3 "bezier" 3
   Patch "bicubic" "P" [
      80.0 0.0 30.0 80.0 44.80 30.0 44.80 80.0 30.0 0.0 80.0 30.0
      80.0 0.0 12.0 80.0 44.80 12.0 44.80 80.0 12.0 0.0 80.0 12.0
      60.0 0.0 3.0 60.0 33.60 3.0 33.60 60.0 3.0 0.0 60.0 3.0
      60.0 0.0 0.0 60.0 33.60 0.0 33.60 60.0 0.0 0.0 60.0 0.0
   ]
   Patch "bicubic" "P" [
      0.0 80.0 30.0 -44.80 80.0 30.0 -80.0 44.80 30.0 -80.0 0.0 30.0
      0.0 80.0 12.0 -44.80 80.0 12.0 -80.0 44.80 12.0 -80.0 0.0 12.0
      0.0 60.0 3.0 -33.60 60.0 3.0 -60.0 33.60 3.0 -60.0 0.0 3.0
      0.0 60.0 0.0 -33.60 60.0 0.0 -60.0 33.60 0.0 -60.0 0.0 0.0
   ]
   Patch "bicubic" "P" [
      60.0 0.0 90.0 60.0 33.60 90.0 33.60 60.0 90.0 0.0 60.0 90.0
      70.0 0.0 69.0 70.0 39.20 69.0 39.20 70.0 69.0 0.0 70.0 69.0
      80.0 0.0 48.0 80.0 44.80 48.0 44.80 80.0 48.0 0.0 80.0 48.0
      80.0 0.0 30.0 80.0 44.80 30.0 44.80 80.0 30.0 0.0 80.0 30.0
   ]
   Patch "bicubic" "P" [
      0.0 60.0 90.0 -33.60 60.0 90.0 -60.0 33.60 90.0 -60.0 0.0 90.0
      0.0 70.0 69.0 -39.20 70.0 69.0 -70.0 39.20 69.0 -70.0 0.0 69.0
      0.0 80.0 48.0 -44.80 80.0 48.0 -80.0 44.80 48.0 -80.0 0.0 48.0
      0.0 80.0 30.0 -44.80 80.0 30.0 -80.0 44.80 30.0 -80.0 0.0 30.0
   ]
   Patch "bicubic" "P" [
      56.0 0.0 90.0 56.0 31.36 90.0 31.36 56.0 90.0 0.0 56.0 90.0
      53.50 0.0 95.25 53.50 29.96 95.25 29.96 53.50 95.25 0.0 53.50
95.25
      57.50 0.0 95.25 57.50 32.20 95.25 32.20 57.50 95.25 0.0 57.50
95.25
      60.0 0.0 90.0 60.0 33.60 90.0 33.60 60.0 90.0 0.0 60.0 90.0
   ]
   Patch "bicubic" "P" [
      0.0 56.0 90.0 -31.36 56.0 90.0 -56.0 31.36 90.0 -56.0 0.0 90.0
      0.0 53.50 95.25 -29.96 53.50 95.25 -53.50 29.96 95.25 -53.50 0.0
95.25
      0.0 57.50 95.25 -32.20 57.50 95.25 -57.50 32.20 95.25 -57.50 0.0
95.25
      0.0 60.0 90.0 -33.60 60.0 90.0 -60.0 33.60 90.0 -60.0 0.0 90.0
   ]
AttributeEnd
# Spout
AttributeBegin
   Basis "bezier" 3 "bezier" 3
   Sides 2
   Basis "bezier" 3 "bezier" 3
   Patch "bicubic" "P" [
```

```
          68.0 0.0 51.0 68.0 26.40 51.0 68.0 26.40 18.0 68.0 0.0 18.0
          104.0 0.0 51.0 104.0 26.40 51.0 124.0 26.40 27.0 124.0 0.0 27.0
          92.0 0.0 78.0 92.0 10.0 78.0 96.0 10.0 75.0 96.0 0.0 75.0
          108.0 0.0 90.0 108.0 10.0 90.0 132.0 10.0 90.0 132.0 0.0 90.0
     ]
   Patch "bicubic" "P" [
          68.0 0.0 18.0 68.0 -26.40 18.0 68.0 -26.40 51.0 68.0 0.0 51.0
          124.0 0.0 27.0 124.0 -26.40 27.0 104.0 -26.40 51.0 104.0 0.0
51.0
          96.0 0.0 75.0 96.0 -10.0 75.0 92.0 -10.0 78.0 92.0 0.0 78.0
          132.0 0.0 90.0 132.0 -10.0 90.0 108.0 -10.0 90.0 108.0 0.0 90.0
     ]
   Patch "bicubic" "P" [
          108.0 0.0 90.0 108.0 10.0 90.0 132.0 10.0 90.0 132.0 0.0 90.0
          112.0 0.0 93.0 112.0 10.0 93.0 141.0 10.0 93.75 141.0 0.0 93.75
          116.0 0.0 93.0 116.0 6.0 93.0 138.0 6.0 94.50 138.0 0.0 94.50
          112.0 0.0 90.0 112.0 6.0 90.0 128.0 6.0 90.0 128.0 0.0 90.0
     ]
   Patch "bicubic" "P" [
          132.0 0.0 90.0 132.0 -10.0 90.0 108.0 -10.0 90.0 108.0 0.0 90.0
          141.0 0.0 93.75 141.0 -10.0 93.75 112.0 -10.0 93.0 112.0 0.0
93.0
          138.0 0.0 94.50 138.0 -6.0 94.50 116.0 -6.0 93.0 116.0 0.0 93.0
          128.0 0.0 90.0 128.0 -6.0 90.0 112.0 -6.0 90.0 112.0 0.0 90.0
     ]
AttributeEnd
# Handle
AttributeBegin
   Basis "bezier" 3 "bezier" 3
   Patch "bicubic" "P" [
          -64.0 0.0 75.0 -64.0 12.0 75.0 -60.0 12.0 84.0 -60.0 0.0 84.0
          -92.0 0.0 75.0 -92.0 12.0 75.0 -100.0 12.0 84.0 -100.0 0.0 84.0
          -108.0 0.0 75.0 -108.0 12.0 75.0 -120.0 12.0 84.0 -120.0 0.0
84.0
          -108.0 0.0 66.0 -108.0 12.0 66.0 -120.0 12.0 66.0 -120.0 0.0
66.0
     ]
   Patch "bicubic" "P" [
          -60.0 0.0 84.0 -60.0 -12.0 84.0 -64.0 -12.0 75.0 -64.0 0.0 75.0
          -100.0 0.0 84.0 -100.0 -12.0 84.0 -92.0 -12.0 75.0 -92.0 0.0
75.0
          -120.0 0.0 84.0 -120.0 -12.0 84.0 -108.0 -12.0 75.0 -108.0 0.0
75.0
          -120.0 0.0 66.0 -120.0 -12.0 66.0 -108.0 -12.0 66.0 -108.0 0.0
66.0
     ]
   Patch "bicubic" "P" [
          -108.0 0.0 66.0 -108.0 12.0 66.0 -120.0 12.0 66.0 -120.0 0.0
66.0
          -108.0 0.0 57.0 -108.0 12.0 57.0 -120.0 12.0 48.0 -120.0 0.0
48.0
          -100.0 0.0 39.0 -100.0 12.0 39.0 -106.0 12.0 31.50 -106.0 0.0
31.50
          -80.0 0.0 30.0 -80.0 12.0 30.0 -76.0 12.0 18.0 -76.0 0.0 18.0
     ]
```

```
  Patch "bicubic" "P" [
    -120.0 0.0 66.0 -120.0 -12.0 66.0 -108.0 -12.0 66.0 -108.0 0.0
66.0
    -120.0 0.0 48.0 -120.0 -12.0 48.0 -108.0 -12.0 57.0 -108.0 0.0
57.0
    -106.0 0.0 31.50 -106.0 -12.0 31.50 -100.0 -12.0 39.0 -100.0 0.0
39.0
    -76.0 0.0 18.0 -76.0 -12.0 18.0 -80.0 -12.0 30.0 -80.0 0.0 30.0
  ]
AttributeEnd
# Lid
AttributeBegin
  Basis "bezier" 3 "bezier" 3
  Patch "bicubic" "P" [
    8.0 0.0 102.0 8.0 4.48 102.0 4.48 8.0 102.0 0.0 8.0 102.0
    16.0 0.0 96.0 16.0 8.96 96.0 8.96 16.0 96.0 0.0 16.0 96.0
    52.0 0.0 96.0 52.0 29.12 96.0 29.12 52.0 96.0 0.0 52.0 96.0
    52.0 0.0 90.0 52.0 29.12 90.0 29.12 52.0 90.0 0.0 52.0 90.0
  ]
  Patch "bicubic" "P" [
    0.0 8.0 102.0 -4.48 8.0 102.0 -8.0 4.48 102.0 -8.0 0.0 102.0
    0.0 16.0 96.0 -8.96 16.0 96.0 -16.0 8.96 96.0 -16.0 0.0 96.0
    0.0 52.0 96.0 -29.12 52.0 96.0 -52.0 29.12 96.0 -52.0 0.0 96.0
    0.0 52.0 90.0 -29.12 52.0 90.0 -52.0 29.12 90.0 -52.0 0.0 90.0]
  Patch "bicubic" "P" [
    -8.0 0.0 102.0 -8.0 -4.48 102.0 -4.48 -8.0 102.0 0.0 -8.0 102.0
    -16.0 0.0 96.0 -16.0 -8.96 96.0 -8.96 -16.0 96.0 0.0 -16.0 96.0
    -52.0 0.0 96.0 -52.0 -29.12 96.0 -29.12 -52.0 96.0 0.0 -52.0
96.0
    -52.0 0.0 90.0 -52.0 -29.12 90.0 -29.12 -52.0 90.0 0.0 -52.0
90.0]
  Patch "bicubic" "P" [
    0.0 -8.0 102.0 4.48 -8.0 102.0 8.0 -4.48 102.0 8.0 0.0 102.0
    0.0 -16.0 96.0 8.96 -16.0 96.0 16.0 -8.96 96.0 16.0 0.0 96.0
    0.0 -52.0 96.0 29.12 -52.0 96.0 52.0 -29.12 96.0 52.0 0.0 96.0
    0.0 -52.0 90.0 29.12 -52.0 90.0 52.0 -29.12 90.0 52.0 0.0 90.0
  ]
AttributeEnd
# Knob
AttributeBegin
  Basis "bezier" 3 "bezier" 3
  Patch "bicubic" "P" [
    0.0 0.0 120.0 0.0 0.0 120.0 0.0 0.0 120.0 0.0 0.0 120.0
    32.0 0.0 120.0 32.0 18.0 120.0 18.0 32.0 120.0 0.0 32.0 120.0
    0.0 0.0 108.0 0.0 0.0 108.0 0.0 0.0 108.0 0.0 0.0 108.0
    8.0 0.0 102.0 8.0 4.48 102.0 4.48 8.0 102.0 0.0 8.0 102.0
  ]
  Patch "bicubic" "P" [
    0.0 0.0 120.0 0.0 0.0 120.0 0.0 0.0 120.0 0.0 0.0 120.0
    0.0 32.0 120.0 -18.0 32.0 120.0 -32.0 18.0 120.0 -32.0 0.0 120.0
    0.0 0.0 108.0 0.0 0.0 108.0 0.0 0.0 108.0 0.0 0.0 108.0
    0.0 8.0 102.0 -4.48 8.0 102.0 -8.0 4.48 102.0 -8.0 0.0 102.0
  ]
  Patch "bicubic" "P" [
    0.0 0.0 120.0 0.0 0.0 120.0 0.0 0.0 120.0 0.0 0.0 120.0
```

```
        -32.0 0.0 120.0 -32.0 -18.0 120.0 -18.0 -32.0 120.0 0.0 -32.0
120.0
        0.0 0.0 108.0 0.0 0.0 108.0 0.0 0.0 108.0 0.0 0.0 108.0
        -8.0 0.0 102.0 -8.0 -4.48 102.0 -4.48 -8.0 102.0 0.0 -8.0 102.0
    ]
    Patch "bicubic" "P" [
        0.0 0.0 120.0 0.0 0.0 120.0 0.0 0.0 120.0 0.0 0.0 120.0
        0.0 -32.0 120.0 18.0 -32.0 120.0 32.0 -18.0 120.0 32.0 0.0 120.0
        0.0 0.0 108.0 0.0 0.0 108.0 0.0 0.0 108.0 0.0 0.0 108.0
        0.0 -8.0 102.0 4.48 -8.0 102.0 8.0 -4.48 102.0 8.0 0.0 102.0
    ]
AttributeEnd
# Lip
AttributeBegin
    Basis "bezier" 3 "bezier" 3
    Patch "bicubic" "P" [
        50.0 0.0 90.0 50.0 28.0 90.0 28.0 50.0 90.0 0.0 50.0 90.0
        52.0 0.0 90.0 52.0 29.12 90.0 29.12 52.0 90.0 0.0 52.0 90.0
        54.0 0.0 90.0 54.0 30.24 90.0 30.24 54.0 90.0 0.0 54.0 90.0
        56.0 0.0 90.0 56.0 31.36 90.0 31.36 56.0 90.0 0.0 56.0 90.0
    ]
    Patch "bicubic" "P" [
        0.0 50.0 90.0 -28.0 50.0 90.0 -50.0 28.0 90.0 -50.0 0.0 90.0
        0.0 52.0 90.0 -29.12 52.0 90.0 -52.0 29.12 90.0 -52.0 0.0 90.0
        0.0 54.0 90.0 -30.24 54.0 90.0 -54.0 30.24 90.0 -54.0 0.0 90.0
        0.0 56.0 90.0 -31.36 56.0 90.0 -56.0 31.36 90.0 -56.0 0.0 90.0
    ]
    Patch "bicubic" "P" [
        -50.0 0.0 90.0 -50.0 -28.0 90.0 -28.0 -50.0 90.0 0.0 -50.0 90.0
        -52.0 0.0 90.0 -52.0 -29.12 90.0 -29.12 -52.0 90.0 0.0 -52.0
90.0
        -54.0 0.0 90.0 -54.0 -30.24 90.0 -30.24 -54.0 90.0 0.0 -54.0
90.0
        -56.0 0.0 90.0 -56.0 -31.36 90.0 -31.36 -56.0 90.0 0.0 -56.0
90.0
    ]
    Patch "bicubic" "P" [
        0.0 -50.0 90.0 28.0 -50.0 90.0 50.0 -28.0 90.0 50.0 0.0 90.0
        0.0 -52.0 90.0 29.12 -52.0 90.0 52.0 -29.12 90.0 52.0 0.0 90.0
        0.0 -54.0 90.0 30.24 -54.0 90.0 54.0 -30.24 90.0 54.0 0.0 90.0
        0.0 -56.0 90.0 31.36 -56.0 90.0 56.0 -31.36 90.0 56.0 0.0 90.0
    ]
AttributeEnd
WorldEnd
```

RIB can be regarded as a set of commands for RenderMan to execute. Each command starts with an uppercase letter and can span several lines. For instance

```
Polygon "P" [0.5 0.5 0.5 0.5 -0.5 0.5 -0.5 -0.5 0.5 -0.5 0.5 0.5]
"st" [0 0 0 1 1 1 1 0]
```

is a command that creates a polygon (a square in this case). The name of the command comes first, followed by additional data for the command. Several commands have two words, both capitalized and with no space between them (e.g. LightSource, FrameBegin, WorldBegin). Speaking of spaces, "whitespace" (tabs, newline characters, extra spaces and blank lines) is ignored by RenderMan. The whitespace is there to aid readability by humans. For RenderMan, the commands

```
Translate 0 0 5
Sphere 1 -1 1 360
```

are equivalent to

```
Translate
0 0 5
Sphere
1 -1 1 360
```

or even

```
Translate
0
0
5
Sphere
1
-1
1
360
```

To the RIB parser, all of the above three variations look like this:

```
Translate 0 0 5 Sphere 1 -1 1 360
```

Note that in between adjacent elements, it is just the extra whitespaces that are ignored. You do need one blank (space) character, just as you would when you write valid prose. The parser is not unlike a human reader in that it uses the space character to tell elements apart. So the following would be invalid:

```
Translate005
```

The character "#" is used to precede comments. RenderMan ignores everything starting with a # till the end of the line containing it. In addition to helping users improve readability, comments can also be used to encode additional "metadata" (more on this shortly). For instance this entire line is a comment line:

```
# This RIB file contains a teapot and a directional light source.
```

The following snippet shows an "inline" comment where a command contains a short annotation next to it:

```
Surface "darkwood" # let's try our new shader!!
```

As just mentioned, the comment facility can be useful for recording additional (non-RIB) information meant not for RenderMan but for other programs that might preprocess RIB files. For instance the RI Specification (Appendix D.1 and D.2) talks about RIB structuring conventions and RIB Entity Files which are RIB files or file fragments that contain standard RIB along with special comments called hints. Hints begin with ## instead of #. This is a sample block of hints:

```
##RenderMan RIB-Structure 1.1
##Scene Animating pendulum
##CreationDate April 12:00am 4/12/03
##For Becky_and_Josh
```

If a **RIB** file is properly structured with adequate hints, **RIB** processors (e.g. programs for shader management, scene-editing and render job distribution which read a **RIB** file, make modifications to it and create new **RIB** output) could specifically look for those embedded hints and take appropriate actions (such as replacing sections of existing **RIB** with custom **RIB**, or simply omitting them).

In most **RIB** files you will notice a line such as

```
version 3.03
```

at the top of the listing. It denotes the version number of the format for the rest of the **RIB**, and is intended for the RenderMan **RIB** parser. The parser is the program that breaks down a **RIB** file into individual "tokens" for use downstream. As the **RIB** format undergoes changes, **RIB** parsers are expected to keep up with the changes. **RIB** parsers of various RenderMan implementations can choose not to deal with **RIB** versions below a certain version number (e.g. 3.0) because the format might be too old and hence might contain commands different from what is currently supported. Likewise an older copy of RenderMan might refuse to parse a **RIB** file with a newer version number. The current **RIB** format version number is 3.04 (as of this writing, in 2003).

3.3.3 Commands

It was mentioned earlier that **RIB** files essentially contain a series of commands for RenderMan to execute. Commands begin with an uppercase letter, e.g. Patch, AttributeBegin. In this subsection we examine the structure of such **RIB** commands.

As you can see from the **RIB** listing just presented, almost every command has additional data that follow the name of the command. These data are separated by whitespaces. For instance

```
Format 640 480 1.0
```

specifies that the output resolution is 640 by 480 pixels, with a pixel aspect ratio (see Chapter 6, "Camera, output") of 1.0.

```
PixelSamples 2 2
```

sets the pixel supersampling grid size to be 2 by 2.

```
Color [1 0.5 0.3]
```

sets the RGB surface color of the primitive(s) that follow the command, to 1, 0.5, 0.3.

```
Basis "bezier" 3 "bezier" 3
```

specifies the spline type of the following patch(es) to be bicubic Bezier (see Chapter 4, "Geometric Primitives").

```
Patch "bicubic" "P" [
    50.0 0.0 90.0 50.0 28.0 90.0 28.0 50.0 90.0 0.0 50.0 90.0
    52.0 0.0 90.0 52.0 29.12 90.0 29.12 52.0 90.0 0.0 52.0 90.0
    54.0 0.0 90.0 54.0 30.24 90.0 30.24 54.0 90.0 0.0 54.0 90.0
    56.0 0.0 90.0 56.0 31.36 90.0 31.36 56.0 90.0 0.0 56.0 90.0]
```

denotes a bicubic spline patch primitive, whose 2D grid of 4x4 control vertices ("P") are specified as an array of numbers bounded by square brackets. Each control vertex is an (x,y,z) triplet, so we have a total of 3x4x4=48 numbers in the array, in the example shown above.

In all these cases, the syntax remains the same. The command comes first, followed by its data. The type of data can be integers (e.g. for PixelSamples), floating point numbers (e.g. the third piece of data for Format), strings (e.g. first and third piece of data for Basis), floating point triplets (e.g. for Color), arrays of arbitrary lengths containing floating point numbers (e.g. for the Patch command) or arrays containing exactly 16 floating point numbers (e.g. for ConcatTransform – see Chapter 5, "Transformations").

Consider the LightSource command which specifies a light source:

```
LightSource "ambientlight" 1 "intensity" .7 "lightcolor" [.4 0 1]
```

The command name is followed by a set of data, as expected. But not all pieces of data are absolutely essential for the command to work. RenderMan will create an ambient light source for us even if we just say:

```
LightSource "ambientlight" 1 # default ambient light
```

"ambientlight" says that we are asking for an ambient light, and 1 is the number we give to the light source (each light in a RIB file needs to be assigned a unique ID, which can be a number or a string). But our light will have a default intensity of 1.0 units and default color of 1,1,1. If we want to override either or both of these defaults, we will have to specify our own values, and that is what is being done above with the extra specification of

```
"intensity" .7 "lightcolor" [.4 0 1]
```

It is as if we are saying "create an ambient light, assign it an ID of 1, and additionally, make its intensity 0.7 and its color 0.4,0,1". You can think of the LightSource command as having user-settable knobs for intensity and color, whose default settings are 1.0 and (1,1,1) respectively. Either or both of the knobs can be changed by the user into a reasonable non-default value. If they are not specified, the built-in defaults are used. So in RIB files it is common to see commands that contain such pairs of knob names followed by their settings. These are referred to as token value pairs. E.g. in the LightSource command above, "intensity" is a token, and .7 is its value.

Token value pairs (which represent optional data) follow the set of minimal data absolutely required by commands. To keep the command syntax simple and consistent, both essential and additional/optional data elements are separated using whitespaces. Note that with the essential data, the ordering of data elements is predetermined. In other words,

```
LightSource "ambientlight" 1
```

is valid RIB, while

```
LightSource 1 "ambientlight"
```

is not. But the optional token value pairs can be specified in any order, as shown in the snippet below which creates two ambient lights.

```
LightSource "ambientlight" 1 "intensity" .7
"lightcolor" [.4 0 1]
LightSource "ambientlight"  2 "lightcolor" [.4 0.8 1]
"intensity" 0.56
```

The token value data can occur in any order, precisely because of their paired grouping. When the parser encounters a token, it will interpret the value(s) immediately following it as belonging to that token.

```
"lightcolor" [.4 0 1]
```

is taken to mean "lightcolor is [.4 0 1]". The whitespace in between the token and value stands for "is".

As an aside, note that using whitespace to separate a token and its value is just one of several possible syntactical notations. Figure 3.8 shows several ways of specifying that a token "color" has a value "blue".

Here is another syntactical detail. Tokens are always enclosed in double quotes. Values on the other hand need to be delimited (bounded) by square brackets. You have seen examples of this above, but here is another one:

```
LightSource "distantlight" "from" [0 1 0] "to" [0 0 0]
```

"from" and "to" are tokens, [0 1 0] and [0 0 0] are their respective values. But in the RIB listing you notice this command (option):

```
Projection "perspective" "fov" 25
```

"fov" is the token (it specifies a perspective camera's field of view) and 25 is the value (in degrees). Should not the value be bounded by square brackets, to read

```
Projection "perspective" "fov" [25]
```

instead? Turns out that if a value is just a single element (number or string), the square brackets are optional. In real-world RIB files you will come across both types of calls, with or without the square brackets. It is however good practice to include the square brackets even though they are optional, since doing so keeps the syntax consistent (by treating single element values and multi element ones in an identical manner).

Figure 3.8 *Several ways to specify values for a token*

So far we have been referring to RenderMan calls generically as commands. Commands can be grouped into the following categories. Options are those commands that are applied globally, for the entire scene or an entire frame. Format (which sets image resolution), Display (which sets the output name, format and type), Projection (which sets camera projection), PixelSamples (which sets supersampling), etc. are commands that are options. In contrast are another group of commands called attributes which are applied on a per-primitive basis. Surface (which specifies a shader), LightSource (which sets up a light), ShadingRate (which specifies shading rate) are examples of attributes. In general, options relate to camera, output image and the renderer itself, while attributes relate to geometry. See the RI Specification for the complete set of options and attributes. In addition to options and attributes, another group of commands manipulate what is known as the graphics state (much more on this topic, in Chapter 5, "Transformations"). Such commands include WorldBegin, WorldEnd, FrameBegin, FrameEnd, TransformBegin, TransformEnd, AttributeBegin and AttributeEnd. The last major group of commands specify geometric primitives and are the topic of the following chapter. Some of these commands are PointsGeneralPolygons, NuPatch, Curve, Point and Cylinder.

We now look at the extensibility of RIB commands. The designers of RenderMan had the foresight to realize that no static set of commands can stay current with the evolution of rendering techniques, the capabilities of modeling software and the increasing needs of users. So they built some extension mechanisms to meet newer requirements. Some of these are available to implementers of RenderMan, and others, to end users.

A pair of such "extension backdoor" commands are Option and Attribute. Appropriately enough, they are meant for RenderMan implementers to add to the built-in set of options and attributes respectively. For instance, PRMan adds a "searchpath" specification facility whereby a RIB file can contain a list of directory names which PRMan will use, when searching for a shader or map. Here is an example:

```
Option "searchpath" "resource" ["C:/tmp:C:/RenderMan/PRMan/shaders"]
```

The above command specifies that the value for the token called "resource" is a single string of colon-separated directories. PRMan would search these directories when it encounters map names and shader names in the rest of the RIB.

Likewise, an attribute to specify if primitive dicing should be binary (equally subdivided) is available in PRMan, and is specified like this:

```
Attribute "dicing" "binary" [0]
```

A value of 0 means that we do not want binary dicing. Similarly, other RenderMan implementations (such as RenderDotC) define several such Options and Attributes meaningful to their renderer.

In addition to the large list of built-in tokens that the RIB parser will recognize, you can define your own using the Declare command which has a pretty simple syntax. You need only to specify the name of your token and what type of data it will hold. Here is a sample block of declarations:

```
Declare "merge" "int"
Declare "stubble" "float"
Declare "skycolor" "color"
Declare "surfpt" "point"
Declare "texmapfile" "string"
```

Once new tokens are declared, they can be used in command invocations, e.g. in an Option or an Attribute command:

```
Declare "tracebreadthfactor" "float"
Declare "tracedepthfactor" "float"
Declare "casts_shadows" "string"
# ....
```

```
Option "user" "tracebreadthfactor" [0]
Option "user" "tracedepthfactor" [0]
# ...
Attribute "render" "casts_shadows" ["opaque"]
```

A few commands such as Display can take on additional implementation-specific token value pairs, tokens for which can be created using the Declare command. For instance:

```
Declare "merge" "int"
# .. intervening commands
Display "test.tiff" "tiff" "rgba" "merge" [0]
```

Shader calls contain token value pairs that customize the behavior of the shader (much more on shaders and shader-writing in Chapter 8, "Shading"). This too can be regarded as an extension mechanism, since the tokens and values originate with shaders which are external programs. Again, the Declare command creates these tokens. Here is a quick example:

```
Declare "Kd" "float"
Declare "Ka" "float"
# ...
Surface "defaultsurface"   "Kd" 0.85 "Ka" 0.27
```

Another end-user extension is the ability to add custom data on to geometric primitives, for shading purposes. A small example will help illustrate this mechanism. Consider the following snippet:

```
Surface "particleRen" "float customAttr" [0.5]
Points "P" [1.8464 0.951407 1.67223 1.27619 -2.5012 -0.90485 0.222985
2.00094 -1.01339]
```

The Points call creates particles whose xyz spatial locations are specified using "P". We are creating three particles which will be shaded using a particleRen shader. particleRen has an input parameter customAttr for which we specify a value of 0.5. All three particles will be shaded using 0.5 for the value of customAttr. Now look at how we can specify a different customAttr for each of the particles:

```
Surface "particleRen" "float customAttr" [0.5]
Points "P" [1.8464 0.951407 1.67223 1.27619 -2.5012 -0.90485 0.222985
2.00094 -1.01339] "vertex float customAttr" [0.72613 0.385704
0.929774]
```

"vertex float customAttr" declares a token called customAttr to be of type "vertex float", which is a specification for data that will be attached to each vertex (or particle, in our case). The declaration is followed by exactly three values, one for each particle. This offers a powerful way to pass data to a shader on a per-vertex or per-particle basis. On a complex polygonal mesh you can supply a different vertex color for each vertex, for example. With particles, you can pass in values for lifespan, age, velocity, etc. for each particle and write your shader to color the particles by taking these values into account. RIB translators for animation packages such as Maya provide straightforward user interfaces that make it very easy to attach such extra data on to primitives.

There is an alternative to using the Declare command to define new tokens for later use, and that is to declare them "inline" at the point of usage. In other words, instead of

```
Declare "merge" "int"
# .. intervening commands
Display "test.tiff" "tiff" "rgba" "merge" [0]
```

you can simply say

```
Display "test.tiff" "tiff" "rgba" "int merge" [0]
```

Here are two more examples:

```
Surface "defaultsurface" "float Kd" 0.85 "float Ka" 0.27
# ...
Surface "darkwood" "color graincolor" [0.35 0.06 0.124]
```

Note however that inlined declarations create throwaway-tokens valid just for the call where they are created. On the other hand, tokens created using the Declare command are added to a token table and are kept around for subsequent use in commands.

3.3.4 Scene structure

Now that you have an idea of how RenderMan calls work, we will explore how these calls are arranged in a typical RIB file. In the teapot.rib listing shown in subsection 3.3.2, you see that at the very top (what is known as the "preamble" section) are commands that specify parameters for the scene camera, output image and renderer. As mentioned in the previous section, these commands are called options. Our RIB listing does not contain global renderer-specific options expressed through the Option command but if they did exist, they would also be at the preamble. Next comes the WorldBegin statement, which signals the start of the actual scene which consists of lights, objects and their materials. The WorldEnd statement denotes the end of the scene description.

In RIB files, no forward referencing is allowed. In other words, you cannot mention something first and then provide a definition for it later in the file. The renderer processes the file from top to bottom just once, so the definitions need to precede usage. In a similar sense the camera parameters and image details (name, resolution, number of channels, output destination, file format if the destination is a disk file) need to be made available before any actual scene definition can begin. In a philosophical sense, the viewer needs to precede the viewed. And even in the world definition, lights come before objects. Within object definitions, materials and transforms come before commands that create the actual primitives.

Given what we know so far about RIB structure, it is interesting to investigate what constitutes a minimal RIB file. Create a completely empty RIB file and try to render it. PRMan complies without any error messages. Of course, you do not get any output. The same happens when you insert just a comment line in the file:

```
# This is a do-nothing RIB file
```

The above two are trivial (and valid) RIB files, but what if our file now contained these lines:

```
Display "test.tiff" "framebuffer" "rgb"
WorldBegin
WorldEnd
```

When you render such a file, you will notice a blank render window pop up. The resolution of the window will be 640x480 which are default values when the Format command is left out. If you change "framebuffer" to "file" you will get a 640x480 blank TIFF file on disk. Next, try rendering a RIB file with just these two lines:

```
WorldBegin
WorldEnd
```

You will get a blank output file on disk called ri.pic. When the Display line is left out in addition to Format, PRman defaults to a 640x480 image called ri.pic, in TIFF format. To view the ri.pic file you can use any TIFF image viewer or manipulation program such as Photoshop, or you can use the "sho" program that ships with PRMan.

Next, add a Sphere call:

```
WorldBegin
    Sphere 1 1 -1 360
WorldEnd
```

This produces a 640x480 ri.pic TIFF file containing a large sphere that just touches the top and bottom of the image frame. Since we left out the Projection option which usually sets up a perspective camera, PRMan defaults to an orthographic projection. Also, our minimal RIB file did not contain a light source, nor was a shader specified for shading the sphere. In the absence of a shader, PRMan uses a default "headlight" matte shader where the light source appears to be located where the camera is, and faces where the camera faces. So the above three line RIB file is the smallest file that renders a non-empty image for us, where left-out options and attributes take on default values.

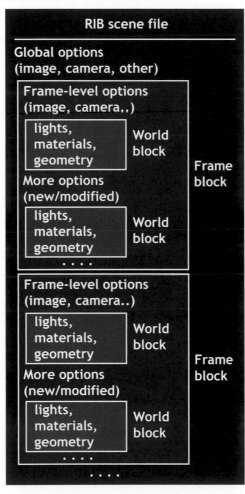

Figure 3.9 *RIB file structure*

Figure 3.9 shows the arrangement of RIB calls, structured as nested hierarchies. At the topmost level we have the global options and attributes as already mentioned. Following this is a frame block specifying a frame's worth of data, bounded by FrameBegin and FrameEnd. The frame block is optional, which is why in our earlier RIB listing it was omitted. Just inside the frame block are options that are specific just to the current frame being rendered. Following this is a world block, which begins the definition of lights, materials, primitives and their attributes.

Inside the world block are a series of nested transform blocks (which are bounded by TransformBegin and TransformEnd) and attribute blocks (which are bounded by AttributeBegin and AttributeEnd). Chapter 5, "Transformations", has more on these two types of blocks. But for now it is sufficient to say that these can enclose calls that create lights, shaders and geometry. The transform and attribute blocks can be arbitrarily nested deep inside each other, but the blocks cannot "cross". In other words, this is fine:

```
# ...
AttributeBegin
 # ...
 TransformBegin
   # ...
 TransformEnd
 # ...
AttributeEnd
```

This is incorrect:

```
# ...
TransformBegin
  # ...
  AttributeBegin
    # ...
TransformEnd # we're ending prematurely before AttributeEnd!
    # ...
  AttributeEnd
```

Figure 3.9 shows that a frame block can contain more than one world block. Between the end of one and the beginning of the next, more options calls can be specified that either add new options or modify existing ones. From Figure 3.9 you can also see that multiple frame blocks are permissible in a single RIB file. The following listing shows such a file.

```
##RenderMan RIB
version 3.03
Format 256 256 1
Projection "perspective" "fov" 20
LightSource "distantlight" 1
Translate 0 0 5
FrameBegin 1
Display "Square.0001.tiff" "framebuffer" "rgb"
WorldBegin
Color [0.4 0.4 0.6]
Translate 0 0 1
Polygon "P" [0.5 0.5 0.5 0.5 -0.5 0.5 -0.5 -0.5 0.5 -0.5 0.5 0.5]
"st" [0 0 0 1 1 1 1 0]
WorldEnd
FrameEnd

FrameBegin 2
```

```
Display "Square.0002.tiff" "framebuffer" "rgb"
WorldBegin
Color [0.4 0.4 0.6]
Translate 0 0 4
Polygon "P" [0.5 0.5 0.5 0.5 -0.5 0.5 -0.5 -0.5 0.5 -0.5 0.5 0.5]
"st" [0 0 0 1 1 1 1 0]
WorldEnd
FrameEnd

FrameBegin 3
Display "Square.0003.tiff" "framebuffer" "rgb"
WorldBegin
Color [0.4 0.4 0.6]
Translate 0 0 8
Polygon "P" [0.5 0.5 0.5 0.5 -0.5 0.5 -0.5 -0.5 0.5 -0.5 0.5 0.5]
"st" [0 0 0 1 1 1 1 0]
WorldEnd
FrameEnd
```

If you render this file, you will get three output windows, one for the Display statement in each frame block. The three images show a square moving away from the camera. If you were to change "framebuffer" to "file" (or equivalently, "tiff") and re-render, you will get an animating sequence of three TIFF files. As primitive as this animation is, it illustrates the idea that a single RIB file can hold data to create an entire animation sequence.

While it is possible for a single RIB file to hold more than one frame of data, in practice, each frame of data in an animated sequence is kept in its own RIB file. This is to keep the file size from getting out of hand, considering that production RIB files can often be several megabytes in size for just one frame of data. Further, by creating a separate RIB file for each frame, a render manager in a render farm can efficiently distribute the files to the different processors that make up the farm.

Whether done through a single RIB file or a series of them, rendering an animated sequence in RenderMan involves describing each frame's data as a self-contained unit. The resulting rendered frames on disk can then be further processed using compositing and other non-linear film/video editing programs to be laid off to tape, recorded on to film or optical storage media, converted to streaming video formats, etc.

3.3.5 External resources

A typical RIB file contains all the scene information needed to render a frame or a series of frames. But that does not mean that all the data needs to be in that single file. If there are shaders that have been applied to objects in the scene, it is just the names of the shaders and their inputs (attribute value pairs) that are stored in the RIB file. The shaders themselves are separate .slo files accessed by RenderMan as needed. Here is a typical shader call which expects the file plastic.slo to be available during rendering.

```
Surface "plastic" "Kd" 0.8
```

In addition, if a shader requires an external image on disk called a map (see Chapter 8), it is just the name of that map that is in the RIB file. Here is an example of such a call:

```
Surface "texShader" "rotAngle" 45 "texFilename" "tulips.tex"
```

In the above call, texShader refers to texShader.slo and tulips.tex refers to a file on disk with the same name.

RIB files containing shader calls, some of which might in turn refer to maps as shown above, can be thought to be "pointing to" these external resources on disk. Maintaining such external references reduces the size and complexity of the RIB and also promotes reuse of shaders and maps.

There is one more reference mechanism that can lead to modular RIB, with further reduction in file size. It is use of the ReadArchive command which is used as follows:

```
Display "test" "framebuffer" "rgb"
Projection "perspective" "fov" 60
Translate 0 0 3
WorldBegin
  LightSource "distantlight" 1
  ReadArchive "TwoSpheres.rib" # "reads in" the contents of
TwoSpheres.rib here
WorldEnd
```

TwoSpheres.rib is not a complete RIB file. It contains just geometry, transforms and shaders, essentially a piece of 3D clip art:

```
# TwoSpheres.rib - a pair of spheres
Surface "plastic" "Ka" 0.5 "Kd" 0.7
AttributeBegin
  Translate -1 0 0
  Sphere 1 -1 1 360
AttributeEnd
AttributeBegin
  Translate 1 0 0
  Sphere 1 -1 1 360
AttributeEnd
#
```

The ReadArchive call opens the TwoSpheres.rib file and simply reads it into the RIB stream at the point of its invocation. The result is equivalent to a RIB file without the ReadArchive call but with the contents TwoSpheres.rib pasted there in its place. As with shaders and maps, the files named in the ReadArchive calls can be thought to be assets external to the parent RIB files where they are called.

Judicious use of ReadArchive (and a related command called DelayedReadArchive) lets you build up asset libraries of characters, props, etc., enabling you to create mix-and-match container RIB files using the ReadArchive calls. The block structuring syntax makes it convenient to build such clip art assets.

Note that our asset RIB files meant for ReadArchive can be regarded as simplified versions of RIB Entity Files mentioned in section 3.3.2. Entity Files are also incomplete like our asset RIBs, but in addition they need to conform to strict document structuring conventions set forth in the Specification. This is because they are created for manipulation by RIB preprocessors which rely on the strict syntax present in the Entity Files. Yet another comparison to make is that while ReadArchive is not a preprocessor hint but an actual RIB command, there is an equivalent hint of the form

```
##Include filename
```

which can be present in preprocessor-oriented RIB files. The mere presence of such a hint does not guarantee that the file referred to will be included in the preprocessor's output. That is up to the preprocessor and the settings specified for its execution.

3.3.6 Errors

In a perfect world every RIB file would be error-free, ready to be turned into imagery. But in reality errors do creep in, and RenderMan has facilities for dealing with them. The default behavior is to print error or warning messages to the window where the RIB render is launched. Depending on the severity of the error, you might get a result image that might still be correct but probably not what you wanted, an incorrect image, or no image at all. In any case the renderer tries to continue past the point of the error without terminating right away.

Errors could be introduced by bugs in translator routines or filter programs, incorrect use of the API function calls or in the case of hand-created files, through user error. RIB errors can be either syntactic or semantic. Syntactic errors are "grammatical" errors (where the RIB is malformed due to missing data or punctuation). Semantic errors on the other hand are errors in the content itself that result from invalid data.

Here are some PRMan examples of both types of errors. You can try to generate these and others by starting with a simple, valid RIB file and making arbitrary, incorrect modifications to it. Becoming familiar with error messages will come in handy later if you encounter problems with bigger production-level RIB files. See Appendix C of the RI Specification for a complete discussion of the variety of errors that can result from bad RIB.

```
WorldBegin
    MyStrangeCmd # bogus command!
WorldEnd
P01001 Unregistered request: "MyStrangeCmd" ...

FrameBegin
 WorldBegin
    Sphere 1 -1 1 360
FrameEnd # we're skipping WorldEnd
R05004 RiEnd called before its proper nesting level. (WARNING)

Surface "matte "Ka" 0.5 # needs to be "matte", not "matte
P01001 Unregistered request: "Ka" (at line ...
P79015 Missing closing quote (at line ...

Color [0.5 0.75] # needs to be an RGB triplet such as [0.5 0.75 0.4]
Sphere 1 -1 1 360
P08001 Wrong number of color samples: 2, expecting: 3 (at line ...
```

Specific RenderMan implementations might generate other errors that result from the details of the particular implementation, such as running out of memory trying to store an array, or reaching an internal limit for string size.

Yet other errors might result from specifics in a scene. For instance if a primitive passes right through the front clipping plane and RenderMan is unable to split the primitive (due to the absence of a high-enough splitting limit), the following error occurs:

```
R56001 Primitive "<unnamed>" will not split at camera plane
(WARNING)
```

3.3.7 Storage formats

How are RIB files stored on disk? Small files (such as the examples we use in this book) can be stored as regular text files, which makes it easy to view, edit, print them. Storing RIB as text also makes it easy to write filter programs (e.g. using a scripting language such as Python, Perl or Tcl) that look for specific elements (see section 3.3.2 above). But it is inefficient to large scenes as text since it results in large file sizes on disk. The RIB format thankfully has a binary counterpart as well, making it a good choice for large production-quality scenes. The downside is that binary RIBs cannot be viewed or edited using a text editor. Should you wish to examine a binary format RIB file, the PRMan distribution ships with a utility called "catrib" that can be used for generating the equivalent text version.

RIB files typically have a .rib file extension. RenderMan does not require that RIB files have this extension but it is common practice anyway. The .rib extension does make it possible to visually pick out RIB files in a crowded directory with mixed file types.

In addition, specific RenderMan implementations also allow RIB files to be compressed using the "gzip" compression format, leading to even smaller files. Such RIB files would have .gz as their extension, so teapot.rib.gz could be a name for our gzip-compressed teapot RIB scene file.

3.3.8 What RIB is not

In the above subsections we have been looking at elements that make up the RIB file format. You can see that it is a pretty straightforward, declarative format where a scene is described in terms of commands with token/value pairs. There is a top to bottom structure to the description, since the file is parsed by RenderMan just once while rendering. Block structured, nested hierarchies allow for description of models of arbitrary complexity.

While it is adequate for scene description, RIB does have some limitations. For instance, new data types other than the built-in float, int, string, point, etc. cannot be created. An entity's usage cannot precede its declaration – it must be declared before it can be referenced. There are no programmatic constructs such as loops, branches or procedure/function calls. Arrays cannot be multi-dimensional. Sections of a RIB file cannot easily be commented out (say, for debugging purposes). All these limitations stem from the fact that RIB is not a general purpose programming language, it is simply a scene description format. If you want full-blown programming support, you are advised to use one of the languages for which RenderMan bindings are available, such as "C", Tcl, Perl, Python or Java (see the RfB site for links and more information).

4
Geometric primitives

In this chapter we catalog the rich set of primitives that serve as shape descriptors for characters, props and effects in RenderMan scenes.

4.1 Surfaces

Artists see the world as an interplay of space, light and form. This chapter is about geometric form or more specifically, about surfaces. Take a moment to look around you and appreciate the varieties of shape and form, both natural and human-made. Objects in the physical world range from atoms to galaxies, spanning a vast scale. Even the range of objects visible to the naked eye span several size magnitudes from tiny specks of dust to huge mountain ranges. In addition to natural forms are human-made objects that make up our familiar material world. Manufactured objects are often angular and sharp, in contrast to nature's macroscopic forms which tend to be more rounded and in some cases, self-similar. A good renderer is expected to handle such diversity of form by providing the user a range of primitives to represent them.

The following subsections present the different geometric representations available in RenderMan. After you become familiar with the RIB syntax for each, feel free to experiment by modifying existing data to create your own imagery (all the RIB files and shaders used to generate the illustrations shown below are available at the RfB site). A good hands-on understanding of what the various primitives can do will help you in picking appropriate ones relevant to your shape modeling needs in the future.

What follows is an informal, by-example presentation and not a rigorous discussion of each primitive. For a more complete treatment read the RI Specification or other references mentioned in Chapter 10, "Resources". Also, for the sake of brevity, only relevant geometry creation commands are presented here and not complete RIB files (again, I refer you to the RfB site for all the RIB files in their entirety). Where possible the RIB commands are annotated to explain their syntax.

4.2 Points

We begin our study of shape commands, starting with a zero-dimensional primitive, namely the point. Although a point occupies no space at all in the mathematical sense, a point rendered using a renderer such as PRMan does take up a small area. While a single point is rarely useful as a renderable primitive, a collection of points is a useful entity for modeling a wide variety of things such as star clusters, dust clouds, fire, sparks, smoke, mist, snow and raindrops. A point collection is also good for rendering the results of chaos simulations where the trajectory of a single point is traced across space and time over a large number of iterations.

A point collection is usually referred to as a particle system and is a staple when it comes to visual effects in the CG production community. In addition to the applications mentioned above, particle systems are also useful for representing crowd systems, splashes etc. that involve a large number of primitives in proximity, whose location, motion , etc. can be abstracted into a particle system for purposes of animation. Doing so keeps the system relatively light-weight and hence more responsive. During rendering, bigger pieces of geometry such as characters and textured sprites are instanced (more on this in section 4.18) at the individual particle locations, effectively becoming replacements for the particles.

Before the introduction of the point primitive, RenderMan users had to fake points using tiny spheres, which was rather expensive in terms of computation. In contrast, the point primitive is very efficient, permitting the rendering of millions of them at a reasonable cost.

In RenderMan you specify a point collection using the Points command. Figure 4.1 shows two sets of nine points arranged in a grid pattern. It was generated using the following command:

```
# "P" specifies xyz coordinates of the particles, e.g. -4 -4 0 # is
the location of the first particle in each set of nine
# particles.
# Left-hand side set:
# "constantwidth" specifies a single particle width for the
# collection
Points "P" [-4 -4 0 0 -4 0 4 -4 0   -4 0 0 0 0 0 4 0 0   -4 4 0 0 4
0 4 4 0] "constantwidth" 0.4
# Right-hand side set:
# "width" is used to specify varying per-particle widths
Points "P" [-4 -4 0 0 -4 0 4 -4 0   -4 0 0 0 0 0 4 0 0   -4 4 0 0 4
0 4 4 0] "width" [1.2 .8 1.2 .8 .5 .8 1.2 .8 1.2]
```

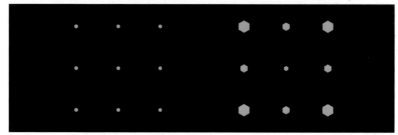

Figure 4.1 *Point grids*

"P" is followed by the specification of XYZ coordinate of each point to be rendered. Note that these coordinates are in "object" space. This is the case as well, for all the other primitives that are discussed in subsequent sections. Each primitive is specified in terms of its native object space, and transformation commands (discussed in the next chapter) are used to position, orient and scale the primitive for scene construction.

Returning to the Points command, notice that the coordinate specification is followed by an attribute called "width" and values for "width". In contrast to their mathematical definition, RenderMan points have user-specifiable widths. The width attribute and its array of values (one for each point in the collection) is for per-particle widths, where all the points are not of the same size. If they are, a different attribute called "constantwidth" can be used like so:

```
constantwidth [.25]
```

The single value that follows the name of the attribute will be uniformly applied to all the points in the collection. Note that in a typical scene, even with a constantwidth specification, all the points in the collection do not need to occupy the same area in the final image – that would depend on how the particles are distributed in space (particles farther away from the camera/viewer would appear smaller due to perspective).

Figure 4.2 shows a spiral particle cloud with a lot more points than in Figure 4.1. The RIB command to generate it is:

```
Points "P"   [-0.0234547 0.169093 -0.141272 0.0384226 0.0524207 -
0.0646742
#.... lot more points ....
] "constantwidth" [0.004]
```

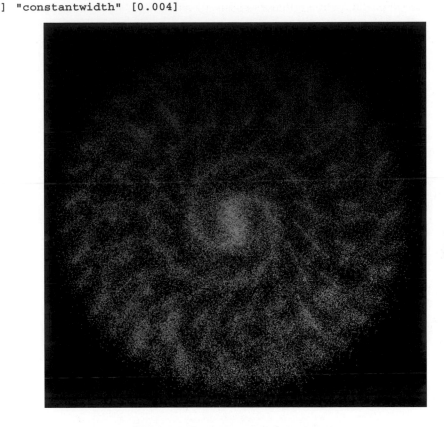

Figure 4.2 *A spiral cloud of particles*

The syntax is identical to that of the first example, except that we have many more points which usually tends to be the case with particle imagery. The coloring comes from a shader called show_xyz. Throughout this chapter, our emphasis will be on shapes, not shading. Shaders will be discussed extensively in Chapter 8.

As a final note, you can see from Figure 4.1 that each rendered point appears to have a hexagonal cross section. This is no accident – PRMan currently implements a point primitive as a pair of semi-hexagonal quadrilaterals placed back to back to create a hexagon (to picture this, imagine cutting a regular hexagon along one of its three diagonals to obtain a pair of mirror-symmetric quadrilaterals – PRMan starts out with such a quadrilateral pair to piece together the hexagon). In typical scenes the sizes of points are kept small enough so that this implementation detail does not become evident to the viewer.

4.3 Curves

Curves are extremely versatile entities, serving as modeling primitives for hair, fur, grass, ribbons, etc. as well as aiding in the construction of spline surfaces (which are discussed in Section 4.7).

This versatility results from a good choice for their representation, namely the use of control vertices (CVs from here on). A non-CV approach is shown in Figure 4.3, where the user specifies some points (blue circles) to use as influencers for curve generation. The generated curve is shown passing through the specified points, but most likely not in a manner that the user expected. The curve is not tense enough and displays slack in the form of curvature (extra curve material) between the input points. The reason is that the curve is generated by fitting a cubic polynomial through the points. This simply means that an equation is generated, whose plot is guaranteed to pass through our input points. But it is that same equation that generates the undesirable bulges, in between the input points.

If the user moves one of the points to alter the curve, a new equation would be generated, and its plot might result in different bulge shapes, making it a nightmare to design curves in a predictable manner. In other words, there is no local control. Further, plots of polynomial curve equations cannot loop back, so it is not possible to design circular or self-intersecting shapes this way.

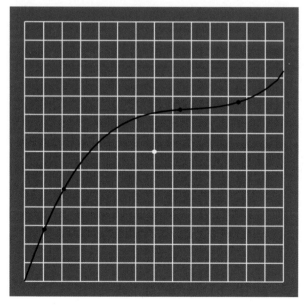

Figure 4.3 *A cubic curve passing through four specified points*

A much better solution (which is practically the only one in use today) is to use CVs, which are points specified by the user (just like in Figure 4.3), which will be used by spline generation algorithms to produce a curve in response. The procedure is more general than curve fitting and offers more local control to the user – changing a CV's position only affects the shape of the curve near the CV.

RenderMan uses the Curve command to generate spline curves. A simple version of a spline curve is a polyline, where the user's CVs are sequentially joined using straight line segments. The result is a curve pulled as tight as possible between adjacent CVs (the curve is said to be a linear one, otherwise known as a degree-1 curve).

If just two CVs are specified for a linear curve, the result is a single line segment. Figure 4.4 shows a shape made from several such line segments (incidentally, the termination points of the lines create an envelope in the form of a hyperbola). You can try generating more complex string-art (symmography) pictures using this technique. Figure 4.4 is obtained using:

```
# Each Curves statement specifies a single line segment
# ("linear") with two CVs ([2]) which are the endpoints
# specified using "P".
# An alternate way to obtain the same image is to combine
# all the segments into a single Curve command, which
# would start with
# Curves "linear" [2 2 2 2 2.......]
# and list all the pairs of CVs using a single "P"
# array beginning with
# "P" [0 1 0 0 0 0  0 0.9473684211 0 0.05263157895 0 0
# 0 0.8947368421 0 0.1052631579 0 0....]
Curves "linear" [2] "nonperiodic" "P" [0 1 0 0 0 0] "constantwidth"
[0.004]
Curves "linear" [2] "nonperiodic" "P" [0 0.9473684211 0 0.05263157895
0 0] "constantwidth" [0.004]
Curves "linear" [2] "nonperiodic" "P" [0 0.8947368421 0 0.1052631579
0 0] "constantwidth" [0.004]
Curves "linear" [2] "nonperiodic" "P" [0 0.8421052632 0 0.1578947368
0 0] "constantwidth" [0.004]
Curves "linear" [2] "nonperiodic" "P" [0 0.7894736842 0 0.2105263158
0 0] "constantwidth" [0.004]
Curves "linear" [2] "nonperiodic" "P" [0 0.7368421053 0 0.2631578947
0 0] "constantwidth" [0.004]
Curves "linear" [2] "nonperiodic" "P" [0 0.6842105263 0 0.3157894737
0 0] "constantwidth" [0.004]
Curves "linear" [2] "nonperiodic" "P" [0 0.6315789474 0 0.3684210526
0 0] "constantwidth" [0.004]
Curves "linear" [2] "nonperiodic" "P" [0 0.5789473684 0 0.4210526316
0 0] "constantwidth" [0.004]
Curves "linear" [2] "nonperiodic" "P" [0 0.5263157895 0 0.4736842105
0 0] "constantwidth" [0.004]
Curves "linear" [2] "nonperiodic" "P" [0 0.4736842105 0 0.5263157895
0 0] "constantwidth" [0.004]
Curves "linear" [2] "nonperiodic" "P" [0 0.4210526316 0 0.5789473684
0 0] "constantwidth" [0.004]
Curves "linear" [2] "nonperiodic" "P" [0 0.3684210526 0 0.6315789474
0 0] "constantwidth" [0.004]
Curves "linear" [2] "nonperiodic" "P" [0 0.3157894737 0 0.6842105263
0 0] "constantwidth" [0.004]
Curves "linear" [2] "nonperiodic" "P" [0 0.2631578947 0 0.7368421053
0 0] "constantwidth" [0.004]
Curves "linear" [2] "nonperiodic" "P" [0 0.2105263158 0 0.7894736842
0 0] "constantwidth" [0.004]
Curves "linear" [2] "nonperiodic" "P" [0 0.1578947368 0 0.8421052632
0 0] "constantwidth" [0.004]
Curves "linear" [2] "nonperiodic" "P" [0 0.1052631579 0 0.8947368421
0 0] "constantwidth" [0.004]
```

```
Curves "linear" [2] "nonperiodic" "P" [0 0.05263157895 0 0.9473684211
0 0] "constantwidth" [0.004]
Curves "linear" [2] "nonperiodic" "P" [0 0 0 1 0 0] "constantwidth"
[0.004]
```

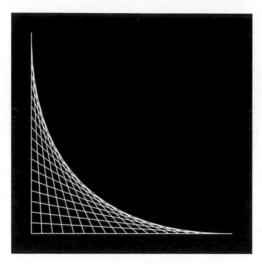

Figure 4.4 *Line segments forming a hyperbolic envelope*

Figure 4.5 shows a single polyline zigzagging through space to form a 3D Hilbert curve which enters the shaded cube enclosure on the top right and exits on the top left. The smaller shaded cube shows a subsection with seven segments, which is repeated seven more times along the rest of the path. The subsection has the same general shape as the whole curve. In other words the Hilbert curve is a space-filling fractal – each subsection can be further divided into eight smaller subsections and so on. In the limit, the result would be a single polyline of infinite length, made up of line segments infinitesimally small, one that would solidly pack the entire cube without any gap. Likewise, a 2D Hilbert curve would fill a square, in the limit. To practice rendering of polylines, look up online, descriptions of other fractal shapes such as Sierpinski curve/gasket, Menger sponge, C curve, Dragon curve and Koch snowflake.

The Hilbert curve in Figure 4.5 results from this Curve command:

```
# A single long polyline passing through 64 points,
# listed using "P"
Curves
"linear" [64]
"nonperiodic"
"P" [0 0 0 -1 0 0 -1 0 -1 0 0 -1 0 -1 -1 -1 -1 -1 -1 -1 0 0 -1 0 0
-2 0 0 -2 -1 0 -3 -1 0 -3 0 -1 -3 0 -1 -3 -1 -1 -2 -1 -1 -2 0 -2 -2
0 -2 -2 -1 -2 -3 -1 -2 -3 0 -3 -3 0 -3 -3 -1 -3 -2 -1 -3 -2 0 -3 -1
0 -3 0 0 -2 0 0 -2 -1 0 -2 -1 -1 -2 0 -1 -3 0 -1 -3 -1 -1 -3 -1 -2
-3 0 -2 -2 0 -2 -2 -1 -2 -2 -1 -3 -2 0 -3 -3 0 -3 -3 -1 -3 -3 -2 -3
-3 -2 -2 -3 -3 -2 -3 -3 -3 -2 -3 -3 -2 -3 -2 -2 -2 -2 -2 -2 -3 -1 -
2 -3 -1 -2 -2 -1 -3 -2 -1 -3 -3 0 -3 -3 0 -3 -2 0 -2 -2 0 -2 -3 0 -
1 -3 -1 -1 -3 -1 -1 -2 0 -1 -2 0 0 -2 -1 0 -2 -1 0 -3 0 0 -3 ]
"constantwidth" .015
```

Figure 4.5 *Polyline Hilbert curve in 3D*

After looking at polylines we are ready to examine cubic (degree 3) spline curves. Figure 4.6 shows the four types of spline curves supported by RenderMan. On the left is the input, which is a set of four CVs. The open shape formed by them is referred to as the CV hull (or just hull). The mathematics of spline evaluation is such that each CV influences, or contributes to, the generation of a section of the output curve. In the figure you can see that the Bezier, Hermite and b-spline curves are contained within the hull, while the Catmull-Rom curve is not.

Note that the same set of four CVs results in different curves, depending on the spline type. In addition to these four, there are many more spline generation algorithms – RenderMan supports just the most popular ones.

Each curve has its own unique properties. The Bezier curve passes through the first and last CV but not the middle ones. The Hermite curve requires the specification of two endpoint CVs and their tangents derived from the middle ones (unlike others that only require CVs). The Catmull-Rom curve passes through the middle CVs and is an example of an interpolating spline while the b-spline does not, being a type of approximating spline. The RIB calls for the curve generation are:

```
# Hull for the CVs:
Curves "linear" [4] "nonperiodic" "P" [-2 -2 0  -1 2 0  1 2 0  2 -2
1] "constantwidth" [0.06]
# The rest of the commands use the same CVs as above to
# generate different cubic spline curves
# Bezier, with a step size of 3
Basis "bezier" 3
Curves "cubic" [4] "nonperiodic" "P" [-2 -2 0  -1 2 0  1 2 0  2 -2
1] "constantwidth" [0.1]
# Hermite, step size 2. Note that unlike with the other
# spline types, the four values specified using "P" are
# really point1, tangent1, point2, tangent2 and not
# four points
```

```
Basis "hermite" 2
Curves "cubic" [4] "nonperiodic" "P" [3 0.5 0   0.5 2.0 0
5.0 0.5 -1   0.5 -2 0    ] "constantwidth" [0.05]
# Catmull-Rom
Basis "catmull-rom" 1
Curves "cubic" [4] "nonperiodic" "P" [-2 -2 0   -1 2 0   1 2 0   2 -2
0] "constantwidth" [0.1]
# B-spline
Basis "b-spline" 1
Curves "cubic" [4] "nonperiodic" "P" [-2 -2 0   -1 2 0   1 2 0   2 -2
0] "constantwidth" [0.1]
```

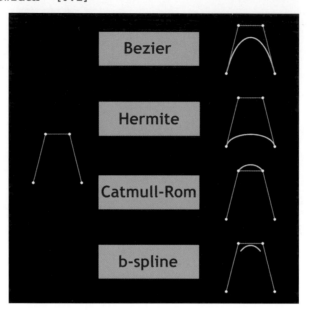

Figure 4.6 *Types of spline curves*

Longer spline curves result from longer CV sequences (made up of more than just four CVs). Overlapping sets of CVs from the sequence are used to generate individual spline segments which are pieced together to yield the final curve. In other words, if there are seven CVs numbered 0,1,2,3,4,5,6, the first Bezier segment is created from CVs 0,1,2,3, and the second, from CVs 3,4,5,6. Note that CV number 3 straddles both segments, providing continuity between them to yield a longer curve. Since the first segment starts at CV 0 and the next one at CV 3, we say that adjoining Bezier segments have a step size of 3. If we had an even longer CV sequence numbered 0 through 9 (ten CVs total), the third segment would start at CV 6.

While Bezier curves have a step size of 3, b-splines and Catmull-Rom curves have a step size of 1, and Hermite curves, 2. Step sizes are specified in the Basis statement along with the spline type, e.g.

```
Basis "bezier" 3
```

Figure 4.7 illustrates the generation of longer splines, using a set of CVs laid out along a square spiral. You can spot the characteristic behavior of the three curves shown – the Bezier curve touches CV endpoints, the b-spline curve approximates the CVs and the Catmull-Rom curve interpolates them. The curves are generated using this block of RIB:

```
# 13 CVs laid out along a square spiral
Curves "linear" [13] "nonperiodic" "P" [
0  0  0
1  0  0
1 -2  0
-2 -2  0
-2  2  0
3  2  0
3 -4  0
-4 -4  0
-4  4  0
5  4  0
5 -6  0
-6 -6  0
-6  6  0] "constantwidth" 0.075


# Bezier, b-spline and Catmull-Rom curves using the above 13
# CVs
Basis "bezier" 3
Curves "cubic" [13] "nonperiodic" "P"
[0 0 0 1 0 0 1 -2 0 -2 -2 0 -2 2 0 3 2 0 3 -4 0 -4 -4 0 -4 4 0 5 4
0 5 -6 0 -6 -6 0 -6 6 0] "constantwidth" 0.1

Basis "b-spline" 1
Curves "cubic" [13] "nonperiodic" "P"
[0 0 0 1 0 0 1 -2 0 -2 -2 0 -2 2 0 3 2 0 3 -4 0 -4 -4 0 -4 4 0 5 4
0 5 -6 0 -6 -6 0 -6 6 0] "constantwidth" 0.1

Basis "catmull-rom" 1
Curves "cubic" [13] "nonperiodic" "P"
[0 0 0 1 0 0 1 -2 0 -2 -2 0 -2 2 0 3 2 0 3 -4 0 -4 -4 0 -4 4 0 5 4
0 5 -6 0 -6 -6 0 -6 6 0] "constantwidth" 0.1
```

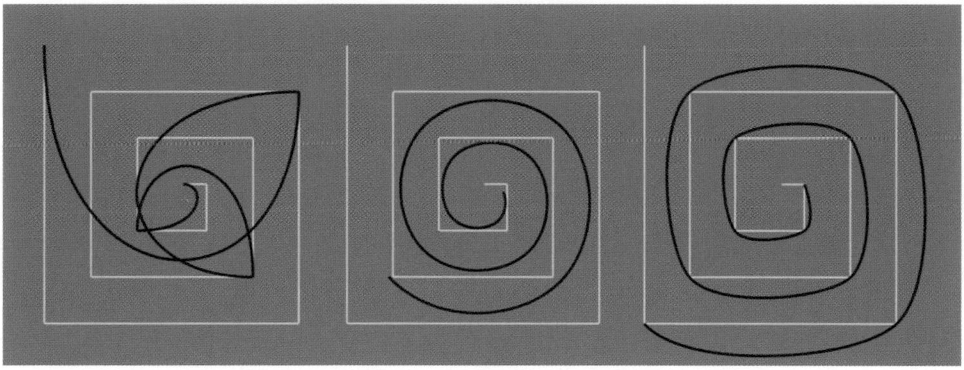

Figure 4.7 *Bezier, b-spline and Catmull-Rom curves*

The spline generation algorithms (built into RenderMan) would need to be given the list of CVs, what type of curve to generate and additional data (such as the overlap between adjacent segments in a long CV sequence). This is schematically shown in Figure 4.8. The type of curve to generate can be bezier, b-spline, catmull-rom or hermite, as shown in the previous examples. Splines are best described in terms of basis matrices, which are matrices that specify how CVs influence the generation process. Basis matrices for the four spline types supported by RenderMan are built-in, so you can simply specify those splines by name. In addition to these, you can also specify alternate spline types using the Basis command by feeding it appropriate matrices for evaluation.

Spline generators work by using the matrices and CVs to calculate several points along the length of the curve which are joined together to produce the curve. Every point lies on the curve's so-called parametric interval which runs from 0.0 to 1.0. Using "u" to indicate the parameter, the starting point of the curve lies at u=0.0 and the endpoint, at u=1.0 (this holds no matter what the shape of the curve is, whether it is long or short, twisted, bent or straight, etc.).

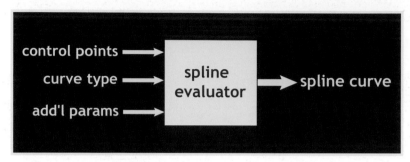

Figure 4.8 *Spline curve evaluation*

To give you an idea of how CVs influence spline generation, let us look at a subdivision technique to generate Bezier curves, invented by Paul de Casteljau of the Citroën car company in the 1960s. Keep in mind that modern Bezier evaluators use more efficient generation techniques – our discussion of the de Casteljau algorithm is for learning purposes only. On the other hand, being a subdivision technique, it will motivate the discussion of subdivision surface primitives in Section 4.6.

In the left of Figure 4.9 are shown four CVs in a zigzag configuration, with three line segments between them. We would like to evaluate a Bezier point at u=0.333 (a third of the way along the parametric interval). Subdivide each of the three segments in a 1/3:2/3 ratio, in other words, pick a point on each segment one third along its length. Join the three points just picked, to produce two new segments. On each of those segments, again pick a one-third point, then join those to obtain a single segment. Finally, pick a one-third point on that last segment. This is the point (shown in red in the right diagram of Figure 4.9) that will lie on the resulting Bezier curve at u=0.333.

So far we have obtained just a single point on what would be the final curve. If we were to repeat the above steps at other u values, such u=0.1, u=0.7, etc., we will get more points to make up our curve (Figure 4.10). The result is a smooth Bezier shape that passes through the end CVs as expected.

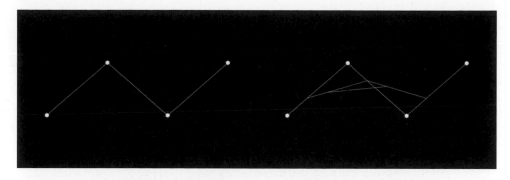

Figure 4.9 *de Casteljau evaluation of a single point*

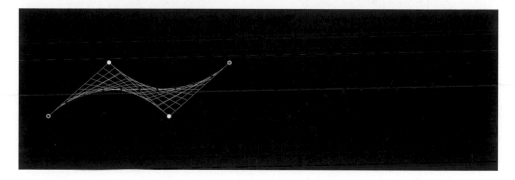

Figure 4.10 *de Casteljau curve tracing*

If we were to reposition one or more of the four CVs, the calculations would have to be repeated to regenerate the Bezier curve. Modern animation packages (such as Maya, Softimage XSI, Houdini, etc.) have excellent tools that let you interactively shape curves by providing tools for CV manipulation.

The curvewidth parameter in the Curve command can be adjusted to produce wider shapes (useful for grass, ribbons, etc.) which can be colored, lit and textured just like any other surface. Shown in Figure 4.11 is a trefoil knot curve with a marble texture. Curves such as the trefoil knot have analytical representations (formulae) that are used to generate them. You can find a variety of such formulae, in *A Catalog of Plane Curves* by J. Dennis Lawrence. The trefoil curve shown here is generated using this RIB:

```
# Points for a trefoil knot
Basis "bezier" 3
Curves "cubic" [664] "nonperiodic" "P"[0 0 -1 0.02849614197
0.04749757081 -0.9996841355
# 662 more points....
] "constantwidth" [0.75]
```

Figure 4.11 *Trefoil knot*

The Curve command allows you to specify a different color, thickness or normal at each
CV, so you can produce curves that taper from one end to the other, curves that twist in
space, curves with color gradations, etc. The curve (b-spline) on the right of Figure 4.12
illustrates such per-CV variations. For comparison, on the left of the figure is the same curve
with no per-CV variation. Per-CV attributes are specified as follows:

```
# Left figure: no per-CV attributes
# Curve - bspline
Basis "b-spline" 1
Curves "cubic" [8] "nonperiodic" "P" [0 0 0 0 1 0 1 1 0 1 0 0  1 0
-1 1 1 -1 0 1 -1 0 0 -1] "constantwidth" 0.02
# Hull
Curves "linear" [8] "nonperiodic" "P" [0 0 0 0 1 0 1 1 0 1 0 0  1 0
-1 1 1 -1 0 1 -1 0 0 -1] "constantwidth" [0.01]
# Right figure, with per-CV color, normal and thickness specified
# using "Cs", "N" and "width", one value per CV for each attribute
# Curve - bspline
Basis "b-spline" 1
Curves "cubic" [8] "nonperiodic" "P" [0 0 0 0 1 0 1 1 0 1 0 0  1 0
-1 1 1 -1 0 1 -1 0 0 -1] "Cs" [0 1 0 0 0 1   1 1 0 1 0 1 0 1 1 0 0
0] "N" [0 1 0 1 1 0 1 0 0  1 0 -1 1 1 -1 0 1 -1] "width" [0.03 0.03
0.06 0.06 0.03 0.03]
# Hull
Curves "linear" [8] "nonperiodic" "P" [0 0 0 0 1 0 1 1 0 1 0 0  1 0
-1 1 1 -1 0 1 -1 0 0 -1]    "constantwidth" [0.01]
```

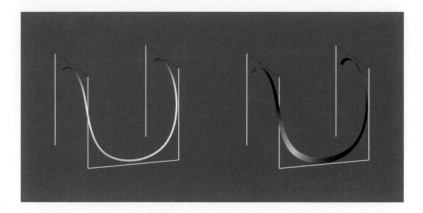

Figure 4.12 *Per-CV normal, color and width*

In all the Curve commands so far, we have specified CV coordinates using the P attribute. It is also possible to use an alternate attribute, Pw, to specify what are called homogeneous coordinates (x,y,z,w). The fourth value w is implicitly assumed to be 1.0 when the P form is used. In Figure 4.13 is a b-spline curve drawn using Pw, with w=1 for all CVs. Such curves (that are specified using P, or equivalently, using Pw with w=1) are called polynomial curves. The Curve command for Figure 4.13 is:

```
Basis "b-spline" 1
# Note the use of Pw instead of P. However we could
# have used P, since w (the fourth value for each CV)
# is 1 for each CV below
# Also, note that the first CV and the last each occur
# four times. This forces the curve to pass through those
# CVs (the replication can occur anywhere, not just at
# endpoints)
Curves "cubic" [17]
"nonperiodic"
"Pw" [
0  0  0  1
0  0  0  1
0  0  0  1
1  0  0  1
1 -2  0  1
-2 -2  0  1
-2  2  0  1
3  2  0  1
3 -4  0  1
-4 -4  0  1
-4  4  0  1
5  4  0  1
5 -6  0  1
-6 -6  0  1
-6  6  0  1
-6  6  0  1
-6  6  0  1
] "constantwidth" [0.075]
```

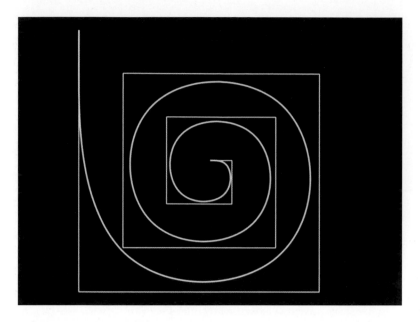

Figure 4.13 *Polynomial b-spline curve (all homogeneous coordinates are 1.0)*

In contrast are rational curves that are specified using Pw, where the fourth value (w) is a value other than 1.0. Figure 4.14 shows a rational b-spline (**RBS** for short) where for CVs numbered 4 and 7, we use a non-unity w value:

```
Basis "b-spline" 1
Curves "cubic" [17]
"nonperiodic"
"Pw" [
0  0  0  1
0  0  0  1
0  0  0  1
1  0  0  1
1 -2  0  1
-2 -2  0  1
-2  2  0  2.5 # non-unity w value
3  2  0  1
3 -4  0  1
-4 -4  0  0.75 # again, w is not 1.0
-4  4  0  1
5  4  0  1
5 -6  0  1
-6 -6  0  1
-6  6  0  1
-6  6  0  1
-6  6  0  1
] "constantwidth" [0.075]
```

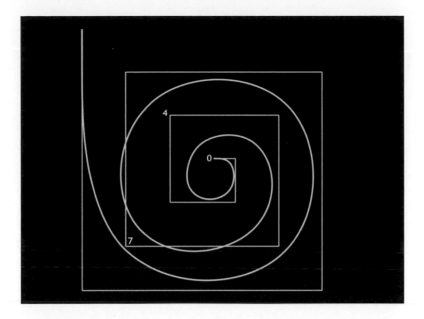

Figure 4.14 *Rational b-spline curve (some homogeneous coordinates are not 1.0)*

Note in Figure 4.14 that the b-spline curve passes through the very first CV. This is because in our RIB command we repeated that CV's coordinates thrice, giving that CV a multiplicity (redundancy) of 3. For a cubic spline curve (the ones supported by RenderMan), repeating a CV thrice will force the curve to pass through that CV.

This is further illustrated in Figure 4.15 where the CV numbered 6 and the last CV (number 12) belonging to a b-spline are repeated thrice. CV number 9 is only repeated twice, so the curve does not quite pass through that CV but passes close to it instead.

By repeating CVs sequentially for a b-spline as shown in figures 4.13 through 4.15 to increase their multiplicity, we are faking the effect of what are called knots whose direct specification is not supported in RenderMan's Curve command. Knots however are supported (indeed, required) for the NuPatch NURBS surface command, so we will discuss them in detail in the section on patches (Section 4.7).

The RIB code used to generate Figure 4.15 is:

```
# We're using Pw with w=1 everywhere, which makes the
# curve a polynomial one. We could have used P
# instead, without the extra w values
Basis "b-spline" 1
Curves "cubic" [18] "nonperiodic" "Pw" [
0  0  0 1
1  0  0 1
1 -2  0 1
-2 -2  0 1
-2  2  0 1
3  2  0 1
# The following CV occurs thrice, forcing the curve to
# pass through it
3 -4  0 1
3 -4  0 1
```

```
3 -4 0 1
-4 -4 0 1
-4 4 0 1
# Following CV is listed twice, attracting the curve
# towards it
5 4 0 1
5 4 0 1
5 -6 0 1
-6 -6 0 1
# endpoint CV occurs thrice, making the curve pass through
# it
-6 6 0 1
-6 6 0 1
-6 6 0 1
]
"constantwidth" [0.075]
```

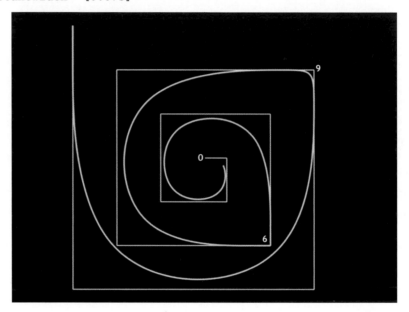

Figure 4.15 *b-spline curve, effect of coincident knots*

4.4 Polygons

A polygon is a straightforward primitive – it is simply a flat shape (face) bounded by straight edges, which meet at corners (vertices). RenderMan has two commands to create polygons. The first is the Polygon command, which creates convex polygons. For example, Figure 4.16 shows a regular (all sides and angles equal) triangle, square, pentagon and hexagon which are all examples of convex polygons.

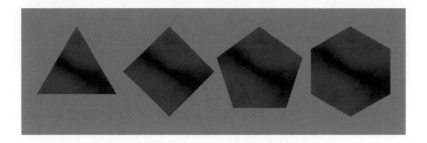

Figure 4.16 *Convex regular polygons*

Intuitively, a convex polygon is a flat shape bounded by straight edges in such a way that its surrounding ("negative") space does not cut back into it. The Polygon command has the following basic syntax:

```
Polygon "P" [...... points..]
```

The primitive variable P is used to represent (x,y,z) vertex data in the form of an array. The number of points in the array is the same as the number of sides in the polygon. The regular polygons in the Figure 4.16 are a result of these commands:

```
# Regular triangle (three vertices)
Polygon "P" [
0  1 0 # vertex 1
-0.8660253367 -0.5000001162 0 # vertex 2
0.8660255063 -0.4999998224 0 # vertex 3
]
# Square
Polygon "P" [-6.320510331e-008 1 0 -1 -1.164102067e-007 0
1.696153101e-007 -1 0 1 2.228204134e-007 0 ]
# Regular pentagon
Polygon "P" [0 1 0 -0.951056549 0.3090168938 0 -0.5877851323 -
0.8090170816 0 0.5877854067 -0.8090168822 0 0.9510564442 0.3090172164
0 ]
# Regular hexagon
Polygon "P" [0 1 0 -0.8660254531 0.4999999145 0 -0.8660253367 -
0.5000001162 0 0 -1 0 0.8660255063 -0.4999998224 0 0.8660252835
0.5000002083 0 ]
```

Figure 4.17. shows a tangram square, an ancient classic toy comprising seven convex polygons. If you cut these shapes out of cardboard, you can make an astonishing variety (several thousand) of figures by rearranging the seven pieces, such as the graceful cat shown in Figure 4.18. If such a thing interests you, look up "Stomachion" or "Loculus of Archimedes" online for a similar dissection puzzle with 14 pieces.

The tangram's initial square configuration can be obtained using these seven Polygon commands:

```
# Tangram pieces - five triangles, two
# quadrilaterals (square and parallelogram)
Polygon "P" [0 0 0 2 2 0 0 4 0]
Polygon "P" [0 4 0 2 2 0 4 4 0]
Polygon "P" [0 0 0 2 0 0 1 1 0]
Polygon "P" [1 1 0 2 0 0 3 1 0 2 2 0]
Polygon "P" [2 2 0 3 1 0 3 3 0]
Polygon "P" [3 1 0 4 2 0 4 4 0 3 3 0]
```

```
Polygon "P"  [2 0 0 4 0 0 4 2 0]
```

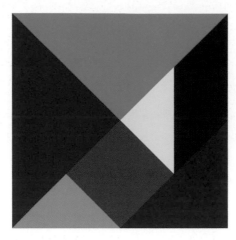

Figure 4.17 *Tangram puzzle, starter configuration*

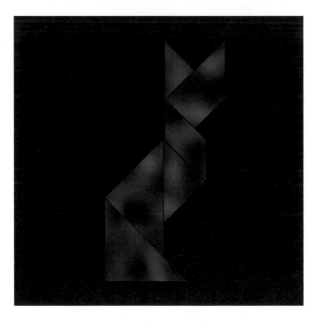

Figure 4.18 *Tangram kitty*

In contrast to convex polygons are concave polygons, whose characteristic is that it contains surrounding regions that cut back into the shape. For instance most islands on earth have a roughly concave shape with waterways extending into the land in the form of bays. The star and cross in Figure 4.19 are examples of concave polygons. On a concave polygon it is always possible to pick at least one spot so that if you draw a straight line starting at that spot, the line will leave the polygon at an edge and then re-enter it by crossing it at another edge (several such crossings can occur in general).

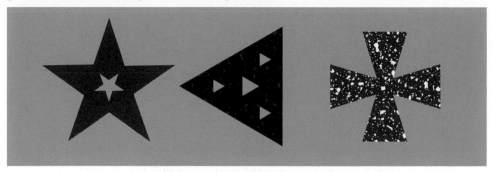

Figure 4.19 *GeneralPolygon shapes*

Both convex and concave polygons can have polygonal holes (negative shapes) cut into them. RenderMan's GeneralPolygon command does double duty by representing concave polygons (with or without holes) and also convex polygons with holes. You can see in Figure 4.19 that the first two polygons have holes. All three figures were generated using these commands:

```
# Star-shaped polygon, with 10 vertices and a
#star-shaped hole also with 10 vertices
GeneralPolygon [10 10] "P"
[0.00306987064 0.9949810505 0 0.2241048515 0.2950369418 0 0.942468524
0.3073166609 0 0.3530419171 -0.1163337231 0 0.5924965143 -
0.8039981127 0 0.00306987064 -0.3803477287 0 -0.5863567591 -
0.7978582382 0 -0.3591819108 -0.1347533017 0 -0.9547483921
0.3011767864 0 -0.2241049707 0.3134565353 0 0.0005537587362 -
0.2301202043 0 -0.05145558058 -0.06851992133 0 -0.2175810314 -
0.07227234985 0 -0.08179825954 0.02645691592 0 -0.1380520371
0.1851937862 0 -0.001193079521 0.08796181035 0 0.134597496
0.185271064 0 0.08289938761 0.03162155483 0 0.2211939456 -
0.06844263669 0 0.0522284704 -0.07221066891 0 ]

# A triangle (3 verts) with four triangular holes (also
# 3 verts each)
GeneralPolygon [3 3 3 3 3] "P"
[-1 0 0 0.5 -0.87 0 0.5 0.87 0 -0.08324998677 -0.1441932106 0
0.1664999846 4.2603818e-008 0 -0.08325003639 0.1441932547 0 -0.506 -
0.097 0 -0.337 0 0 -0.506 0.097 0 0.168 -0.487 0 0.337 -0.389 0
0.168 -0.292 0 0.337 0.389 0 0.168 0.487 0 0.168 0.292 0 ]

# Maltese cross shape with 12 verts and no holes
GeneralPolygon [12] "P" [0.1395230957 0.1385857179 0 0.4043791595
0.9938444968 0 -0.4043028509 0.9938827359 0 -0.1395231805
0.1385857179 0 -1.002029874 0.3998560053 0 -1.002029874 -0.4088260051
0 -0.1503951209 -0.1440845421 0 -0.4079650737 -0.9993050607 0
0.4007551759 -0.9992668215 0 0.1395230957 -0.1440845421 0
0.9984440445 -0.4088260051 0 0.9947435825 0.3997796119 0 ]
```

The GeneralPolygon command has this syntax:

```
GeneralPolygon
[num_poly_vertices
```

```
num_vertices_in_first_hole
num_vertices_in_second_hole .....]
"p"
[....point data...]
```

The first array of integers specifies how many vertices are in the polygon (which could be concave or convex) and also the number of vertices of every hole present. The occurrence of holes is optional (the command does not require that they be present). That is why in Figure 4.19, the command for the cross shape contains [12] for the integer array. You can think of the polygon as a positive shape and the holes it might contain, as negative shapes. So the integer array at the beginning of the command lists the number of vertices in the positive shape and if holes are present, their vertex counts as well. This is followed by point data using P. Again, the points of the enclosing polygon are listed first, and if holes are present, their point data as well.

The shape in the left side of Figure 4.20 is an example of a fairly complex concave polygon with four regions cutting into it. This figure is discussed in Joseph O'Rourke's book *Computational Geometry in C*.

On the right is the same shape shown sectioned into triangles (which are always convex). Note that many renderers internally break up a concave polygon into convex polygons for rendering purposes.

The command for O'Rourke's polygon is:

```
# Concave poly, with 18 vertices
# and no holes
GeneralPolygon [18]
"P"
[
0  0  0
10  7  0
12  3  0
20  8  0
13  17  0
10  12  0
12  14  0
13  11  0
7  11  0
6  14  0
10  15  0
6  18  0
-1  15  0
1  13  0
4  14  0
5  10  0
-2  9  0
5  5  0
1  2  3
]
```

Figure 4.20 *A rather complex concave polygon*

Polygons are especially useful for rendering tessellation (tiling) patterns. Figure 4.21 shows the beautiful Penrose tile pair (dart and kite) on the left. As the figure on the right shows, kites and darts can be arranged to create intricate aperiodic patterns with rotational symmetry. Such five-fold symmetry is very common in nature (e.g. in flowers and starfish) but rather unusual in tessellations and crystal structures.

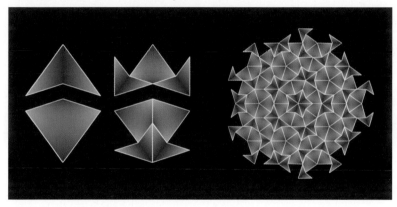

Figure 4.21 *Penrose tiles, deflation and a tessellation*

The dart and kite shapes shown on the left of Figure 4.21 can be obtained using these commands:

```
# Penrose tile, dart shape
GeneralPolygon [4] "P" [0 0 0 95.10565186 -30.90168953 0 0 100 0 -
95.10565186 -30.90168953 0 ]
# Penrose tile, kite shape
Polygon "P" [0 0 0 161.8034058 0 0 130.9017029 95.10565186 0
49.99999237 153.8841858 0 ]
```

The middle illustration in Figure 4.21 shows how a parent dart shape can be "deflated" (or decomposed) into a smaller kite and two smaller dart shapes, and likewise, a parent kite into two darts and two kites. The deflation operation can be repeatedly (recursively) carried out on an initial arrangement, leading to increasingly fine, intricate tessellations that display captivating shapes and symmetries.

See if you can render some tessellation patterns by getting hold of vertex coordinates for them (an online search should turn up several examples). If you are interested in tessellations or mathematical art in general, David Eppstein's "Geometry Junkyard" site on the web is a good resource. Also, *Tilings and Patterns: An Introduction* by Grunbaum and Shephard is a classic text on the subject.

4.5 Polygonal meshes

A polygonal mesh (also known as a polyhedron, polymesh or mesh) is simply a collection of polygonal faces adjacent to one another that share vertices and/or edges. It is an intuitive and easy to understand modeling primitive that is useful (especially in hardware game engines) for representing everything from characters and terrain to vehicles and props.

In the previous section we saw how to specify individual polygons. If several such polygons are laid out to form larger entities (such as the tetrahedron in Figure 4.22), it is inefficient (wasteful) to specify the arrangement as being made up of these individual polygons. What is better is to take into account the fact that vertices and edges are shared by adjacent polygons, list them just once and make the adjoining faces share them. The tetrahedron in Figure 4.22 is made up of four triangular faces, where each face is in contact with three others along shared edges. Also, three faces come together at every corner (vertex). As a result, just four vertices (labeled 0,1 2,3 in the figure) are sufficient to describe the four faces. But if we were to specify each triangle separately, we would need 4x3=12 vertices (what we call 0,1,2 and 3 will each need to be specified thrice). Clearly the shared-vertices form is more compact and efficient, since both RenderMan and the user can consider the collection as a single unified entity.

There are several ways to represent polymeshes. Here we will only consider RenderMan's way, called the points-polygons specification. The idea is to list the vertices first, then describe each face as being comprised of vertices from the list.

Returning to Figure 4.22 where the vertices are numbered 0 through 3, the four faces are created from vertices (2,1,0), (1,0,3), (2,0,3) and (2,1,3). We have specified the topological (structural) connectivity between the vertices. Note that the vertices for each face are listed in counter-clockwise order. In other words, imagine holding the vertex-labeled tetrahedron in your hand, rotating it to look at each of the four faces in turn, and reading off the vertices in counter-clockwise order. Vertex ordering of a face is what determines its surface normal direction. By convention, counter-clockwise ordering makes the normal of a polygon face outward. So consistent ordering is essential to ensure that the normals of all the faces in a mesh are oriented appropriately (inward or outward). Shading calculations are often based on normals, so flipped normals might make parts of a surface incorrectly appear dark even if a light source were to be positioned nearby to illuminate it.

For completeness, note that the six edges that result from the arrangement are (1,3), (3,2), (2,1), (1,0), (0,2) and (0,3). Again we are using vertex indices to describe edges.

To complete the polymesh description, all we need is an (x,y,z) coordinate for each of our four vertices. A list of such coordinates is referred to as a vertex array. For our tetrahedron it looks like this:

```
0.664      0.000        -0.469       # vertex 0
0.000      -0.664        0.469       # vertex 1
0.000      0.664         0.469       # vertex 2
0.664      0.000        -0.469       # vertex 3
```

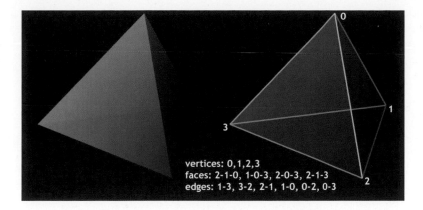

Figure 4.22 *A tetrahedral polymesh*

The polymesh description is packaged using the PointsPolygons command, as follows:

```
# Tetrahedron shown in Figure 4.22
PointsPolygons
[3 3 3 3] # 4 faces, each with 3 verts, 12 total
[2 1 0 1 0 3 2 0 3 2 1 3] # indices of the 12 verts
# following is the vertex array with (x,y,z) positions
# of the four vertices, referred to as 0,1,2 and 3 in the
# indices array above
"P" [
      0.664       0.000      -0.469
      0.000      -0.664       0.469
      0.000       0.664       0.469
     -0.664       0.000      -0.469
]
```

PointsPolygons is a generalization of the Polygon command which creates convex polygons, so it can be used only for polymeshes comprised of convex polygons. Most of the polymeshes you encounter are likely to fit in this category, since most polymeshes are created using triangles or quadrilaterals, both of which are convex polygons. Polymeshes created from triangles and quadrilaterals are referred to as triangle meshes and quad meshes respectively.

RenderMan does provide an equivalent generalization for GeneralPolygon, called PointsGeneralPolygons. As you might expect, this is the command to use for creating polymeshes from concave polygons and/or polygons with holes. For example, Figure 4.23 shows a cube that has a regular pentagon, hexagon and septagon cut out from three faces. If it were not for these holes, the shape would be described using PointsPolygons. But here we would employ PointsGeneralPolygons instead, like this:

```
PointsGeneralPolygons
# 6 faces - first has a hole, second
# doesn't, third does, and so on. Three
# faces have a hole each, other three don't.
# Total number of polys + holes is
# 2+1+2+1+2+1=9
[2 1 2 1 2 1]
# Number of vertices for each face and
# for a hole in it where one exists, a
```

```
# total of 9 entries
[4 5 4 4 7 4 4 6 4]

# Indices into the vertex array, for
# each face and hole
[
2 3 1 0 8 9 10 11 12 # face and pentagonal hole
4 5 3 2    # face
6 7 5 4 13 14 15 16 17 18 19 # face and septagonal hole
0 1 7 6  # face
3 5 7 1 20 21 22 23 24 25 # face and hexagonal hole
4 2 0 6 # face
]

# (x,y,z) vertex array
"P" [
# cube vertices
-1.5 -1.5 1.5
1.5 -1.5 1.5
-1.5 1.5 1.5
1.5 1.5 1.5
-1.5 1.5 -1.5
1.5 1.5 -1.5
-1.5 -1.5 -1.5
1.5 -1.5 -1.5

# pentagon
0 1 1.5
-0.951 0.309  1.5
-0.5877  -0.809  1.5
0.5877 -0.809 1.5
0.951 0.309 1.5

# septagon
0 1 -1.5
-0.7818312645 0.6234900951 -1.5
-0.9749280214 -0.2225204557 -1.5
-0.4338842928 -0.9009686112 -1.5
0.4338830709 -0.9009692073 -1.5
0.9749277234 -0.2225217819 -1.5
0.781832099 0.6234890223 -1.5

# hexagon
1.5 1 0
1.5 0.5000 0.866
1.5 -0.5   0.866
1.5 -1 0
1.5 -0.500 -0.8660
1.5 0.5 -0.8660
]
```

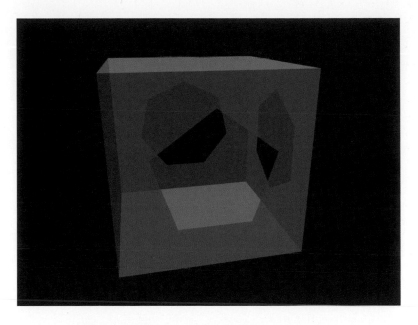

Figure 4.23 *A cube, with holes on three faces*

A polymesh does not always need to be closed or even three-dimensional. Figure 4.24 shows a flat, open polymesh that is shaped like a triangle. The flat coloring does not reveal the mesh structure, but in Figure 4.25 you can see the eleven convex polygons that make up the mesh. As a side note, this is a Voronoi polygon mesh, where the interior vertices always contain three edges that emanate from them. Voronoi polygons and their meshes are widely used in several fields ranging from astronomy to zoology. For instance crack propagation leading to brittle fractures can be modeled by splitting Voronoi polygons along their edges, resulting in the generation of realistic-looking fragments. See Christopher Gold's excellent site www.voronoi.com for much more information on Voronoi polygons.

Figure 4.24 *A flat polymesh*

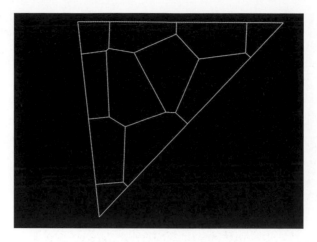

Figure 4.25 *Voronoi polygons*

Each vertex in a polymesh can be associated with arbitrary user-defined data, in addition to the "P" variable used to specify coordinates. For instance a finite-element method (FEM) simulation of temperature distribution over an aircraft wing might calculate a temperature value (scalar) at every vertex of the wing's polymesh. This data can be sent to RenderMan as a custom "T" variable for example, to be processed using an associated custom shader that can turn the temperature values into colors. In addition to such user-defined data, there are additional RenderMan-defined built-in variables you can specify, one of which is Cs (other common ones are N for vertex normals, and s and t for texture coordinates). A Cs value specified for each vertex will be used as that vertex's color. This is illustrated in Figure 4.26, which is generated using the following code:

```
# Voronoi polymesh with 23 vertices. We use # PointsGeneralPolygons
to describe the mesh, but PointsPolygons # could have been used also
PointsGeneralPolygons [1 1 1 1 1 1 1 1 1 1 1]
# 11 polygons: 6 pentagons, 3 quads and 2 hexagons
[5 5 5 4 5 6 5 6 4 5 4]
# indices into the vertex array, for the 23 vertices
[4 3 2 1 0 0 1 7 6 5 12 11 10 9 8 8 9 14 13 17 6 7 16 15 15 16 19
10 11 18 19 16 7 1 2 2 3 14 9 10 19 5 6 17 20 13 14 3 4 21 18 11 12
22]
# vertex array
"P"
[70.7105 0 170.711
69.5083 8.20932 167.808
# 21 more vertices, not shown here
# ....
]
# RGB color values, using Cs. There needs to be one value for
# each vertex, so a total of 23 values are needed
"Cs" [
0.7299169931 0.3638440628 0.75273698635
0.3911505674 0.3733838236 0.9096705964
# 21 more RGB triplets, not shown
# ...
]
```

The vertex colors are smoothly interpolated across each face, leading to colors that blend nicely. In Figure 4.26 the color smoothing is reduced on purpose, to enable you to pick out different colors where the vertices lie. Such vertex coloring is commonly used in low-end game engines to shade simple characters, where they serve as an alternative to more expensive texture-map based coloring.

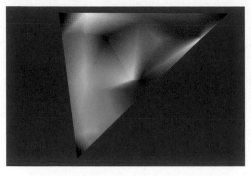

Figure 4.26 *Per-vertex mesh coloring*

Polymeshes are also ideal for procedurally generating surfaces (using equations that describe their shapes). If you have a programming background, you can try outputting RIB code using Python, Java, Perl, etc. to generate polymeshes of a variety of popular parametric surfaces such as Boy's surface, Klein bottle, Kuen's surface, Verrill minimal surface, etc. See Paul Bourke's personal pages on the web for striking images and parametric formulae for these and several other surfaces.

Figure 4.27 illustrates the beautiful Boy's surface. Smoothness of shape is achieved using a large number of tiny triangles (in other words, with a dense mesh), a portion of which can be seen in Figure 4.28.

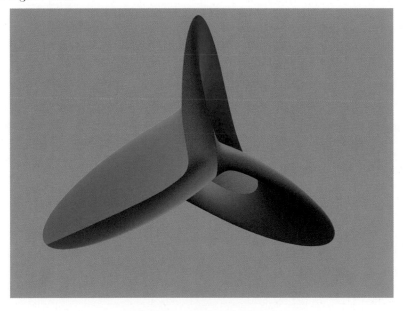

Figure 4.27 *Boy's surface*

Figure 4.28 *Boy's surface, detail*

If you are captivated by the beauty of parametric surfaces such as Boy's, you might be interested to know that such forms can be turned into physical 3D objects. Look up the works of Helaman Ferguson, Stewart Dickson, Brent Collins and Carlo Sequin for examples of mathematical shapes brought to life using stereolithography, casting and sculpting techniques.

Apart from procedurally generating meshes, it is possible (and is a common practice) to generate them interactively, using polygon and mesh editing tools to create and extrude faces, split faces and edges, merge coincident vertices, etc. Such tools are found in every major animation package, in addition to being available in high end modeling programs.

4.6 Subdivision surfaces

The notion of subdivision surfaces has been around since the late 1970s (in 1978, two schemes to generate them were proposed, one by Catmull and Clark and the other, by Doo and Sabin). Today's CG production community is re-discovering their importance, making them a current favorite especially for modeling characters. The revival is largely due to Pixar's Oscar-winning 1998 short *Geri's Game*, where Geri's head was modeled as a single subdivision surface. Since then Pixar has used the technique in their wildly popular animated feature films such as *A Bug's Life*, *Toy Story 2* and *Finding Nemo* and has also made subdivision surfaces available to all PRMan users.

What are subdivision surfaces and why are they good for modeling? Let us take a look. Figure 4.29 illustrates a very simple case, where an open polymesh (top figure) consisting of just two triangles is used as the generator for the subdivision algorithm. The overall idea is that the user specifies the polymesh as the input, and the system outputs a smooth subdivided result (bottom figure) in response. The user is able to use familiar polygon modeling tools to create the input mesh, which can be of arbitrary topology (which means that it can contain holes or open faces like the ones in our figure, can have an arbitrary number of faces meeting at a common vertex, can be made of polygons with any number of sides, etc.). The result is always guaranteed to be a smooth, topologically valid subdivided surface.

The middle rows of Figure 4.29 shows the steps involved in the subdivision process. The two triangles from our input mesh are split using Y-shaped edge triplets into quadrilaterals (quads). This is done by taking the midpoints along the triangle edges and joining those midpoints with the face centers. Note that this first splitting step will always generate quads, regardless of the number of sides the mesh polygons might have. In our example each triangle yields three quads, for a total of six for both. This first-level quad mesh has eleven vertices, up from the four vertices that our starter mesh had (verify this for yourself). The next step is to displace these eleven vertices to new positions which are derived from the configuration of the quads just generated. This displacement step results in some of the eleven vertices being peeled off the parent faces, and an accumulation of such displacement is what leads to eventual smoothing. The six quads are now split into smaller ones whose vertices get further displaced (to smaller extents than before), and the process continues. Each split-displacement combination results in increasingly finer levels of subdivision, which in the limit yields the smooth surface shown at the bottom of Figure 4.29.

Note that both the face splitting and the subsequent vertex displacement step are equally essential to the subdivision process. The splitting step refines the model, much like a block of wood being whittled down into a bunny shape using increasingly finer cuts. The mathematics of the displacement step ensures optimum smoothness, as the faces get finer. If it were not for displacements, all we will be left with at the end is still the parent polymesh, each face now tiled with a large number of small quads. The refinement explanation presented above is just for instructional purposes. While it is a valid way to achieve subdivision, in actual practice the implementation of an algorithm such as Catmull-Clark's would combine both steps into a single one, for efficiency reasons.

Subdivision surfaces offer the following advantages. First, the user only needs to deal with lightweight, easy to model polymeshes which also have a compact representation. A smooth output of topologically good quality is automatically generated by the subdivision algorithm, the absence of which would require a dense, heavy polymesh to represent an equivalent result. The overall polymesh model can be kept simple, with additional detail modeled just where extra subdivision is desired (e.g. for generating facial features on a head shape). Another big advantage is that subdivision surfaces always retain their smoothness regardless of their distance to the camera. A polymesh on the other hand might look smooth from sufficiently far away, but might begin to show faceting when it gets close to the camera. A final bonus is that subdivision meshes do not suffer from patch cracking problems the way spline surfaces might, since they are not comprised of patches to begin with.

In Figure 4.29, the pair of triangles at the top is rendered using the following RIB code:

```
PointsGeneralPolygons
[1 1] [3 3] [1 2 0 0 2 3]
"P" [0.5 0.5 0.5 -0.5 0.5 -0.5 0.5 0.5 -0.5 0.5 -0.5 -0.5]
```

To use the triangles as input for subdivision, we would use the SubdivisionMesh RIB command as follows:

```
# Subdivision of a pair of triangles. "catmull-clark" is
# currently always the first argument, since that is the
# only scheme currently implemented.
SubdivisionMesh "catmull-clark"
# two faces, each with 3 vertices; indices into vertex array
[3 3] [1 2 0 0 2 3]
# "interpolateboundary" is one of several tags used to
```

```
# specify additional properties for the subdivision. It
# takes 0 integer inputs and 0 float inputs, which is
# why it is followed by [0 0]. The two empty arrays []
# again mean 0 integer inputs and 0 float inputs
["interpolateboundary"] [0 0] [] []
# vertex array for the 4 verts making up our simple mesh
"P" [0.5 0.5 0.5 -0.5 0.5 -0.5 0.5 0.5 -0.5 0.5 -0.5 -0.5]
```

"interpolateboundary" means that the subdivided surface should be extended out to open edges and vertices. Specifying this is what makes our result drawn out to the two corners. Other tags currently defined are "hole", "corner" and "crease", all three of which are illustrated in Figure 4.33.

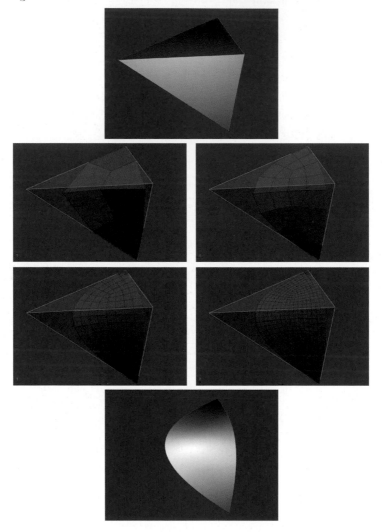

Figure 4.29 *Subdivision of a pair of triangles*

Figure 4.30 shows the rendered result of subdividing a cube polymesh. The symmetry of the cube results in a symmetric sphere-like surface. Note that the subdivision is not a perfect sphere – you can detect a little bit of flattening where the cube's faces would be.

The following SubdivisionMesh command is used to subdivide the cube:

```
# subdivision of a cube
SubdivisionMesh "catmull-clark"
[4 4 4 4 4 4]
[2 3 1 0 4 5 3 2 6 7 5 4 0 1 7 6 3 5 7 1 4 2 0 6]
["interpolateboundary"] [0 0] [] []
"P" [-0.5 -0.5 0.5 0.5 -0.5 0.5 -0.5 0.5 0.5 0.5 0.5 0.5
-0.5 0.5 -0.5 0.5 0.5 -0.5 -0.5 -0.5 -0.5 0.5 -0.5 -0.5]
```

Figure 4.30 *A subdivided cube*

The first three steps in the subdivision are shown in wireframe form in Figure 4.31. Each of the cube's six faces is split into four quads whose vertices subsequently get displaced. Those twenty four quads are further split and displaced, and so on.

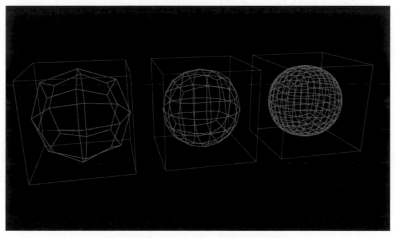

Figure 4.31 *Cube being progressively subdivided*

Smooth, closed subdivision surfaces are nice, but what if we need to introduce holes, creases or sharp corners into our models? PRMan's subdivision implementation does let us specify such features. In Figure 4.32 is shown a pentagonal torus mesh and its subdivision surface. At the top of the figure the subdivision surface is drawn out to coincide with two vertices, creating corners. Also at the top, an inner torus edge creates a crease in the subdivision surface. The rendered version in Figure 4.33 shows the corners and the crease, and also a hole in the subdivision.

The crease, corners and hole are specified in the SubdivisionMesh command as follows:

```
SubdivisionMesh "catmull-clark"
# pentagonal torus mesh, made up of all quads
[4 4 4 4 4 4 4 4 4 4 4 4 4 4 4 4 4 4 4 4 4 4 4 4 4]
# indices into vertex array
[6 5 0 1 7 6 1 2 8 7 2 3 9 8 3 4 5 9 4 0 11 10 5 6 12 11 6 7 13 12
7 8 14 13 8 9 10 14 9 5 16 15 10 11 17 16 11 12 18 17 12 13 19 18
13 14 15 19 14 10 21 20 15 16 22 21 16 17 23 22 17 18 24 23 18 19
20 24 19 15 1 0 20 21 2 1 21 22 3 2 22 23 4 3 23 24 0 4 24 20]

# tags are specified in a string array, followed by inputs
# for each tag
["crease" "corner" "hole" "interpolateboundary"]
# each pair of ints below specify the number of int and
# float inputs for each tag above. "crease" and "corner"
# need two int inputs and one float input (2 1), "hole" two
# and none (2 0), "interpolateboundary" none and none (0 0)
[2 1 2 1 2 0 0 0]

# int values for crease, corner and hole
# edge joining vertices 20 and 21 forms a crease
# vertices 15 and 16 form corners
# (adjoining) faces 17 and 18 are for creating a hole
[20 21 15 16 17 18]

# float values for crease and for corners
# 5 is the crease's sharpness. 0 means smooth, 10 and above
# mean very sharp, so 5 is somewhere in-between
# 20 is the sharpness value (infinitely sharp) for
# both corners
[5 20] # note that the value '20' is used for both corners

# vertex array
"P" [
0.154509 0 -0.475528 -0.404509 0 -0.293893 -0.404509 0 0.293893
0.154508 0 0.475528 0.5 0 0 0.261271 0.475528 -0.80411 -0.684017
0.475528 -0.496968 -0.684017 0.475528 0.496967 0.261271 0.475528
0.80411 0.845492 0.475528 0 0.434017 0.293893 -1.33577 -1.13627
0.293893 -0.82555 -1.13627 0.293893 0.825549 0.434017 0.293893
1.33577 1.40451 0.293893 0 0.434017 -0.293893 -1.33577 -1.13627 -
0.293893 -0.82555 -1.13627 -0.293893 0.825549 0.434017 -0.293893
1.33577 1.40451 -0.293893 0 0.261271 -0.475528 -0.80411 -0.684017 -
0.475528 -0.496967 -0.684017 -0.475528 0.496967 0.261271 -0.475528
0.80411 0.845491 -0.475528 0
]
```

Note that the flexible tag syntax makes it possible for more subdivision features to be introduced in future implementations.

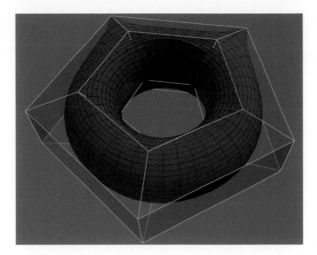

Figure 4.32 *Subdivision of a pentagonal torus*

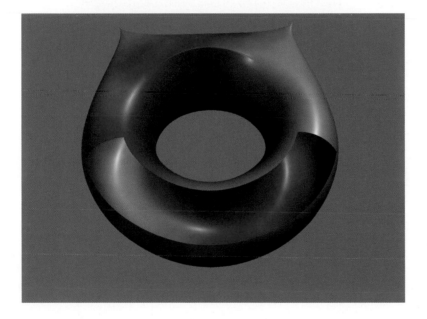

Figure 4.33 *Subdivision mesh containing a crease, two corners and a hole*

4.7 Patches

Patches are somewhat like subdivision surfaces, in the sense that simpler control geometry is amplified into a more complex result, leading to ease of construction and subsequent manipulation. Whereas the control mesh in a subdivision surface could be an arbitrary polygonal mesh, a spline patch control mesh is a grid of control vertices (CVs). Patches have a special place in the world of modeling, as they offer ways to generate complex surfaces such as those required in product design (e.g. automobiles) and character animation. Just like with curves, animation packages offer interactive ways to edit CVs that are used to create patches.

RenderMan handles spline patches using the Patch command, assemblies of them with the PatchMesh command and NURBS patches (a special class of patches) through the NuPatch command. An overview of each of these commands follows.

Two types of patches are supported in RenderMan, namely bilinear and bicubic. These are analogous to the linear and cubic splines creatable through the Curve command. Figure 4.34 shows a simple bilinear patch obtained using this RIB command:

```
# Simple bilinear patch produced from just
# 4 CVs listed using the P variable
Patch "bilinear" "P"
[
-1 1 1
1 1 -1
-1 -1 -1
1 -1 1
]
```

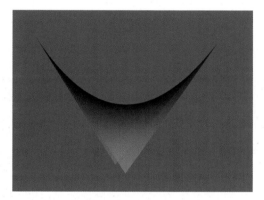

Figure 4.34 *A bilinear patch*

The idea is that the surface is generated using just four CVs which become the corners of the 3D surface generated. Note that unless the four CVs lie on a plane, it is not possible to generate a flat polygon out of them using the Polygon command. With bilinear patches there is no such restriction – the CVs can lie in any configuration, in particular they can be non-planar.

Bilinear surfaces are examples of so-called ruled surfaces. Imagine four stakes on the ground that are all of different heights. Now imagine running a rope along their tops, to produce a non-planar quadrilateral (a figure with four straight-line edges). The surface with linear cross sections that spans the quadrilateral's edges would be a bilinear surface. To put it differently, it is a surface obtained by linearly interpolating one straight line segment to another. This is illustrated in Figure 4.35 where a bilinear surface is visualized as being generated by sweeping a line segment (say, left to right) through space across a pair of end segments, using segments at the top and bottom (not pictured) as guides. As it makes its way from one end to the other, the segment that is swept is allowed to elongate or shrink, but not bend. Note that you would get the same surface if you were to sweep from top to bottom, using the segments on either side as guides.

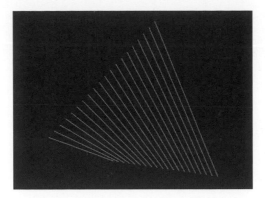

Figure 4.35 *Bilinear patch visualized as the sweep of a line segment*

Bilinear patches are commonly instanced at particle locations in a particle system to generate sprites (camera-facing at every frame), which can be appropriately colored and textured to produce animations of fire, splashes, etc. Figure 4.36 shows a collection of bilinear patches created from a particle system. Although our figure does not show it, it is common to make each patch somewhat curved instead of keeping them flat. The advantage of curving is that the bend in the surface helps catch light better, imparting a rich volumetric look when there is a collection of such sprites appropriately lit and textured.

Figure 4.36 *A collection of bilinear surface sprites*

Next we look at bicubic patches. As mentioned before these are surface analogs of spline curves and are generated using a grid (or net, or hull) of CVs. Recall that a single cubic spline curve segment requires four CVs. Likewise a single surface patch is generated by a grid of 4x4=16 CVs. Whereas the parametric space for a spline curve is a straight line, for a spline patch it is a two-dimensional region, with orthogonal axes labeled u and v. Our 4x4 grid of CVs form a corresponding 4x4 uniform grid of coordinates in uv parameter space. It is as if the sixteen (u,v) points in parametric space are laid out on a square sheet of very elastic material which can be distorted to conform to the sixteen spatial CV locations. In other words, you can think of every spline patch hull as a severe distortion of a rectangular area. As a side note, the resulting patch is a so-called tensor product surface where any spatial cross section corresponding to a cross section along the parametric u or v direction is a spline curve. So the four boundaries of a spline patch are spline curves, as are cross sections along u and v. Compare this to a bilinear surface which has straight line boundaries and whose cross sections are also straight lines.

Figure 4.37 shows a simple surface that results from this RIB code:

```
# Simple bicubic Bezier patch, specified using
# a 4x4 grid of 16 CVs
Basis "bezier" 3 "bezier" 3
Patch "bicubic" "P"
[
-1  1  2   -.5  1 -.5   .5  1  2   1  1 -.5
-1 .5 -.5  -.5 .5 -3   .5 .5 -3   1 .5 .5
-1 -.5 .5  -.5 -.5 3   .5 -.5 3   1 -.5 -.5
-1 -1  1   -.5 -1 -.5   .5 -1  1   1 -1 -.5
]
```

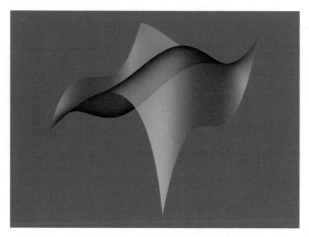

Figure 4.37 *A bicubic patch*

Note that the spline basis (type) for the patches can be b-spline, Catmull-Rom, etc. just as with the Curve command. If the basis is not specified in the RIB, the default is Bezier, as is the case with the Curve command. Figures 4.38 and 4.39 show the classic Utah teapot comprised of discrete bicubic Bezier patches (the surface was hand-generated by Martin Newell in 1974). The patches are carefully aligned so as to produce smooth surfaces. The RIB file simply contains a collection of Patch commands each containing a 4x4 CV matrix for a single patch.

Figure 4.38 *Bicubic patches making up the Utah Teapot*

Figure 4.39 *Utah teapot from Figure 4.38, rendered with a marble shader*

Figures 4.40 and 4.41 show another CG icon, the Gumbo elephant dataset, also made up of Bezier bicubic patches. Incidentally Gumbo was modeled by Ed Catmull. At the RfB site you will find the complete dataset for the Utah teapot and Gumbo. You are encouraged to use them in your own RenderMan renders, especially for experimenting with lighting and shading.

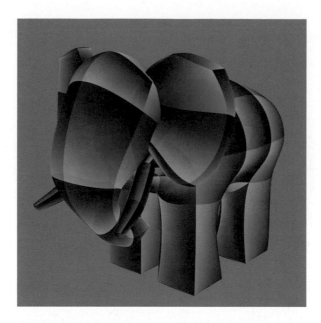

Figure 4.40 *The Gumbo model as a set of a bicubic patches*

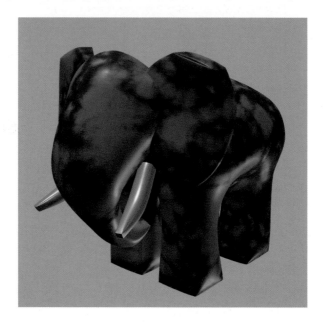

Figure 4.41 *Gumbo from Figure 4.40 rendered using a marble shader*

The Patch command can also be fed scalar (single valued) height-field data instead of 3D CVs. In other words, instead of an (x,y,z) value for each CV specified using P, we can input just a single floating point number using Pz instead. This value will be interpreted as a height over the parametric domain, and a surface will be generated to span those heights.

Height surfaces can also be bilinear or bicubic just like regular spline patches. Figure 4.42 shows a bilinear height surface generated using:

```
# A bilinear Pz surface created with just four floats,
# representing heights at four corners. Note the use
# of Pz instead of the usual P.
Patch "bilinear" "Pz" [.25 .5 1.5 2.0]
```

Note that you need only four height values, one for each corner of the surface. If the height values are those of tent poles arranged along a square's vertices, the bilinear Pz surface would be a tight weave spanning the tips of the poles.

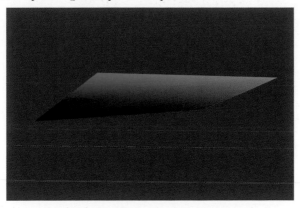

Figure 4.42 *A simple bilinear height mesh*

A bicubic Pz patch is shown in Figure 4.43. Input is a set of sixteen height values (whose control hull is shown in gray) and the result is the colored spline surface. The RIB code is as follows:

```
# Bicubic Pz height mesh, specified using a 4x4
# grid of 16 height values. Result is the curved, colored
# surface in Figure 4.43
Basis "bezier" 3 "bezier" 3
Patch "bicubic" "Pz" [.2 .4 .4 .2 .4 .8 .8 .4 .4 .8 .8 .4 .2 .4 .4
.2]
```

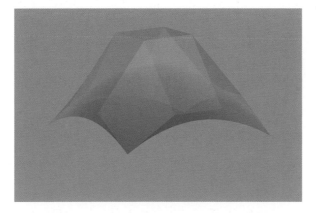

Figure 4.43 *A simple bicubic height mesh*

While an individual patch is capable of representing a certain amount of non-trivial detail, it is surely not adequate for modeling complex shapes such as humanoid characters. To model something like that, a patchwork of meshes is created by specifying a larger grid (higher than 4x4) of CVs, with CVs overlapping. This is a lot like the case of curves where a long sequence of CVs is used to generate a smooth curve with multiple segments that match at endpoints. RenderMan allows you to specify patch meshes using the PatchMesh command. Where the edges of adjacent patches touch, CVs are shared, meaning they are specified just once overall (not twice, once for each patch). This keeps the representation compact and also makes the patch mesh to function as a unified primitive. This is also comparable to polymeshes where adjoining faces share vertices without having to specify them multiple times.

Figure 4.44 shows a bent surface created from triangles. In Figure 4.45 is shown a corresponding bilinear patch mesh, generated using the triangle vertices from Figure 4.44 as CVs. You can see that the patch mesh version is smoother compared to the polymesh case. This is because each bent quadrilateral is decomposed into a pair of triangles in the polymesh version, resulting in two flat areas with a crease in between. The bilinear patch mesh version on the other hand is able to sweep out a smoother continuous surface across the quadrilateral edges.

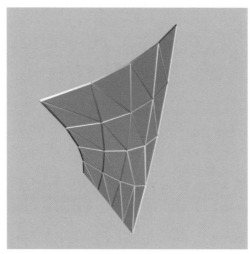

Figure 4.44 *A bent surface modeled as a triangle polymesh*

The patch mesh in Figure 4.45 is produced using this RIB:

```
# bilinear patch mesh produced using a 5x5 grid of
# CVs supplied to the PatchMesh command
PatchMesh "bilinear" 5 "nonperiodic" 5 "nonperiodic" "P"
[
0.336697 -0.076095 1.048288
0.354482 -0.051168 1.023498
0.370659 -0.024122 0.999421
0.384790 0.005053 0.976263
0.396345 0.036287 0.954190
# ... 20 more CVs ...
]
```

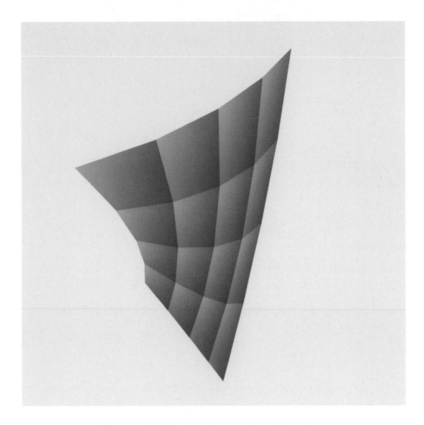

Figure 4.45 *Bilinear patch mesh surface*

In Figure 4.46 is a bicubic patch mesh, with Bezier basis which you recall has a step size of 3. So to obtain two patches in the u direction, we need four CVs for the first patch and three new ones for the second, for a total of seven (there is a shared CV in between). The patch mesh is therefore described by a grid of 7x7 CVs:

```
# Bicubic patch mesh. The Bezier basis matrix is
# explicitly specified here using matrix form, instead
# of the more common
# Basis "bezier" 3 "bezier" 3
Basis [-1 3 -3 1 3 -6 3 0 -3 3 0 0 1 0 0 0]
3 [-1 3 -3 1 3 -6 3 0 -3 3 0 0 1 0 0 0] 3
# patch mesh is comprised of
# 7x7=49 CVs
PatchMesh "bicubic" 7 "nonperiodic" 7 "nonperiodic" "P"
[
0.336697 -0.076095 1.048288
0.348713 -0.059710 1.031693
0.360073 -0.042390 1.015382
0.370659 -0.024122 0.999421
0.380338 -0.004906 0.983869
0.388956 0.015242 0.968778
0.396345 0.036287 0.954190
# ... 42 more CVs ...
]
```

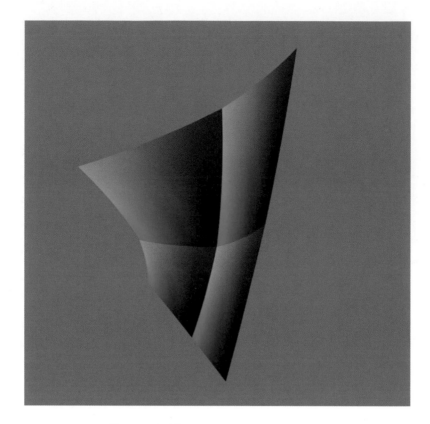

Figure 4.46 *Bicubic Bezier patch mesh*

As mentioned in the section on curves, the Basis command can be used to specify a custom basis matrix to use for computing splines. To illustrate this, Figure 4.47 shows a bicubic surface with custom spline types along u and v. The same grid of 7x7 CVs as in Figure 4.46 is used here, but the patch mesh looks different because of our custom base matrices. The RIB code is:

```
# Bicubic patch mesh using a custom basis matrix. Compare
# the matrix below with the Bezier basis from the previous
# RIB snippet, and compare the resulting Figure 4.47 with
# the Bezier surface in Figure 4.46
Basis [-.5 1.5 -1.5 .5 4 -8 4 0 -1.5 1.5 0 0 1 0 0 0] 3 [-.5 1.5 -
1.5 .5 4 -8 4 0 -1.5 1.5 0 0 1 0 0 0] 3
# same set of 7x7 CVs used in the Bezier version. The
# point is that for a given set of CVs, different
# basis matrices produce different spline surfaces
PatchMesh "bicubic" 7 "nonperiodic" 7 "nonperiodic" "P" [
0.336697 -0.076095 1.048288
0.348713 -0.059710 1.031693
0.360073 -0.042390 1.015382
0.370659 -0.024122 0.999421
0.380338 -0.004906 0.983869
0.388956 0.015242 0.968778
0.396345 0.036287 0.954190
# ... 42 more CVs ...
```

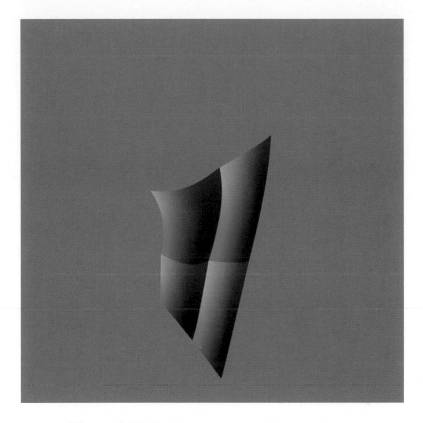

Figure 4.47 *Bicubic patch mesh with custom bases*

Patch meshes can also be produced using Pz heightfield values. This turns out to be very useful if you have sampled data collected along regular grid points (e.g. terrain elevation data from satellite telemetry). A Pz patch mesh can be used to fit a smooth surface across the data. You could obtain a grid of Pz values by sampling brightness/luminance values in an image at uniform intervals, as shown in Figure 4.48. The gray lines overlaid on the image represent luminance values, used to generate a bicubic b-spline patch mesh. The result is shown in Figure 4.49, which is reminiscent of craft figures hammered from thin copper sheets. The RIB code is:

```
# b-spline bicubic patch mesh Pz surface
# the 65x65 grid of height values was obtained by
# sampling DustyKitty's photo (Figure 4.48)
# at uniform intervals along x and y
Basis "b-spline" 1 "b-spline" 1
PatchMesh "bicubic" 65 "nonperiodic" 65 "nonperiodic" "Pz" [0.0701999
0.0658738 0.0654863 0.0651615 0.0664454 0.0671352 0.0763301 0.0715386
0.073642 0.0763271 0.0750778 0.0803917 0.0845983 0.0866315 0.081909
0.081161 0.0815414 0.0793773 0.0796774 0.0780938 0.0761933 0.0752231
0.0753482 0.0768823 0.0785448 0.0810467 0.0802221 0.0734633 0.0731184
0.0776101 0.0865952 0.0716137 0.0686921 0.0748872 0.0754161 0.0803547
0.0823655 0.0874012 0.0881696
# ... many more CVs representing luminance values
# sampled at regular pixel intervals ...
#]
```

Figure 4.48 *Sampling pixels to create a heightfield grid*

Figure 4.49 *Heightfield patch mesh surface*

Next we look at NURBS surfaces. NURBS stands for Non Uniform Rational B Spline. In the section on curves (Section 4.3) I mentioned that rational b-splines are curves specified using (x,y,z,w) Pw coordinates instead of the usual P, where some of the w (homogeneous) values might be non-unity. In RenderMan, any spline surface is allowed to be rational (it can be an RBS) , since it can be generated by specifying Pw (instead of just P) with non-unity w values. NURBS surfaces bring the notion of non-uniformity (NU) to RBS, through what are called knots (discussed below). In simple terms, what this means to the user is more control, specifically local control. A single NURBS patch can contain a large grid of CVs (not just 4x4 as required by the standard spline patches), analogous to bicubic patch meshes discussed above. But unlike those patch meshes, a NURBS surface can contain subsections of mixed spline types such as Bezier and b-splines. This is one of the features that makes NURBS more powerful than standard bicubic patch meshes.

Also, uniform b-splines (whether rational or not) can only serve as approximations when it comes to generating conic shapes such as circles, parabolas, cones, cylinders and spheres. The full machinery of NURBS (knots, CVs and their non-unity weights) is required for their exact mathematical representation. This becomes important in computer-aided design (CAD) applications where precise generation of curves and surfaces is called for.

The notion of NURBS surfaces has been around since the mid 1970s, and they were first used at Boeing in the late 70s. However it was Alias corporation in the 1980s that brought NURBS to the forefront of modeling, both for industrial and product design as well as for entertainment applications.

Figure 4.50 shows a basic NURBS surface, generated using the following NuPatch command:

```
# A simple NURBS patch
NuPatch
# 6 CVs in the 'u' parametric direction, order 4
# (order 4 is the same as degree 3, i.e. cubic)

# The non-decreasing sequence of numbers inside
# the [] are called knots. There are 6+4=10 knots
# in the sequence. Note how they are evenly spaced
# and how endpoint knots are repeated multiple times.

# Repeating an endpoint knot value 4 times when order
# is 4 clamps the surface down (makes it pass through
# the corresponding endpoint CV)

# The 0 1 following the knot sequence defines the parametric
# range (interval) used to render the NURBS

6 4
[0 0 0 0 0.333333 0.666667 1 1 1 1] 0 1

# 6 CVs also along parametric 'v', so 10 knots again
6 4 [0 0 0 0 0.333333 0.666667 1 1 1 1] 0 1

# 6x6=36 CVs, expressed using Pw (xyzw) instead of P
"Pw" [
-0.516963 -0.516963 -0.516963 1
-0.409862 -0.526965 -0.526965 1
# ... 34 more CVs
]
```

Figure 4.50 *A simple NURBS patch*

Figure 4.51 shows a collection of **NURBS** surfaces (six, with three in the front) in contact. This kind of positional continuity between adjacent patches is labeled C0 continuity. C0 means that adjacent patches touch along an edge without a gap, but there is no smoothness (we see creases where the surfaces come together). In contrast are C1 continuity where tangent planes smoothly transition from one patch to the adjacent, and C2 continuity where in addition to C1 tangent smoothness there is also continuity in curvature (direction of bulge).

Figure 4.51 results from these commands:

```
# First patch, 19x19 CVs, 19+4=23 knots in each sequence
# renderable 'u' and 'v' ranges 0 to 1.
NuPatch 19 4 [0 0 0 0 0.0625 0.125 0.1875 0.25 0.3125 0.375 0.4375
0.5 0.5625 0.625 0.6875 0.75 0.8125 0.875 0.9375 1 1 1 1] 0 1 19 4
[0 0 0 0 0.0625 0.125 0.1875 0.25 0.3125 0.375 0.4375 0.5 0.5625
0.625 0.6875 0.75 0.8125 0.875 0.9375 1 1 1 1] 0 1
# 19x19 grid of CVs
"Pw" [
-0.506667 0.506667 0.506667 1
# ... more CVs
]
# Second patch, also 19x19 CVs
NuPatch 19 4 [0 0 0 0 0.0625 0.125 0.1875 0.25 0.3125 0.375 0.4375
0.5 0.5625 0.625 0.6875 0.75 0.8125 0.875 0.9375 1 1 1 1] 0 1 19 4
[0 0 0 0 0.0625 0.125 0.1875 0.25 0.3125 0.375 0.4375    0.5 0.5625
0.625 0.6875 0.75 0.8125 0.875 0.9375 1 1 1 1] 0 1 "Pw" [-0.506667 -
0.506667 0.506667 1
# ... more CVs
]
# 4 more patches similarly defined below
# ...
```

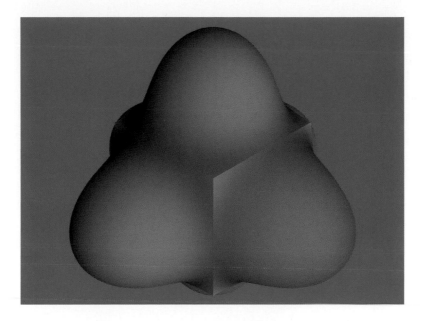

Figure 4.51 *A collection of NURBS surfaces*

Animation packages such as Maya, Softimage XSI, 3D Studio Max and dedicated surface creation programs such as Rhino have a rich collection of interactive modeling tools to generate NURBS surfaces. Three such common modeling techniques are shown here. The beauty of such modeling operations is that a relatively complex surface can result from simple inputs.

Figure 4.52 contains a NURBS surface obtained through a lofting operation, where a small number of cross section curves are specified (these can be open or closed, can have variable spacing and can be of different lengths) and a surface spanning those cross sections is produced in response. The surface shown here is lofted using triangular, square and pentagonal and hexagonal cross sections which are all twisted about a perpendicular axis with respect to each other. Lofting is also referred to as skinning, and is useful for constructing a variety of objects such as characters, machine parts and terrains.

The surface in Figure 4.52 is generated from:

```
# lofted surface with 12x13 CVs. Note that the order along
# u is 4 (degree 3 or cubic) while the order along v
# is 2 (degree 1, or linear). It is a feature of NURBS
# surfaces that the order (degree) can differ in u and v
# Consequently there are 12+4=16 knots along u and
# 13+2=15 knots along v
NuPatch 12 4 [0 0 0 0 0.111111 0.222222 0.333333 0.444444 0.555556
0.666667 0.777778 0.888889 1 1 1 1] 0 1 13 2 [0 0 0.166667 0.2 0.25
0.333333 0.4 0.5 0.6 0.666667 0.75 0.8 0.833333 1 1] 0 1 "Pw" [
1 0 -0.5 1 1 0 -0.444444 1
# ... more CVs
]
```

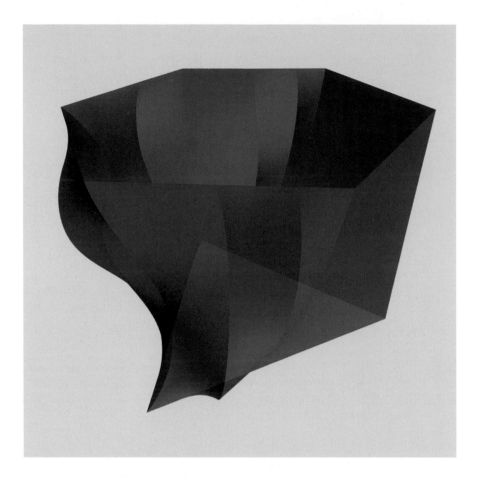

Figure 4.52 *A NURBS surface due to lofting*

Figure 4.53 illustrates the sweep operation, where a cross sectional profile (circle in our example) is translated along a curve (spiral) to sweep out a surface. Note that a profile curve is more accurately referred to as a generatrix, and the curve it travels along, as a directrix. By the way, extrusion operation is a simpler case of sweep where the profile is translated along a straight line.

The spiral surface NURBS is generated using this RIB:

```
# 199 CVs along u (along the spiral), degree 1
# 11 CVs along v (circular cross section), degree 3
NuPatch
199 2
[
# ... 201 knots ...
]
0 1
11 4
[-0.25 -0.25 -0.125 0 0.125 0.25 0.375 0.5 0.625 0.75 0.875 1 1.125
1.25 1.25]
0 1
"Pw" [
-5.39896 0 -5.39896 1
```

```
-5.39896 -0.372348 -5.39896 1
# .. more CVs ...]
```

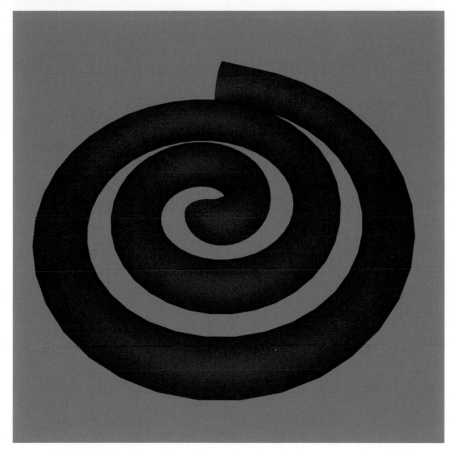

Figure 4.53 *A NURBS surface resulting from extrusion along a curve (sweeping)*

A surface of revolution results from spinning a profile curve about an axis. To generate the urn shape in Figure 4.54, the approximately-S-shaped curve is revolved around the vertical axis. This operation is analogous to throwing a pot using a potter's wheel where the circularly-symmetric surface gets shaped via its profile.

The NuPatch command to generate the shape in Figure 4.54 is as follows:

```
# 11x14 bicubic CV grid
NuPatch
11 4
[-0.25 -0.25 -0.125 0 0.125 0.25 0.375 0.5 0.625 0.75 0.875 1 1.125
1.25 1.25]
0 1
14 4
[0 0 0 0 0.0909091 0.181818 0.272727 0.363636 0.454545 0.545455
0.636364 0.727273 0.818182 0.909091 1 1 1 1]
0 1
"Pw" [
-0.00025314 0 0 1
```

```
# ... more CVs ...
]
```

Figure 4.54 *A NURBS surface of revolution*

Recall that RenderMan only supports bilinear and bicubic (degree 3) spline surfaces. Another advantage a NURBS surface has over a standard spline surface is that it can be of any degree, including 2, 4, 5, 7, etc. Further, the degree can be different in u and v, e.g. linear in u and cubic in v. Most of the time (especially in animation work) a degree 3 NURBS surface along both u and v is sufficient, but the flexibility is there should you need it. Figure 4.55 illustrates NURBS torus surfaces with degrees 1, 2 and 3. As expected the lower degree surfaces have more angular shapes. The RIB code to generate the tori is:

```
# Degree 1 (linear) torus shown on the left of Figure 4.55
# 5x5 CVs
NuPatch 5 2 [0 0 0.25 0.5 0.75 1 1] 0 1 5 2 [0 0 0.25 0.5 0.75 1 1]
0 1 "Pw" [1 -0.5 0 1 0 -0.5 1 1
# ...
]
# Degree 2 (quadratic) torus, middle of Figure 4.55
# 6x6 CVs
NuPatch 6 3 [-0.25 -0.25 0 0.25 0.5 0.75 1 1.25 1.25] 0 1 6 3 [-0.25
-0.25 0 0.25 0.5 0.75 1 1.25 1.25] 0 1 "Pw" [0.507057 -0.4867 -
0.499125 1 0.501266 -0.4867 0.498614 1
# ...
]
Degree 3 (cubic) torus, right of Figure 4.55
# 7x7 CVs
NuPatch 7 4 [-0.5 -0.5 -0.25 0 0.25 0.5 0.75 1 1.25 1.5 1.5] 0 1 7 4
[-0.5 -0.5 -0.25 0 0.25 0.5 0.75 1 1.25 1.5 1.5] 0 1 "Pw" [0 0 -
0.375 1 0.375 0 0 1
# ...
]
```

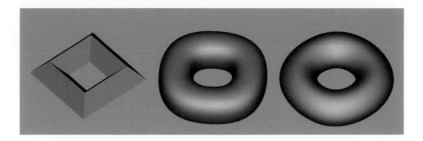

Figure 4.55 *Linear, quadratic and cubic NURBS tori*

It was mentioned earlier that knots can impart non-uniformity to rational b-splines. A standard bicubic surface can be generated given the type, a set of CVs and weights (w coordinates) for them. In addition to these, a NURBS surface also requires what is called a knot-sequence, which is a non-decreasing array of floating point values. Non-decreasing means that the values can either increase or stay constant but not decrease, like a runaway train gaining speed. For instance [0 0 0 0 1 1 1 1] and [0 0 0.25 0.5 0.75 1 1] are valid knot sequences but [0 0 0.25 0.5 0.75 0.5 1] is not.

But what are knots in the first place? They are discrete values along the u or v parametric interval. Recall that every spline curve, no matter how complex or long, can be generated by stepping across a parametric interval (conventionally, along the u axis) and evaluating points on the curve at a series of u values (see Figures 4.9 and 4.10 for an example of Bezier curve generation). Similarly every spline surface can be generated by evaluating points on it using a set of (u,v) values over the surface's rectangular parametric domain. If we fix the u value at say, 0.25 and vary v from 0 to 1 in steps of say, 0.1, we will have a sequence of isoparametric values (so-called, since parameteric u is the same value 0.25 on all of them) (0.25,0), (0.25,0.1), (0.25, 0.2), (0.25,0.3) all the way up to (0.25,1.0). If we evaluate our surface at these eleven (u,v) values, we will get eleven corresponding points that lie on the surface. If these points are joined in sequence, the resulting surface-lying curve is called an isoparametric curve or an 'isoparm'.

Since a knot sequence is a series of u or v values, every distinct knot value in a sequence can be used to create a distinct isoparm on the surface. Doing this for both u and v knots yields the familiar wireframe-like nets that shape NURBS surfaces (e.g. Figure 4.57). Isoparm lines therefore serve as visual indicators of knot distribution.

What is special about knots is their spacing, in other words, difference between adjacent knot values. In a Bezier bicubic spline curve for example, a curve obtained from a long CV sequence is considered to be uniform, since the step size is always 3 across the sequence of CVs. In NURBS by contrast, knot values and their spacings determine both subcurve types and step sizes, thereby providing a flexible way to intermix any variety of them in the same curve or surface. For instance a knot sequence such as [0 0 0 0 1 1 1 1] with all 0s and 1s mimics Bezier. The multiplicity of a knot value is the number of times it is repeated, so in our [0 0 0 0 1 1 1 1] example the multiplicity of the knots with values 0 and 1 are 4 and 4. For a cubic curve or a bicubic surface, this means that the curve or surface will pass through the endpoint CVs, as is the case with Bezier curves and surfaces. NURBS can thus represent classical spline types such as b-spline and Bezier through appropriate knot sequences.

We now know that knots are what make NURBS special, so where do knots come from? They are created for you by the modeling package you work with, as you go about using the various NURBS tools. As a good default, those initial knot sequences tend to be evenly spaced (with possible multiplicities), as can be seen from the corresponding evenly spaced isoparm lines that get created.

Since direct editing of knot sequences is not very intuitive, you would alter them (e.g. add or remove knots, vary their spacing) indirectly by working with corresponding isoparms instead. For instance to add detail in a geometric model, you might insert an isoparm line in between two existing ones, causing corresponding knot insertion. This is shown in Figure 4.56 where an undulation has been added to a featureless sheet. The initial knot sequence for the flat sheet was [0 0 0 0 0.25 0.5 0.75 1 1 1 1], giving rise to four evenly spaced vertical isoparms. An extra isoparm was inserted midway between knots at 0.25 and 0.5, creating a new knot value 0.375 and a new sequence [0 0 0 0 0.25 0.375 0.5 0.75 1 1 1 1].

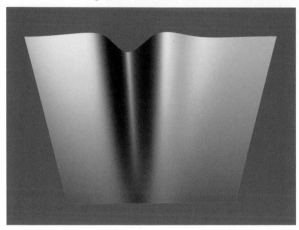

Figure 4.56 *NURBS surface with non-uniform knot spacing*

You can see this in Figure 4.57 where the extra isoparm is shown with a blue dot on top, leading to an unevenness (bunching) in spacing. The knot/isoparm insertion also causes an extra column of CVs to be inserted, and these were pulled out to create the fluted shape. If the knot sequence is slightly altered, e.g. to be [0 0 0 0 0.25 0.35 0.5 0.75 1 1 1 1] instead, that would cause a subtle change in the appearance of the surface, compared to Figure 4.56.

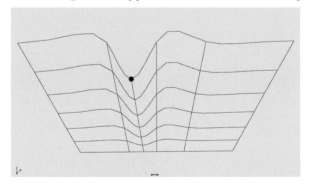

Figure 4.57 *Wireframe view, showing non-uniform knot (isoparm) spacing*

A simple relationship exists between the number of visible segments (spans between isoparms), number of CVs and number of knots. The number of CVs is the number of segments plus the degree of the NURBS. In our example in Figure 4.57, there are five segments after the knot insertion, and we are dealing with a degree 3 NURBS surface. So there are eight columns of CVs (5+3). The number of knots in the sequence is the number of CVs plus the order of the NURBS, where order is defined to be degree plus one (order is four in our example). So our knot sequence can be predicted to contain 8 + 4 = 12 knots, and that is the case with the obtained sequence [0 0 0 0 0.25 0.375 0.5 0.75 1 1 1 1]. That is why, increasing detail by adding isoparms necessitates addition of rows or columns of CVs. The unique thing about NURBS is that the detail increase can occur anywhere in the parametric u or v, thanks to the mathematics behind NURBS evaluation. This means that the length of the knot sequences (number of values in each sequence) can be different along u and v.

Earlier I mentioned that Rhino is a dedicated, standalone NURBS surface modeler. It happens to be easy to learn and so is an excellent choice for further exploring the idea of knots.

NURBS surfaces also provide another valuable modeling feature, and that is the ability to trim away sections of a surface using curves lying on the surface in a manner analogous to cookie cutting. In Figure 4.58 a simple curved patch is shown with a circular region trimmed away. The trim region is expressed as a set of curves that lie end-to-end in the surface's parametric space, forming a closed loop (compare this to declaring holes in a polygon, using the GeneralPolygons command). You can either keep the trimmed region, or keep the remainder after discarding the trimmed piece (the latter choice is shown in Figure 4.58).

Trim curves are expressed using the TrimCurve command, as follows:

```
# the trimcurve attribute is used to specify whether
# to render the outside (what is left after trimming)
# or inside (the piece trimmed away)
Attribute "trimcurve" "sense" "outside"

# trim curve definition follows
TrimCurve
# just one element in the array below, which means
# the trim curve has just one loop. That single element
# is 4, which means the loop is made of 4 curves lying
# end to end (forming a closed loop)
[4]
[4 4 4 4] # order of each of the 4 curves

# knot values. Each curve has order 4 and also has 4 CVs
# (see below), so has 4+4=8 knots. There are 4 curves,
# which makes a total of 4x8=32 knot values in the sequence
[-8 -8 -8 -8 -6 -6 -6 -6 -6 -6 -6 -6 -4 -4 -4 -4 -4 -4 -4 -4 -2 -2
-2 -2 -2 -2 -2 -2 0 0 0 0]

# min and max parametric value for each curve. In other
# words, first curve has a range (-8,-6), second has
# (-6,-4), etc.
[-8 -6 -4 -2] # min
[-6 -4 -2 0] # max

# number of CVs in each curve making up the loop
[4 4 4 4]

# CVs, u values for all curves in our loop, a total
```

```
# of 4+4+4+4=16 values
[0.5 0.365881 0.298821 0.298821 0.298821 0.298821 0.365881
0.5 0.5 0.634119 0.701179 0.701179 0.701179 0.701179 0.634119 0.5]

# CVs, v values
[0.701179 0.701179 0.60059 0.5 0.5 0.39941 0.298821 0.298821
0.298821 0.298821 0.39941 0.5 0.5 0.60059 0.701179 0.701179]

# w values for the CVs
[1 1 1 1 1 1 1 1 1 1 1 1 1 1 1 1]

# the trim curve definition would be followed by
# an NuPatch command defining the NURBS surface
# over which the trimming will occur
# ...
```

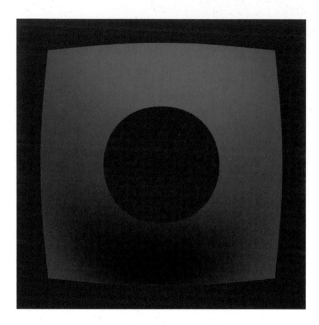

Figure 4.58 *A simple NURBS patch with a circular region trimmed out*

As is clear from the annotation in the preceding RIB code, multiple trim loops can be specified on a surface, as shown in the aria (lantern) shape in Figure 4.59 The TrimCurve command to create the cutouts begins as follows:

```
TrimCurve
# 3 distinct loops (each cuts out a star), made of
# 4, 13 and 14 curves
[4 13 14]
# order of the 4+13+14 curves making up all 3 loops
[2 2 2 2 4 4 4 4 4 4 4 4 4 4 4 4 4 4 4 4 4 4 4 4 4 4 4 4 4 4 4]
# ... knots, u v min max, u v w CV arrays ...
# ...
```

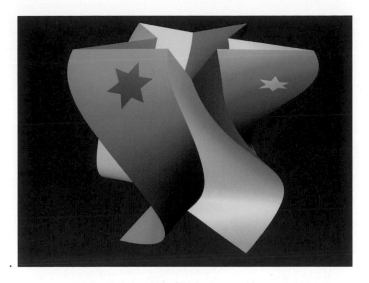

Figure 4.59 *Star-shaped trim regions over a NURBS surface*

If you would like to learn more about NURBS, I refer you to *The NURBS Book* by Piegl and Tiller. This book remains one of the best sources for comprehensive NURBS information, especially its mathematical underpinnings.

4.8 Spheres

This section and the following five (ending with Paraboloids) describe what are called quadric surfaces, which can be described analytically using second degree polynomials. They are all hollow surfaces (not solid) and are centered around the Z axis by default. So in the code snippets you will see transformation commands to translate, rotate and scale them to orient them for better viewing (we will cover transformations in detail in the next chapter – here they are only used for presenting the subject matter better).

Note that these are convenience primitives that save you the trouble of having to explicitly model them using polymeshes, subdivision surfaces or spline patches. By the same token, you cannot subject them to arbitrary nonlinear deformations. For example you cannot use the sphere primitive to model an apple shape or a red blood cell. For those you need to resort to explicit modeling using polygons, patches, etc.

We start with an ubiquitous quadric primitive, namely the sphere. You can think of a sphere as a surface swept out by a circle as it is spun about an axis passing through a diameter. RenderMan creates spheres using the Sphere command which has the following syntax:

```
Sphere <radius> <zmin> <zmax> <sweep_angle>
```

The resulting sphere is centered at the origin, with its two hemispheres extending along the + and - Z axes. Their extents are specified using zmin and zmax. In other words, you can render just a sliced-off section of a sphere by making zmin and/or zmax to be numerically less than the radius value. Also, sweep_angle specifies how much of a wedge you want. A value of 360 (degrees) specifies a wedge going all the way around, while 330 specifies a nearly-complete sphere that is missing a 30-degree wedge. See Figure 4.60 for some examples. The spheres in the figure result from these commands:

```
# A complete sphere on the left, radius 1.0 unit
Sphere 1 -1 1 360
# Middle sphere, radius 0.8, with a wedge missing
# (sweep angle only goes to 300, instead of 360 degrees)
Sphere 0.8 -0.8 0.8 300
# Right sphere: full sweep, but sectioned off at
# top and bottom with -0.6 and 0.25, instead of
# going out all the way to -.7 and .7
Sphere 0.7 -.6 .25 360
```

Figure 4.60 *Spherical shapes*

Spheres can of course be used to construct a multitude of shapes (particularly in conjunction with other primitives) such as molecules, pearls, stylized tree tops, fruits and snowmen.

4.9 Cylinders

A cylinder in RenderMan can be imagined to be a surface resulting from sweeping a line segment parallel to and a certain distance away from the Z axis, along a circular path. This makes it hollow and also open at the top and bottom (think of rolling up a newspaper into a tube). A RenderMan cylinder primitive is obtained using this command:

```
Cylinder <radius> <zmin> <zmax> <sweep_angle>
```

Again, the sweep_angle parameter is used to specify how open the cylinder should be. A half-cylinder would be the result of specifying 180 (degrees) for sweep_angle.

The following block of RIB code is used to generate the cylinders in Figure 4.61. Cylinders, just like spheres, are also useful modeling primitives, for representing rods, tubes, pipes, tree trunks, etc. With a thin-enough radius, several short ones can be joined end to end to render things like fibers and hair (before the introduction of the Curves primitive, this was the preferred way in RenderMan to render hair and fur).

```
# Left cylinder, radius 0.8, zmin and zmax -.8 and .8
Cylinder 0.8 -.8 .8 360
# Middle cylinder, thin-looking with radius smaller
# than height
Cylinder 0.4 -.9 .9 360
# Right cylinder (large radius, small height) is incomplete
# because the sweep angle is 240 degrees, not 360.
Cylinder .9 -.4 .4 240
```

Figure 4.61 *Cylinders constructed using the "Cylinder" command*

4.10 Cones

Cones are created using the Cone command which has this syntax:

```
Cone <height> <radius> <sweep_angle>
```

See Figure 4.62 for some examples which are a result of these commands:

```
# left: cone with height (1.25) equal to diameter (2*0.625)
Cone 1.25 .625 360
# middle: tall thin cone, with radius a tenth of the height
Cone 2 0.2 360
# section of a cone, sweep angle 300 deg.
Cone 1.2 .6 300
```

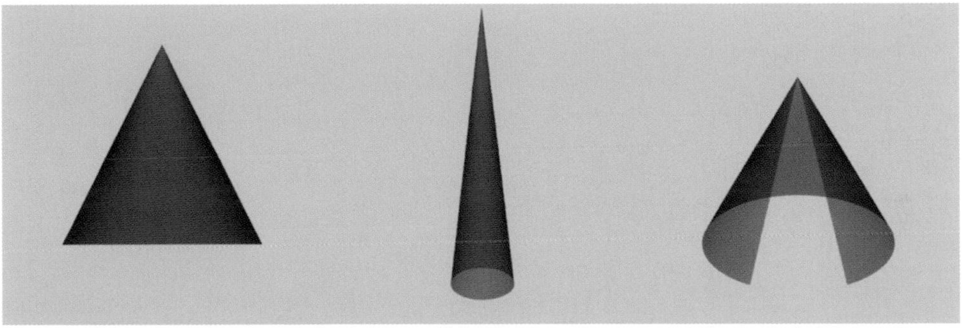

Figure 4.62 *Conical shapes*

4.11 Tori

If you sketched a circle the size of your palm, took a small round coin, stood it on the circle and swept it a full revolution along the circle's circumference, the resulting surface would describe a torus. Informally, it is a donut-shaped surface with a characteristic hole through the middle. The Torus command is used to create such a torus, with the following syntax:

```
Torus <major_radius> <minor_radius> <start_angle> <end_angle>
<sweep_angle>
```

The two radii specify the sizes of the sweeping path circle and the swept circle. The start and end angles can be used to limit the sweeping shape to just an arc of a circle, while the sweep angle is used to limit the extent of the sweep itself.

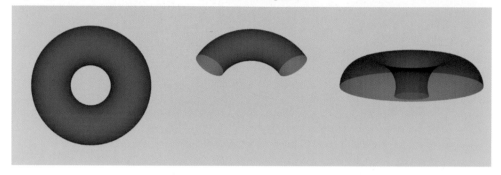

Figure 4.63 *Toroidal shapes*

The surfaces in Figure 4.63 were created using these commands:

```
# left: full torus, classic donut shape
Torus .5 .25 0 360 360

# middle: limited sweep angle (120 deg.) produces a
# 'piece' of torus
Torus .6 .2 0 360 120

# right: sliced-off torus results from start_angle and
# end_angle being 0 and 200 deg. instead of 0 and 360.
Torus .55 .35 0 200 360
```

Note that more complex surfaces are possible if the cross section of the sweeping (profile) curve is allowed to be an arbitrary shape instead of a circle. Modeling programs usually provide such a feature as part of their shape generation toolset, and the resulting shape would likely be a patch, polymesh or subdivision surface.

4.12 Hyperboloids

Draw a vertical line, then place a pencil across it at an angle. If you now imagine the pencil rotating about the vertical line so that the pencil's two ends sweep out circles, the resulting surface is a hyperboloid. More generally, a line segment rotated about an axis creates a hyperboloid surface. As we have seen before, if the line is parallel to the axis of rotation, a cylinder results. If one endpoint lies on the axis of revolution, the result is a cone.

Here is the syntax of the Hyperboloid command which creates hyperboloid shapes:

```
Hyperboloid <x1> <y1> <z1> <x2> <y2> <z2> <sweep_angle>
```

(x1,y1,z1) specifies one endpoint of our line segment and (x2,y2,z2), the other.

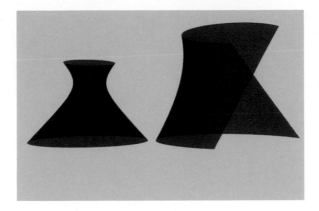

Figure 4.64 *A couple of hyperboloid surfaces*

Figure 4.64 results from the following commands:

```
# Left: line segment joining (0.15,-0.8,-0.5) and
# (0.25, 0.25, 0.6) is revolved a full 360 degrees
# which creates a closed (along the sides) surface
Hyperboloid 0.15 -0.8 -.5 0.25 .25 .6 360

# Right: line segment is revolved only 235 degrees,
# leading to an open shape
Hyperboloid -.4 1.0 -.5 .5 .5 1.0 235
```

4.13 Paraboloids

A paraboloid is obtained by revolving a parabola (roughly a cross between a "U" and a "V" shaped curve) lying in the XY plane, about the Z axis. Doing so creates a symmetric surface that curves down to a point, or sections of it. The Paraboloid command creates paraboloids, as follows:

```
Paraboloid <radius_at_zmax> <zmin> <zmax> <sweep_angle>
```

The paraboloid is contained within zmin and zmax, and at zmax, has the largest cross section (the cross sections are circles). If zmin is 0.0, the paraboloid tapers down to a point. Figure 4.65 is created using these commands:

```
# Left: a complete paraboloid (zmin is 0.0, sweep angle
# is 360 deg.)

Paraboloid 0.6 0.0 1.0 360

# Right: paraboloid slice (zmin is 0.25), incomplete
# around the z axis (sweep angle is 330 degrees)

Paraboloid 1.0 0.25 0.9 330
```

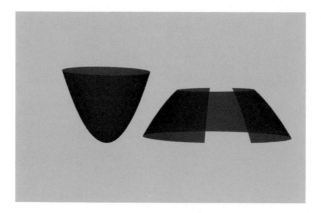

Figure 4.65 *Paraboloids*

As an aside, circles (and ellipses), parabolas and ellipses (which generate spheres, paraboloids and ellipsoids respectively when revolved about a central axis) are referred to as conic curves or simply conics. They are so called because they result from the intersection of a plane with a regular (upright) cone. The angle at which the plane slices the cone determines the type of conic generated (see the online RfB page for illustrations).

By way of wrapping up quadrics, Figure 4.66 shows "RfB" constructed using the six quadric shapes. The slanted leg of "R" is a paraboloid, while a hyperboloid creates the horizontal arm of "f". Note that combinations of quadric surfaces are particularly useful in describing machine parts and assemblies.

Figure 4.66 *Use of quadrics to spell out "RfB"*

4.14 Disks

A disk is simply a flat circular shape (like the pieces of paper produced using a hole punch). In RenderMan they are commonly used to cap off cylinders, cones and other quadric surfaces which are open when constructed using their respective commands. Disks are also useful as pointillistic primitives to produce dot-oriented artwork.

Disks are created using the Disk command:

```
Disk <height_along_z> <radius> <sweep_angle>
```

All you need to specify are the radius of the disk, height above/below the Z axis where the disk will be situated and as usual, the sweep angle.

Figure 4.67 *Use of the "Disk" command*

Figure 4.67 shows disk shapes produced using these commands:

```
# Left: Disk, at z=0
Disk 0 0.5 360
# Middle: Disk, at z=1.5
Disk 1.5 0.5 360
# Right: Partial disk (sweep angle 300 deg.) at z=-0.5
Disk -.5 .75 300
```

Figure 4.68 is a color blindness test image constructed using Disk primitives. See if you can make out the numeral "7" in the middle of the figure.

4.15 Blobbies

Imagine an isolated point in space being surrounded by a uniform spherical field. The visualization of such a uniform field will naturally look like a sphere (Figure 4.69, leftmost shape). The middle column of Figure 4.69 shows what might happen if two such points come together. When they are sufficiently far apart, the points' fields do not interact. As the points get closer, the space in between gets subjected to both fields. When the points are just at the right distance for this to start happening, the field visualization shows the individual spherical fields being drawn out to a point at the center. As the points get closer, there is an increasingly greater field overlap in between, leading to the formation of a neck-like region in the middle. Such field visualizations are called blobbies or metaballs or soft objects. Blobbies are attributed to Jim Blinn who came up with the concept for approximating atomic field interactions, while creating images of DNA for Carl Sagan's famous *COSMOS* series.

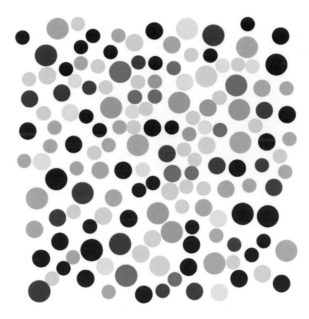

Figure 4.68 *Color blindness test image*

The image on the right side of Figure 4.69 shows the result of three interacting blob centers. The attraction of the blobby surface for modeling is that the user does not explicitly need to model the smooth connector regions. These are automatically calculated by the underlying software. All the user provides are the locations and strengths of the blob centers.

As is evident, blobbies are useful for describing smooth surfaces (that do not have sharp corners or edges). They are ideal for animating the splashing of fluids, where individual droplets can be rendered as blobs to convincingly depict their merging and separation.

PRMan's Blobby command is used to specify blobs. The Blobby command is a container for a mini-language that lets you specify different kinds of blobbies (such as segment and ellipsoid) and operations on their fields (such as addition, maximum). Here we will only cover the basic syntax (please see Application Note #31 in the PRMan documentation for complete usage). The single spherical surface in Figure 4.69 is the result of the following command:

```
# a single blob
Blobby

1 # no. of blobs

# 1001 means an ellipsoid blob
[1001
```

```
# 0 below is the offset into a 4x4 transformation matrix
# to situate our ellipsoid blob
0

# 0 below means we're adding blobs. There is only one
# blob (1) with index (blob #) 0
0 1 0
]
# below is the transformation matrix, which places
# the blob at (-3,0,0)
[1 0 0 0 0 1 0 0 0 0 1 0 -3 0 0 1]

[] # empty string array
```

The central column of blobs approaching each other is generated by these commands:

```
# top figure - large separation between two blobs
# 1001 (ellipsoid) code occurs twice, once for each blob.
# what follows each 1001 is an index into the
# transformation array - first blob's matrix starts at
# position 0, the other's, at position 16
# 0 2 0 1 means we're adding (0) two (2) blobs 0 and 1 (0 1)
Blobby 2 [1001 0 1001 16 0 2 0 1]
# 32 element transformation array, first 16 values are
# for blob 0, the rest 16 for blob 1. The transformations
# situate our first blob at (-0.7,3,0) and the second,
# at (0.7,3,0)
[1 0 0 0 0 1 0 0 0 0 1 0 -0.7 3 0 1
 1 0 0 0 0 1 0 0 0 0 1 0 0.7 3 0 1] []


# pair of blobs, just touching (point contact in between)
Blobby 2 [1001 0 1001 16 0 2 0 1]
# transforms to locate the blobs at (-0.6425,1,0) and
# (0.6425,1,0), where they make point contact
[1 0 0 0 0 1 0 0 0 0 1 0 -0.6425 1 0 1
1 0 0 0 0 1 0 0 0 0 1 0 0.6425 1 0 1] []


# pair of blobs, starting to fuse
Blobby 2 [1001 0 1001 16 0 2 0 1]
# now the matrices bring the blobbies even closer, to
# (-0.635,-1,0) and (0.635,-1,0)
[1 0 0 0 0 1 0 0 0 0 1 0 -0.635 -1 0 1
1 0 0 0 0 1 0 0 0 0 1 0 0.635 -1 0 1] []


# pair of blobs, close enough to form a thick neck in between
Blobby 2 [1001 0 1001 16 0 2 0 1]
# now our blobs are at (-0.5,-3,0) and (0.5,-3,0)
[1 0 0 0 0 1 0 0 0 0 1 0 -0.5 -3 0 1
1 0 0 0 0 1 0 0 0 0 1 0 0.5 -3 0 1] []
```

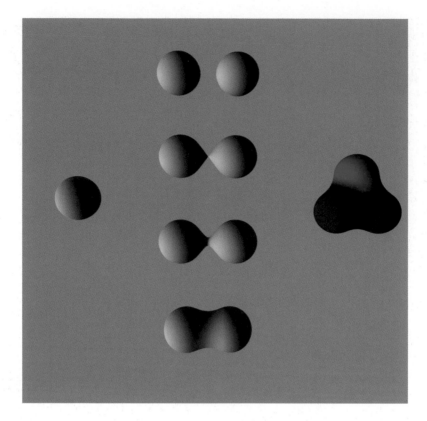

Figure 4.69 *Metaball (blobby) shapes*

The trio of blobs at the right of Figure 4.69 are generated using:

```
# 3 ellipsoid (1001 code) blobbies, added (operation 0),
# each situated using transformations starting at
# 0,16 and 32 in the transformations array. There is also
# a per-blobby RGB color specified using Cs
Blobby 3 [1001 0 1001 16 1001 32 0 3 0 1 2] [1 0 0 0 0 1 0 0 0 0 1
0 3 -0.3 0 1 1 0 0 0 0 1 0 0 0 0 1 0 4 -0.3 0 1 1 0 0 0 0 1 0 0 0
0 1 0 3.5 0.57 0 1] [] "varying color Cs" [1 0 0 0 0 1 0 1 0]
```

Figure 4.70 shows a spiralling-spiral wire sculpture modeled using ellipsoid blobs to specify successive locations of points along the curve. The spherical fields of these close-lying points merge (again using the addition operation as in the simple cases above) together to produce a smooth wire shape, which appears to be rounded off at the endpoints of the curve. The points on the curve were generated using equations for a "Pendulum harmonograph", an old Victorian-era toy that traces fascinating curve shapes. You can use the underlying idea to try to generate your own images of other curve shapes. A simple way to obtain curve coordinates is to photocopy a curve you like on to a graph paper and then read off the (x,y) values of points along the curve.

Finally, Figure 4.71 shows an ornament-like blobby surface obtained by using the vertices of a Penrose tessellation (see Figure 4.21) as blob centers. Such a surface with gentle undulations is reminiscent of imagery of small atomic clusters produced by a scanning tunneling microscope or STM (do a web search to come across such images).

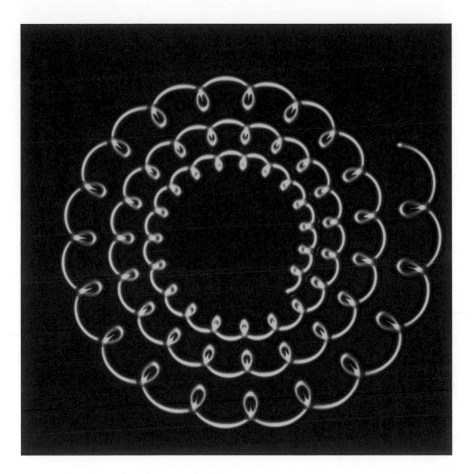

Figure 4.70 *Union of blobbies forming a bent-wire sculpture*

We have not explored other blob types or operations possible with the Blobby command. Please refer to the application note mentioned above for further details. Here we will simply mention what else is available. In addition to the ellipsoid blob primitive, there is a segment blob type which can be used to create cylindrical blob shapes. In addition to being able to add the fields of two blobs, you can also subtract, multiply or divide them or use the maximum of the two or their minimum. Also you can negate a single blob's field.

The very last array in all our Blobby examples was empty. RenderMan blobbies can be repelled by ground planes which are specified in the form of depth image files. The last array in the command is used to hold the names of such depth-map files.

Figure 4.71 *Blobbies forming a fivefold-symmetric surface*

4.16 Constructive Solid Geometry (CSG)

CSG makes it possible to apply the Boolean operations of union, intersection and difference, on geometric shapes. This gives us the ability to construct complex, composite shapes out of simpler primitives, in a hierarchical fashion. These complex shapes can themselves serve as inputs for further CSG operations, and so on.

Figure 4.72 illustrates the basic idea. On the left are two separate, overlapping spheres. We can derive three new shapes from this arrangement, as shown to the right of the overlapping spheres.

The first shape illustrates the CSG "difference" operation. We are subtracting (chipping away) the part of the overlapping right sphere from the left, thereby making a concavity where the spheres overlap. Likewise if we subtracted an overlapping cylinder from a sphere, a hole on the sphere would result. If the overlapping cylinder were to pass through the sphere and come out on the opposite side, the difference operation would yield a hole all the way through the sphere. The creation of chipped surfaces and holes underscores the fact that the shapes used in CSG operations are solid (filled), not hollow. Doing a difference operation is like taking a bite out of an apple or a candy bar – inner surfaces become exposed due to the operation.

The next shape is the intersection of the overlapping spheres. This double convex surface is common to both the spheres, which is what the intersection operation provides.

Finally, the shape on the right is the union (summation, or merging) of the two spherical shapes. Note that this is not the same as merely overlapping the separate spheres. The union is a single shape made up of material from both the overlapping shapes.

Here is the RIB syntax to create the chipped difference image:

```
# CSG difference of two primitives
SolidBegin "difference"
# First primitive, a solid sphere
TransformBegin
Translate -.75 0 0
SolidBegin "primitive"
Sphere 1 -1 1 360
SolidEnd
TransformEnd
# Second primitive, a smaller solid sphere
TransformBegin
Translate .85 0 0
SolidBegin "primitive"
Sphere .75 -.75 .75 360
SolidEnd
TransformEnd
SolidEnd
```

Notice that each of the two Sphere primitives must first be converted into CSG primitives by enclosing them in a SolidBegin "primitive"/SolidEnd block. This is true for any other surface (such as polymeshes, NURBS surfaces etc.) as well. You cannot use these non-CSG shapes as-is. The SolidBegin/SolidEnd enclosure promotes the formerly-hollow surfaces into filled solids, getting them ready for the CSG operations of union, intersection and difference.

The double convex intersection surface is created using:

```
# CSG intersection
SolidBegin "intersection"
# same first primitive as before
TransformBegin
Translate -.75 0 0
SolidBegin "primitive"
Sphere 1 -1 1 360
SolidEnd
TransformEnd
# same second primitive as before
TransformBegin
Translate .85 0 0
SolidBegin "primitive"
Sphere .75 -.75 .75 360
SolidEnd
TransformEnd
SolidEnd
```

The union of the spheres results from this:

```
SolidBegin "union"
TransformBegin
Translate -.75 0 0
SolidBegin "primitive"
Sphere 1 -1 1 360
SolidEnd
TransformEnd
TransformBegin
Translate .85 0 0
SolidBegin "primitive"
Sphere .75 -.75 .75 360
SolidEnd
TransformEnd
SolidEnd
```

Note that while the union and intersection operations are commutative (it does not matter in what order the participating shapes are specified), the difference operation is not – you would get a different shape if you subtract solid B from solid A, as opposed to subtracting A from B (try it).

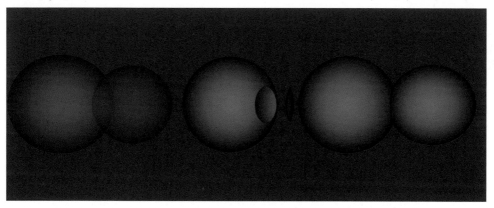

Figure 4.72 *Difference, intersection and union of two spheres*

Figure 4.73 shows surfaces resulting from hierarchically applying combinations of union, intersection and difference operations. The primitives used in this example are instanced (see Section 4.18 for a discussion of instancing). On the left is a hollow cube with thin walls, produced using this code:

```
# difference of nested cubes to produce a thin-walled cube
SolidBegin "difference"
Opacity [.5 .5 .5]
# outer cube
SolidBegin "primitive"
Scale 1.25 1.25 1.25
Translate -.5 -.5 -.5
ObjectInstance 1 # cube model
SolidEnd
# inner cube
SolidBegin "primitive"
Scale 1.2 1.2 1.2
Translate -.5 -.5 -.5
ObjectInstance 1 # same cube model as above
```

```
SolidEnd
SolidEnd
```

Next is a union of three similar cylinders lying along X, Y and Z axes which results from these commands:

```
SolidBegin "union"
SolidBegin "primitive" # first rod
Color [1 1 1]
ObjectInstance 2 # cylinder capped by two disks
SolidEnd
SolidBegin "primitive" # second rod
Color [1 1 1]
Rotate 90 0 1 0
ObjectInstance 2
SolidEnd
SolidBegin "primitive" # third rod
Color [1 1 1]
Rotate 90 1 0 0
ObjectInstance 2
SolidEnd
SolidEnd
```

The third figure shows the result of subtracting the cylinder union from the hollow cube. Here is how that is done:

```
SolidBegin "difference"
Opacity [.5 .5 .5]
# RIB for difference of nested cubes from previous
# discussion.
# ...
# RIB for union of cylinders from above
# ...
SolidEnd
```

The final figure results from taking the intersection (common regions) of the hollow cube and the cylinder union. The code outline to produce it is:

```
SolidBegin "intersection"
Opacity [.5 .5 .5]
# RIB for difference of nested cubes from previous
# discussion.
# ...
# RIB for union of cylinders from above
# ...
SolidEnd
```

CSG operations are extremely useful for generating shapes related to mechanical design, such as flanges, gaskets, nuts and bolts, lathe beds, etc. Such shapes employ regular spheres, cylinders cuboids and other symmetric primitives in their construction, and contain features such as grooves and holes. Try generating CSG images of some of these and also of other objects such as bowling balls, pills and capsules, postal stamps with perforated edges, etc.

On a side note, the Boolean operations of union, intersection and difference are also referred to as set-theoretic operations. In elementary texts on mathematics these are illustrated using Venn diagrams that usually involve a pair of overlapping circles which denote sets.

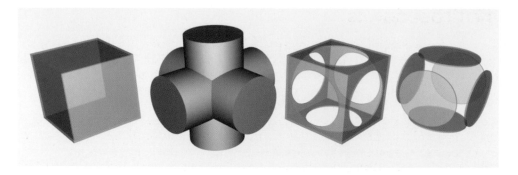

Figure 4.73 *Hierarchies of difference, union and intersection operations*

Figure 4.74 shows an abstract shape obtained by taking the difference between two identical but slightly rotated trefoil knot **NURBS** surfaces (see Figure 4.11 for a trefoil knot). The commands to generate it are:

```
# intersection of two copies of the same surface rotated
# with respect to each other
SolidBegin "intersection"
SolidBegin "primitive"
ObjectInstance 1 # contains NURBS trefoil surface
SolidEnd
SolidBegin "primitive"
Rotate 40 1 0 0
Scale 1 1 1
ObjectInstance 1
SolidEnd
SolidEnd
```

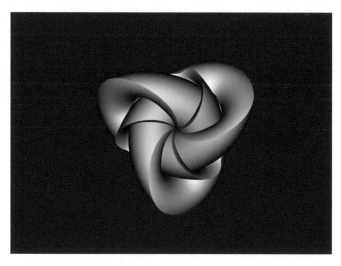

Figure 4.74 *Intersection of a pair of trefoil knot surfaces*

4.17 Procedurals

In this chapter we have looked at the rich set of geometric primitives available in RenderMan. But what is provided is by no means exhaustive. For instance, Coons patches (which are surfaces derived from four arbitrary boundary curves) and alpha shapes (which are blobby-like primitives with polygons as their backbones) are not available in RenderMan. Also unavailable are procedural ways to generate shapes such as fractals, terrains and botanical forms. What is provided instead is a "back door' RIB command called Procedural that lets you extend RenderMan's shape catalog by specifying your own routines for generating custom geometry. These external routines are invoked by RenderMan during rendering. The geometry that they output (described in terms of built-in RenderMan primitives) are treated just like built-in primitives specified directly in RIB files. You can use this technique to implement your own primitive types, subdivision schemes, procedural surface generators, particle replacers, etc. Feel free to skip the rest of this section if you do not plan on writing your own RIB generators.

The technique is powerful, flexible and easy to use. Figure 4.75 shows the dataflow.

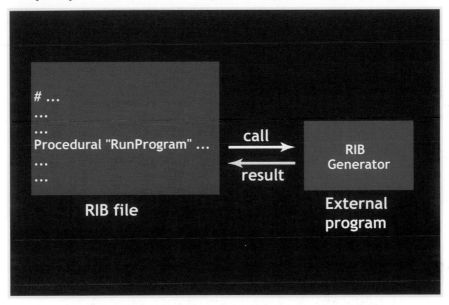

Figure 4.75 *RIB generation via an external program*

So how does it work? The Procedural command's syntax is as follows:

```
Procedural "RunProgram" [<external program plus inputs>] [<bounding
box>]
```

"RunProgram" is one of the three keywords following Procedural (the other two are mentioned below). "RunProgram" is followed by the name of the external program to invoke, along with inputs to that program, if any. The last thing needed is a bounding box in object space in the form <xmin xmax ymin ymax zmin zmax>. The bounding box is a cuboid that would tightly enclose the actual geometry to be rendered. RenderMan converts such a bounds specification into a single number which corresponds to the area in the output image, in pixels, occupied by the generated geometry. This single number is also passed by RenderMan to your external program in addition to any inputs it requires.

The external program could use this number (referred to as the detail parameter) to decide an appropriate level of simplification for the generated object. A character that occupies most of a rendered image's area needs to be generated in sufficiently high detail, while one that only occupies a handful of pixels can be vastly simplified.

Figure 4.76 shows a regular triangle, square, pentagon and hexagon, obtained through an external program called genRegPoly which generates a regular polygon (using the built-in Polygon RIB command) given the number of sides.

Figure 4.76 *Regular polygons generated via an external program*

The four figures shown are a result of these invocations.

```
# Invocation of the external 'genRegPoly' program to
# create regular polygons. The program needs a single
# input - num. sides for the poly it will generate.
# The Procedural call requires a bounding box in addition
Procedural "RunProgram" ["genRegPoly" "3"]  [-1 1 -1 1 -1 1]
Procedural "RunProgram" ["genRegPoly" "4"]  [-1 1 -1 1 -1 1]
Procedural "RunProgram" ["genRegPoly" "5"]  [-1 1 -1 1 -1 1]
Procedural "RunProgram" ["genRegPoly" "6"]  [-1 1 -1 1 -1 1]
```

genRegPoly was written in "C" and then compiled to produce a binary (executable) version. The program looks like this:

```c
#include <stdio.h>
#include <stdlib.h>
#include <math.h>
void doPolyGen(int nSides)
{
    int i;
    float angStep, currAng;
    printf("Polygon \"P\" [");
    if (nSides<3)nSides=3;
    angStep= 2.0*M_PI/nSides;
    for(i=0;i<nSides;i++)
    {
        float x,y,z;
        currAng = 0.5*M_PI + i*angStep;
        x = cos(currAng);
        y = sin(currAng);
        z = 0.0;
        printf("%f %f %f ",x,y,z);
    }
    printf("]\n");
}/* doPolyGen() */
int main()
{
    void doPolyGen(int nSides);
    char buffer[256];
    double detail;
    int nSides;
    while(fgets(buffer,256,stdin))
    {
        sscanf(buffer,"%f %d",&detail,&nSides);
        doPolyGen(nSides);
        fprintf(stdout,"%c", '\377');
        fflush(stdout);
    }
}/* main() */
```

Notice that the above program ignores the detail parameter passed in. We can afford to do so in simple cases, but if the geometry generation is sufficiently involved, it would be wise to scale the complexity in relation to the detail parameter.

You can also write the same program using Java, C++, Python, Perl, Tcl or any other general purpose programming language of choice. RenderMan needs to be able to invoke your program with at least one input (the "detail" parameter, derived from the bounding box specified in the Procedural command), more if your program requires additional inputs to use during geometry generation.

Note that your external program can itself contain Procedural command calls which in turn can invoke other external programs, and so forth.

I mentioned earlier that there are two other forms of the Procedural command. One is the DelayedReadArchive version, an example of which would look like this:

```
Procedural "DelayedReadArchive" ["polyhedra.rib"] [-1 1 -1 1 -1 1]
```

In the above case, polyhedra.rib is an external RIB file, which would get read in only if/when required as determined by the bounding box specification. Compare this with the ReadArchive command introduced in Chapter 3, where the contents of the associated RIB file would get read in, no matter what. The DelayedReadArchive is a more intelligent version, where the user-supplied bounding box is used by RenderMan to make decisions about the file inclusion.

The last type of Procedural command is the "DynamicLoad" kind. Here, just like with "RunProgram", an external program is invoked by RenderMan. The difference is that in this case, the external program needs to be compiled into a shared object. Doing so makes the RIB generation more efficient. By the way the syntax is identical for both RIB generation commands.

4.18 Instancing

As mentioned in Section 4.1, it is common to use instancing in conjunction with particle systems. For example, volumetric-looking splashes can be created by instancing bilinear patches at particle locations and texturing them with animated splash image sequences. Bilinear patches are preferable to polygons for this purpose since the patches can be created to be non-flat, thereby catching light better than all-flat shapes. In crowd systems entire characters are instanced at particle locations. This makes for a highly efficient scheme for rendering large numbers of them without making the scene overly heavy in geometry (which would be the case if the characters are duplicated and not instanced at each location).

Take a look at Figure 4.77, which shows the seven tangram pieces (Figure 4.17) arranged to form the letters R, F and B. A naive way to describe this arrangement would be to specify the geometry of the seven pieces thrice, once for each letter. But doing so does not take into account the fact that the letters are made of the same pieces. It would be better if we could specify the seven pieces just once in a sort of master definition, and then describe each letter as being made of instances from that master definition. The master definition is like a mold or rubber stamp, helping create arbitrary numbers of copies as needed.

RenderMan's instancing mechanism permits us to define such master objects (retained models, in RenderMan terminology) using an ObjectBegin/ObjectEnd block, and create copies of them using the ObjectInstance command.

The tangram pieces are defined as follows:

```
# Each ObjectBegin/ObjectEnd block below encloses a
# single GeneralPolygon definition, i.e. a single
# tangram piece. Each ObjectBegin command is followed
# by an identifier number to be used when instancing
# the object later
ObjectBegin 1
##|Inst|TanPiece_BgT1
GeneralPolygon [3] "P" [-2 -2 0 0 0 0 -2 2 0 ]
ObjectEnd
ObjectBegin 2
##|Inst|TanPiece_BgT2
GeneralPolygon [3] "P" [-2 2 0 0 0 0 2 2 0 ]
ObjectEnd
ObjectBegin 3
##|Inst|TanPiece_SmT1
GeneralPolygon [3] "P" [-2 -2 0 -1 -1 0 0 -2 0 ]
ObjectEnd
ObjectBegin 4
##|Inst|TanPiece_Sqre
GeneralPolygon [4] "P" [0 -2 0 -1 -1 0 0 0 0 1 -1 0 ]
```

```
ObjectEnd
ObjectBegin 5
##|Inst|TanPiece_SmT2
GeneralPolygon [3] "P" [1 -1 0 0 0 0 1 1 0 ]
ObjectEnd
ObjectBegin 6
##|Inst|TanPiece_Rhmb
GeneralPolygon [4] "P" [1 -1 0 1 1 0 2 2 0 2 0 0 ]
ObjectEnd
ObjectBegin 7
##|Inst|TanPiece_MidT
GeneralPolygon [3] "P" [0 -2 0 2 0 0 2 -2 0 ]
ObjectEnd
```

Once defined, the pieces can be instanced like this:

```
# Instancing of the 7 shapes is shown for letter 'R' in
# Figure 4.77. Similar commands are used for the 'f'
# and 'B'. Each ObjectInstance command creates an
# instance of the specified (via its identifier) shape
TransformBegin
Translate -5.474 5.703 0
Rotate -225 0 0 1
ObjectInstance 1
TransformEnd
TransformBegin
Translate -5.481 0.012 0
Rotate -45 0 0 1
ObjectInstance 2
TransformEnd
TransformBegin
Translate -3.412 4.849 0
ObjectInstance 3
TransformEnd
TransformBegin
Translate -2.627 5.657 0
ObjectInstance 4
TransformEnd
TransformBegin
Translate -4.428 1.823 0
Rotate 90 0 0 1
ObjectInstance 5
TransformEnd
TransformBegin
Translate -3.204 1.592 0
Rotate 180 0 0 1
Scale -1 1 1
ObjectInstance 6
TransformEnd
TransformBegin
Translate -3.62 4.641 0
ObjectInstance 7
TransformEnd
```

The rubber stamp/mold analogy mentioned above is not entirely accurate, since instanced models also can be scaled or skewed in addition to being instanced in a rigid rubber stamp or mold-like fashion.

Instancing is particularly effective for gathering into a single aggregate, a complex model such as a droid or soldier. Armies can then be created by instancing individuals, each with their own geometric transformations as well as attributes such as color, opacity and shading. Instancing is primarily done for efficiency reasons – it is better to carry around in memory a single master definition of a complex object instead of identical multiple ones offset only by transformations. It is also a scheme beneficial to the user, since changes can be made to the model in just one location and automatically be available everywhere the model is instanced.

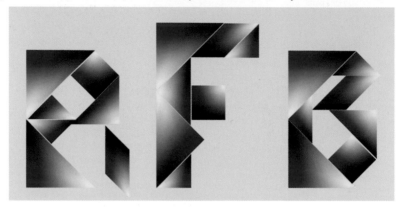

Figure 4.77 *Tangram pieces instanced to form "RfB"*

4.19 Reference geometry

In an animated sequence involving a piece of geometry that undergoes deformations, the shape in one of the frames (usually the first frame) can be designated to serve as reference geometry for other frames. For instance, for a character undergoing complex deformations, the classic da Vinci pose can serve as a reference. For a flexing cube, the reference can simply be the undistorted version.

Being able to specify reference geometry is especially useful for texturing deforming primitives such as blobbies, on a per-frame basis. This is because blobbies do not come with a built-in texturing scheme. Though we have not covered texture mapping yet (we will, in Chapter 8), I am mentioning it here since it is the context where referencing is most used. The idea is to apply texture (e.g. using a 3D paint program) to a reference, undeformed shape, and use it to texture that shape in other frames when it undergoes deformations.

Here is a simple example to illustrate how this works. Figure 4.78 shows a section of an annulus (ring) surface that has been textured with colorful bands across, from yellow on the left to cyan on the right.

The annulus is generated using RIB that looks like this:

```
# Annulus created from adjoining quads
PointsGeneralPolygons [1 1 1 1 1 1 1 1 1 1] [4 4 4 4 4 4 4 4 4 4]
[3 2 1 0 7 6 5 4 11 10 9 8 15 14 13 12 19 18 17 16 23 22 21 20 27
26 25 24 31 30 29 28 35 34 33 32 39 38 37 36] "P" [0.707107 0.707107
0 1.41421 1.41421 0 1.17557 1.61803 0
```

```
# ... more points
]
```

Now imagine that this surface gets squeezed on either side. Without the use of reference geometry, the new surface will look incorrect, like in Figure 4.79. The problem is that the surface does not appear squeezed, rather it looks like the sides were chopped off.

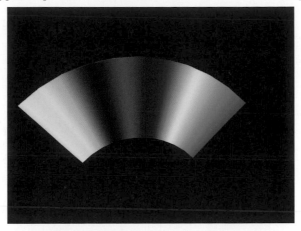

Figure 4.78 *A section of an annulus*

Figure 4.79 *Compressed annulus section, no reference geometry*

Figure 4.79 is generated using RIB that looks like the following. We have the same topology as before but the vertices are now closer together.

```
# Compressed annulus, using a new set of P values
PointsGeneralPolygons [1 1 1 1 1 1 1 1 1 1 1] [4 4 4 4 4 4 4 4 4 4 4]
[3 2 1 0 7 6 5 4 11 10 9 8 15 14 13 12 19 18 17 16 23 22 21 20 27
26 25 24 31 30 29 28 35 34 33 32 39 38 37 36] "P" [0.34202 0.939693
0 0.68404 1.87939 0 0.551275 1.92252 0
# ... more points
]
```

The expected result that uses reference geometry is shown in Figure 4.80, where you can see that the colored bands, narrower than before, correctly span yellow to cyan as in the original figure.

Reference geometry is very easy to specify. We simply use the RIB extension scheme of being able to append arbitrary data on to primitives, to attach a copy of the original geometry to its deformed versions:

```
PointsGeneralPolygons # ... usual vertex counts, indices ...
# same compressed annulus geometry as the previous case
  "P" [0.34202 0.939693 0 0.68404 1.87939 0 0.551275 1.92252 0 # ....
more points ...
]
# We're using Pref below - note that the vertices that follow
# are the same as the P values in the undeformed geometry
"Pref" [0.707107 0.707107 0 1.41421 1.41421 0 1.17557 1.61803 0 #
... rest of the points from the original geometry
]
```

Attaching reference geometry using Pref as shown above is by itself not enough to get the shading right. The shader attached to the geometry needs to be written to make use of this information. Please look in the online RfB pages for an example of this.

Figure 4.80 *Compressed annulus section using reference geometry*

4.20 Handedness, sides

RenderMan's native coordinate system is a left-handed one. Look at Figure 4.81 for what this means. On the left photograph, the X-Y-Z axes form a right-handed coordinate system, where if the X and Y axes point to the right and up respectively (like you see in math textbooks), the Z axis comes out towards you. Given the orientation of X and Y, you can derive Z's orientation by imagining that you are grabbing the X axis, rotating it along the XY plane to make it coincide with Y, then repeating that motion on a jar's lid – the direction of the lid's travel gives you the (positive) Z axis. But as shown in the right of Figure 4.81, RenderMan uses a left-handed system instead, where if X and Y are laid out as usual, then Z points away from you, along your view direction. Another way of saying this is that if your eye is the camera looking at an image plane straight ahead, your view direction defines the positive Z axis.

Figure 4.81 *Right-handed and left-handed (RenderMan default) coordinate systems*

Usually we would like surfaces to be defined so that their normals point along what would be considered the outside of the surface (the side opposite outside is naturally enough, the inside). If you hold a tennis ball in your hand, at every point on the ball the surface normal is imagined to point outward, away from the ball's center. The inside surface would be invisible to you since the ball is opaque and closed. Further, the portion of the ball visible to you is said to be frontfacing, and the hidden part, backfacing. If you now pick up a glass sphere, you would see the frontfacing surface as usual and in addition be able to see the inside of the backfacing surface since the sphere is transparent.

An orientation can be associated with a geometric primitive to fix its sense of inside and outside. Given a surface definition (say, a certain consistent ordering, clockwise or counterclockwise, of vertices of every polygon in a polymesh), the meaning of "outside" and "inside" is based on the surface's specified orientation.

RenderMan uses the Orientation command (orientation is an attribute, meaning that it can be specified per primitive) to specify orientations, and ReverseOrientation to reverse the sense of existing orientations. The Orientation command can specify one of "outside", "inside", "rh" or "lh" to be the orientation of surfaces that follow.

Surfaces in RenderMan can be defined to be single-sided where only the outside is visible to the renderer, or two-sided where both sides are visible. Sidedness is specified using the Sides command.

Through appropriate choices for the surface orientation and number of sides, you can specify which side of a surface (inside or outside or both) you would like to render. It is customary to define opaque, closed surfaces as being single sided with normals facing outward, whereas transparent and/or open surfaces are usually double-sided in order to expose their insides to the renderer.

Consider the single-sided cube on the left in Figure 4.82. Only the frontfacing outside surfaces are visible, and the backfacing surfaces are obscured. But in the figure on the right, the situation is reversed by flipping the cube's orientation. The previously-visible surfaces become culled, exposing the inner back walls which are now considered frontfacing.

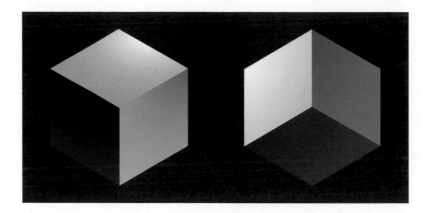

Figure 4.82 *Outside and inside of a cube*

The first cube is rendered using:

```
# single-sided cube, "lh" orientation
Sides 1
Orientation "lh" # default orientation
PointsGeneralPolygons [1 1 1 1 1 1]
[4 4 4 4 4 4]
[2 3 1 0 4 5 3 2 6 7 5 4 0 1 7 6 3 5 7 1 4 2 0 6]
"P" [-0.5 -0.5 0.5 0.5 -0.5 0.5 -0.5 0.5 0.5 0.5 0.5 0.5 -0.5 0.5 -
0.5 0.5 0.5 -0.5 -0.5 -0.5 -0.5 0.5 -0.5 -0.5]
```

The command "Sides 1" specifies that the cube is a single-sided surface, where only the outside is rendered by the renderer.

The inside-out cube on the right of Figure 4.82 is produced using this **RIB**:

```
# single-sided cube, reverse orientation
Sides 1
# instead of ReverseOrientation, we could explicitly
# say Orientation "rh" and get the same result
ReverseOrientation # opposite of "lh"
PointsGeneralPolygons [1 1 1 1 1 1]
[4 4 4 4 4 4]
[2 3 1 0 4 5 3 2 6 7 5 4 0 1 7 6 3 5 7 1 4 2 0 6]
"P" [-0.5 -0.5 0.5 0.5 -0.5 0.5 -0.5 0.5 0.5 0.5 0.5 0.5 -0.5 0.5
-0.5 0.5 0.5 -0.5 -0.5 -0.5 -0.5 0.5 -0.5 -0.5]
```

The surfaces are still single-sided as in the previous case, and in addition, the ReverseOrientation command turns the surfaces inside out (the orientation is the opposite of what it was in the previous case).

Note that turning a surface inside out does not mean a surface eversion in the topological sense where a shape change occurs. It simply means that the directions of surface normals get reversed, that is all. The overall shape still stays the same.

Also, if "Sides 2" is specified, both the inside and outside of a surface would be rendered regardless of the orientation the surface happens to have.

Many 3D animation packages (e.g. Maya) employ a right-handed coordinate system. When objects from these programs are exported to RenderMan via RIB translators, their sense of inside and outside becomes reversed because of RenderMan's left-handed axes convention.

So it is common to see a ReverseOrientation command at the top of these translated RIB files, placed there to make the surface sense compatible between RenderMan and the host animation programs. Such a global ReverseOrientation flips the orientation of all the surfaces in the scene, providing in effect an equivalent coordinate system reversal. To force an actual reversal of the coordinate system, the Scale transformation command (see Chapter 5, "Transformations") can be used with negative arguments. However this does not substitute for the ReverseOrientation command – the geometry may look right but the normals might still point in the wrong direction. We will illustrate this with an example in Chapter 5.

Shown in Figure 4.83 is a rather tricky surface called a tritorus, invented by Roger Bagula. It contains three twists along its surface and has front and back facing surfaces intertwined.

Figure 4.83 is rendered with "Sides 2" so that you can see both surfaces at once. The individual single-sided versions, which happen to be mirror images of each other for this surface, are shown in Figure 4.84 and Figure 4.85. Superposing them (Figure 4.86) shows that the two are intertwined, each obscuring half the other.

The double-sided tritorus in Figure 4.83 is a result of this RIB:

```
# tritorus, double-sided
Sides 2
Color [.61 .21 .73]
ReadArchive "TriTorus.dat" # polymesh RIB
```

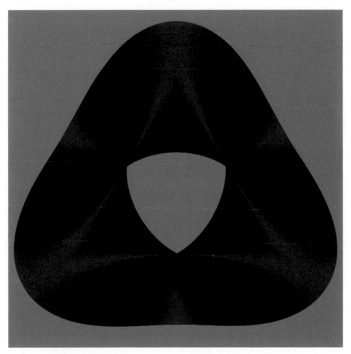

Figure 4.83 *A tritorus rendered with both sides*

Figure 4.84 results from this code:

```
# tritorus, lh orientation
Sides 1
Orientation "lh"
```

```
Color [.63 .17 .16]
ReadArchive "TriTorus.dat" # polymesh RIB
```

Figure 4.85, the opposite-side version, is obtained using the following:

```
# tritorus, rh orientation
Sides 1
# We could also use ReverseOrientation instead, to
# obtain Figure 4.85
Orientation "rh"
Color [.10 .18 .47]
ReadArchive "TriTorus.dat" # polymesh RIB
```

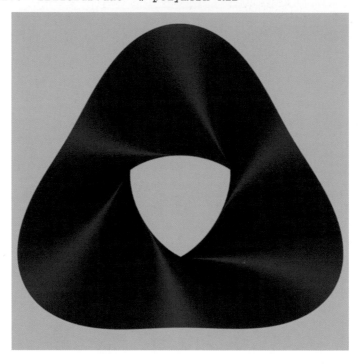

Figure 4.84 *Tritorus showing a single side*

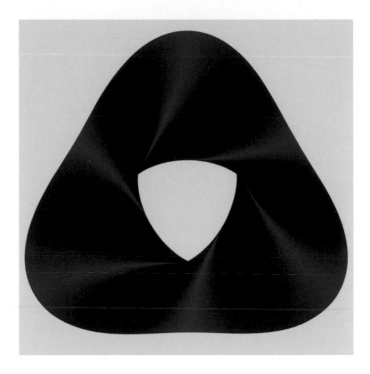

Figure 4.85 *Tritorus now showing the opposite side*

Superposing the two single-sided versions to obtain Figure 4.86 is simply a matter of rendering the surface twice:

```
# ...
Sides 1
Orientation "lh"
Color [1 0 0]
Opacity [.65 .65 .65]
ReadArchive "TriTorus.dat"
# ...
Sides 1
Orientation "rh"
Color [0 0 1]
Opacity [.65 .65 .65]
ReadArchive "TriTorus.dat"
```

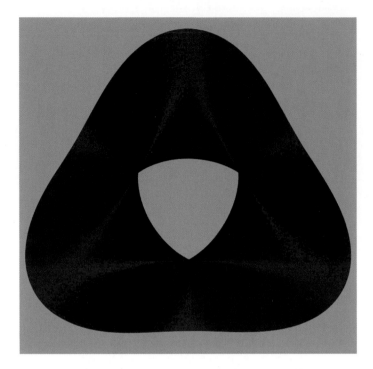

Figure 4.86 *Superimposed single-sided tritori*

Our final example is a Mobius strip shown in Figure 4.87. A Mobius strip is topologically a single-sided surface. Rendering both sides produces the classical view in the left of Figure 4.87, but rendering each of the two sides separately and superposing them (right side of the figure) reveals two complementary forms that comprise the Mobius strip. The interesting thing is this – because the overall surface is one-sided, both single-sided views have camera-facing parts in the front portion of the strip as well as in the back.

Figure 4.87 *Mobius strips, full (left) and superimposed partials (right)*

We are now done taking a tour through the various geometry generation RIB commands, sometimes paying obsessive attention to syntax. The goal was to provide you with enough familiarity with the commands, enabling you to use them in creative ways for shape synthesis.

5
Transformations

This chapter presents commands to locate (position, orient and scale) entities such as models, lights and cameras in space which help create useful scenes for rendering.

5.1 Coordinate systems

A coordinate system, also known as a reference frame or coordinate space or simply space, is a central concept in computer graphics. Conceptually it provides a measurement system consisting of an origin, some reference directions (X, Y and Z axes in three-dimensional space) and uniformly-spaced tick marks along these directions with respect to which elements can be constructed. Elements created with reference to a certain coordinate system coexist in the space laid out by that system. Points in this space can be assigned values (e.g. x,y,z triplets in rectilinear 3D space) measured in terms of the coordinate system. The origin provides a starting location for measuring, the axes provide orientation, and the tick marks provide scale.

It is common to have multiple coordinate systems in a scene, each serving as its own starting point for a cluster of elements (geometry, lights, materials, cameras) defined with respect to it. Furthermore, these coordinate systems need not be all independent, they can be made to relate to each other.

To make these ideas concrete, we will start with a simple example. Figure 5.1 shows three panels, in each of which is a unit white square and a unit blue square. The squares exist in the 2D plane of the paper.

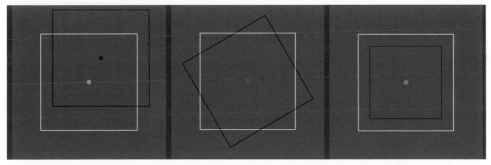

Figure 5.1 *A square undergoing translation, rotation, scaling*

The white square in each case defined with respect to an origin at the center (the white circle) and horizontal (X) and vertical (Y) axes laid out in the usual textbook way. The square is obtained by joining the four points (-0.5,-0.5), (-0.5,0.5), (0.5,0.5) and (0.5,-0.5).

Now imagine making a copy of this coordinate system and sliding the copy's origin off towards the top and right, keeping the X and Y horizontal and vertical. Such an origin shift is called a translation. The new coordinate system, represented by the blue circle, can now be used to trace out a blue unit square similar to the white one. The new square is understandably shifted (translated) with respect to the original one by the same amount as the origin translation. The point is that translating the origin leads to a translation of all elements defined in relation to that origin.

Likewise, the middle panel in Figure 5.1 shows a rotation transformation. The original coordinate system is again duplicated, but this time the new origin stays coincident with the old one while the new XY axes are rotated counterclockwise. The new unit square now appears rotated with respect to the old one.

Finally, the rightmost panel in Figure 5.1 illustrates scaling. The new coordinate system's origin and axes orientations stay the same, but the tick marks are scaled down. So our blue unit square now looks smaller, scaled-down compared to the white one.

Translation, rotation and scaling are three of the most common transformations that coordinate systems can undergo, and we study each individually and in combinations in the following sections. As you will see these transformations turn out to be incredibly useful in model construction, motion description and scene assembly. Without them, every piece of geometry, light and even the observer (camera) in a scene would appear to be piled on top of each other, as expressed in this anonymous quote: "Time is what keeps everything from happening at once; space is what keeps everything from happening to you".

To put it differently, it is as if every character, prop, light, etc. in a scene starts out at a common initial origin, and is then located, oriented and sized appropriately using a series of transformation commands.

5.2 Translation

The translation command is straightforward:

```
Translate <amount_along_x> <amount_along_y> <amount_along_z>
```

The Translate command needs a triplet of (x,y,z) values to use as an offset for translation.

Figure 5.2 shows a human figure constructed by translating two types of hexagons (flat top and angled top) to create the tiled shape. Each hexagon is declared inside an ObjectBegin/ObjectEnd block, and is instanced as follows:

```
WorldBegin
# ...
# hexagon at the default (origin) location
TransformBegin
# Translate 0 0 0
ObjectInstance 1 # flat-top hexagon
TransformEnd

# a translated hexagon
TransformBegin
# our translations are planar in XY,
# so the z component of the translations are 0
Translate -1.50433 -2.6249 0
ObjectInstance 1
TransformEnd

# .. more hexagons ..
# another translated hexagon
TransformBegin
Translate 0.84218 3.41579 0
```

```
ObjectInstance 2 # pointed-top hexagon
TransformEnd
# .. more hexagons
# ...
WorldEnd
```

In between each TransformBegin/TransformEnd pair is a Translate command which translates the world origin, followed by an ObjectInstance command to place a hexagon using the translated coordinate system. So there are several coordinate systems active at once, each responsible for defining a single hexagon. Each coordinate system can be imagined to be a 3D cursor which started out to be coincident with the RenderMan world origin and subsequently got translated by a Translate command. Once a 3D cursor is in a new location, a hexagon is instanced in relation to it. A collection of such translated 3D cursors and instanced shapes relative to them is what creates our tiled figure.

Figure 5.2 *A figure made of hexagons*

In Figure 5.3 is shown a tiling of bird outlines, abstracted from Escher's "Day and Night" woodcut. The bird outline is a cubic b-spline curve, which is replicated as follows:

```
# goose outline in its default location
ReadArchive "EscherGoose.dat"

# goose, translated
Translate 3.2 -0.3 0
ReadArchive "EscherGoose.dat"

# another translation
Translate 3.2 -.3 0
ReadArchive "EscherGoose.dat"

# .. more translated geese
```

Notice that the Translate commands are not enclosed in TransformBegin/End blocks, the way they were for Figure 5.2. The result is that the translations accumulate. In other words, the first (3.2,-0.3,0) translation situates the new coordinate system at that point, while a subsequent (3.2,-0.3,0) translation locates the next coordinate system at (6.4,-0.6,0). The second translation happens in relation to the first.

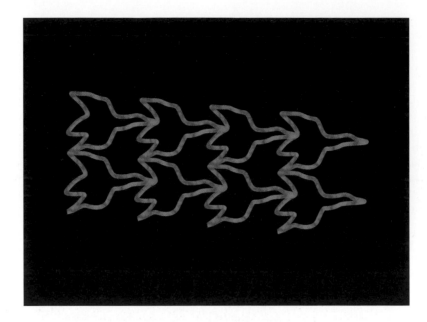

Figure 5.3 *Tiling of bird shapes*

A further example seeks to illustrate this. We would like to locate four spheres along the X axis, at (-2,0,0), (-1,0,0), (1,0,0) and (2,0,0), as shown at the top of Figure 5.4. If you try to do so using the following RIB, you will get the incorrect result at the bottom of the figure:

```
Translate -2 0 0
Color 1 0 0
Sphere 0.5 -0.5 0.5 360
Translate -1 0 0
Color 0 1 0
Sphere 0.5 -0.5 0.5 360
Translate 1 0 0
Color 0 0 1
Sphere 0.5 -0.5 0.5 360
Translate 2 0 0
Color 1 1 0
Sphere 0.5 -0.5 0.5 360
```

The reason is that the first Translate command correctly places the red sphere at (-2,0,0), but the second one does not place the green sphere at (-1,0,0). It is instead placed at ((-2)+(-1)),(0+0),(0+0), which is (-3,0,0). The green sphere incorrectly ends up at the left of the red one instead of at the right. The blue and yellow ones compound the error and are also incorrect. The way to obtain the arrangement at the top of Figure 5.4 is to use this **RIB** instead:

```
# first sphere
TransformBegin
Translate -2 0 0
Color 1 0 0
Sphere 0.5 -0.5 0.5 360
TransformEnd
# second sphere
TransformBegin
```

```
Translate -1 0 0
Color 0 1 0
Sphere 0.5 -0.5 0.5 360
TransformEnd
# .. two more spheres, also inside TransformBegin/End pairs.
```

The TransformBegin/TransformEnd pairs (also called transform blocks) rectify the situation by making each translation independent of the others. The general case is that transformation commands (there can be more than one) inside a block accumulate, but when blocks occur sequentially, each block localizes its transformations (accumulation does not continue from one block into the next). You can think of each block as a sealed box which isolates its contents from subsequent ones. In addition to occurring sequentially as shown in the snippet above, blocks can also be nested, leading to hierarchies of them. We will deal with nested blocks in section 5.12.

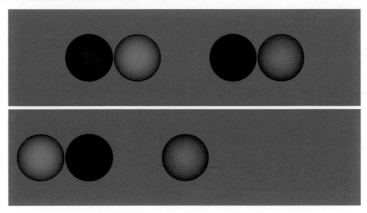

Figure 5.4 *Linear translation of spheres*

5.3 Scale

The RenderMan scale command is

```
Scale <scale_in_X> <scale_in_Y> <scale_in_Z>
```

The command takes three inputs, one value to scale along each component axis. In other words when a coordinate system is scaled to produce another, the new set of axes can be made to have different lengths of tick marks along the different axes. So if you scale a sphere using different scale factors along X, Y and Z, you will obtain an ellipsoid. Uniform scaling is a special case where all three axes are scaled by the same amount.

In Figure 5.5 are shown a set of nested squares with diamond holes. The figure is produced by starting with a GeneralPolygon shape and repeatedly uniform-scaling it by 50%, like so:

```
# parent shape: square, with a diamond hole
GeneralPolygon [4 4] "P" [1 1 0 -1 1 0 -1 -1 0 1 -1 0   0 1 0 -1 0
0 0 -1 0 1 0 0]

# first scaled copy
Scale 0.5 0.5 0.5
GeneralPolygon [4 4] "P" [1 1 0 -1 1 0 -1 -1 0 1 -1 0   0 1 0 -1 0
0 0 -1 0 1 0 0]
```

```
# second copy, 50% of prev. poly and hence 50%*50%=25% of the
# parent poly
Scale 0.5 0.5 0.5
GeneralPolygon [4 4] "P" [1 1 0 -1 1 0 -1 -1 0 1 -1 0   0 1 0 -1 0
0 0 -1 0 1 0 0]

# .. more nested polys
```

Since the Scale commands are not enclosed in blocks, they accumulate. Every new concave polygon is therefore scaled 0.5 times the previous value, giving rise to the nested set pictured.

Figure 5.5 *Repeated scaling of a square containing a diamond hole*

A set of concentric hemi-torus shapes is shown in Figure 5.6. The following RIB produces the shapes:

```
Torus 2   .2 0 180 360

Scale 1 1 -1
Torus 1.6 .2 0 180 360

Scale 1 1 -1
Torus 1.2 .2 0 180 360

# ... more tori
```

The major radius of each subsequent torus is smaller by 0.4 units. In addition, the tori are scaled by -1 along Z, which causes every other one to be flipped about the Z axis to create a rippling wave effect. An implicit "Sides 2" declaration is why both the unflipped and flipped versions are visible. Try rendering the RIB with "Sides 1" to see the flipped ones drop out.

Figure 5.6 *Repeated scaling of hemi-tori*

In Figure 5.7 is shown two versions of the Boy's surface parametric shape. The RIB files for the shapes are identical except for an extra Scale command for the right shape:

```
# ...
Scale -1 1 1
# Boy's surface mesh data
# ...
```

Scaling by -1 along X creates the mirror geometry. Both pieces of geometry are colored by the same shader which turns surface normals into colors, so the shading is not mirrored – only the geometry is.

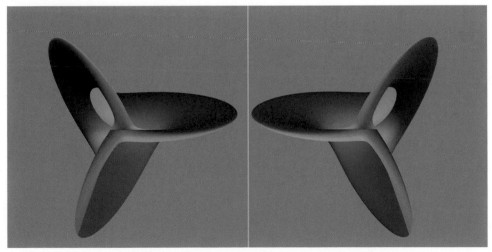

Figure 5.7 *Boy's surface - original and mirrored geometry*

5.4 Rotation

RenderMan uses an axis-angle representation to effect rotations, as follows:

```
Rotate <angle_in_degrees> <3d_axis_vector>
```

Given a shape, you would rotate it by specifying an axis (a direction about which to rotate) as well as an amount (angle, in degrees) of rotation. This is a flexible way to rotate, which enables you to rotate things not just about X, Y and Z axes but also about any arbitrary axis.

Let us look at some simple examples. A Star of David can be obtained by taking an equilateral triangle frame and superposing a 180-degree-rotated copy over it, like so:

```
# Equilateral triangle with a smaller triangle cut out,
# leaving just a thin frame
GeneralPolygon [3 3] "P"
[0 1 0 -0.8660253367 -0.5000001162 0 0.8660255063 -0.4999998224 0
0 .75 0 -0.6495 -0.375 0 0.6495 -.375 0]
# Same triangle rotated 180 degrees about Z, i.e. turned upside down
Rotate 180 0 0 1
GeneralPolygon [3 3] "P"
[0 1 0 -0.8660253367 -0.5000001162 0 0.8660255063 -0.4999998224 0
0 .75 0 -0.6495 -0.375 0 0.6495 -.375 0]
```

Since the default Z axis is perpendicular to the plane of the paper, a 180 degree rotation around it causes our triangle to be turned upside down. Try generating related shapes, e.g. a series of 12 triangles each rotated 30 degrees in relation to the one before.

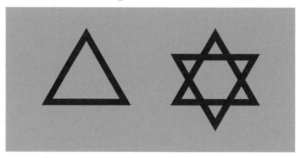

Figure 5.8 *Star obtained using a triangle and its rotation*

In Figure 5.9 are shown three "golden rectangles" (rectangles with an aesthetically-pleasing length to height ratio of about 1.618, a quantity known as the "golden mean") placed on the XY, YZ and XZ planes and passing through the origin. The RIB code to create them is as follows:

```
# First rectangle
AttributeBegin
Color [1 1 .47]
Opacity [.5 .5 .5]
PointsGeneralPolygons [1] [4] [2 3 1 0] "P" [-0.809 -0.5 0 0.809 -
0.5 0 -0.809 0.5 0 0.809 0.5 0]
AttributeEnd
# Second rectangle, obtained by rotating the coordinate system
# twice - first about Y (0 1 0), then about X (1 0 0)
AttributeBegin
Rotate 90 0 1 0
```

```
Rotate 90 1 0 0
Color [.64 .83 .76]
Opacity [.5 .5 .5]
PointsGeneralPolygons [1] [4] [2 3 1 0] "P" [-0.809 -0.5 0 0.809
-0.5 0 -0.809 0.5 0 0.809 0.5 0]
AttributeEnd
# Third rectangle, also obtained through two rotations
#(about Z, then X)
AttributeBegin
Rotate 90 0 0 1
Rotate 90 1 0 0
Color [.28 .0 .47]
Opacity [.5 .5 .5]
PointsGeneralPolygons [1] [4] [2 3 1 0] "P" [-0.809 -0.5 0 0.809
-0.5 0 -0.809 0.5 0 0.809 0.5 0]
AttributeEnd
```

Each plane is placed using an AttributeBegin/AttributeEnd pair, which is an expanded version of the TransformBegin/TransformEnd block, where attributes such as color and opacity can be localized for each block. The first plane is placed as is, while the second and the third are created after rotating the original coordinate system twice (see the comments in the RIB snippet). Again, inside each block, the two rotations are compounded (accumulated). Note that any rotation (arbitrary axis, arbitrary angle) can be synthesized by accumulating a finite series of incremental rotations about X, Y and Z. Figure 5.9 shows an interesting fact – the twelve corners of the three golden rectangles happen to form the vertices of a regular icosahedron (a Platonic solid with twenty equilateral triangular faces).

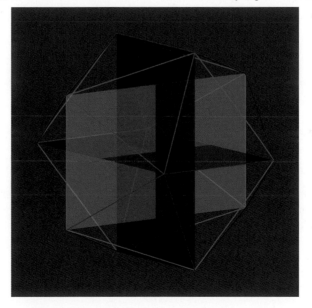

Figure 5.9 *Three orthogonal golden rectangles*

The right portion of Figure 5.10 shows the beautiful Costa minimal surface (a mathematical shape) obtained by calculating one half of the surface (shown at the left of the figure) and generating the other half through rotation.

```
# Left half, calculated using differential geometry equations
ReadArchive "Costa_semi.dat"

# right half, obtained through rotation about Z. The shape is left
# unsealed (on purpose, for illustration)by using 179 degrees for
# rotation instead of the exact value of 180 degrees.
Rotate 179 0 0 1
ReadArchive "Costa_semi.dat"
```

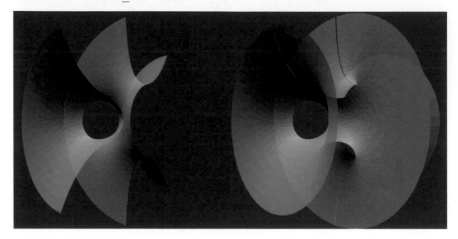

Figure 5.10 *A Costa minimal surface (right)*

As our final example, Figure 5.11 contains eight copies of a concave polygon, rotated 45 degrees every subsequent copy, with two colors that alternate. The RIB snippet is:

```
# Starter polygon, blue
Color [.22 .32 .58]
PointsGeneralPolygons [1] [5] [0 1 2 3 4] "P" [0 0 0 0 1 0 -.4142
1.0 0 0 1.414 0 0.7071 0.7071 0]

 # next poly, pink
Color [.96 .77 .72]
Rotate 45 0 0 1
PointsGeneralPolygons [1] [5] [0 1 2 3 4] "P" [0 0 0 0 1 0 -.4142
1.0 0 0 1.414 0 0.7071 0.7071 0]

# back to blue
Color [.22 .32 .58]
Rotate 45 0 0 1
PointsGeneralPolygons [1] [5] [0 1 2 3 4] "P" [0 0 0 0 1 0 -.4142
1.0 0 0 1.414 0 0.7071 0.7071 0]

# .. five more copies of alternately colored polys
# ...
```

As a side note, the shape is said to possess antirotational symmetry (as opposed to rotational) since the colors alternate each step.

Figure 5.11 *An antirotational pattern*

5.5 Perspective

Given a field of view angle, the Perspective command does a perspective projection of a shape, along the Z axis. The command is simple to specify:

```
Perspective <field_of_view>
```

Though rarely used in a RIB file outside the context of a camera, the Perspective command is useful for projecting shapes along an arbitrary axis. For example, Figure 5.12 shows four cubes being projected such that their vanishing points are near the center of the image but are not coincident. This is because each cube has its own projection axis, which is really the Z axis that has been reoriented. The commands to project one of the cubes are as follows:

```
# Bot. rt. cube
AttributeBegin
# we first perspective-project, then reorient the Z projection axis
# along our preferred direction before creating our cube
Perspective 45
Translate 1 -1 2
Rotate 45 0 1 0
Rotate 45 0 0 1
Color [.73 .73 1.0]
Opacity [.5 .5 .5]
Surface "plastic" "Kd" .75 "Ka" .2
# standard unit cube
PointsGeneralPolygons [1 1 1 1 1 1] [4 4 4 4 4 4] [2
3 1 0 4 5 3 2 6 7 5 4 0 1 7 6 3 5 7 1 4 2 0 6] "P" [-0.5 -0.5 0.5
0.5 -0.5 0.5 -0.5 0.5 0.5 0.5 0.5 0.5 -0.5 0.5 0.5 0.5 0.5 -0.5
-0.5 -0.5 -0.5 0.5 -0.5 -0.5]
AttributeEnd
```

In the above snippet, the Perspective command is given a field of view (FOV) of 45 degrees. A larger angle would make the projection more pronounced, while a smaller value will make it less so. The ability to project objects in this manner is useful for forced-perspective effects and for creating artistic imagery with multiple vanishing points situated on projection axes of your choice.

Perspective is more commonly specified as a camera projection to create the output image, a topic we will explore in Chapter 6, "Camera, output".

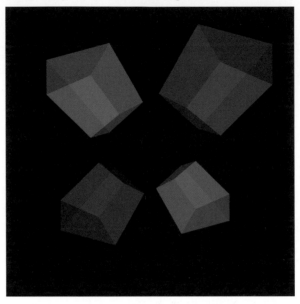

Figure 5.12 *Four cubes in perspective*

5.6 Skew

A skewing transformation linearly distorts a coordinate system's axes, thereby distorting objects defined using that coordinate system. RenderMan's Skew command implements skewing and is specified as follows:

```
Skew <distortion_angle> <source_axis> <target_axis>
```

The source and target axes are vectors. The idea is that the source axis is bent towards the target axis, by <distortion_angle> degrees. In general this creates a warped coordinate system where the axes are no longer perpendicular to each other, so objects defined in such a coordinate system also appear warped.

Figure 5.13 contains a six panel visual proof (one among dozens of proofs) of the famous Pythagoras theorem. We wish to show that the area of the tilted blue hypotenuse square equals the sum of the areas of the two smaller squares. The second and the third steps indicate the square being cut up and slid towards the smaller squares. The third step contains two parallelograms sharing an edge. The fourth and fifth steps are of interest to us here, since they illustrate skewing. The two parallelograms are skewed in steps four and five, to turn them into squares shown in the last step.

In step four the parallelograms are skewed by 10 degrees, as follows:

```
TransformBegin
Skew 10   0 -1 0 -1 0 0
Translate 4 -3 0
Polygon "P" [0 0 0 3 0 0 -1 3.037 0 -4 3 0]
TransformEnd
TransformBegin
Translate 3 0 0
Skew 10   1 0 0 0 1 0
Translate -3 0 0
Translate 4 -3 0
Polygon "P" [3 0 0  3 4 0 -1 7 0 -1 3.037 0]
TransformEnd
```

The same parallelograms are skewed by 40 and 20 degrees in the next step, to warp them even more into the squares:

```
TransformBegin
Skew 40   0 -1 0 -1 0 0
Translate 4 -3 0
Polygon "P" [0 0 0 3 0 0 -1 3.037 0 -4 3 0]
TransformEnd
TransformBegin
Translate 3 0 0
Skew 20   1 0 0 0 1 0
Translate -3 0 0
Translate 4 -3 0
Polygon "P" [3 0 0  3 4 0 -1 7 0 -1 3.037 0]
TransformEnd
```

As an exercise you could try creating a smooth animation of the proof by carrying out the steps (especially the skewing) in finer increments.

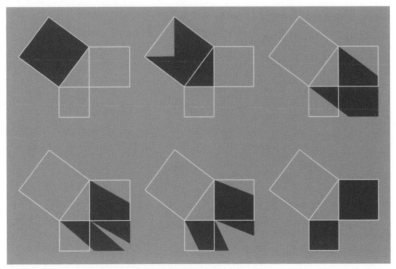

Figure 5.13 *A visual proof of the Pythagoras theorem (also see Figure 5.22)*

Figure 5.14 shows another application of the skew transform, an anamorphic warp. A square containing a texture map is shown on the top left, and a warped version is shown on the bottom. The warping is achieved as follows:

```
AttributeBegin
Surface "tex" "tmap" "DustySq.tex"
Rotate 180 0 1 0
Skew 20 1 0 0 1 1 4
Rotate 180 0 1 0
Skew 20 1 0 0 1 1 4
Scale 2.5 1 1
Polygon "P" [1 1 0 -1 1 0 -1 -1 0 1 -1 0] "st" [1 1 0 1 0 0 1 0]
AttributeEnd
```

A sequence of rotations, skews and a scale produce an anamorphic-warp coordinate system, where a unit square appears distorted as shown. If you hold the page almost perpendicular to your line of sight and look at the warped square at a glancing angle, your eye will recreate the undistorted kitty image. Hans Holbein's "The Ambassadors" contains one of the best examples of classic anamorphic art, a skull warped to look like a whalebone.

The 45-degree warp at the top right of Figure 5.14 (which is not an intermediate step for anamorphic projection) is created using:

```
# bend Y towards X, by 45 degrees
Skew 45 0 1 0 1 0 0
# unit square with texture map
# ...
```

Figure 5.14 *Image distortion obtained by skewing*

While the warps shown above can also be achieved in RenderMan using a bilinear patch, polygon or even using a drawing program such as Illustrator, the Skew command could also be applied to true 3D geometry as well (e.g. to a model of a cat) and not just to flat planes.

5.7 Rotation, scale

Now that we have looked at translation, rotation and scale in isolation, we can examine effects of combining them. First we study the rotation/scale combination.

Figure 5.15 contains ten right triangles. We start with the small blue one and obtain subsequent triangles by rotating and scaling up (and alternating color). The rotation and scale are encoded in a single 4x4 transformation matrix, a set of 16 numbers specified as a linear array in RenderMan. The magic of transformation matrices is that any sequence (however long) of a mix of rotations, translations and scales in any order can always be collapsed into a single 4x4 entity. The matrix is specified as an input to the ConcatTransform RIB command:

```
# First (small blue) triangle
Color [.22 .32 .58]
# The [1 0 0 0 0 1 0 0 0 0 1 0 0 0 0 1] matrix is a do-nothing
# "no-op" transformation
ConcatTransform [1 0 0 0 0 1 0 0 0 0 1 0 0 0 0 1]
PointsGeneralPolygons [1] [3] [2 1 0] "P" [0 0 0 1 0 0 1 0.7265 0]
# second triangle, pink, rotated and scaled
Color [.96 .77 .72]
ConcatTransform [0.999945 0.726503 0 0 -0.726503 0.999945 0 0 0
1.236 0 0 0 0 1]
PointsGeneralPolygons [1] [3] [2 1 0] "P" [0 0 0 1 0 0 1 0.7265 0]
# third, blue
Color [.22 .32 .58]
ConcatTransform [0.999945 0.726503 0 0 -0.726503 0.999945 0 0 0
1.236 0 0 0 0 1]
PointsGeneralPolygons [1] [3] [2 1 0] "P" [0 0 0 1 0 0 1 0.7265 0]
# ... nine more triangles
# ...
```

The sequence of ConcatTransform commands serve to accumulate (or more accurately, concatenate) the rotation and scaling, where each previous transformation is used as a starting point for the current one. Only the color alternates each time (just for cosmetic effect). The transform matrix as well as the right triangle definition are identical for all the nine additional copies of the starter right triangle.

The dictionary definition of the word "concatenate" is "to connect or link in a series or chain". Conceptually, it is as if each ConcatTransform statement places its transformation matrix at the end of an existing chain of matrices, thereby lengthening the chain by one matrix. Either a Transform or ConcatTransform statement could be used to start the chain. In the above code snippet, a ConcatTransform with an identity "do nothing" matrix begins the concatenation. Alternately, a Transform statement with an identity matrix could have also been used. Each new link in the matrix chain inherits the accumulated transformations of all the links prior to it. In other words, matrix concatenation leads to transformation accumulation. In our example the links are all identical (except the first one), where each contains the same matrix for rotation and scaling up. This is what leads to a whirling, zooming effect where the starter triangle is repeatedly rotated and enlarged.

Figure 5.15 *Whirling right triangles*

The rotation and scaling combination is ideal for creating beautiful kaleidoscope patterns (which can be animated) out of any RIB geometry. Figure 5.15 shows one such pattern, made using a Boy's surface mesh. A classic hexagonal kaleidoscope pattern is obtained by taking a shape and its mirror copy, and creating additional copies of the shape/mirror pair by rotating it 120 degrees and 240 degrees. The RIB code to do this involves scales and rotations:

```
# original shape and its mirror
# Unit
TransformBegin
ReadArchive "BoysSurf.dat"
TransformEnd
# Unit, refl.
TransformBegin
Scale 1 -1 1
ReadArchive "BoysSurf.dat"
TransformEnd
# shape/mirror pair, rotated 120 degrees
# Rot 120 deg
TransformBegin
Rotate 120 0 0 1
# Unit
TransformBegin
ReadArchive "BoysSurf.dat"
```

```
TransformEnd
# Unit, refl.
TransformBegin
Scale 1 -1 1
ReadArchive "BoysSurf.dat"
TransformEnd
TransformEnd
# shape/mirror pair, rotated 240 degrees
# Rot 240 deg
TransformBegin
Rotate 240 0 0 1
# Unit
TransformBegin
ReadArchive "BoysSurf.dat"
TransformEnd
# Unit, refl.
TransformBegin
Scale 1 -1 1
ReadArchive "BoysSurf.dat"
TransformEnd
TransformEnd
```

Notice that "Scale 1 -1 1" is used to create a reflected copy. Also, for the additional rotated copies at 120 and 240 degrees, we are using nested transformations by enclosing the shape/mirror combination in a block that contains a rotation.

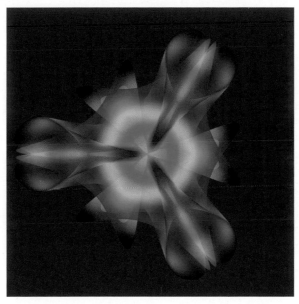

Figure 5.16 *Boy's surface kaleidoscopic pattern*

You could try creating your own kaleidoscope images by using the above code block as a template, substituting your own geometry in place of the Boy's surface shape.

Note that a kaleidoscope pattern results from the rotational and reflectional symmetries of a regular hexagon. On a side note, the Pentagon building in Washington, D.C. and the dome of St. Peter's Basilica in Rome also display reflectional and rotational symmetries.

As Figure 5.16 and several other figures in this chapter illustrate, you can use simple geometrical observations to generate a variety of images. Geometry is one of the most visual areas of mathematics, and a good grounding in it can help you get a lot out of computer graphics. There are many good books on geometry as it relates to natural form and the visual arts. For example *Symmetry: A Unifying Concept* by Istvan Hargittai and Magdolna Hargittai is an excellent book filled with drawings and photographs that illustrate the occurrence/use of symmetry in nature, art and architecture.

5.8 Translation, scale

As an example of a translation/scale combination, Figure 5.17 shows a set of stacked torus shapes. Starting with the very bottom one, the tori are constructed like this:

```
# set of stacked tori to illustrate combination
# of translation and scale

# first, tilt the axes so Z points up:
# [the default Z points into the plane of the paper,
# so we point it 'up' instead by using a counter-clockwise
# (-100 degrees) rotation about the X axis]
Rotate -100 1 0 0

TransformBegin
# Base (Ring0)
Color 1 0 0
Torus 3 .5 0 360 360
TransformEnd

TransformBegin
# Ring1
Color 0 1 0
Translate 0 0 .8
# the base torus was full scale, we make each subsequent
# one 20% smaller
Scale .8 .8 .8
Torus 3 .5 0 360 360
TransformEnd

TransformBegin
# Ring2
Color 0 0 1
Translate 0 0 1.44
# 0.64 = 0.8*0.8
Scale .64 .64 .64
Torus 3 .5 0 360 360
TransformEnd

# more tori
# ...
```

The same torus shape is used for each of the stacked objects. Each new torus is smaller than the previous one and is also offset further along Z (which now points upwards).

Figure 5.17 *Stacked tori, reminiscent of a baby toy*

A Disk primitive is scaled and translated to create the seven osculating (kissing) circles called Farey's circles, in Figure 5.18. Farey's circles touch each other tangentially and are also tangential to a horizontal line at the bottom. The circles are obtained using:

```
TransformBegin
# Translate 0 0 0
# disk, at default position
Disk 0 0.5 360
TransformEnd

TransformBegin
# translated disk
Translate 1 0 0
Disk 0 0.5 360
TransformEnd

TransformBegin
# smaller disk at the center, translated and scaled
Translate 0.5 -.375 0
Scale .25 .25 .25
Disk 0 0.5 360
TransformEnd

# four more disks, all translated and scaled
# ...
```

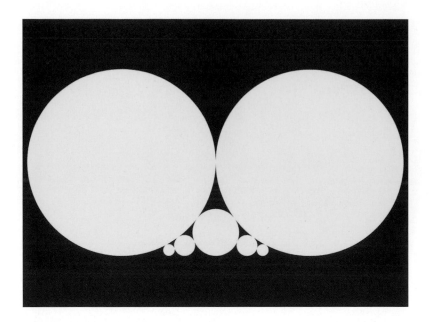

Figure 5.18 *Farey's circles tangential to a horizontal line at the bottom*

In Figure 5.19, the unit square is translated and scaled differently nine times to create a tiling of squares. The tiling itself is almost a square (it is 32x33 units). The squares are obtained using:

```
AttributeBegin
# 0,0
Color .25 .25 .25
Scale 18 18 1
Polygon "P" [0 0 0 1 0 0 1 1 0 0 1 0]
AttributeEnd

AttributeBegin
# 18,0
Color .5 .5 .5
Translate 18 0 0
Scale 14 14 1
Polygon "P" [0 0 0 1 0 0 1 1 0 0 1 0]
AttributeEnd

AttributeBegin
# 18,14
Color .75 .75 .75
Translate 18 14 0
Scale 4 4 1
Polygon "P" [0 0 0 1 0 0 1 1 0 0 1 0]
AttributeEnd

# six more squares of different sizes
```

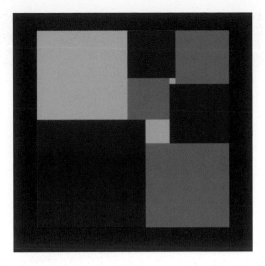

Figure 5.19 *Squares of various sizes tiled to form an almost-square rectangle*

5.9 Rotation, translation

The rotation/translation combination is particularly useful for creating images of tilings and construction toys. Pleasing arrangements of shapes and patterns can be obtained through appropriate translations and rotations of rigid shapes (there is no scale change involved).

Five examples illustrate what can be done using rotation and translation alone. On the left of Figure 5.20 is the classic Truchet tiling pattern, published by Sebastien Truchet in 1704. The tiling is obtained using copies of the single square tile shown isolated. A flip of a coin decides if a copy is placed as is or after a 90 degree turn. Such a randomized placement still shows pleasing arrangements of closed loops and meandering curves stretching across tiles. Since there are exactly two placement choices (as is, or rotated 90 degrees) at each tile location, the Truchet tiling is a binary pattern. The tiles are placed using:

```
# ...
# rotated tile
AttributeBegin
Translate 0 -2 0
Rotate 90 0 0 1 # flips the pattern on the tile
ReadArchive "TruchetUnit.dat"
AttributeEnd

# unrotated tile
AttributeBegin
Translate 2 -2 0
ReadArchive "TruchetUnit.dat"
AttributeEnd
# ... more tiles..
```

A ternary (composed of three) extension to the Truchet tiling is shown at the right of Figure 5.20. A decorated hexagon is now used to form the tiling, where at each location it can be placed as is or rotated by either 120 degrees or 240 degrees. Since there are three choices to pick from, hence we now have a ternary pattern as opposed to Truchet's pattern which is binary.

The hexagons are placed using RIB code such as this:

```
AttributeBegin
Translate 0 -1.73202 0
Color [0.5 0.5 0.5]
# rotated by 120 deg.
Rotate 120 0 0 1
ReadArchive "TernTruchetUnit.dat"
AttributeEnd

AttributeBegin
Translate 1.5 -0.86601 0
Color [0.5 0.5 0.5]
# unrotated copy
ReadArchive "TernTruchetUnit.dat"
AttributeEnd

AttributeBegin
Translate 3 -1.73202 0
Color [0.5 0.5 0.5]
# rotated by 240 deg.
Rotate 240 0 0 1
ReadArchive "TernTruchetUnit.dat"
AttributeEnd

# ... more tiles
```

Figure 5.20 *Truchet tiles (left) and their ternary analogs (right)*

The next example, Figure 5.21, shows a hinged tessellation, so called because each square appears to be rotated about a corner, causing the simple tiling of squares to open up. The squares in the tiling are defined to be symmetric about the origin, like so:

```
PointsGeneralPolygons [1] [4] [3 2 1 0] "P" [1 1 0 -1 1 0 -1 -1 0 1
-1 0]
```

So doing a rotation about Z will cause the squares to spin about their own centers. But we want a corner to act as the pivot for rotation, not the center. This is achieved by bracketing the rotation with a pair of translations. The first translation makes the corner the new origin, the rotation uses this new origin as a hinge, and the second translation negates the first by restoring the origin to its former location. The code to hinge-rotate the top-left square is:

```
AttributeBegin
Translate -2.17 2.17 0 # translate to top-left corner
Translate -0.5 -0.5 0 # temporarily make -.5,.5 the new origin
Rotate 10 0 0 1 # rotate by 10 degrees, effecting a hinge-rotation
Translate 0.5 0.5 0 # move origin back to where it was
ReadArchive "UnitSquare.dat" # draw a square centered at the origin
AttributeEnd
```

The other squares are hinged in a similar fashion, using a corner for rotation instead of the center.

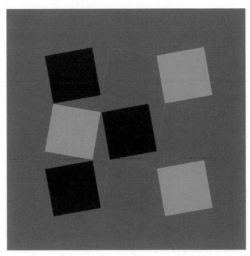

Figure 5.21 *Hinged tessellation of squares*

Figure 5.22 presents a four-copy proof of the Pythagoras theorem, where a right triangle is replicated three more times to create a hypotenuse square at the center (top left figure). The area of this square needs to be shown to be the sum of the squares on the other triangle sides. The proof proceeds by using triangle corners as rotation hinges to create a pair of rectangles in the bottom left figure. One of those rectangles is rotated 90 degrees, revealing squares on the two triangle sides. The original hypotenuse square area has been redistributed to be the areas on the squares of the sides. The code to hinge-rotate the first triangle is:

```
TransformBegin
Translate -1 3 0 # temporarily shift origin
Rotate -90 0 0 1
Translate 1 -3 0 # shift origin back
Polygon "P" [3 3 0 -1 3 0 3 1 0]
TransformEnd
```

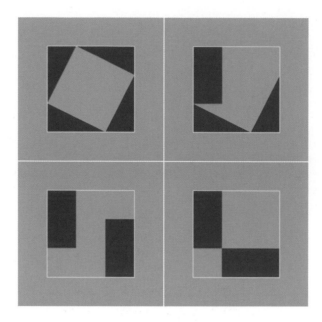

Figure 5.22 *Another proof of the Pythagoras theorem (also see Figure 5.13)*

Figure 5.23 shows a spirolateral curve. Spirolaterals result from carrying out simple instructions such as these, starting with the pen-down position on a piece of paper:

```
Go forward 1 unit
Turn left
Go forward 2 units
Turn left
Go forward 3 units
Turn left
Repeat the above six instructions three more times
```

Try the above yourself to see that you obtain the pattern in Figure 5.23. It can be created using RIB by interspersing drawing commands (that draw unit-length straight lines) with translation and rotation commands for the going forward and turning left part. The six instructions shown above are written this way in RIB:

```
# start at the blue dot shown in Figure 5.23
# Forward 1
Curves "linear" [2] "nonperiodic" "P"
[0 0 0 0 1 0]
"constantwidth" 0.05
Translate 0 1 0
# Left
Rotate 90 0 0 1
# Forward 2
Curves "linear" [2] "nonperiodic" "P"
[0 0 0 0 2 0]
"constantwidth" 0.05
Translate 0 2 0
# Left
Rotate 90 0 0 1
# Forward 3
```

```
Curves "linear" [2] "nonperiodic" "P"
[0 0 0 0 3 0]
"constantwidth" 0.05
Translate 0 3 0
# Left
Rotate 90 0 0 1
```

LOGO is a popular language used to teach computer programming to children. It uses the concept of a 2D turtle which can be given commands like those that generated our spirolateral. As the turtle executes the commands, it traces out the desired shape. Do an online search for small LOGO programs and try to render them using RIB. As mentioned in Chapter 3, "RIB syntax", RIB does not have the concept of code loops, so you will have to "unroll" any loop (in other words, sequentially replicate commands inside it) in the LOGO programs you find.

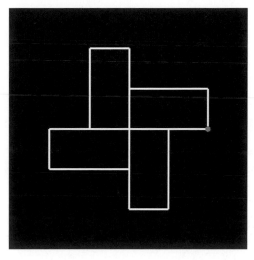

Figure 5.23 *A simple spirolateral*

A two-block tetrahedron puzzle is pictured in Figure 5.24. The idea is to arrange two identical wedge shapes to form a tetrahedron. First the pieces are made to coincide using a simple translation of the purple piece (top right):

```
# first piece
# ...
Translate 0 0 -.5
# second (purple) piece
```

Next, a 180 degree rotation about X is carried out (bottom left):

```
# first piece
# ...
Rotate 180 1 0 0
Translate 0 0 -.5
# second piece
```

Finally, the puzzle is solved by rotating our piece 90 degrees about Z (bottom right):

```
# first piece
# ...
Rotate 90 0 0 1
```

```
Rotate 180 1 0 0
Translate 0 0 -.5
# second piece
```

Notice that for the three solution steps, the transformations were applied to the object (purple block) instead of the coordinate system. Notice too for each new step, the additional transformation was specified before existing ones, reading top to bottom. To put it differently, each new transformation occurs after existing ones, reading bottom to top starting with the object (second piece). Coordinate system transformations are read (and applied) top to bottom ending with the geometry placed in the new set of axes, while object transformations are read bottom to top starting with the object in question. Both of these produce identical results, which is to situate objects appropriately in space. Sometimes it is convenient to think in terms of transforming coordinate axes (like in our spirolateral example) while at others, it is more intuitive to picture transformations being applied to objects instead (e.g. in the tetrahedron puzzle example).

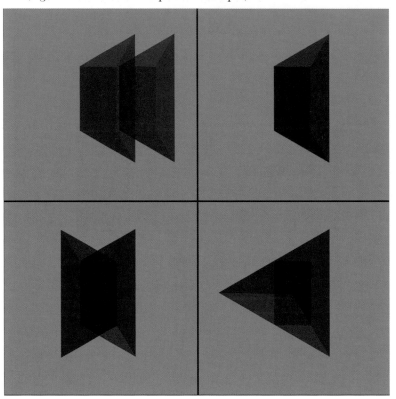

Figure 5.24 *A tetrahedron constructed from two identical pieces*

If you enjoy building with construction toys, check out www.ldraw.org which contains a variety of freeware programs for creating virtual LEGO® models and scenes in the LDraw ".DAT" format. Part of the software collection is l2rib (a program by Julian Fong, a Pixar employee) which creates RIB files out of .DAT files. The book *Virtual Lego* by Tim Courtney et. al. might be a good starting point for your explorations.

5.10 Rotation, scale, translation

Many transformations consist of multiple rotations, scales and translations, each applied an arbitrary number of times and in arbitrary order. A simple example is shown in Figure 5.25 where at first only a translation is applied to a square, followed by translation and rotation, and finally, translation, rotation as well as scale. The RIB code to apply all three is:

```
AttributeBegin
Color [1 .8 0]
Translate .5 .25 0
Rotate 40 0 0 1
Scale .6 .6 .6
ReadArchive "UnitSq.dat"
AttributeEnd
```

As noted in the previous section, you can interpret the above sequence of transforms in two ways. Reading from top to bottom, the coordinate system is translated, rotated and then scaled. The square is created in this altered coordinate system. Alternately, you can read the sequence bottom to top, starting with the scaling. The square is first scaled, then rotated and finally translated into the destination location. The sequence of transforms that scale the coordinate axes is the inverse of the sequence that transforms the object instead. This is true for any block of transforms, whether they consist of a dozen calls or just two.

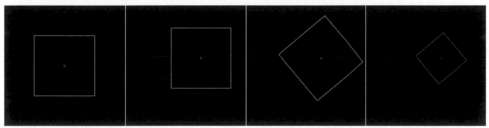

Figure 5.25 *Sequential transformations (translation, rotation, scale) of a square*

In Figure 5.26 the large square on the left of the figure is repeatedly translated, rotated and scaled to produce a tiled golden rectangle. The transformation calls are:

```
# First square (large one on the left of Figure 5.26)
PointsGeneralPolygons [1] [4] [0 1 2 3] "P" [-0.5 -0.5 0 0.5 -0.5 0
0.5 0.5 0 -0.5 0.5 0]
"st" [0 0 1 0 1 1 0 1]
# second square
Translate .809 .191  0
Rotate -90 0 0 1
Scale .618 .618 .618
PointsGeneralPolygons [1] [4] [0 1 2 3] "P" [-0.5 -0.5 0 0.5 -0.5 0
0.5 0.5 0 -0.5 0.5 0]
"st" [0 0 1 0 1 1 0 1]
# third square
Translate .809 .191  0
Rotate -90 0 0 1
Scale .618 .618 .618
PointsGeneralPolygons [1] [4] [0 1 2 3] "P" [-0.5 -0.5 0 0.5 -0.5 0
0.5 0.5 0 -0.5 0.5 0]
"st" [0 0 1 0 1 1 0 1]
```

```
# .. more squares.
```

Note that the calls for creating each additional square are identical. The transformations accumulate, so each smaller square is created in relation to the one before it.

Figure 5.26 *Whirling squares filling out a golden rectangle*

Tiling patterns can be created by rotating, translating and at times scaling copies of a single unit tile. If scaling is involved, it is in the form of a reflection (a -1 scale about an axis). Figure 5.27 shows how a right triangle (seen against a white hexagon) can give rise to a tessellation. Twelve triangles can be fitted inside a hexagon through reflection and rotation, and the hexagons themselves can be placed via translations so that they tile.

Figure 5.27 *A tessellation constructed from the unit triangle at bottom left*

An Origami paper stack is sometimes presented in the manner shown in Figure 5.28. Each sheet of paper in the stack is slightly rotated in relation to the ones above and below it. The RIB code that achieves this is:

```
# First square
Color [0.6059156488 0.02576022293 0.0216564229]
Polygon "P" [0 3 0 -3 0 0 0 -3 0 3 0 0]
# second
Color [0.2215023425 0.4502362759 0.02143815019]
Scale 0.923 .923 .923
Rotate 5 0 0 1
Translate 0 0 .1
Polygon "P" [0 3 0 -3 0 0 0 -3 0 3 0 0]
# third
Color [0.4861902168 0.09465779778 0.7166934369]
Scale 0.923 .923 .923
Rotate 5 0 0 1
Translate 0 0 .1
Polygon "P" [0 3 0 -3 0 0 0 -3 0 3 0 0]
# more squares..
# ...
```

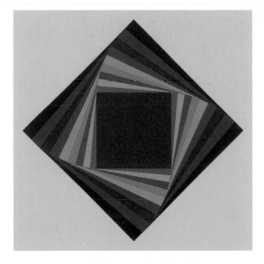

Figure 5.28 *A stack of Origami sheets*

Does command ordering matter, in a sequence of transformations? Yes, it does. Look at Figure 5.29 which shows two views of a torus which have the same orientation but are at different locations in space. The left figure is obtained by specifying a rotation followed by translation:

```
# R, then T
TransformBegin
Rotate -45 2 0 1
Translate 0 -1 1
Torus .5 .25 0 360 360
TransformEnd
AttributeEnd
```

The right side figure contains the same set of RIB commands but translation comes before rotation:

```
# T, then R
TransformBegin
Translate 0 -1 1
Rotate -45 2 0 1
Torus .5 .25 0 360 360
TransformEnd
AttributeEnd
```

Translation followed by rotation does not produce the same result as rotation followed by translation. In other words the operations are not commutative (commutation is when the operations are interchangeable, e.g. addition of a pair of numbers). A triplet of translation (T), rotation (R) and scale (S) commands has six permutations RST, RTS, TRS, TSR, SRT and STR. In general each of these arrangements will yield a different result.

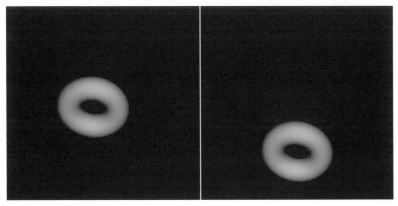

Figure 5.29 *Translation and rotation are not commutative*

A pair of translation commands are commutative (e.g. translating first by (0,1,0) followed by (1,2,3) is the same as translating by (1,2,3) followed by (0,1,0)). Similarly, a pair of scaling transformations are also commutative. But a pair of rotations are not, if they occur about different axes. For instance on the left of Figure 5.30 is a torus that results from this snippet:

```
TransformBegin
Rotate -45 2 0 1
Rotate 60 0 1 -1
Torus .5 .25 0 360 360
TransformEnd
```

The torus on the right of the figure results from the rotations being swapped:

```
TransformBegin
Rotate 60 0 1 -1
Rotate -45 2 0 1
Torus .5 .25 0 360 360
TransformEnd
```

The point is that it is important to specify proper ordering of transformations to get the result you want. Otherwise you run the risk of mispositioning your geometry or incorrectly aiming your camera or lights, etc.

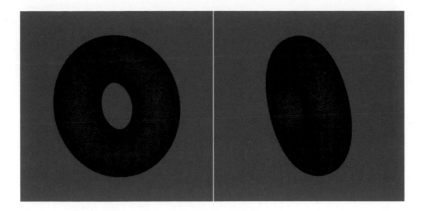

Figure 5.30 *Rotations about different axes are not commutative*

5.11 Concatenating transforms

So far we have illustrated transformations through individual rotation, translation and scale commands, with the exception of using the ConcatTransform command to discuss rotating right triangles in Figure 5.15. In this section we look at ConcatTransform again, along with a couple of related commands, which are Transform and Identity.

Look again at Figure 5.25 where a unit square is situated using a translation, rotation and scale command in sequence. The combination of the three transforms are expressed via this 4x4 matrix:

```
0.459627 0.385673 0 0
-0.385673 0.459627 0 0
0 0 0.6 0
0.5 0.25 0 1
```

The Transform command takes as input a matrix such as the one above, and carries out the transformations encoded in the matrix. The following code that uses the above matrix transforms our unit square to its destination in a single step instead of three (Figure 5.31):

```
AttributeBegin
Color [1 .8 0]

# Single transformation matrix that encapsulates our
# translation, rotation as well as scale operation. Note that
# the translation values 0.5 0.25 0 appear as the first 3 entries
# in the last row of the matrix

Transform
[
0.459627 0.385673 0 0
-0.385673 0.459627 0 0
0 0 0.6 0
0.5 0.25 0 1
]
ReadArchive "UnitSq.dat"
AttributeEnd
```

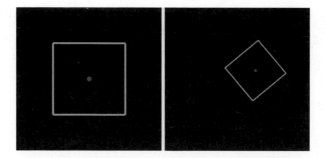

Figure 5.31 *A square translated, rotated, scaled using a single transform matrix*

A series of rotations, scales and translations occurring together get progressively concatenated, as mentioned before. But if a Transform command occurs at the end of such a set of commands, the concatenated transformation is discarded and is instead replaced with the Transform command's own matrix.

On the other hand, a ConcatTransform command's matrix does get compounded with the current transformation matrix (CTM) which exists just before the occurrence of the command. This is illustrated in Figure 5.32 (which is similar to Figure 5.26) where a series of squares are transformed to obtain a golden rectangle. Here each square is decorated with a red arc, and the arcs from adjacent squares join up to create a spiral. A sequence of ConcatTransform commands are used to repeatedly rotate, scale and translate squares.

The ConcatTransform commands are as follows:

```
# First (biggest) square
ReadArchive "GoldenRectSpiral.dat"

# second square
# all ConcatTransform statements contain the same transformation
# matrix which rotates, translates as well as scales the arc.
# The arcs joined end-to-end form a spiral
ConcatTransform [0 -0.618 0 0 0.618 0 0 0 0 0.618 0 0.809
0.191 0 1]
ReadArchive "GoldenRectSpiral.dat"

# third square
ConcatTransform [0 -0.618 0 0 0.618 0 0 0 0 0.618 0 0.809
0.191 0 1]
ReadArchive "GoldenRectSpiral.dat"

# .. more squares using the same matrix shown above
# ...
```

Note that the transformation matrix following the ConcatTransform commands in the above code snippet is equivalent to the trio of translation, rotation and scale commands that were used to position the squares in Figure 5.26.

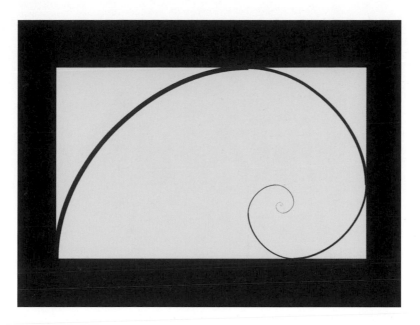

Figure 5.32 *A spiral obtained by repeated translation, rotation and scaling of an arc*

The "RepTile" (Sphinx) puzzle shape is shown at the left of Figure 5.33 can be constructed using four smaller copies of itself, as shown in the right of that figure. To situate four copies of a unit RepTile, the following code is used:

```
# first piece
AttributeBegin
Transform [-0.5 6.12303e-017 0 0 6.12303e-017 0.5 0 0 0 0 -0.5 0
1.30106 -0.249518 0 1]
Color [0.60 .67 .96]
# Polygon data for the RepTile shape..
# ...
AttributeEnd
# second piece
AttributeBegin
Transform [-0.5 6.12303e-017 0 0 6.12303e-017 0.5 0 0 0
0 -0.5 0 0.00356455 -0.245954 0 1]
Color [.23 .54 .23]
# Polygon data for the RepTile shape..
# ...
AttributeEnd
# third piece.
# ...
Transform [0.5 0 0 0 0 -0.5 0 0 0 0 -0.5 0 0.434875
2.22045e-016 0 1]
# ...
# fourth piece
# ...
Transform [-0.25 -0.433013 0 0 0.433013 -0.25 0 0 0
0.5 0 0 0.499037 0 1]
# ...
```

Inside each attribute block, a Transform command is used to set the transformation that places a RepTile copy in its correct position and orientation.

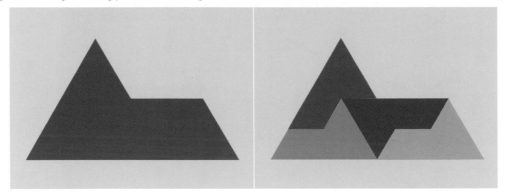

Figure 5.33 *A "RepTile" shape constructed from four identical smaller ones*

The WorldBegin statement at the top of a RIB establishes the world coordinate system at its default location, scale and orientation. It is as if the following Transform command was issued right after WorldBegin:

```
Transform
[1 0 0 0
 0 1 0 0
 0 0 1 0
 0 0 0 1]
```

The above matrix is called an identity matrix, and the Identity command is a shortcut notation for the above Transform command with the identity matrix argument. The CTM's value right after WorldBegin is identity as well, since we are just starting things off. The translation, rotation, scale and ConcatTransform calls that follow transform the default coordinate system into other coordinate systems. A "Transform [1 0 0 0 0 1 0 0 0 0 1 0 0 0 0 1]" or "Identity" at the end of such a sequence will reset the CTM to identity, regardless of what its value happens to be at the time. So the Identity command offers a way to backtrack in one step, all the way up to the world level.

5.12 Transformation hierarchies

So far we have been examining sequences of transformations enclosed in TransformBegin/TransformEnd or more generally, AttributeBegin/AttributeEnd blocks. A block's transforms are not visible to other blocks before or after it. Consider the following RIB code:

```
TransformBegin # block A
Translate 0 1 5
Scale .5 .5 .25
# geometry..
TransformEnd
TransformBegin # block B
Rotate 45 0 0 1
Rotate 60 1 0 0
# more geometry..
TransformEnd
```

The translation and scale commands inside block A only affect geometry in that block, and the two rotations only transform geometry declared in block B. If blocks were not available as a shielding mechanism, we would have to manually undo (reverse) the first pair of transforms before invoking the second, with RIB such as this:

```
Translate 0 1 5
Scale .5 .5 .25
# geometry
# ...
# now undo the translation and rotation
Scale 2 2 4
Translate 0 -1 -5
# ready for the next set..
Rotate 45 0 0 1
Rotate 60 1 0 0
# more geometry..
```

This makes the commands verbose and unwieldy. Blocks are seen to offer a clean way to contain and group sets of related transforms. You can think of a block as a folder (or a box) and its contents as pieces of paper that belong in the folder (or things that go in the box). What we are talking about is the notion of containment.

Another way to look at blocks is in terms of the CTM and the 3D cursor concept. When a new TransformBegin/End (or AttributeBegin/End) block is encountered, RenderMan creates a new set of coordinate axes, a new 3D cursor. Blocks that are adjacent to each other (as in the code snippet above) each get their own cursors. After the first cursor gets created there is no need to manually back it out (which is what the reverse transformations would do) before creating another one.

RenderMan blocks can be arbitrarily nested (blocks can contain more blocks), and this leads to some powerful, flexible functionality. Let us first consider the idea of block nesting a little more. While blocks alone offer containment, nesting them also creates a hierarchy, a parent-child relationship between the nested blocks. In terms of the folder/paper analogy, it is as if folders can contain other folders in addition to sheets of paper. Likewise, boxes can contain more boxes inside them in addition to loose objects.

Figure 5.34 illustrates these ideas. On the left are a hierarchical set of blocks (rectangles). At the outermost level (also called the top level or root) is a single block, which contains three blocks as its offspring. The first of these is childless (also called a leaf or terminal block), the second one contains two leaf blocks. The third one contains a single child which in turn contains a single child. Such a hierarchy of blocks, or hierarchies in general, can be illustrated using a tree diagram. Trees contain nodes (white circles in our diagrams, which stand for terminal and non-terminal entities) and branches which connect them. Three alternate tree representations are seen in Figure 5.34, all of which correspond to our hierarchical blocks. The first is left-to-right view useful for describing trees using plain text characters. Next is the inverted-tree view, the most common representation, with the root node on top. Last is a tree in the botanical sense, with the root on the bottom. Such notations can also be used to describe other hierarchies such as file systems and organizational charts for companies, armed forces and religious bodies.

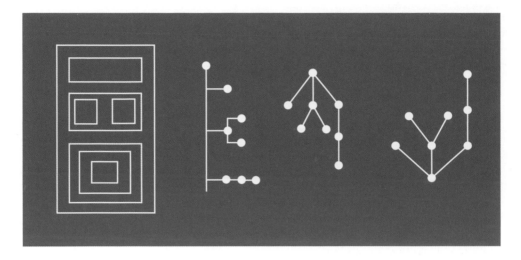

Figure 5.34 *Different ways to represent a hierarchy of blocks*

In RenderMan, nested blocks of transforms can lead to concatenation. Consider this code:

```
TransformBegin #A
# .. A-level rotation/scale/translate commands
TransformBegin #B
# .. B-level commands
TransformBegin #C
# .. C-level commands
TransformEnd # C
# .. more B-level commands
TransformBegin #D
# .. D-level commands
TransformEnd # D
TransformEnd # B
TransformEnd # A
```

Block A contains block B, which contains both C and D. C and D are siblings, children of B. When block B begins, it inherits the CTM just before its TransformBegin command. As long as B contains Translate, Rotate, Scale or ConcatTransform commands, the transformations they contain are concatenated with the existing CTM (a Transform command on the other hand sets the CTM to its own value, ignoring what came before it). When block C starts, it inherits B's CTM. When the block for C ends, the CTM reverts to that of B's, no manual backtracking using additional commands is necessary. After some B-level commands, the D block begins, which inherits B's newer CTM. D ends, the CTM reverts to B's, and when B ends, the CTM is restored to that of A's. C and D are branches off level B, and they in turn could serve as roots for their own hierarchies.

This kind of hierarchical CTM creation and auto-reverting to previous CTMs is what makes block nesting powerful, making it possible to compose transforms (and attributes) to create static modeling as well as motion hierarchies. Note that TransformBegin/End blocks can be nested inside AttributeBegin/End blocks, and vice-versa. Let us look at some examples to illustrate block nesting.

In Figure 5.35 is shown a pair of tangram tulips. The tulip shapes look identical, but they have different colors and are also scaled, translated and rotated differently. If the tulip shape is defined in a file called tulip.dat, the pair of tulips pictured are created using:

```
# bigger
AttributeBegin
Color [1 0 0]
Translate 0.135 -0.405 0
Rotate 15 0 0 1
ReadArchive "Tulip.dat"
AttributeEnd
# smaller
AttributeBegin
Color [1 1 0]
Translate 2.655 -0.743 0
Rotate -20 0 0 1
Scale 0.75 0.75 0.75
ReadArchive "Tulip.dat"
AttributeEnd
```

Each tulip is in its own attribute block. As mentioned before, attribute blocks save and restore transformation like transformation blocks, but in addition they save/restore attributes as well. Here we are using them to give each tulip its own color. The first tulip is translated and rotated, but not scaled, from its default definition. The second one has all three transforms applied to it. It is as if we are taking the whole tulip hierarchy (defined separately in tulip.dat) and embedding them in two different hierarchies, with transforms and an attribute at the root of each new hierarchy. Such hierarchical embedding leads to reuse of existing blocks, and offers a flexible, parts-based approach to modeling. Such modeling parallels real-world construction, where objects ranging from space shuttles to construction toys can be put together using hierarchy-based construction plans. It is a good conceptual tool, helping us synthesize a whole object from progressively bigger, more complex parts.

Figure 5.35 *Tangram tulips*

In addition to static models, motion can be hierarchically expressed as well. Imagine that a child is on a swing, which sits on a rotating platform. In her hand is a toy seesaw with a teetering boy and girl. For an observer on the ground, the toy boy's motion is a complex one, a result of three different motions. Such a motion is most naturally expressed in terms of the composition of the platform, swing and toy's individual motions. That makes it tractable, both for an analytical solution and for describing such a scene to a renderer. Figure 5.36 is a photograph of a pair of K'nex® figures which are jointed. The figures are posed by rotating the sections at the joints. The rotations are hierarchical – rotation at the shoulder causes the whole arm to move (the elbow and wrist inherit the rotation) whereas bending the elbow only affects parts down its hierarchy, which are the forearm and wrist.

Figure 5.36 *K'nex® figures illustrating joint rotations*

Two frames from a tangram walk cycle are shown in Figure 5.37. The head on the left is the default pose, modeled using:

```
TransformBegin # head
TransformBegin # big tri.
ConcatTransform [-0.939693 0.34202 0 0 -0.34202 -0.939693 0 0 0 1
0 1.84153 -0.687617 0 1]
PointsGeneralPolygons [1 1 1 1 1] [3 3 4 4 4] [5 4 3 1 2 0 3 4 1 0
4 5 2 1 5 3 0 2] "P" [2 -2 0 2 0 0
0 -2 0 1.96464 -1.96464 0.1 1.96464 -0.0646447 0.1 0.0646447
-1.96464 0.1]
TransformEnd
TransformBegin # small tri.
ConcatTransform [-0.422618 0.906308 0 0 -0.906308 -0.422618 0 0 0 0
1 0 1.34804 -0.500921 0 1]
PointsGeneralPolygons [1 1 1 1 1] [3 3 4 4 4] [5 4 3 1 2 0 3 4 1 0
4 5 2 1 5 3 0 2] "P" [1 1 0 0 0 0
1 -1 0 0.985355 0.95 0.1 0.0353553 1.25316e-10 0.1 0.985355 -0.95
0.1]
TransformEnd
```

```
TransformEnd # head
```

The head is tilted up in the second frame using a transformation at the root level:

```
TransformBegin # head
# Rotate the head - the ConcatTransform repositions
# both tris as a single unit
ConcatTransform [0.939693 0.34202 0 0 -0.34202 0.939693 0 0 0 0 1 0
0 0 0 1]
TransformBegin # big tri.
ConcatTransform [-0.939693 0.34202 0 0 -0.34202 -0.939693 0 0 0 0 1
0 1.84153 -0.687617 0 1]
PointsGeneralPolygons [1 1 1 1] [3 3 4 4 4] [5 4 3 1 2 0 3 4 1 0
4 5 2 1 5 3 0 2] "P" [2 -2 0 2 0 0
0 -2 0 1.96464 -1.96464 0.1 1.96464 -0.0646447 0.1 0.0646447
-1.96464 0.1]
TransformEnd
TransformBegin # small tri.
ConcatTransform [-0.422618 0.906308 0 0 -0.906308 -0.422618 0 0 0 0
1 0 1.34804 -0.500921 0 1]
PointsGeneralPolygons [1 1 1 1] [3 3 4 4 4] [5 4 3 1 2 0 3 4 1 0
4 5 2 1 5 3 0 2] "P" [1 1 0 0 0 0
1 -1 0 0.985355 0.95 0.1 0.0353553 1.25316e-10 0.1 0.985355 -0.95
0.1]
TransformEnd
TransformEnd # head
```

Likewise the feet are animated by specifying different matrices each frame, in the blocks containing the parallelogram and the square/triangle pair.

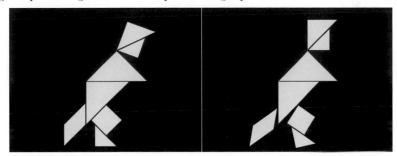

Figure 5.37 *Frames from a tangram walk cycle*

Another simple example of motion is a pair of polygon groups breaking apart. In Figure 5.38 two groups of polygons are moved apart through transforms on their groups:

```
# frame 1
Color [.07 .35 .76] # for both groups
# right piece
ReadArchive "RtPiece.dat"
# left piece
TransformBegin
Translate .385 0 0 # .4 starts the crack
ReadArchive "LtPiece.dat"
# frame 3
Color [.07 .35 .76] # for both groups
# right piece
```

```
ReadArchive "RtPiece.dat"
# left piece
TransformBegin
Translate .3 0 0
Rotate 12 0 0 1
ReadArchive "LtPiece.dat"
```

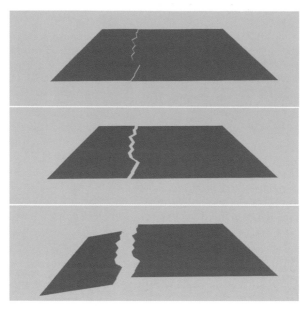

Figure 5.38 *Separation of Voronoi polygon groups*

The last example in this section illustrates the fact that lower levels in a hierarchy inherit attributes and transforms from higher levels, but these can be overridden if necessary. Figure 5.39 shows four versions of a simplified pinwheel shape which contains a smaller pinwheel on one of its blades. The top-left figure is the default pose:

```
AttributeBegin # root
# color and opacity for both pinwheels
Color [1 0 0]
Opacity [.5 .5 .5]
# larger shape
GeneralPolygon [16] "P"
[0 0 0 6 0 0 9 3 0 3 3 0 0 0 0 0 6 0 -3 9 0 -3 3 0
0 0 0 -6 0 0 -9 -3 0 -3 -3 0 0 0 0 0 -6 0 3 -9 0 3 -3 0]
# Nested little pinwheel, inherits color and opacity
# from enclosing block
TransformBegin
# local translation, to situate it on a blade tip
Translate 9 3 0
GeneralPolygon [16] "P"
[0 0 -1 2 -.75 -1 2 .75 -1 0 0 -1 0 0 -1 .75 2 -1 -.75 2 -1 0 0 -1
0 0 -1 -2 .75 -1 -2 -.75 -1 0 0 -1 0 0 -1 -.75 -2 -1 .75 -2 -1 0 0
-1
]
TransformEnd
AttributeEnd
```

In the top-right version, the whole shape is rotated by rotating at the root:

```
AttributeBegin # root
Rotate 45 0 0 1 # animates both wheels..
Color [1 0 0]
Opacity [.5 .5 .5]
# .. rest identical to the code above
```

Since the 45 degree rotation is on the enclosing block, the smaller pinwheel inherits it and is carried along with the blade to which it is attached. At the bottom-left, the parent pinwheel is at rest, only the smaller one is rotated. This is done by specifying a rotation just at the child level:

```
AttributeBegin # root
# color and opacity for both pinwheels
Color [1 0 0]
Opacity [.5 .5 .5]
# larger shape
# ...
# Nested pinwheel
TransformBegin
# local translation
Translate 9 3 0
Rotate 45 0 0 1 # to rotate just the smaller pinwheel
# ... shape
]
TransformEnd
AttributeEnd
```

Both color and rotation are changed at the child level on the bottom-right:

```
AttributeBegin
Rotate 45 0 0 1 # animates both wheels..
Color [1 0 0]
Opacity [.5 .5 .5]
GeneralPolygon [16] "P"
[0 0 0 6 0 0 9 3 0 3 3 0 0 0 0 0 6 0 -3 9 0 -3 3 0
0 0 0 -6 0 0 -9 -3 0 -3 -3 0 0 0 0 0 -6 0 3 -9 0 3 -3 0]
# Nested pinwheel
AttributeBegin
Color [.46 .04 .25] # own color
Opacity [1 1 1]
Translate 9 3 0 # local translation
Rotate -45 0 0 1 # local rotation to cancel out parent rotation
 GeneralPolygon [16] "P"
[0 0 -1 2 -.75 -1 2 .75 -1 0 0 -1 0 0 -1 .75 2 -1 -.75 2 -1 0 0 -1
0 0 -1 -2 .75 -1 -2 -.75 -1 0 0 -1 0 0 -1 -.75 -2 -1 .75 -2 -1 0 0
-1
]
AttributeEnd
AttributeEnd
```

Note that the smaller shape is given its own color using an inner attribute block. If attributes are not overridden in this way, shapes in inner blocks inherit attributes from their enclosing blocks. In our example, the smaller shape is given a counter-rotation of -45 degrees to nullify the overall 45 degree rotation. As a result the smaller shape is in the same orientation as in the default pose at the top-left.

Figure 5.39 *Inheritance and overriding of motion and color*

5.13 Custom spaces

The last topic for this chapter has to do with defining and using custom coordinate systems. Anywhere in a hierarchy of transformations, you can use the CoordinateSystem command (which takes a name as an input) to make RenderMan store the CTM for future use. Several named, custom coordinate systems can be created this way, usually near the top of a RIB file. Just like the Transform command which sets the CTM to be its input matrix, the CoordSysTransform command sets the CTM to be its name input, assuming that a CoordinateSystem command was issued with the same name earlier.

Figure 5.40 shows another kaleidoscope pattern, created using a torus and a cone. The six rotation and reflection axes were defined first, then were invoked to position the objects. The RIB code is as follows:

```
# We are defining 6 coordinate systems below, for use
# later. Each CoordinateSystem call "marks" the current
# transformation to be recalled later
TransformBegin
CoordinateSystem "Default"
TransformEnd
TransformBegin
Scale 1 -1 1
CoordinateSystem "Refl"
```

```
TransformEnd
TransformBegin
Rotate 120 0 0 1
CoordinateSystem "Rot120"
TransformEnd
TransformBegin
Rotate 120 0 0 1
Scale 1 -1 1
CoordinateSystem "Rot120Refl"
TransformEnd
# two more axis definitions..
# ..
# We are now going to use the 6 spaces defined above, to
# create a kaleidoscopic image. Note that the spaces
# can be recalled in any order (not necessarily in order
# they were defined). Also, they can be used multiple times,
# though we're only using each once in our example.
# Each CoordSysTransform call SETS the current transformation
# to be the one named in the command.
# Rot120, refl.
CoordSysTransform "Rot120Refl"
ReadArchive "Pieces.dat"
# Rot 240 deg
CoordSysTransform "Rot240"
ReadArchive "Pieces.dat"
# Unit, refl.
CoordSysTransform "Refl"
ReadArchive "Pieces.dat"
# three more axis invocations..
# ..
```

Figure 5.40 *Objects placed in six named coordinate spaces*

We have now examined a variety of ideas involving translation, rotation and scaling transformations (and briefly looked at perspective and skew). Note that these are linear transformations, so-called since they preserve straight lines and not bend them. Rotations, scales and translations also preserve parallel lines and are hence affine transformations. In addition, rotations and translations are rigid-body transformations since they do not cause a scale change.

Nonlinear transformations cannot be expressed using combinations of translations, rotations and scales alone. Common examples of nonlinear transformations (deformations) include twist, taper, bulge, bend, curl, crack, crumple, fold, wrinkle, pucker, tear and telescope. These operations are carried out in host animation software and the deformed geometry is output frame by frame to the renderer. In other words, nonlinear deformations are baked into an object's geometry definition itself before it reaches the renderer.

In this chapter, all the transformations we encountered were applied just to geometry. These transformations can also be applied to cameras and lights in order to locate and orient them appropriately. In addition they can be applied to shader invocations. Coordinate spaces such as world, camera, shader and object are especially useful inside shaders for transforming spatial coordinates and vectors (e.g. the location of the point being shaded), for purposes of lighting and shading. We will look at an example of this in the chapter on shading (Chapter 8, "Shading").

6
Camera, output

A camera is an essential component of a renderer since it enables image synthesis from custom viewpoints. In this chapter we examine the basics of CG cameras and image formation.

6.1 Proxy viewpoints

Cameras act as substitute eyes, showing us images that we cannot see with our own eyes. Our visual culture is defined by images gathered from ubiquitous cameras. Cameras are used in a variety of fields and endeavors including news gathering, medicine, surveillance, industrial process monitoring, basic scientific research, advertising, interpersonal communications and of course, entertainment. The digital revolution is a big enabler of the plethora of images that surround us, by making still as well as video cameras smaller, cheaper and easier to use compared to their analog counterparts.

The world of moviemaking (and photography too) has been on the forefront of imaging technology right from the start. The evolution of motion pictures has paralleled that of image synthesis, as the movie makers have always been eager to incorporate the latest imaging advances into their work in order to wow audiences. Also, movie making, being a highly creative and experimental art form, has itself inspired picture-related innovations. Examples include camera design, film stock, projection technologies, camera rigs including remote-control cameras and motion control, blue-screen process, etc. It is no wonder that filmmaking and computer graphics (and digital imaging technology in general) have a similar symbiotic relationship.

Every renderer necessarily includes camera specification as part of its feature set. In other words, part of a scene description includes specifics about a camera which will be used as the viewpoint from which the output image is rendered. This is a crucial feature, as it lets us place and move our virtual camera at will through a synthetic environment. While being able to synthesize a still frame from any desired viewpoint is in itself useful, being able to do so when the camera is moving is even more advantageous. When you move your head from side to side, there is continuity in the images that you see, derived from your presence in the scene and motion of your "camera". A renderer likewise lets you derive CG imagery of a scene, using point-of-view (POV) and camera motion of your design. The images can be photoreal, meaning they are often indistinguishable from what a real camera might produce. This places enormous power in your hands, enabling you to derive imagery that can work in conjunction with, or at times replace, real-world images. At one extreme you can even use a CG renderer to output images impossible for real-world cameras to create. For instance you can set up your CG camera to rove through galaxies, rapidly making its way through the solar system on to earth, descending to human level to make its way inside an infant and ultimately into one of its red blood cells. The whole sequence can be done in a seamless fashion as one continuous move. Note that the magnitude of distance and scale spanned by such a CG camera is unachievable in the real world, so the camera move mentioned above might be good for a science documentary or a science-fiction movie but is not acceptable for conveying everyday reality. At the other extreme a renderer can be used to make subtle changes to existing imagery, where the alterations are so minor that they go unnoticed by the viewer. Or it can be used to render convincing stills for print advertisements, obviating the need for product photography (think liquor bottles, cordless shavers and watches).

Live action/CG integration forms the basis of the Hollywood visual effects industry, which it has perfected over the last 25 years. Effects that used to be tedious, expensive and dangerous to create using live actors and props are now routinely done inside the computer. RenderMan has been a big part of this shift in moviemaking, as you can see from the list of Oscar-nominated/awarded blockbuster films where it has been employed. Camera matching between live action and rendered images is vital to making their integration seamless. To that end, this chapter shows how you can manipulate RenderMan's camera.

By the way if you are intrigued by this line of work (CG imagery for movies or visual effects as a whole), read *Cinefex* magazine on a regular basis (every issue and every article is a treasure trove of effects techniques). Also, Ron Brinkmann's *The Art and Science of Digital Compositing* is a very good book that deals with specifics of working with digital images originating from CG as well as the real world.

6.2 Camera angles, moves

The default RenderMan camera is located at the world origin and points along the positive Z axis in a left-handed coordinate system (see Figure 4.81). Objects need to be placed in front of the camera in order to get rendered. This is accomplished by specifying an initial transformation that leaves the camera as-is and moves the world origin away from it to a location in front. Objects are then defined with respect to the transformed world origin.

This initial world transformation can either be specified before the WorldBegin statement, or immediately after, or both. This is illustrated in Figure 6.1 which shows a sphere with three highlights. The sphere is located two units away from the camera along the Z axis. The figure on the left can be obtained using one of several variations. The translation can be specified before WorldBegin:

```
Display "SplitTranslation.tiff" "tiff" "rgb"
Imager "background" "color" [0.94 0.94 .06]
Format 450 450 1.0
PixelSamples 3 3
Projection "perspective" "fov" 60
# Translate the world origin
Translate 0 0 2

WorldBegin

# light source, sphere
# ...
```

Alternately the translation can happen right after WorldBegin:

```
Display "SplitTranslation.tiff" "tiff" "rgb"
Imager "background" "color" [0.94 0.94 .06]
Format 450 450 1.0
PixelSamples 3 3
Projection "perspective" "fov" 60

WorldBegin

# Translate the world origin
```

```
Translate 0 0 2
# light source, sphere
# ...
```

The translation can even be split across WorldBegin, for example:

```
Display "SplitTranslation.tiff" "tiff" "rgb"
Imager "background" "color" [0.94 0.94 .06]
Format 450 450 1.0
PixelSamples 3 3
Projection "perspective" "fov" 60
# partial translation
Translate 0 0 1

WorldBegin

# more translation
Translate 0 0 1
# light source, sphere
# ...
```

In all three cases the image on the left of Figure 6.1 results. Likewise, an additional rotation about the Z axis (right of Figure 6.1) can also occur on either side of WorldBegin:

```
Display "SplitTranRot.tiff" "tiff" "rgb"
Imager "background" "color" [0.94 0.94 .06]
Format 450 450 1.0
PixelSamples 3 3

Projection "perspective" "fov" 60

# The rotation can be either here or across WorldBegin or
# split in seq. here or split across WorldBegin
Rotate 45  0 0  1

WorldBegin

# The translation can be either here or across WorldBegin or
# split in seq. here or split across WorldBegin
Translate 0 0 2
```

Where this initial world transform is specified does not matter because in all cases the world is ultimately transformed to camera space (where the camera is by definition at the origin) before the rest of the imaging steps can occur. The location of the initial transform does have conceptual value. If it occurs before WorldBegin, we imagine that it is the camera which is being transformed (where it is peeled away from the world origin and placed in the scene just like any other object or light). If the same transformation occurs after WorldBegin instead, we like to think that the camera is left in its default location and orientation and that the rest of the world is transformed to lie in front of the camera for rendering. RIB translators such as MTOR take the transforms that have been applied to the camera in the host animation software and convert them to equivalent world transforms to be placed before WorldBegin in RIB files. We will be following this convention for all the examples in this chapter (which again are online at the RfB site).

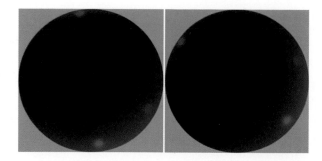

Figure 6.1 *Equivalence of camera or world positioning (see text)*

We are now ready to look at a set of basic camera moves such as zoom, pan, dolly and orbit. In a camera move, some aspect of the camera is varied over time, resulting in imagery that reflects this change.

Figure 6.2 shows the effect of zooming (note that a zoom is not technically a camera move but we will loosely refer to it as one). In a real camera zooming is obtained by varying the focal length of the lens. Lenses with short focal length (wide angle lenses) take in more of the scene spanning a wider viewing angle (left image, Figure 6.2). By aiming at the same spot while increasing the focal length (employing a narrow angle or telephoto or zoom lens) we are able to bring a small part of the distant scene into a closeup view, as can be seen in the other two images in Figure 6.2.

In RenderMan, you do not directly specify the focal length. Instead, the field of view (FOV) which has an inverse relationship with focal length is what is specified:

```
Projection "perspective" "fov" <field of view, in degrees>
```

The FOV is specified as an attribute of the Projection command which is used to select either perspective or orthographic projection. Of the two, only the perspective version has an FOV attribute. The wide FOV image at the left of Figure 6.1 is obtained using this RIB code:

```
Display "Zoom_40.tiff" "file" "rgb"
Imager "background" "color" [.36 .36 1.0]
Clipping 0.1 1000
Projection "perspective" "fov" [48.4555] # 40 mm
ScreenWindow -1 1 -0.74902 0.74902
ConcatTransform [1 0 0 0 0 1 2.98023e-008 0 0 0 -1 0 0 -2 15 1]
WorldBegin
# ...
```

The Projection command specifies an FOV of 48.45 degrees which is equivalent to a 40 mm lens (the actual formula that relates the two quantities involves the size of the image plane as well, and we will not go into that here). The middle image employs this line of RIB:

```
# ..
Projection "perspective" "fov" [18.59] # 110 mm
```

We are seeing less of the scene with a smaller FOV of only 18 degrees compared to 48.45 degrees in the previous case. The zoomed-in image calls for an even smaller FOV:

```
# extremely narrow lens
Projection "perspective" "fov" [11.75] # 175 mm
```

Wide angles are used in establishing shots where characters are shown situated in their locales. Note that extreme wide angles can introduce severe perspective distortions (e.g. the faces of a cuboid can appear to intersect at sharp angles instead of true 90 degrees). They must therefore be used within limits. Zooming into a scene is a useful compositional device where the wide-angle view establishes a shot's location, enabling subsequent views to zoom in on the character or action. In real life zoom lenses are useful when it is not possible to physically get close to the subject, as is the case when photographing war scenes, wildlife, celebrities or sports events. A zap zoom is a variation where the zooming is carried out so rapidly that the images show nothing but radial streaks spanning the edges of the frame to the center.

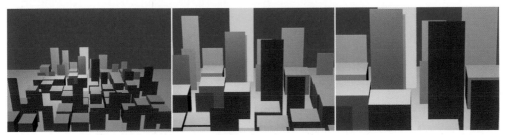

Figure 6.2 *Zoom*

The next camera move is a pan, where the camera is rotated from side to side. The top row of images in Figure 6.3 illustrate this move. The FOV is kept the same, as is the location (translation value) of the camera. The only change is in the rotation angle about an axis perpendicular to the view (turn your head from side to side while looking straight ahead and standing still). The images in Figure 6.3 are obtained from RIB files that are identical except for just the ConcatTransform statement that rotates the camera:

```
# first view
ConcatTransform [1 0 0 0 0 1 1.19209e-007 0 0 -1.49012e-008 -1 0 0 -
3 10 1]
# second view
ConcatTransform [0.984808 -2.62748e-009 -0.173648 0 4.96705e-008 1
1.58946e-007 0 -0.173648 -1.49012e-008 -0.984808 0 1.73648 -3 9.84808
1]
# third view
ConcatTransform [0.939693 -5.42358e-009 -0.34202 2.16943e-009
7.94729e-008 1 7.94729e-008 -1.77636e-015 -0.34202 -1.49012e-008 -
0.939693 5.96047e-009 3.4202 -3 9.39693 1]
```

Notice that the sizes or relationships between the objects do not change in a pan. Only their placement in the picture frame changes. Panning is useful for showing the surrounding areas of a main location or for going back and forth between two characters engaged in dialog. In our simple pan example the tops of the buildings are level with the image frame. A variation of this called the Dutch Tilt where the camera is inclined so that the subject matter and horizon are tilted. This is usually done for dramatic impact and variety.

The pan camera move is accomplished using pure rotation about the camera's "up" vector. This is also referred to as yaw. Likewise, in a roll the camera rotates about the view direction (this is when you cock your head or at the extreme, look at something upside down). Finally the pitch rotation is what occurs when you look up and down. The terms yaw, pitch and roll are normally used to describe an airplane's rotation about its center of gravity.

Just like a zap zoom, a swish pan is where the panning occurs so rapidly that it blurs all content. It is often used as a way to transition between scenes involving change of location.

Tilt-pan is a variation of the simple pan move and is shown at the bottom row of Figure 6.3. Here, there is some pitch in addition to the usual pan. Imagine panning left to right while looking down from the top of a tall building. Just like in a regular pan objects move across the image frame, but in addition they have a tilt when they are on the sides (but not at the center) of the frame. As an object passes from one side to the other its tilt changes orientation appropriately, straightening out as it passes through the center. Tilt-pans are naturally suited for tall viewpoints. The resulting tilt changes are used to add visual interest to what might be an otherwise unremarkable pan. As with the pan example, RIB files containing a tilt-pan will differ only in their camera placement ConcatTransform command.

Figure 6.3 *Pan, tilt-pan*

In Figure 6.4 are frames showing a dolly (also called truck) move. Here the objects look bigger as the camera physically gets closer to them. Compare this with zooming where the camera stays put. You can obtain dollying by translating your camera towards or away from the scene. Once again, only the camera's ConcatTransform will differ from frame to frame in the RIB files.

The words dolly or truck (or track) refer to the fact that a live action camera move of this nature involves placing the film camera on a platform with wheels and pulling it along towards the composition focus. Note that a dolly move yields a visually different result compared to a zoom. In a zoom, the relative sizes and positions of the objects do not change frame to frame. All the objects get uniformly bigger or smaller – in other words there is no change in perspective. In a dolly move, they do, as the distance change resulting from dollying causes a perspective change.

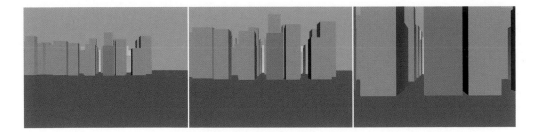

Figure 6.4 *Dolly/truck*

We just saw that unlike a pan which involves only a rotation, the dolly move requires net camera movement. Another such move is the orbit (Figure 6.5) which requires the camera to go around an object of interest all the while aiming at it (this is like a police helicopter circling overhead with its lights trained at a suspect on the ground).

Once again no RIB code is shown here because only the camera's ConcatTransform values change in an orbiting move (pan, tilt-pan, dolly and orbit involve only camera rotations and/or translations, which are compactly encoded in ConcatTransform statements).

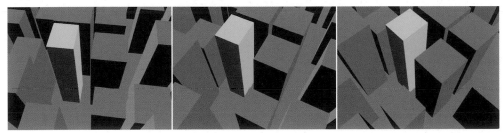

Figure 6.5 *Orbit*

Long shot, medium shot and closeup (LS, MS and CU) refer to framing of characters in a scene (Figure 6.6). In a long shot the subjects appear small and far away, with their surroundings visible. A medium shot is a little "tighter", the focus now being on the subject matter. A closeup employs even tighter framing, with the subject often filling the frame. In RenderMan you can obtain these shots by adjusting camera placement and/or FOV. Such stereotypical shots are a common part of the moviemaking vernacular and have been used in hundreds of movies and TV shows for identical purposes, namely setting locale (LS), establishing figures (MS) and showing expressions/detail.

Figure 6.6 *Long shot (LS), medium shot (MS), closeup (CU)*

So far our camera illustrations have employed the perspective projection in the form of the argument to the Projection RIB command. We have a natural affinity for perspective imagery since our own eyes act as perspective cameras. But there are situations where non-perspective projections are more suitable. The only such projection supported by RenderMan is the orthographic projection:

```
# ortho. projection - NO add'l attributes
Projection "orthographic"
```

The image on the left of Figure 6.7 shows an orthographic view of a set of buildings. Note that they appear totally flat. There are no perspective cues regarding the relative depth of the objects. Similarly-sized buildings very far from the camera will appear just as big as the ones nearby. It is as if the "z" (depth) axis has been discarded, which is basically what happens mathematically in an orthographic projection. It is the mathematical limit of a perspective projection where the FOV becomes zero and the focal length becomes infinite.

While a plain straight-on orthographic projection is not very informative, a variation called isometric projection (Figure 6.7, right) is useful in situations where perspective distortion of angles and shortening of lines gets in the way of comprehension. Note the precise 120 degree angles between orthogonal lines (which meet at 90 degrees in real space). Sometimes architectural drawings are shown this way. So are bar charts that have bars emanating from an area. Isometric views are also found in certain videogames (e.g. simulation games) where a "God's eye" viewpoint is used to depict a large area without distortion. Isometric views are most useful in engineering drawing where they are used to show mechanical parts without angular distortion.

Here is how you can create an isometric view. Try to use it with your own object definitions to see the result for yourself.

```
# ...
Projection "orthographic"
# ...

WorldBegin

TransformBegin
# the following rotations provide an isometric view
# the magic numbers are 30, 35.26 and 45 degrees, which are
# rotation values applied to Z, Y and X respectively.
Rotate 30 0 0 1
Rotate 35.26 0 1 0
Rotate 45 1 0 0
# usual object definition
# ...
TransformEnd

# ...
```

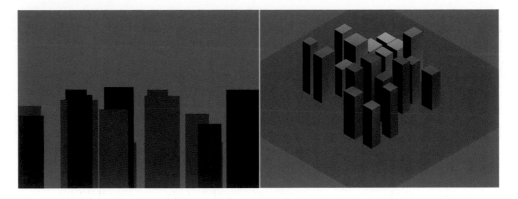

Figure 6.7 *Orthographic views: regular and isometric*

In Figure 6.8 are shown three frames illustrating Alfred Hitchcock's famous camera move from his *Vertigo* movie. Static printed frames are certainly not adequate to convey the startling nature of this move, you need to try it for yourself. The idea is that a zooming-in enlargement can be nullified by an appropriate dollying-out, and vice-versa. The result is unsettling as it violates common sense. Imagine running towards a building and finding that it does not grow bigger as expected. To add to the spookiness the buildings behind it would appear to undergo a larger-than-life perspective change, rapidly disappearing from your peripheral vision.

This camera move is referred to as a contrazoom or zolly or simply the "Vertigo effect". It is used to create a sense of falling or as a narrative device to show a character's altered sense of reality, e.g. when they experience life flashing before their eyes. You can easily mimic this effect by first creating a zoom and then compensating for foreground size change using a dolly move, adjusting the dolly to just cancel out any size change. You can also apply it to moving objects for even more impact.

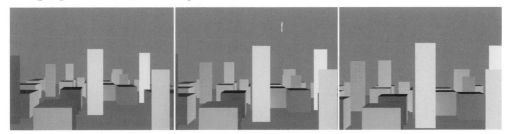

Figure 6.8 *Contra-zoom or "Vertigo effect"*

Several basic camera moves were illustrated in the above paragraphs. Proper positioning and movement of the CG camera are particularly essential in live action footage/CG integration, where the rendered imagery needs to look as if it were part of the scene filmed by the live action camera. While camera matching is a big factor in a successful blend of rendered images and live action footage, it is not the only aspect. Many other things have to match as well, such as scale, lighting conditions, shadows, reflections, motion blur, depth of field and even film grain, dust and scratches (which have to be added to the CG imagery as a post process).

Consult books on cinematography for a more in-depth look at the mechanics of camera placement/motion as well as for their motivating factors such as choice of subject matter or emotional impact on the viewer. Useful books include *The Five Cs of Cinematography* by Kris Malkiewicz, *Film Directing: Shot by Shot* by Steve Katz and *The Visual Story* by Bruce Block.

6.3 Camera artifacts

Motion blur is a phenomenon in which relative motion between camera and the subject causes loss of definition of the imaged subject, making it appear blurry or streaked. In other words, a camera, whether film or still, digital or analog, exposes its image plane for a short time interval to record its subject. If the subject stays still during this interval, a relatively clear picture is obtained. But if the subject and/or camera undergoes motion (translation or rotation, and in addition, arbitrary shape change for the subject) within the time interval, multiple overlapped copies of the subject gets imaged, and this shows up as blurs or streaks depending on the relative motion. It is a temporal sampling problem where the action is too fast for the camera. If it is a moving camera, capturing the action at a higher frame rate can alleviate the problem (when it indeed is a problem). For a still camera, using a faster shutter will help freeze the subject in the image plane, as is done in sports photography.

Our eyes do not exhibit motion blur, except maybe for motion trails ("acid trails") caused by hallucinogens. It is an artifact of still and film cameras and is sometimes used as a design element. Since we are so used to seeing them, at a subconscious level imagery that displays it somehow registers as true in our minds. CG renderers therefore need to provide this feature as well, although their cameras do not have shutters in the physical sense. The blur is algorithmically calculated, basically by simulating the relative camera subject motion, obtaining multiple temporal pixel samples representing shifted subject positions and averaging them via filtering.

RenderMan supports two types of blurs. The first is object-related, where the blur is the result of an object undergoing transformation and/or shape change. The other type is the camera blur where everything in the scene gets blurred because of an apparent camera motion. Both types of blurs are allowed to occur simultaneously.

Motion blur is very easy to specify in RIB, and is done via a motion block. A motion block is delimited by MotionBegin/MotionEnd statements and is similar in spirit to a transform or attribute block inside which it is usually nested.

Figure 6.9 shows motion blur resulting from spinning the letters making up "RenderMan". The rotation occurs perpendicular to the viewing plane, and the blur is classified as an object transformation one.

In the camera section of the RIB code, a Shutter statement defines the time interval during which the shutter is open. The smaller the interval, the lesser the blur will be. The image on the top left is created using the following Shutter statement:

```
# relatively fast shutter
# the first number is almost always 0, so the second value
# defines the shutter open time
Shutter 0 0.00231481
```

Next, in the world block, inside the attribute or transform block where the object is defined, the geometry definition is preceded by a motion block, which looks like this in our case:

```
AttributeBegin
MotionBegin [0 0.000462963 0.000925926 0.00138889 0.00185185
0.00231481]
ConcatTransform [1 0 0 0 0 1 0 0 0 0 1 0 -725 8.8784e-014 0 1]
```

```
ConcatTransform [0.999289 0.0376902 0 0 -0.0376902 0.999289 0 0 0 0
1 0 -724.485 -27.3254 0 1]
ConcatTransform [0.997159 0.0753268 0 0 -0.0753268 0.997159 0 0 0 0
1 0 -722.94 -54.6119 0 1]
ConcatTransform [0.994951 0.100362 0 0 -0.100362 0.994951 0 0 0 0 1
0 -721.339 -72.7622 0 1]
ConcatTransform [0.990461 0.13779 0 0 -0.13779 0.990461 0 0 0 0 1 0
-718.085 -99.898 0 1]
ConcatTransform [0.984564 0.175023 0 0 -0.175023 0.984564 0 0 0 0 1
0 -713.809 -126.892 0 1]
MotionEnd
TransformBegin
Opacity [1 1 1]
Color [0.999998274 1.000 0.137]
Surface "metal" "float Ka" [ 1 ] "float Ks" [ 1.600 ] "float
roughness" [ 0.200 ]
TransformEnd
PointsGeneralPolygons [1 # ...
# .. rest of geometry specification
AttributeEnd
```

The MotionBegin statement contains six discrete time values that span the shutter open interval. The ConcatTransform statements represent object transformations (rotations of our wheel-shaped object) at each time sample specified with MotionBegin. The motion block is followed by the usual material and geometry definition. RenderMan will use the ConcatTransform statements one at a time to create six snapshots of the rotation and average them to produce what you see. Note that the six ConcatTransforms are not used cumulatively, as would be the case if they were enclosed in an attribute or transform block instead. Because it is in a motion block, each ConcatTransform represents an instantaneous rotation at a discrete instant of time. The middle image in the top row of Figure 6.9 shows more blurring because the shutter was open for a longer time, and likewise for the rightmost image:

```
# values for middle image, top row, Figure 6.9
Shutter 0 0.00810185


# values for right image, top row, Figure 6.9
Shutter 0 0.0138889
```

You can experiment with transform blur using simpler combinations of Translate, Rotate and Scale commands if you like. If you do so, each statement needs to be in its own motion block, e.g.:

```
# Two consecutive motion blocks, indicating object translation and
rotation
# we provide three motion samples in each block
MotionBegin [0  0.5 1]
Translate 2 0 0
Translate 4 0 0
Translate 6 0 0
MotionEnd
MotionBegin [0  0.5 1]
Rotate 30 0 0 1
Rotate 45 0 0 1
Rotate 60 0 0 1
MotionEnd
```

```
#  ... geometry definition
#  ...
```

In our rotation example, we specified six time values and a rotation transform for each. The idea is that RenderMan images the six increasingly-larger rotations to average the result. As you can imagine, the more the intermediate samples we provide, the smoother will be the result. This facility is called multi-segment motion blur, and RenderMan supports it for transform blurs (but not for shape-change blurs discussed below). The bottom three images of Figure 6.9 show the effect of varying the number of intermediates. At the left we only specify two samples, two being the smallest possible sample count (there can be no blur without more than a single sample), the middle image is generated with three samples and the rightmost one, using six. Our situation is analogous to approximating a circle with a regular polygon. A square is a poor approximation, a pentagon and hexagon are better, but a 100-sided polygon (centagon?) is a much closer approximation since the vertices are more numerous and closely spaced.

As expected the quality of the blur increases with increasing sample count, and so does rendering time. Be aware that complex multi-segment blurs with several nested motion blocks can take a very large amount of time to render. This is partly because the number of subpixel samples (input using the PixelSamples command) might need to be cranked way up in order to generate an acceptable image, at times to even as much as 10x10. Alternately you could use smaller subpixel counts and use a blurrier filter such as Gaussian, for a smoother, smeared-out blur. Note that **PRMan** imposes an arbitrary upper limit of six, for the number of motion samples that can be provided.

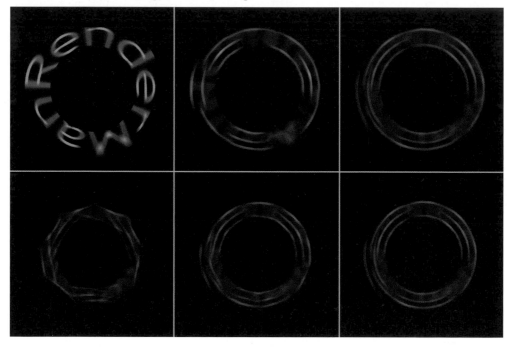

Figure 6.9 *Motion blur due to object transformation*

Motion blurring can also happen due to a shape change that happens via geometry definition as opposed to a transform-related change. The geometry change can be as simple as a sphere's radius increasing, or it can be a complex deformation involving **NURBS CVs** generated in your host animation program. In either case the idea is to use a motion block to enclose the pair of object definitions (remember, only two alternative shapes can be specified, not more). Shape change blurs are also referred to as deformation blurs.

Figure 6.10 shows our RenderMan letter object undergoing a shape change where the letters spread away from each other. The RIB calls to generate the blur are:

```
# ... camera section
Shutter 0 1

# world section
# ...

AttributeBegin
Opacity [1 1 1]
Color [0.999998274 1.000 0.137]
Surface "metal" "float Ka" [ 1 ] "float Ks" [ 1.600 ] "float
roughness" [ 0.200 ]
# motion blur related to shape change
MotionBegin [0 1]
ReadArchive "shape1.dat"
ReadArchive "shape2.dat"
MotionEnd
AttributeEnd
```

The individual shape definitions reside in external data files brought in via ReadArchive calls.

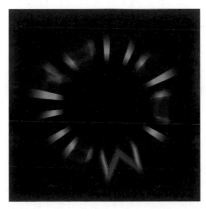

Figure 6.10 *Motion blur due to object shape change*

If there is a camera shake or a fast move (such as whip-pan mentioned earlier), everything in the scene gets blurred as a result. Figure 6.11 shows an example of this where the alphabet object is kept stationary, and the camera is spun (rolled). The core of the shapes appear intact, only their edges get streaked. The blur is specified just like for transform-based object blurs, except that the motion block is now in the camera section, before WorldBegin:

```
# ...
Shutter 0 0.0347222
Format 600 600 1
Display "Moblur_Cam.tiff" "file" "rgb"
# ...
Projection "perspective" "fov" [54.4322]
```

```
# ...
# camera-based blur
MotionBegin [0 0.0347222]
ConcatTransform [1 0 0 0 0 1 0 0 0 0 -1 0 0 0 14 1]
ConcatTransform [0.989475 -0.144702 0 0 0.144702 0.989475 0 0 0 0 -1
0 0 0 16.2187 1]
MotionEnd
WorldBegin
# .. lights, geometry, materials...
# ...
```

Figure 6.11 *Motion blur due to camera*

In the general case, the camera can undergo a motion while objects in the scene might also undergo transform blurs or shape blurs or both. Figure 6.12 contains such an example. The camera has a slight roll, the "RenderMan" object is undergoing a shape change while the "Rendering" object is moving left to right. You can see that the camera motion does alter the shape-based blurs. For instance the left to right motion plus camera roll makes the letters in "Rendering" appear to smear from top-left to bottom-right and not strictly left to right. The shape-change blur likewise is subjected to extra smearing thanks to the camera motion.

As mentioned earlier motion blur is a very important visual cue in motion footage, so if you attempt to composite a CG element onto motion-blurred live action imagery, you need to absolutely make sure to motion blur your CG element appropriately. At times this may seem like you are throwing away good modeling and animation by blurring it all. To add insult to injury, it takes a long time to calculate the apparent defacement. To offset things a little, you can make the shading rate for the motion blurred elements more blocky than usual, since fine details are going to be blurred away. You can even let RenderMan itself decide the level of coarsening, using the motionfactor approximation:

```
# no scaling of shading rate, which is the default
GeometricApproximation "motionfactor" 1.0

# shading rate scaled up, i.e. coarsened (values greater than 1.0
# cause shading rate to be scaled up)
GeometricApproximation "motionfactor" 2.5
```

Figure 6.12 *Motion blur due to object as well as camera*

Another camera artifact (or more precisely, lens artifact) is depth of field (DOF). Every lens has a depth range within which objects are in sharp focus. On either side of the range, they appear out of focus and hence blurry. Just like with motion blur, this optical limitation has been turned into a means of artistic expression and compositional device. If you want your viewer to focus on a certain subject, place them in the DOF range. The viewer has no choice other than to train their eyes on what is there, since there is not much to look at in other parts of the image. In motion picture work this technique of selective shallow focusing is known as focus pulling.

In real-world lenses, depth of focus is related to the camera opening or aperture just like motion blur is related to shutter open times. Aperture is measured in f-stop units. A very tiny opening that approximates a pinhole camera will give you a large DOF, while larger apertures will reduce the DOF range. f-stop numbers are inversely related to opening diameters, so larger the f-stop number, larger the DOF range and vice-versa. For a given object to camera focusing distance and an f-stop value, using a lens with a short focal length (macro lens) will give you a bigger DOF than a lens with a bigger focal length. So the focal length indirectly affects DOF.

RenderMan's DepthOfField RIB command specifies DOF as follows:

```
DepthOfField <f-stop> <lens' focal length> <focus distance [object to
camera]>
```

We would like to specify how deep the clear zone is, and where it should be centered. The first and third parameters to the command let us do just that.

Note that there is some redundancy in the command. Focal length is usually specified in the form of FOV via the Projection command (recall that focal length and FOV are inversely related). It therefore helps to treat the focal length value here in the DepthOfField command as a multiplier for the actual value specified via Projection. It is probably best to leave it at 1.0, but it can be altered if necessary to scale the DOF range up or down. Also, in real cameras, stopping down the aperture (making it smaller, i.e. increasing f-stop) will obviously cause less light to enter, making the image proportionately darker (this can be offset by keeping the shutter open longer, provided of course the subject and camera remain static). The RenderMan DepthOfField command however does not cause any brightening or darkening based on changes in f-stop values. The Reyes algorithm is not a true simulation of real-world lens optics, so naturally-linked effects can be decoupled this way. There is a separate Exposure RIB command that does control brightness, and we will be looking at that command in a bit.

Figure 6.13 shows DOF comparisons on a Spirograph™ NURBS surface render. The focus distance is kept constant at 2.5 units, and the focal length, at 1.0. The f-stop is the only thing that varies in the RIB files for the four renders.

The image at the top left is produced using:

```
Display "DOFSpiro_1.tiff" "framebuffer" "rgb"
# small aperture, wide DOF range
DepthOfField 6 1 2.5
Clipping 0.001 100000
Projection "orthographic"
# ...
WorldBegin
# ...
```

Note that DOF, being a camera-related effect, is applied to the scene as a whole (contrast this with motion blur which can be object-based) and is therefore specified before WorldBegin.

A value of 6.0 denotes a small aperture, and you can see that the entire object is in focus since the DOF range is quite high.

The other three images are created with f-stop values of 2.0, 1.0 and 0.675. A 0.675 value for f-stop signifies a fairly large opening, and this reduces the DOF range to a thin slice on the view direction. As a result only a small portion at the front of the surface is in focus, the rest are very blurry.

Figure 6.13 *Depth of field, effect of aperture change*

For a given aperture of 5.0 units and focal length of 3.5, the focus distance or lookat point can be varied over a scene (focus can be pulled) to bring selective parts into clear view. This can be seen in Figure 6.14, where the focus distance is moved from near to far, from 4.2 to 5.6 units. The images were created using these commands:

```
# makes 'Rendering' to be in focus
DepthOfField 5 3.5 4.2

# makes 'for' to be in focus
DepthOfField 5 3.5 5.0

# makes 'Beginners' to be in focus
DepthOfField 5 3.5 5.6
```

Figure 6.14 *Depth of field, focal distance change*

The RenderMan camera lets you use an arbitrary number of clipping planes inside your scene, to clip away parts of objects. While the near and far clipping planes are mandatory for a Reyes-like renderer for clipping unwanted objects, these auxiliary clipping planes are useful for some simple effects whereby you can make objects materialize/dematerialize in a scene. An example is shown in Figure 6.15 where a trefoil knot comes into view. The full surface was present in all four frames, and a clipping plane was moved from front to back over the four frames. The top left image was created using:

```
Display "ClippingPlaneSlice_1.tiff" "framebuffer" "rgb"
Imager "background" "color" [.53 .04 .04]
# this specifies the near and far clipping planes
Clipping 0.1 1000
Projection "perspective" "fov" [61.9275]
ScreenWindow -1 1 -0.75 0.75
ConcatTransform [1 0 0 0 0 1 0 0 0 0 -1 0 0.519097 -0.0519097 -
22.0139 1]
# user defined clipping plane!
TransformBegin
ConcatTransform [1 0 0 0 0 1 0 0 0 0 1 0 0 0 -29.3 1]
ClippingPlane 0 0 1 0 0 0
TransformEnd
WorldBegin
# .. rest of scene description
# ...
```

The ClippingPlane command is used to create a custom clipping plane:

```
ClippingPlane <plane_normal> <point_on_plane>
```

The plane normal identifies a direction (orientation) along which clipping should occur, while the point on the plane determines where in space the plane passes through (specifying just a normal is not adequate, since there is an infinity of parallel planes with that same normal). All surfaces lying in front of the clipping plane as determined by the plane normal are clipped away.

Note the the ClippingPlane command can be wrapped in a transform block, so it is wise to start with a default clipping plane pointed along Z and passing through the origin as shown in the above code block, and use Transform or ConcatTransform or Translate/Rotate statements to locate it appropriately). In our frames, the clipping plane is translated along Z, start with a value of -29.3, and on to -29.9, -30.5 and finally -32 units.

You can create multiple clipping planes and animate their locations and orientations, to obtain unique effects such as a gemstone being faceted.

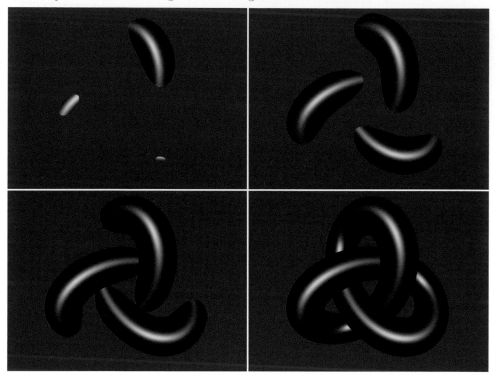

Figure 6.15 *Slicing an object using a clipping plane*

6.4 Output: frame

From cameras we now turn our attention to the rendered image. In this section we deal with the sizes and shapes of the output images and in the next, what type of pixel information is created.

Look around you for the variety of squares and rectangles used in day-to-day life. From building walls and door frames to posters to TV sets to books, rectangles serve as useful design elements. Rendered images are rectangular collections of pixels, so it is useful to consider rectangles in that context.

Figure 6.16 shows a collection of rectangles of various sizes and shapes. The square is of course a special-case rectangle where the width (breadth) equals height (length). From here on we will talk about rectangular frames in terms of width (along X axis) and height (along Y axis). In Figure 6.16 some of the rectangles (e.g. U.S. currency and Crown Quarto book) are specified in terms of absolute dimensions whereas for others (e.g. widescreen TV and CinemaScope film frame) are in terms of width to height ratio, also known as aspect ratio or more specifically, frame aspect ratio (FAR). Length and width dimensions can of course be divided by each other to be expressed as aspect ratios as well. For instance, currency notes in the U.S. can be seen to have an aspect ratio of 6.14"/2.61"=2.35, same as that of a CinemaScope movie frame.

Digital image sizes are measured in terms of resolution, which are pixel counts along width and height. For instance a 1K film resolution is 1024x768 pixels, a size which is known as XVGA when applied to monitor resolution. In conjunction with a pixel density value, e.g. 2400 dpi or dots/inch, pixel resolution can be equivalently expressed in linear dimension units, as is common in printing. For instance a 2400x3000 pixel image at 300 dpi is equivalent to 2400/300 by 3000/300, or 8x10 inches. Also, the total pixel count (pixels along width times pixels along height) is a measure used to quantify resolutions of digital still and video cameras.

In RenderMan the Format command in the camera section is used to specify pixel count along width and height:

```
Format <num_horizontal_pixels> <num_vertical_pixels>
<pixel_aspect_ratio, or PAR>
```

Ignore the PAR input for now, we will get to that shortly. The first two values are used to specify the output image size in number of pixels. In that sense, RenderMan is resolution independent. A scene can be rendered as a small 320x240 image for quick preview, 640x480 image for expanded preview and finally at high quality at 4096x3072 for output to a film recorder. The FAR in each case is the same (4/3 or 1.33), so we are keeping the composition the same and only scaling the pixel count up or down.

While not directly related to RenderMan, here is an interesting aside. A variety of digital content is increasingly created for viewing on widescreen TVs, which have a wider aspect ratio of 16:9 (4:3 squared along both dimensions) compared to standard NTSC ratio of 4:3. Widescreen enhances the viewing experience, especially while watching movies. The extra space is used by storytellers to stage their scenes better. What happens if you want to view standard 4:3 content (e.g. from an old videotape) on a widescreen TV? The common solution shown at the top of Figure 6.17 (implemented in hardware in the widescreen TV sets) is to position the narrower content at the center of the wider frame, leaving black vertical bars on either side in a practice known as pillarboxing. Conversely, how to convert widescreen content into fare for standard TV sets? The bottom row in Figure 6.17 shows two common alternatives. In the middle image, the widescreen frame has undergone a "pan and scan" (in the hands of a human editor) to undergo selective loss of content. In other words, a narrower 4:3 window is digitally overlaid on to the 16:9 image stream to crop out the area of interest in each frame. This is a subjective decision and can at times lead to content loss. The other solution shown at the right of Figure 6.17, called letterboxing, is to uniformly scale down the widescreen content to make it all fit in a 4:3 frame. The downside of course is that the images look smaller. TV broadcasters tend to use letterboxing to transmit widescreen content to older NTSC sets.

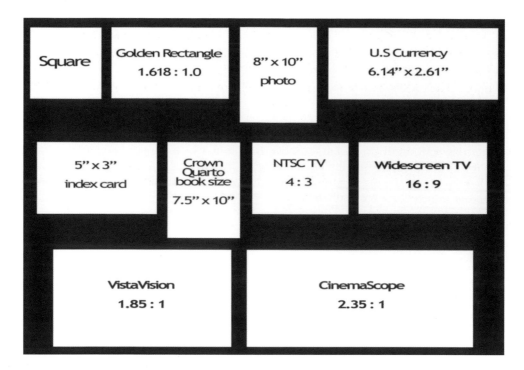

Figure 6.16 *Collage of rectangles with different aspect ratios*

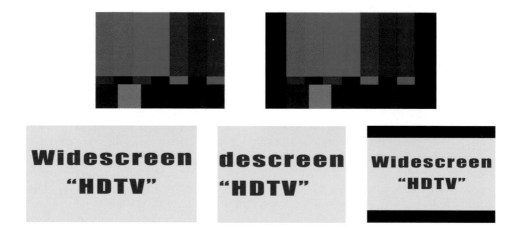

Figure 6.17 *Pillarbox, pan and scan, letterbox*

Another RIB command related to image frames is CropWindow. Regardless of actual resolution or frame aspect ratio, it is sometimes convenient to think of an image as having dimensionless unit width and height, in other words, as stretching from 0 to 1 horizontally left to right and also 0 to 1 vertically top to bottom. That puts (0,0) at the top-left corner and (1,1) at the bottom right. A subwindow can now be expressed in terms of this unit space by specifying fractional values for its diagonal corners. The CropWindow command takes such a subwindow as input, and causes RenderMan to render only the pixels belonging to that subwindow:

```
# Note that the corner values (xmin,ymin) and (xmax,ymax)
# are specified in a different order, namely xmin xmax first,
# followed by ymin ymax
CropWindow <xmin> <xmax> <ymin> <ymax>
```

Figure 6.18 shows a videowall-like collage of individual crop windows from nine RIB files. The CropWindow commands in the RIBs look like these:

```
# top left
# ...
Format 1200 900 1
CropWindow 0.00 0.33 0 0.33
Display "Teapot_CropWin_00.tiff" "framebuffer" "rgb"
# ...

# piece at the very center
# ...
CropWindow 0.33 0.67 0.33 0.67

# bottom row, middle image
CropWindow .33 .67 .67 1.00
```

The CropWindow command is useful in partitioning a single frame into subwindows, for simultaneous rendering on multiple machines. If the frame is complex and takes a long time to render, the time saved by rendering the pieces in parallel more than offsets the overhead of replicating the RIB data for all the processors and having to piece together the resulting cropwindow renders. A cropwindow is also useful if you want to isolate just a section of your scene for fine-tuning. You can keep rendering just the cropwindow over and over while working on its contents and not waste time rendering the rest of the frame.

Figure 6.18 *Assembly of crop windows*

We saw earlier that the Format command has three arguments, namely xresolution, yresolution and pixel aspect ratio (PAR). When we think of a pixel (either in the context of displaying it on screen or printing it onto paper) we correctly imagine it to be a little square. The PAR value in the Format command is most commonly left at 1.0 to reflect this. But there are cases when a non-square pixel (the use of which will make an image appear stretched or squashed when viewed on a regular monitor which has square pixels) is specifically called for.

For instance the NTSC D-1 broadcast resolution requires that each frame be 720x486 pixels, with each pixel having an aspect ratio of 10/11 or roughly, 0.9. 720/486 gives us a FAR of 1.481, and 1.481 times 0.9 is 1.33 which is the NTSC aspect ratio. A lot of times it is possible to get away with rendering 640x480 square pixels using

```
# bad way to create an NTSC frame
Format 640 480 1
```

but the right thing to do is this:

```
# correct NTSC frame, with proper resolution and PAR
Format 720 486 0.9
```

The two cases are shown in Figure 6.19 which contains a rendered sphere at the center. While the 640x480 image looks correct to us, the 720x486 is preferable since it conforms to broadcast quality specifications. Note that in the good image the sphere looks elongated by about 10%, as a result of each pixel being non-square. For broadcast the pixels are made square, so the sphere will appear correctly on TV monitors.

Figure 6.19 *Square and non-square pixel aspect ratios*

Another place where non-square PAR comes in handy is during the creation of anamorphic CG elements for CinemaScope. CinemaScope (or C-Scope) is an unusually wide movie format with a 2.35:1 frame aspect ratio. Shooting imagery in this format would call for non-standard camera and film size, raising costs. What is done instead is this. An "anamorphic" lens is placed in front of the recording camera, and lens squeezes the wide image to fit into a regular film frame of 1.33 aspect ratio. The squeeze factor is 2.35/1.33=1.767. During projection, another lens unsqueezes the image to make it come out right on the screen.

If you need to render CG to blend with squeezed C-Scope imagery, you could use a Format command with a PAR of 1.767. Alternately you could use the ScreenWindow RIB command:

```
ScreenWindow <xmin> <xmax> <ymin> <ymax>
```

For a landscape-format frame (where the width is more than height), <xmin> and <xmax> are -FAR and FAR, while <ymin> and <ymax> are -1 and 1. For example for a 640x480 image, the default ScreenWindow command would be:

```
# default values for a 640x480 image
```

```
# note that (xmax-xmin) / (ymax-ymin), which is 2.66/2.0, equals FAR
ScreenWindow -1.33 1.33 -1 1
```

Using the default values (or leaving it out) would produce square pixels with default framing if the Format command contains a 1.0 PAR. Any other values for ScreenWindow would alter the contents of the output image. Specifically if the ratio between the x range (xmax-xmin) and y range (ymax-ymin) is altered to not be FAR anymore, there will be a net squeezing or stretching of the image.

The image at the left of Figure 6.20 shows such an anamorphic C-Scope render. The image contains 400x300 pixels which gives it a FAR of 1.33. The ScreenWindow command looks like this:

```
ScreenWindow -1 1 -0.425532 0.425532
```

x range over y range is 2.0/0.851=2.35, which gives us the desired result of wanting to fit a 2.35:1 image on to a 4:3 frame. For comparison, the image at the right of Figure 6.20 shows the unsqueezed version. The ScreenWindow command is the same as before but the FAR now matches:

```
# FAR is 2.35
Format 705 300 1
Display "CScopeUnsqueezed.tiff" "framebuffer" "rgb"
Imager "background" "color" [.48 .02 .03]
Clipping 0.1 1e+006
Projection "perspective" "fov" [83.9744]
# (xmax-xmin)/(ymax-ymin) is also 2.35, so
# no distortion occurs
ScreenWindow -1 1 -0.425532 0.425532
```

Figure 6.20 *CinemaScope: anamorphic warp, no warp*

You can play with the values for ScreenWindow to pan, zoom or nonuniformly scale the default image formed on the film plane. See Figure 6.21 which contains frames with a FAR of 1.33. The top left image is the control case, with the following default ScreenWindow:

```
# 1.33 ratio, same as FAR, so no distortion
ScreenWindow -1.33 1.33 -1 1
```

The middle figure in the top row shows a zoomed in version, because of this ScreenWindow:

```
# 1.33 ratio as before, but zoomed in (smaller x and y range)
ScreenWindow -1 1 -0.75 0.75
```

At the top right is a zoomed-out version which is obtained by increasing the ScreenWindow's x and y ranges:

```
# bigger screenwindow, so more gets included in the output
# (the ratio is still 1.33 though)
ScreenWindow -2 2 -1.5 1.5
```

Note that the zoomed out image contains more content compared to the default image at the top-left. The same scene elements are used in all cases, and the default framing was unable to include letters on the periphery. Specifying a wider screenwindow causes more to come into view, at a smaller size.

At the bottom left is an image where the contents have been shifted by sliding the ScreenWindow away from the default center, while keeping the zoom factor and aspect ratio the same:

```
# instead of -1.33 to 1.33, we specify 0 2.66 instead
# to shift what's viewed
ScreenWindow 0 2.66 -1 1
```

In the image at the middle of the bottom row, the letters are squashed horizontally by increasing just the X range:

```
# Horizontal squashing by including MORE than the default -1.33 to
1.33 for X
ScreenWindow -2.5 2.5 -0.75 0.75
```

Finally, the bottom-right image shows vertical stretching by reducing the vertical range alone:

```
# Vert. stretching by including LESS than the default of -.75 to .75
ScreenWindow -1.33 1.33 -.5 .5
```

To summarize, the ScreenWindow command can be used to pan, zoom in/out or stretch/squash pixels by suitably altering its x and y ranges. A smaller range (compared to the default) in X or Y enlarges, while a larger range shrinks the result. Note that these image changes are not true zooms and pans in the camera sense. Rather, they are manipulations over the image plane. It is as if the image plane is elastic and you can cut any axis-aligned rectangle out of it and stretch/squash it to fit the output frame.

Figure 6.21 *Use of ScreenWindow to shift and zoom over the image plane*

6.5 Output: channels

Now we consider the Display statement which lets us specify just what to render and where to send the result. The basic syntax of Display is as follows:

```
# look up your RenderMan documentation additional options
Display <name of the image> <destination> <channels>
```

Since it applies to an image as a whole, the Display statement occurs near the top of each FrameBegin/End block and near the top of the RIB file for just a frame of data.

The first parameter names the image. This will be the name given to your image file if you choose to render to disk. The second parameter is what controls where the output goes. It names a display driver, which handles the rendered pixels. The two most common choices for the driver are "framebuffer" and "tiff". "framebuffer" will cause the pixels to appear on the screen in a rectangular window (whose size of course is decided by values in the Format statement). Nothing gets written to disk. The "tiff" or equivalently the "file" driver on the other hand creates an image on disk, in the popular and versatile TIFF format, and nothing appears on the screen. There might be additional image format drivers available (consult your documentation) whose names you can specify in the Display statement. For instance PRMan ships with drivers for writing out images in the Cineon, Maya IFF and Targa file formats.

Additional drivers can be created by end users with some programming experience. Not counting shader-writing, this is an example of end users being able to extend RenderMan (writing external programs to use with the Procedural command is another, as discussed in Chapter 4). For instance drivers could be written to directly send the render to a printer or even mail it to an email address. Or a display driver could blend the render with existing imagery and display the composite on screen to help make aesthetic choices about the render. It is more common however to write drivers for other image formats.

The third parameter in the Display tells RenderMan what information to render, and can be combinations of "rgb", "a" and "z", e.g. "rgb", "rgba", "a" or "az". Let us explore what these mean.

If the parameter value is "rgb", a standard three-channel image is created. RenderMan outputs the three common channels R, G and B by default, and this is quite adequate most of the time. If you need to obtain additional color components, using the ColorSamples call will let you do so.

In addition to the visible RGB channels, a fourth alpha channel can also be output, using "rgba" instead of "rgb" in the Display statement. Or if you need only the alpha channel you can specify it with just "a" instead of "rgba". A simple explanation for an alpha channel is that it holds information as to which pixels in the rectangular output contain actual rendered data, and which are filler (empty) pixels. The alpha channel is indispensable if you are going to use the rendered image in a compositing pipeline.

It works like this. Imagine a child drawing a tree on a piece of construction paper to create a collage. If she simply pastes the whole piece of paper on to the collage, the left over extra paper around her tree would also end up on the collage, blocking things underneath. Her solution would be to cut out the tree with scissors and use that for the collage. Her situation would not be bad if her tree was on a rectangular sticker, with clear plastic surrounding it. Then she could paste the whole rectangle on to existing artwork and still be fine. This is what we would like to do with digital images also. Somehow we want the non-useful pixels to drop out.

If our digital image is a photograph or a scanned live action frame, we need to somehow separate our elements from unwanted background. If the elements are surrounded by relatively flat color areas (e.g. if they were shot against a bluescreen or greenscreen), we can tell our image manipulation software to key out those colors, isolating our elements. In the worst case we can use selection tools such as the lasso to cut out our elements by hand, a very tedious process that also needs to be very precise. What we are talking about is somehow creating the alpha or matte channel, when one does not already exist.

With a renderer, it is possible to have the alpha channel generated as part of the rendering pipeline so that it does not need to be created as part of a post-render process. Since the renderer does calculations at the subpixel level, it can output a high quality matte which might even be impossible to manually recreate during post-processing.

Note that I used the terms alpha channel, matte and key to describe the same thing, which is that a fourth image channel can be used to hold coverage information for pixels in the RGB channels. The fourth channel is also referred to as the support, transparency channel or opacity channel (transparency and opacity are opposites). RenderMan stores the opacity of pixels in the alpha channel. A value of 1.0, or 255 in an 8-bit alpha channel signifies that the pixel is solid, i.e. fully opaque. If a pixel's alpha is 0 instead, it is a non-opaque, fully transparent pixel which will drop out during compositing. Values other than 1 or 0 signify fractional opacities, where the pixel's color will be partially visible and so will any background behind it.

Figure 6.22 shows a simple composite. At the top left is a photo and on its right, a teapot rendered with alpha channel as an RGBA TIFF file. The image is shown opened in Photoshop which uses the alpha information to drop out the non-teapot background, replacing them with its own checkerboard pattern. This tells us that the image is ready for compositing. If we had rendered only an RGB image and opened that, we would not see any checkerboard squares at all – the entire rectangle of the image would be considered opaque, and that would make it unsuitable for compositing.

The teapot is shown composited on the photo to make it appear to rest on Ian's RenderMan book. As mentioned earlier a host of factors need to be accounted for in order to make a truly credible composite. Ours is passable, and it illustrates the idea. With the matte channel, only the teapot is pasted. Without it, the whole image rectangle will be.

If the edges of a matte are sharp, the composited element will appear to stand out from its new background, ruining the illusion. This was a bigger problem in the old pre-digital filmmaking era when matting was done optically, where distracting matte lines around monsters or spaceships would break the intended suspension of disbelief. Collage artists soften their elements by tearing out edges by hand rather than with a sharp knife, and editors of supermarket tabloids use feathering to insert their fake elements into photos. RenderMan thankfully does a great job at anti-aliasing matte edges (alpha channels are treated identical to RGB channels for this purpose), so edge quality is usually never a concern.

Figure 6.22 *Alpha channel, compositing*

The "z" channel is specified using a special zfile driver, like so:

```
# 'z' depth image using the zfile driver
# alternately, "shadow" can be used instead of "zfile"
Display "teapot.z" "zfile" "z"
```

Instead of "rgb" or "rgba" we now have "z", and in place of "framebuffer" or "tiff", we have "zfile". The zfile driver produces a single channel image, where depth from the background at each pixel is encoded as a grayscale value. Surfaces closest to camera are brighter and those closer to the background, darker. Figure 6.23, top-left, shows a z-depth image of the Utah teapot.

The most common reason for computing depth images (which are also called depth maps) is for faking shadows during rendering. We will look at this in more detail later (Chapter 8, "Shading"). The z-depth image will be turned into a shadow map, which will then be used for shadow generation. Instead of first creating a depth image and then turning it into a shadow map using the MakeShadow RIB call, an alternative is to directly output the shadow map using the "shadow" driver:

```
Display "teapot.shd" "shadow" "z"
```

Depth maps are also useful in z-compositing, which is an operation featured in many image processing programs. The idea is to combine rendered RGB images using their depth channels instead of alpha channels. The operation uses the depth values to sort pixels front to back so that elements from different renders appear properly situated, depthwise. For instance a pillar can obscure one person in a crowd but not another, if its depth value happens to lie in between those of the two characters.

A more frivolous use is shown in the bottom of Figure 6.23, where you can see a color field stereogram (CFS). The CFS is computed using the depth image and a texture block (top right) which is tiled throughout the CFS, the tiling being suitably altered using the teapot's depth values. If you cross your eyes as you look at the CFS the teapot will appear to float in front of it. RenderMan offers the possibility of creating animated CFS imagery using z-depth sequences obtained through camera moves and/or shape transformation.

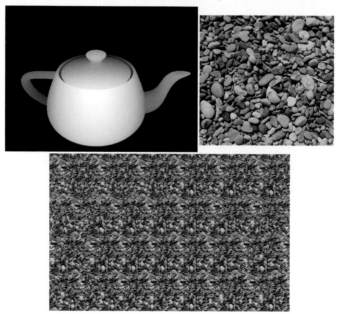

Figure 6.23 *Depth image from the "z" driver (top left), color-field stereogram (bottom)*

The bottom row of Figure 6.24 shows two different monotones of the Gumbo model. The one on the left was created using the rendered version shown above it, and the bottom-right image was obtained using the so-called normal vector image on the top right. A normal vector image is one where at each pixel, the surface normal is encoded as an RGB color (the surface normal, being a 3D vector, conveniently has three components from which R, G and B can be derived).

In older versions of PRMan, you would have to render the two images at the top row of Figure 6.24 separately. In other words, two separate render passes were required. PRMan now supports auxiliary output buffers, which means that in addition to the regular RGB image, any number of additional images (via auxiliary buffers) can be output in a single pass. This translates to huge savings in rendering time, especially if more additional images are needed. For example to render 3D scenes as if they were inked and painted in the style of traditional animation, it is common to obtain about ten different versions of a scene in each frame, image process the resulting ten images each frame to combine their information, deriving ink lines and paint regions in the process. The result of the so-called toon rendering process is that the final results look as if the images were painstakingly drawn and painted one frame at a time, when in truth all the effort went into setting up the 3D scene. Some of the pieces of information needed in each frame are as follows: shaded version, flat color without shading, brightness/luminance, texture coordinate distribution over the surface, normal distribution, depth from a given back plane.

It is very easy to set up PRMan for auxiliary buffer output. The shaded and normal vectors in Figure 6.24 were obtained using:

```
# ...
# regular RGB image
Display "Elephant.tiff" "framebuffer" "rgb"

## aux.buffer(s): the type of data that is written out
## first needs to be declared; also, the image name needs to
## begin with a '+' character; finally, the data needs to be
## quantized (scaled up and discretized from the internal 0.0 to 1.0
## floating point range)
Declare "Nn" "varying normal"
Display "+Elephant_AuxBuf_Nn.tiff" "framebuffer" "Nn" "quantize" [0
255 0 255]
# rest of the camera/image section, and then the
# scene after WorldBegin, as usual
Imager "background" "color" [.3 .3 .7]
Projection "perspective" "fov" 30
# ...
```

The magic is in the second Display statement, where the image name has a + in front of it. The + flags the output as an auxiliary one. Destination can be framebuffer or file as usual. The next parameter "Nn" specifies the type of data (surface normals, in our case) to be written out in image form. Following that is the "quantize" attribute which tells RenderMan to convert decimal values between 0 and 1, to integers between 0 and 255 (we will discuss quantization shortly). "Nn" is an always-positive version of the standard surface normal. I wrote a small shader to export this Nn data to RenderMan, for use in the Display statement above. What this exactly means will become clear in the chapter on shading. Any number of auxiliary attributes can be specified. Each needs to be in its own Display statement, and the first Display command always needs to be a regular ("rgb", "z" etc.) one. In other words you cannot request just auxiliary output.

One use for auxiliary buffers was mentioned above, which is toon rendering. Another is to separate out components of lighting into different images on disk. Ambient, diffuse and specular are three standard components which come together to create light distributions on surfaces (again, more on these in Chapter 8, "Shading"). By rendering these as separate images, we will have control over how to combine them in a compositor. Each can be blurred, tinted, lightened or contrast-enhanced independently and then combined. On the other hand if you do not separate them, you would need to incur expensive re-rendering costs if a small change needs to be made to just one component (e.g. the specular highlight needs to be softened a bit).

The technique of rendering multiple images in a single pass using auxiliary buffers is also referred to in literature as AOV (Arbitrary Output Variables) or MRT (Multiple Render Targets).

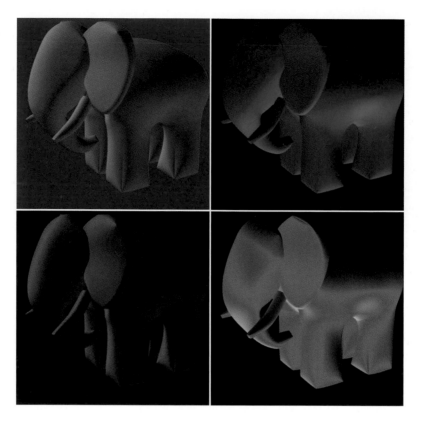

Figure 6.24 *Regular and normal vector (N) images (top) and their monotones (bottom)*

RenderMan features the use of what are called matte objects, which are pieces of geometry you would place in a scene to punch out holes in the matte channel. These objects do not show up in the render, and in addition they make the matte behind them completely transparent. The holes in the matte can be used to reveal other elements later in a compositing step. Any surface can be turned into a matte object using the Matte RIB command, like so:

```
AttributeBegin
# matte object
Matte 1
# geometry definition, e.g. a multi-sided polygon with
# rounded corners, to punch out a single sprocket hole
# ...
AttributeEnd
```

The film strip render at the top left of Figure 6.25 is created using matte objects to cut out the sprocket holes at the top and bottom, and to cut out the central area for another picture to show through. Note that in our simple case, this same image could also have been obtained in other ways, e.g. if the film strip were to be a NURBS surface, trim curves could have been used to cut out the shapes from the geometry. But in a more general case, arbitrary 3D geometry can act as matte objects, and their effect on the matte would be hard to obtain any other way.

The second row from the top shows how another image can show through the transparent, matted out areas in the film strip render. In a way the effect on the matte due to a matte object is the opposite of what you would like in a typical rendered element. For example in our teapot render for Figure 6.22, we only wanted the pixels belonging to the teapot and wanted to discard the rest. In the case of a matte object we want to discard the pixels belonging to the matte object by making the matte behind it transparent, and want to keep the rest of the rendered pixels.

What was illustrated above was a solid, fully opaque matte object whose effect is to make a clean hole in the alpha channel. You can also insert fractional matte objects in to a scene, where matte object is not totally opaque. For example it may have a shader attached to it where the shader calculates partial opacities for the matte object. Such a fractional matte object (again, made into one using the same "Matte 1" command) will not make the matte behind it totally transparent, but only fractionally so. A totally opaque matte object will make the alpha behind it totally transparent, and vice versa where a totally transparent matte object will leave the alpha behind it as is. In between these extremes, fractional results are obtained. The right image in the third row of Figure 6.25 shows the effect of a star-shaped fractional matte object. Behind the star, the transparency is not 100%. Rather, the colorful render of the square is partly visible. If this image is composited with a photo as shown in the last row, you can see that the photo does not totally show through, the way it did earlier with a fully matted out region. Here, both the photo is seen through the left-over, semi-transparent matte created by our fractional matte object.

In the auxiliary buffer Display statement discussed earlier, you saw how the "quantize" attribute was used to turn normal vector components into shades in the 0 to 255 range. The Quantize RIB command lets you set such quantization levels for the entire image:

```
Quantize <channels> <one> <min> <max> <dither>
```

RenderMan's default is to create 8-bit imagery, as if the following command were present in the RIB:

```
Quantize "rgba" 255 0 255 0.5
```

You can look up the documentation for precisely what the values mean, but here is a general discussion. The color (and alpha) information is written out with 8 bits or 256 shades of gray per red, green and blue channel, producing 24 bit RGB (8+8+8) images which can display any of 256x256x256 or about 16.7 million unique colors. Currently most monitors display color using 8 bits per channel or bpc, so rendering 8-bpc images is fine for these purposes. But film stock has a higher dynamic range or contrast, which is another way of saying it can record finer shades of gray, even upto 16 bpc or 65,536 unique values for each channel. Note that 65,536 shades per red, green or blue channel can combine to yield 281, 474, 976, 710, 656 colors (about 281 trillion). Working with a higher bpc is like being able to mix more subtle tints and shades of a given color. If RenderMan-derived 8-bit imagery is composited with images scanned from film at 16 bpc, at times the disparity in bit depth between the two can sometimes stand out. The situation somewhat like painting over a smooth airbrush contour with relatively flat poster paint, where the difference in contrast levels would call attention. The lack of bit depth in 8-bpc imagery becomes especially apparent at the low end of the contrast range. In other words if you composite a 8-bpc CG monster over a 16-bpc scan of candle-lit scene shot on film, you will likely notice some banding on the CG creature. 256 shades per channel from our 8-bpc image is simply not smooth enough to match film's fine gradations. To alleviate this, the CG image needs to also be rendered at 16 bpc. RenderMan internally computes everything using high precision floating point good for up to 64 bpc, so outputting 16 bpc is not a problem and can be requested as follows:

```
# use this statement in the image (camera) block of the
```

```
# RIB, to cause RenderMan write out 16 bpc images.
# if the output goes to disk, be sure to use the "tiff" or
# "file" driver
Quantize "rgba" 65535 0 65535 0
```

While the default quantization for RenderMan is 8bpc, the values in the Quantize statement shown above will produce 16 bpc instead. Note that the TIFF format is capable of holding 16-bpc values, so after quantizing channels the images can be written out as 16-bpc TIFF for processing in high-end compositing programs that can handle this bit depth.

The last value in the Quantize statement is a dither amount, which tells RenderMan by how much to randomly alter (or "perturb") the color and alpha of each pixel before doing the quantizing. A value of 0 represents no dithering, and a value of 0.5, a common choice for this attribute, specifies that dithering should be limited to a single shade up or down. Why take a nice rendered image and purposefully alter pixel values randomly in this way? It is done to reduce banding which sometimes crops up in the renders of smooth surfaces. The regular edges between the band contours are destroyed when pixel values are randomly, imperceptibly altered. This is somewhat similar to smudging a charcoal drawing using a stump to blend contours and smooth the shading. The idea is to exploit the observation that visual noise is a less objectionable artifact compared to banding.

RenderMan passes the raw floating point pixel values through an exposure calculation before doing the quantization discussed above. The core Reyes algorithm is oblivious to the characteristics of the output devices which will receive its calculated pixel values, and it should be. But after the calculations are done it would be nice for us to do an exposure correction on the result before committing the values into integer RGB data. Exposure correction means that we want to alter the brightness and/or contrast of the pixels to better suit them to the way the output device handles intensities. Exposure is specified using the Exposure RIB command:

```
# default is 1 and 1, meaning pixels are
# left unaltered
Exposure <brightness factor> <gamma>
```

The brightness factor, also called gain, is a simple multiplier for the brightness of all pixels. Gamma is a so-called non-linear factor, meaning that the same value of gamma alters brighter pixels differently compared to darker ones. Real-world things such as film, monitor, and printers have a nonlinear relationship between their input and output, and the gamma factor aims to model this sort of output response.

Figure 6.26 shows some exposure wedges so you can see the effect of gain and gamma. The top row which is our control data shows a strip of eleven squares whose colors vary from black (0.0) on the left to white (1.0) on the right, in steps of 0.1. No exposure correction is applied to these pixels. In the second row, the pixels have been brightened using:

```
# make each pixel 50% brighter
Exposure 1.5 1
```

You can see that all pixels have been brightened, and at the top range the gradations have all washed out to white. In the third row, the gamma is set to 2.0, leaving the gain as is:

```
# gamma correction, gain is unaltered
Exposure 1 2.0
```

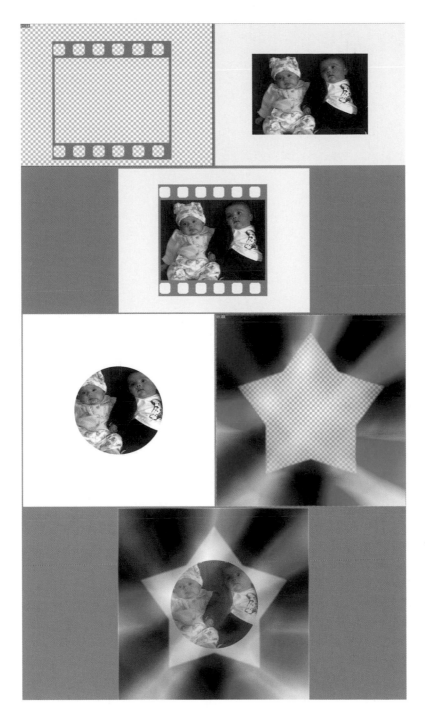

Figure 6.25 *Matte objects, solid and fractional*

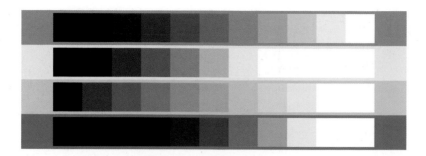

Figure 6.26 *Exposure wedges*

The gamma correction makes the contrast between adjacent steps higher, compared to the control case. Finally, the last row shows the result of both increasing brightness and decreasing gamma:

```
# simultaneous incr. in gain, decr. in gamma
Exposure 1.4 0.5
```

The decrease in gamma lessens contrast, and this coupled with the brightening causes values to flatten out both in the dark as well as bright areas. Only the middle four or five squares are resolvable as individual ones.

It is common to alter gamma for film work where the CG image needs to look as if it were really shot on film, but it comes in handy while viewing images on your monitor as well. If your renders appear to be too dark or in low contrast, try experimenting with gamma values between 1.7 and 2.7 in your RIB file. You should see a perceptible improvement in the displayed image.

6.6 Fun with cameras

In this section we will look at four relatively uncommon aspects of using a CG camera. The first of these is to use the camera to do a 360 degree nodal pan around a scene. In Figure 6.27 is shown such a cylindrical pan. The camera was rotated in increments on 30 degrees around its center, to obtain twelve renders of the buildings surrounding it. Since 30 degrees is a relatively small rotation, adjacent renders have buildings that overlap, making it easy to line them up in a program such as Photoshop. Note that wider angles would cause warping at the ends, making it more challenging to align the segments. The top row in Figure 6.27 shows the first six images pieced together, and the middle row shows the next six. These two pieces can be joined together for the full panorama shown at the bottom row. The full panorama represents an unwrapped cylinder. It is as if the scene surrounding us is projected on to the interior of a giant cylindrical ring which we cut open to break the circularity and make it flat. You could cut this panorama out from paper and glue the ends together, recreating the projection cylinder. The gluing can be done in one of two ways. The panorama can on the cylinder's inside, vaguely identical to Disney's "CircleVision 360" wraparound panoramas. Or it can be on the outside, reminiscent of the Zoetrope device which formed an early mechanical basis for cinema.

Figure 6.27 *Cylindrical (full 360 degrees) panorama*

Stereo renders can be obtained by rendering a scene from a pair of slightly different viewpoints. The top of Figure 6.28 shows a standard left-eye/right-eye stereo pair, of the trefoil knot surface. It was obtained by rotating (as in a pan) the left and right eye viewpoints relative to each other. Stereo pairs can also be generated by linearly separating the viewpoints or equivalently the scene itself, and we will see an example of this in the chapter on shading.

Relax your eyes and look in between the two trefoil surfaces in Figure 6.28, to make them fuse together. If you would rather do cross-eyed viewing you can turn the book around and focus your right eye on the left image and vice versa. Alternately if you have a stereo viewer it will make it easy to experience the stereo effect. Stereo rendered images are routinely used in high profile location-based entertainment (in so-called ride films), so this is a fruitful area to explore. By making small changes to the Projection and Transform commands in the camera section, you can experiment to your heart's content with optimal view parameters for stereo.

In the bottom of Figure 6.28 is an anaglyph stereo image, which requires red-cyan glasses to show the stereo effect. An anaglyph can be generated from a stereo pair by combining the R channel from the left image and the GB channels from the right. These glasses are easier to come by than stereo viewers, and you can even make your own with colored cellophane paper. The drawback of course is that the images are no longer in full color. You can try generating anaglyph sequences of animations in your scenes. They are fun to watch on the monitor but are even more impressive when projected on to a large screen.

Figure 6.29 shows a simple recreation of the classic slit-scan effect. This technique was pioneered by John Whitney and was modified by Doug Trumbull, Con Pederson and others for use in the trippy, unforgettable Stargate sequence in *2001: A Space Odyssey*. The effect is easy to describe. A large flat piece of vertically-mounted artwork is photographed with a motion-controlled camera standing in front, in a series of exposures all on the same film. The film is fully covered except for a small slit aperture which makes its away across the film end to end, in perfect step with the camera which edges closer and higher for each exposure. The resulting image has a wonderful curved perspective which can signify endless expanse of sky or earth. By optically layering a variety of images, magical sequences of colors and patterns can be produced, which you can see in the movie.

For *2001* the images were created using motion-control cameras and real-world artwork (which consisted of a medley of op-art, moire patterns, architectural renders, electron microscope images of organic and inorganic forms, etc.). As Figure 6.29 shows you could now set this up entirely in the computer. The classic technique involved flat artwork and a slit undergoing a simple linear motion but you can experiment with alternate surface shapes, multilayered textures and more complex relative motion between surface and camera. If you are interested, look up Greg Ercolano's pages on the web where he has deconstructed images from the Stargate slit-scan sequence using his own software, in an attempt to guess the source artwork.

The top of Figure 6.29 shows an enlargement of a single strip that went into creating the whole image. I set up the alphabet shapes in Maya and keyed the camera to approach the shapes while climbing, and rendered a sequence of 1024x2 (Format 1024 2 1) thin-strip images. I used the ImageMagick image-processing package to assemble the strips together (this resembles accidentally shredding an important piece of paper and piecing the strips together to recover the document). I needed to blur the assembled strips a little, to hide small mismatches at the edges.

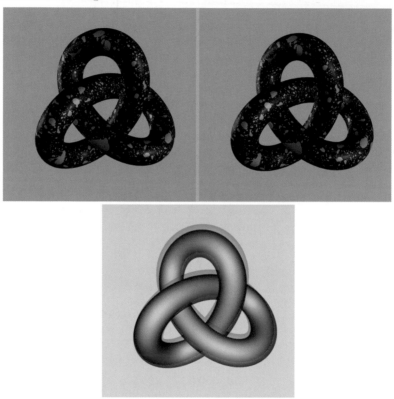

Figure 6.28 *Stereo images: left eye/right eye pair, anaglyph*

Figure 6.29 *Slit scanning*

Figure 6.30 shows sprites (also known as billboard textures) which are are small, relatively flat camera-facing surfaces. They can be polygons, bilinear surfaces or even patches. The idea is to texture each with an animated image sequence, e.g. of water splashes, foam, flames, smoke, etc. Complex volumetric-looking effects can be obtained by using a large number of sprites to fill the image frame and animating the sprites each frame. The combined animation of the sprites themselves and textures they contain leads to visually rich imagery which would be expensive to compute any other way. There is one other requirement to make this work, and that is to ensure that each sprite faces the camera in each frame. Sprites are usually generated using host animation software such as Maya, where the RIB translator inserts an appropriate ConcatTransform for each sprite to align it with the camera. So out of the infinity of possible viewpoints, the sprite collection looks correct only from that of the scene camera.

The top left image in Figure 6.30 shows such camera-aligned sprites. The image to its right shows the same, except that the underlying square shape containing the texture is purposely made visible in order to start giving away the illusion. You can see that the darkened shapes are all squares in various rotations, scales and translations. The bottom two images thoroughly spoil the effect by showing the sprites from other viewpoints obtained by moving the camera away to a sidewise location and to another in the back of the sprite group. Seen from these non-optimal viewpoints, the sprites are revealed for what they are, and it is not at all flattering to see the textures edgewise. It should be clear from looking at the bottom row that the sprites consistently need to be camera-facing, every one of them, in every frame.

In addition to camera applications mentioned above, there are several others to explore. Look up the term "multiperspective panorama" for a clever panorama technique that merges images containing multiple perspectives on to a single big layout. Also, animated 360 degree cylindrical imagery can be sequenced for playback to cycle through successive camera viewpoints, creating a freeze-frame effect popularized in *Matrix*. If you have access to a digital projector, experiment with large format images, stereo animations and projections on to curved surfaces. The experience could be useful someday for use with commercial formats such as IMAX, IMAX 3D or OMNIMAX (these are restricted trademarks).

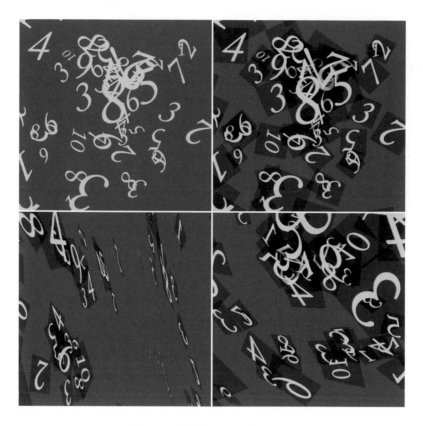

Figure 6.30 *Sprite imagery*

7
Controls

In this chapter we explore the knobs that come with RenderMan, for trading off rendering speed versus image quality or memory consumption.

7.1 Tradeoffs in rendering

Manufactured objects as well as human endeavor involve a familiar balance between quality, time and resource consumption. Conventional wisdom is that you can have two of "faster, cheaper, better" but not all three at once. If each of these measures is located at a triangle corner, the ideal compromise is to end up right in the center of the triangle.

This turns out to be the case in rendering as well, which involves tradeoffs between execution speed on one hand and memory usage or image quality on the other. Execution speed refers to the time it takes to render an image. Memory is the amount of RAM plus disk-based swap space required for image computation. Image quality is a subjective measure of what constitutes "good enough" in the rendered result.

The following sections deal with the controls that enable tradeoffs. Keep in mind as you read along, that a tradeoff is exactly that. A low-quality render is not necessarily an absolutely bad thing. If you are blocking out a scene by placing geometry, adjusting camera angles or fine tuning light locations, a poor-quality render that has a quick turnaround time is just fine. Conversely, if you are rendering final frames in a production environment for output to film, quality is of the utmost concern even if the frames take a longer time to render. The important thing is that RenderMan hands you these controls instead of locking them away deep inside code, out of your reach.

Several of the images in this chapter involve side-by-side comparisons of controls provided by RenderMan. I chose this format since it is an effective way to talk about them. Also, as usual, all the RIB files used to creates the images are online, and only relevant snippets of them are shown in the sections below.

7.2 Image-related controls

As you know by now the Reyes algorithm dices geometric primitives into grids of micropolygons whose vertices are shaded to create colors and opacities for output image pixels. Note for the record that a micropolygon is technically a bilinear patch but we will talk about it as if it were a polygon. Shading rate refers to the maximum area, in pixels, the micropolygons are allowed to have. It is the single most important control you have over image quality. The larger the shading rate, the more pixels a micropolygon will encompass in the rendered image and the larger the gap between adjacent micropolygon centers. It means that we are coarsely approximating our surface using fewer micropolygons that are larger, leading to a rather faceted look. Since shading is carried out at micropolygon vertices, rendering time is faster since there are fewer micropolygons to shade. Also, fewer hidden surface calculations are carried out, resulting in a smaller memory consumption to store the results of the calculations. At the other extreme, a small shading rate means smaller micropolygons that occur in larger numbers are used to better approximate the surface. Many more shading and hidden surface computations are needed, with a resultant increase in image quality and in rendering time as well. If you are not comfortable with the term "shading rate" it might help to think of it as shading frequency. Larger rates mean coarser frequencies while finer rates entail more frequent shading.

The effect of varying shading rate is illustrated in Figure 7.1 which shows three blobs rendered using the Blobby RIB command. The blobs at the top left are rendered with a shading rate of 1.0, which means that the largest micropolygon area will be about a single pixel. This produces an acceptable image in many cases. You would need to go to a smaller value such as .5 or even .25 if your render involves heavy displacements or detailed texture mapping. At the top right of Figure 7.2, the blobs have a shading rate of 100, so each micropolygon is about 10 pixels wide (square-root of 100). At 10 pixels in length individual micropolygons start to become discernible in the output (the image has a faceted look). As we continue to increase the shading rate to 300 and then to 3000 (bottom images, Figure 7.1) the micropolygons become much more prominent. The faceted silhouette at the bottom right is a telltale sign of too large a shading rate.

Shading rate is specified using the ShadingRate RIB command (an attribute):

```
# acceptable shading rate
ShadingRate 1.0
# .. geometry specification
# ...


# preview (lower quality) shading rate
ShadingRate 400
# ...
```

Figure 7.2 shows the same blobbies rendered with the same shading rates used in Figure 7.1, namely 1, 100, 300 and 3000. The images look significantly smoother, especially when the shading rate is 100 or 300. This is because the ShadingRate command is followed by a ShadingInterpolation command:

```
# preview rate with smooth shading
ShadingRate 300
ShadingInterpolation "smooth"
```

ShadingInterpolation command takes one of two values, "smooth" or "constant". The value "constant" means that a single color is used for an entire micropolygon, which gives the image a faceted look. This was the default, used in Figure 7.1. A value of "smooth" on the other hand specifies that at the interiors of a large micropolygon that spans several pixels, the colors at interior pixels need to be interpolated from the values calculated at the four corners by the shading process. It is such color interpolation that irons out the faceting. Gouraud shading is the term used to refer to color interpolation from polygon vertices, so the ShadingInterpolation "smooth" command causes Gouraud shading to happen at the micropolygon level (as opposed to shading primitives at the scene level). Note that a shading rate of 3000 is so coarse that even with Gouraud shading, interior faceting is still evident, and the silhouette too remains faceted.

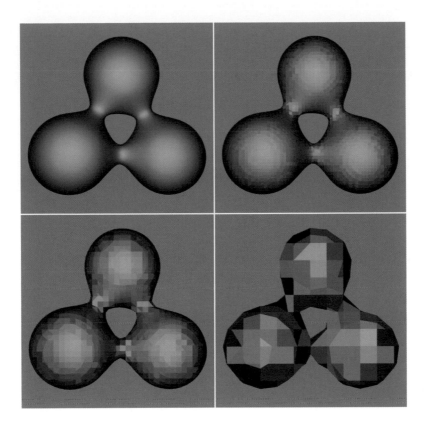

Figure 7.1 *Effect of coarsening shading rate*

Figure 7.3 shows three views of an idealized starfish shape made from five Penrose darts. On the left is a simple shaded view. The middle figure shows micropolygon grids. Each distinctly colored area shows a single grid (which contains an array of micropolygons bounded by shading rate). The rightmost image shows the micropolygons themselves (rendered with ShadingInterpolation "constant" to permit picturing of individual micropolygons). Keep in mind that every one of your primitives gets diced into such micropolygons for shading purposes.

The ShadingRate command is an attribute, which means it can be specified on a per-primitive basis:

```
# an attribute block with a shading rate specification
AttributeBegin
 ShadingRate 1.0
 # ... color, etc.
 # geometry..
 # ...
AttributeEnd
```

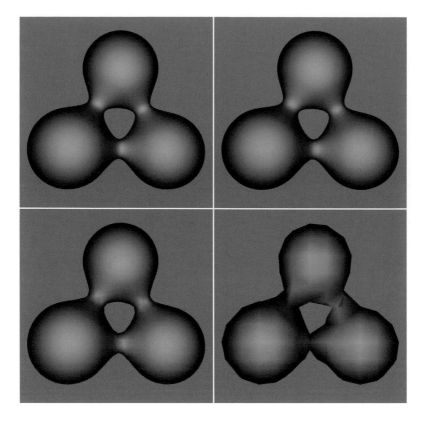

Figure 7.2 *Coarsening shading rate, with smooth interpolation*

Figure 7.3 *Penrose stars: shaded, micropolygon grids, micropolygons*

Figure 7.4 contains interlocked Borromean rings, where each ring holds the other two from coming apart. Notice that each ring in the image has a different shading rate (5, 300 and 800). It is of immense benefit to be able to customize shading rate per surface in this manner. If you are experimenting with inserting a new primitive into an otherwise-approved scene, the primitive can have a large initial rate during placement. Conversely if you are focusing on a single object (e.g. a character) you can make its shading rate smaller, leaving nearby objects with a coarser rate. Even in final renders, a chandelier with minute detail could be rendered with a fine shading rate, while the flat, smooth ceiling it is hanging from will render perfectly well with a much coarser rate.

Figure 7.4 *Borromean rings: each ring has its own shading rate*

Once micropolygons are shaded, the resulting colors and opacities somehow need to be transferred to pixels making up the output image. This involves the twin steps of sampling and reconstruction, which any digitizing process needs to reckon with. A small digression into basic digital signal processing is in order.

Figure 7.5 shows a 1D version of sampling and reconstruction. At the top-left is a signal, a graph of energy/strength/amplitude (say, audio) plotted against time in the horizontal axis. Maybe it pictures a single syllable spoken into an old-fashioned analog microphone. The important thing is that the waveform (signal, our curve) is smooth and continuous, generated by a real-world source. Imagine that we would like to convert the signal to a digital form suitable for recording to a CD. First we need to sample the signal, which means that we measure its strength at fixed time intervals. The middle figure in the top row illustrates this step. We take eleven measurements (white bars) where each measurement gives us a signal strength (proportional to the height of the bar). We can now throw away the original signal, since we have captured its essence in these eleven samples. We reconstruct the original curve by connecting the tops of our bars with a smooth curve, shown in orange (middle and right figures). The orange curve is now our sampled and reconstructed digital version of the original signal. The digital version does roughly follow the original, but certain fluctuations in the original are lost to the digitizing process. The digital reconstruction is smoother. Fluctuations in audio correspond to pitch (frequency), so if we played back the digital copy, we would not be able to hear the high frequency parts of the original signal. They have become a victim of the digitizing process. The bottom figures in Figure 7.5 show an even worse scenario – here we only extract five values, and the digitized curve looks almost nothing like the original. All the high frequency content is gone, what are left are low frequency "aliases". If you imagine a high-pitched note from a violin to be poorly sampled like this, the digitized low frequency output would sound like a bass/cello instead. The situation is not unlike the story of the six blind men who each touched different parts of an elephant and based on what they felt, argued about what it might look like. Again, there were not enough samples for an adequate reconstruction.

So how do we capture the input signal perfectly? The comparison in Figure 7.5 suggests that we need a lot of samples, an infinity of them for a perfect capture. A better question to ask is how not to lose the highest frequencies. If the sample spacing (also called sampling rate or sampling frequency) is high enough to capture every peak and valley in the signal, we are in business.

Formally, the Nyquist sampling theorem (proposed by Harry Nyquist in 1928) states that for adequate sampling, the sampling frequency needs to be twice or more than the highest frequency in the input signal. Conversely, for a given sampling rate (which maybe dictated by equipment, storage costs, time consumed, etc.), the sampled signal needs to contain as its highest frequency, half the sampling rate or less. If higher frequencies are present in the input, they will end up as low frequency proxies (aliases) in the output.

Incidentally, the high end of adult human hearing is around 22KHz (a high frequency whistle tone bordering on ultrasonic), so to properly sample everything that a human ear can hear, the sampling frequency has to be at least twice that value. This is why the CD-Digital Audio (CD-DA) "red book" standard from 1980 specifies a sampling rate of 44.1KHz.

The important consequence of the Nyquist theorem is that sampling rate imposes a limit on content to be sampled and conversely, the content places a lower bound on acceptable sampling frequency that will yield a faithful reconstruction. This is the case for any form of digitizing, be it audio, video, images, typography or CG rendering. Informal examples serve to illustrate the problem. You would be hard-pressed to paint a rich scene inside a 10x10 grid of squares (remember, each square can only hold a single color). Likewise for being able to sculpt a human face in detail using just 100 polygons. Or try to construct a straight line at 10 degree inclination using a coarse grid of squares. Take a 2 megapixel digital image and resize it down to 64x64 pixels. Finally, obtain video of a fast-spinning wheel and play it back to watch the spokes spin slowly backwards (the playback speed will affect the result, so 30 fps, 24 fps and 15 fps will all produce different variations of the artifact). What is common to all the above is that there is too much detail (high frequencies) and too little space or time steps (low sampling rate). The lack of adequate spatial sampling leads to stair-step artifacts called "jaggies". They are distracting enough in a still image but get worse with motion – the jaggies pop on and off at pixel locations or appear to crawl across moving imagery.

How does all this relate to rendering in particular? A scene with relatively smooth, continuous geometry needs to be rendered into a set of pixels, which is where the sampling and reconstruction come in. Once micropolygon grids are shaded, the grids get "busted" into individual micropolygons containing colors, opacities at the corners. Already some digitization has occurred as a result of this, and it is about to be compounded when the micropolygons' values need to end up inside pixels. As you know from Chapter 2, shaded micropolygons are sampled at pixel locations to extract color/opacity values from them. A single pixel can end up with contributions from multiple micropolygon vertices, and all these values are collapsed into one final color/opacity for that pixel. We now examine exactly how this is done.

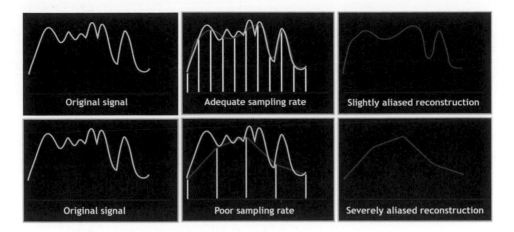

Figure 7.5 *Signal sampling and reconstruction*

Sampling amounts inside a pixel is specified using the PixelSamples RIB command at the top of a RIB file, like this:

```
PixelSamples <number of horiz. samples> <number of vertical samples>
```

In other words PixelSamples needs two integer inputs (usually the same value, e.g. 1 1 or 3 3, etc.) which are used to dice each pixel into smaller subpixel grids. PixelSamples 1 1 means that each pixel is retained as is, while PixelSamples 4 4 specifies that every pixel be divided into a 4x4 grid of 16 subpixels.

Each subpixel is examined for micropolygon contribution and colors/opacities potentially collected and accumulated for each. The logic is that fine subpixel features not near the center of a pixel will be missed if only one central sample is taken, but they have a better chance of being accounted for if several well-distributed samples are taken within the pixel.

As you can imagine this can lead to a lot of data, especially for finer subpixel grids. The tradeoff is that the resulting pixel color is more representative of the micropolygon fragments falling inside a pixel. Note that the procedure is also somewhat confusingly referred to as supersampling, even though the resulting grids are subpixel.

Sampling is illustrated in Figure 7.6. On the left, a 1x1 grid was used, leading to a characteristic jagged appearance at the edges. The same mesh was sampled using a 3x3 grid for the image on the right. The nine color samples inside each pixel were averaged together to produce the image (done with a box filter, discussed below). The result is markedly better. The pixels at the edges display a range of colors (specifically a range of values) which make the edges seem smoother. This is known as antialiasing (getting rid of the aliases or sharp discontinuities) through supersampling. We obtain better edge quality at the expense of more computations, about nine times as much for a 3x3 case compared to 1x1.

When a pixel is gridded and a sample collected from each grid cell, it matters where inside each cell the samples come from. If you look at the 2x2 grid in Figure 2.12, you can see that the four color samples C1, C2, C3 and C4 are obtained from an off-center, randomized location inside each cell. The regularity stemming from obtaining those samples at the centers of the subpixels leads to artifacts, so the sample locations are randomly shifted ("jittered") off-center inside each cell, leading to what is called stochastic sampling. Jittering manages to replace regularity-induced artifacts with noise (random variations) which is less objectionable to our visual system.

Jittering is specified at the top of a RIB file, like so:

```
# The Hider command specifies the hidden-surface algorithm
# "jitter" [1] turns jittering on, "jitter" 0 turns it off
Hider "hidden" "jitter" [1]
```

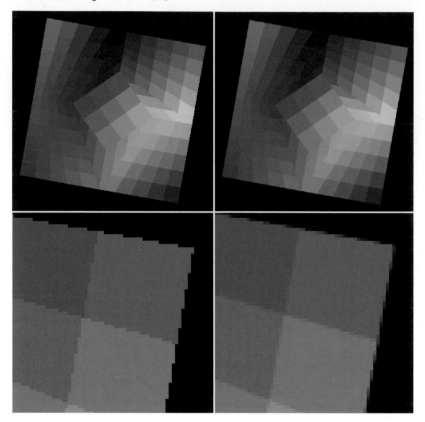

Figure 7.6 *Filtering, without and with supersampling*

Incidentally in Figure 7.6, the 1x1 sampling (single sample calculation per pixel) for the image on the left was done with jittering turned off. Turning it on for this case would have resulted in very ragged looking, broken edges (try it).

Note that supersampling increases the apparent sampling resolution (we use a finer grid) and not the actual target resolution (which might be fixed, at say, 640x480 pixels). In other words we calculate more than we need and systematically collapse the extra values into pixel colors and opacities. This might seem counter-productive but it does produce a better result than not supersampling at all. The reason is that the finer supersampling grid provides us with a higher Nyquist frequency limit which lets us sample finer details.

Supersampling is not a solution to totally eliminate aliasing. Aliasing is a fundamental artifact of the digital point-sampling process and will always be with us no matter how high of a target resolution we use or how fine our individual pixel dimension gets. Strategies such as supersampling help us reduce aliasing to more acceptable levels but never completely get rid of it.

Given a collection of pixels each with subpixel grids of colors and opacities, there are many ways to collapse subpixel values into a single color/opacity for each pixel. Such a pixel reconstruction step is also known as filtering, and RenderMan uses the PixelFilter command to specify what type of filter to use:

```
PixelFilter <filter type> <filter width,pixels> <filter height,pixels>
```

Figure 7.7 shows renders of a synthetic resolution target which is simply a collection of thin triangles arranged in a circle. At the perimeter the circles are separated enough but towards the center they converge, making contact in the mathematical sense only at the center. But we are dealing with discrete pixels, and near the center the pixels experience high frequency variations (triangle edges straddle them in close proximity) that exceed the Nyquist limit. This of course gives us a good way to compare how the various reconstruction filters behave.

At the top left is the 1x1 box filter, specified using:

```
# 1x1 box filter
PixelSamples 1 1
PixelFilter "box" 1 1
```

The filter width (how many pixels to take into account for reconstruction averaging) is usually matched with the PixelSamples values, here we have 1 1 for both. A single sample is taken inside each pixel and is simply output as the value for that pixel. This of course is the quickest and simplest possible reconstruction but gives poor results at high frequencies. In the middle of our top-left figure, the box filter creates a noisy output void of any detail.

Next up is the triangle filter, shown at the top right in Figure 7.7:

```
2x2 triangle filter
PixelSamples 2 2
PixelFilter "triangle" 2 2
```

Four subpixel values from sets of four pixels are blended together. The result looks better than the box filter but problems remain at the very center which looks just as bad as before.

The bottom images show the Catmull-Rom and Gaussian filters which involve progressively more blending and produce better results:

```
# 3x3 catmull-rom filter
PixelSamples 3 3
PixelFilter "catmull-rom" 3 3

# 4x4 gaussian filter
PixelSamples 4 4
PixelFilter "gaussian" 4 4
```

The 3x3 Catmull-Rom filter is a very good choice if you want to balance quality versus speed. A lot of sharp detail is visible almost right down to the center. The more expensive 4x4 Gaussian filter produces a softer look, where the pixels at the center form a mass of constant color (the high frequency noisy values have been averaged out and blended into a smoother result, too smooth in fact for some tastes).

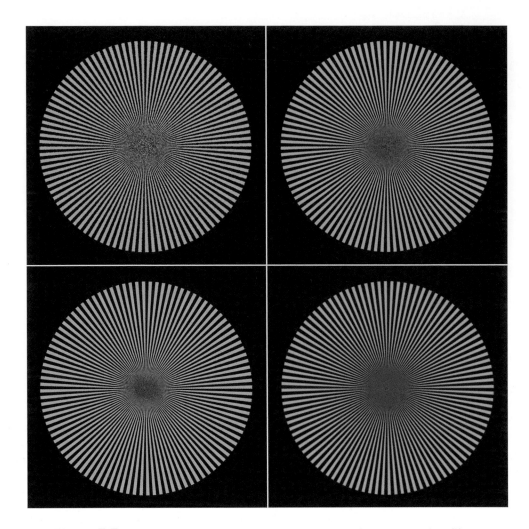

Figure 7.7 *Box, triangle, Catmull-Rom and Gauss pixel reconstruction filters*

Is a 1x1 box filter always bad? Not necessarily. Remember that pixel filters average samples produced using the PixelSamples command. This decoupling between sampling and reconstruction lets you play with different settings for each, making it possible to create a variety of looks. For instance a combination such as

```
# high supersampling, narrow box
PixelSamples 5 5
PixelFilter "box" 1 1
```

produces a sharp render as shown at the left of Figure 7.8, whereas

```
# low supersampling, wide filter
PixelSamples 2 2
PixelFilter "gaussian" 8 8 # !!
```

gives a softer, photograph-like render. Experiment with different combinations of sampling rates and filter types/widths to discover which you like best. For instance a different kind of sharp image will result from:

```
PixelSamples 4 4
PixelFilter "sinc" 4 4
```

While sharpness is achieved using a box filter by restricting it to a single pixel, the sinc filter performs sharpening using a 4x4 pixel grid of 4x4 subpixel values inside each pixel.

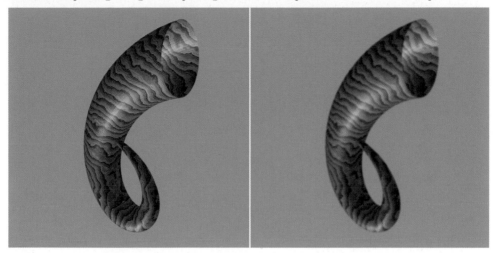

Figure 7.8 *Sharp vs. soft look effected through different sample and filter settings*

PixelSamples and PixelFilter are RIB options, meaning they are applied to an image as a whole (not per-object). They therefore appear at the top of RIB files in the image and camera specification section, before WorldBegin.

We saw that supersampling is one way to deal with aliasing. Another way to make sure that the scene being rendered does not contain high frequencies (details) in relation to the image resolution. To restrict content this way is of course not always possible. Alternately the image could be rendered at a higher resolution (actual pixel count) than necessary and then resized down to the actual desired resolution using an image-processing program. If the resizing is done using a wide filter such as a bicubic one, the result will be a softer, slightly-blurry image as compared to an image rendered at the desired resolution (in which case resizing is unnecessary). This works because resizing smears out the high frequency artifacts into neighboring pixels, reducing sharp contrasts into gentler ones.

7.3 Object-related controls

RenderMan offers a level-of-detail (LOD) facility which makes it possible to specify a set of representations of varying complexity for a single object. They are defined in such a way that the renderer can choose between them, depending on the object's distance to the camera. As a character runs away or objects recede from the camera, you can make RenderMan automatically switch to lower resolutions (say, polygon count) versions as the character occupies less and less pixel area in the output. It is a good time-saving device that can also reduce aliasing somewhat, since we are not forcing the renderer to turn a detailed model into a small blob of pixels as the object recedes.

Figure 7.9 shows an example where a sphere's distance from camera gets larger, and its representation switches between three inputs, from a smooth one to a faceted one and finally to an octahedron. Five steps in the animation are shown, each rendered from a different RIB file. The only thing that changes in the five RIB files is the object-to-camera distance. RenderMan automatically picks the right object based on pixels occupied by the object. The five images are read left to right, top to bottom. You can see that the second image shows a blend between the smooth and faceted spheres, and the fourth image likewise is a blend between the faceted sphere and the octahedron. It is as if the three objects are laid out next to each other and RenderMan travels from first one to the last, cross-dissolving between them as it passes in between.

LOD is very easy to specify:

```
#########################################
# The following translation is used to vary object-to-camera
# distance to make the various LOD alternatives kick in
# Z=3: Sph1
# Z=6.75: Sph1+Sph2
# Z=7: Sph2
# Z=9: Sph2+Sph3
# Z=11: Sph3
Translate 0 0 11
#########################################
WorldBegin
ShadingRate .5
AttributeBegin
Color [1 1 1]
Surface "show_sto" "blu" .5
# Detail is used to specify an object space bounding box (cuboid)
# which will be projected on to the image to determine pixel area
# occupied by our object. This pixel area is what will drive which
# of the alternative representations gets picked
Detail [-1 1 -1 1 -1 1] # bounding box
# LOD is just a series of DetailRange commands followed by
# geometry definition. LeechSph3.dat contains the octahedron,
# LeechSph2.dat contains a faceted sphere and LeechSph1.dat
# is the smoothest version.
# DetailRange takes four inputs, which are pixel counts (area)
# interpreted as follows:
# 1. if the object's actual pixel count is less than the first
# value, the representation is ignored. Sph3 is ignored below a
# pixel count of 0 (when the object disappears!), Sph2 is ignored
# below 30000 pixels, Sph1 is ignored below 80000 pixels
# 2. likewise if the pixel count is higher than the last value,
# the alternative is ignored as well. Sph1 drops out after
# 50000 pixels, Sph2 after 90000 and Sph3 after 1e38
# (1,00000....38 zeroes total, in other words, infinity)
# 3. if the pixel count falls between the second and third values
# of a DetailRange, the corresponding choice is the one
# (and only) that is picked. In between 0 to 30000 pixels,
# Sph1 is picked, in between 50000 to 80000 Sph2 is picked
# instead, and between 50000 and infinity, Sph3 is picked
# 4. finally, if the pixel count were to fall between values 1
# and 2 or values 3 and 4, the appropriate choice makes a
# fractional contribution. E.g. if our sphere occupies exactly
# 40000 pixels, Sph3 will contribute 50% and so will Sph2.
# by making these low and high transition regions overlap at
# adjacent DetailRange commands as shown, we can smoothly
```

```
# transition between the various choices.
DetailRange [0 0 30000 50000]
ReadArchive "LeechSph3.dat"
DetailRange [30000 50000 80000 90000]
ReadArchive "LeechSph2.dat"
DetailRange [80000 90000 1e38 1e38]
ReadArchive "LeechSph1.dat"
AttributeEnd
WorldEnd
```

The magic happens via DetailRange commands as explained in the above annotated RIB snippet. Each DetailRange command has two transition ranges, two dropoff (endpoint) values and a full strength range (all interpreted from four values). By overlapping the transition ranges and varying the size of the full-on range, we can precisely control which choice or choice pairs will be used as the object distance animates.

In addition to Detail and DetailRange, there is RelativeDetail option which acts as a global LOD scale factor:

```
RelativeDetail <LOD scale value>
```

Lower the scale value, more the emphasis towards the DetailRanges with smaller pixel counts. This command can therefore be used to cross-dissolve between LOD alternatives even as the object to camera distance remains fixed. Figure 7.10 illustrates this using our set of three spheres (incidentally, the sphere vertices were calculated using a triangle subdivision algorithm by Jon Leech):

```
#########################################
# Try these values for RelativeDetail: 1.0, .5, .4, .2 and .1
RelativeDetail 1.0
#########################################
Translate 0 0 5
WorldBegin
ShadingRate .5
AttributeBegin
Color [1 1 1]
Surface "show_sto" "blu" .5
Detail [-1 1 -1 1 -1 1]
DetailRange [0 0 30000 50000]
ReadArchive "LeechSph3.dat"
DetailRange [30000 50000 80000 90000]
ReadArchive "LeechSph2.dat"
DetailRange [80000 90000 1e38 1e38]
ReadArchive "LeechSph1.dat"
AttributeEnd
WorldEnd
```

When RelativeDetail takes on values of 1.0 (full detail, normal LOD), 0.5, 0.4, 0.2 and 0.1, the cruder approximations are weighted more, causing the object to dissolve in place from one LOD choice to an adjacent one.

Figure 7.9 *Level-of-detail, varying distance to camera*

GeometricApproximation is a command that might come in handy if your object is a subdivision surface which contains severe displacements. The command is used to specify a flatness threshold, which causes RenderMan to approximate primitives such as subdivision surfaces so that the approximations (which could be bilinear patches, polygons, etc.) are flatter than the given threshold. In other words, a small value for flatness will force a finer object tessellation. Note that we are talking about actual object tessellation, not micropolygon gridding. So if you notice that your primitives are not as smooth as you would expect or if there seem to be artifacts related to displacements, you could try lowering the flatness threshold.

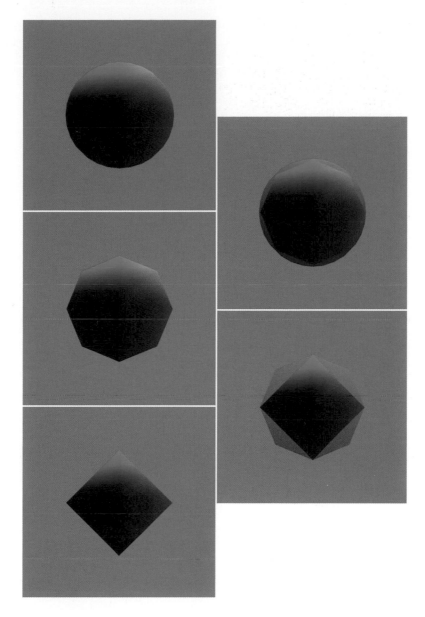

Figure 7.10 *Level-of-detail, varying the RelativeDetail value*

An example is shown in Figure 7.11 where a conical subdivision surface has been displaced using PRMan's "threads" shader:

```
# shader
Displacement "threads" # ....
# flatness threshold: 0.1 is "good" (right column, Figure 7.11),
# 3.5 is "ok" (left column)
GeometricApproximation "flatness" .1
# geometry specification
SubdivisionMesh "catmull-clark" # ....
```

The pair of images on the left illustrate the effect a coarser threshold of 3.5, and the pair on the right are rendered using a threshold of 0.1. You can see that the images on the left display artifacts (look at the serrations on the top left, near the tip of the cone). The top image uses a marble shader and the bottom one, a diagnostic shader that creates fine stripes. The images on the right show that the artifacts disappear at a finer approximation threshold of 0.1. The difference in our example is not very dramatic. But when it is, the control is there to address the problem.

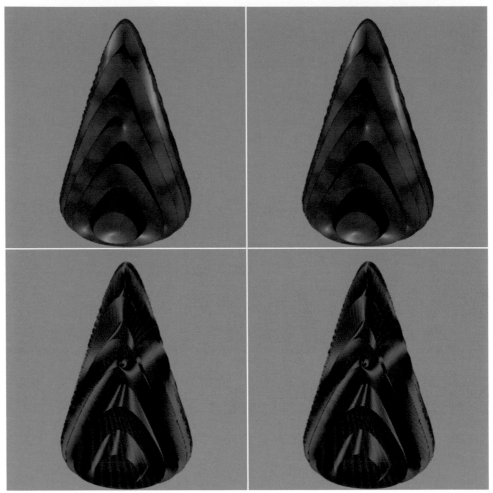

Figure 7.11 *Affecting tessellation through GeometricApproximation*

7.4 REYES-related controls

In addition to the image and object controls we have seen so far, PRMan's Reyes algorithm offers some other controls as well.

A feature of Reyes is that it renders an image in rectangular pixel blocks called buckets (Figure 7.12). This is a memory-related feature, in that micropolygon collections and (sub)pixel sample lists are dealt with on a bucket by bucket basis, placing an upper bound on memory consumption. When micropolygons straddle pixels across adjacent buckets, they are forwarded to the neighboring bucket to continue being processed there. Large bucket sizes enable large grids of micropolygons to be held in memory and processed at once, which makes for efficiency. The downside is that the process is memory-intensive. Conversely very small buckets are easy on memory, but they can only hold small collections of micropolygons and are hence not as efficient. On one extreme the entire image (say, 1024x768 pixels) can be a single large bucket and on the other, each bucket can be specified to hold just a one pixel. Neither of these limits is practical, and real-world choices fall in between.

Figure 7.12 shows renders with two bucket sizes. The images are screenshots of the renders happening on screen. The step at the bottom of each image shows the next bucket about to be painted on screen. The image on the left uses 32x32 buckets, specified at the top of the RIB file using:

```
Option "limits" "bucketsize" [32 32]
```

The right image uses larger buckets of 64x64 pixels:

```
Option "limits" "bucketsize" [64 64]
```

The optimal bucket size depends on how much memory you can spare, and the general advice to make the bucket size as large as possible (values in excess of this will degrade performance by causing disk thrashing). 16x16, 32x32, 64x64 are usually acceptable values.

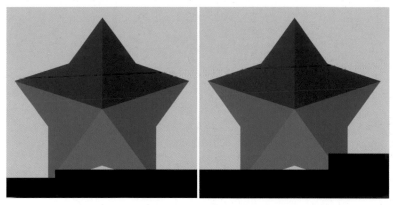

Figure 7.12 *Small and large bucket sizes*

Another control closely related to bucket size and shading rate is grid size. While shading rate is equivalent to micropolygon area, grid size is simply an integer micropolygon count. As you know primitives are diced into grids which are collections of micropolygons, and shading occurs at the vertices of these grids (where adjacent micropolygons share vertices before being busted apart for sampling). You also now know that rendering occurs in pixel blocks called buckets. For maximum efficiency, we would like to create grids with just enough micropolygons to fit inside a bucket so that they would not need forwarding to adjacent buckets. Given that bucket size and shading rate are both measured in pixel units, the optimum grid size is simply "bucket size/shading rate". For 16x16 bucket size and a shading rate of 1.0, the ideal grid size is 16x16/1 which is 256. Since each pixel on average will contain a micropolygon (which is what a shading rate of 1.0 implies), we are saying that each grid should hold 256 micropolygons so that they completely occupy a bucket. On the other hand a 16x16 bucket size and a shading rate of 32 (bigger micropolygons) would imply a smaller grid size of 16x16/32=8. The micropolygons are so big that a grid containing just eight of them will fill a bucket.

Grid size is specified with the gridsize option, e.g.:

```
# each grid needs to hold about 1024 micropolygons
Option "limits" "gridsize" 1024
```

Grid sizes can be nicely visualized using a built-in shading language call, as shown in Figure 7.13 where we are zoomed into a teapot lid. Given a shading rate of 2.0 and a bucket size of 16x16, the ideal grid size is 16x16/2 which is 128. This is shown at the upper left in Figure 7.13. Each small colorful piece is a distinct grid, which will hold about 128 different micropolygons each about 2 pixels in area.

Since the ideal grid size in our situation is 128, what would happen if we specify a grid size of 32 instead?

```
# suboptimal grid size
Option "limits" "gridsize" 32
```

RenderMan will make grids any size you want, and the 32-micropolygons grid can be seen at the top right of Figure 7.13. The grids are smaller (remember, the micropolygon sizes have not changed, only their count has) and hence more numerous. As was pointed out above, smaller grids are less efficient – since all micropolygons in a grid are shaded at once, the bigger the better.

Alternately, the grid size value can be increased beyond the optimum value, e.g. to 512 and 1024 in our case:

```
# superoptimal grid size
Option "limits" "gridsize" 1024 # or 512
```

You can see the results at the bottom of Figure 7.13. If there is sufficient memory to hold all the data, these larger grids are preferable to grid sizes of 128.

Note that bucketsize and gridsize are memory-related performance controls that have no bearing on image quality. The different settings discussed above will all yield the same quality, some more efficiently than others. Image quality is mostly dictated by shading rate and pixel sampling and filtering specifications.

There are situations where a piece of geometry will get uncomfortably close to the renderer's camera, at times passing right through it. In other words the geometry leaves the viewing frustum (see Figure 1.22), penetrates the near clipping plane, travels through the buffer zone separating the clipping plane from film (imaging) plane and finally passes through the image plane so its tip ends up behind the camera. This can happen, for example, when you render space debris or big rocks that fly past the camera. It can also happen if you place the camera close to the ground plane almost parallel to it. The math underlying perspective projection assumes that objects being projected lie in front of the camera, not behind. Parts of our object become unrenderable because of this, and the renderer needs to deal with the eventuality.

The standard solution to this in scanline rendering is to use the near clipping plane like a knife and make a smooth cut through the offending geometry, separating it into two parts – one that is now totally contained in the frustum and therefore renderable, and the other that falls outside and can be discarded. But the standard solution does not work with the Reyes algorithm where primitives need to be split until they are small enough to dice and shade. So a single cleave through the clipping plane is approximated via a series of splits – the primitive is repeatedly split in two, creating a cascade of smaller and more numerous pieces in each splitting step. The resulting pieces are examined to decide which to keep for shading and which to discard.

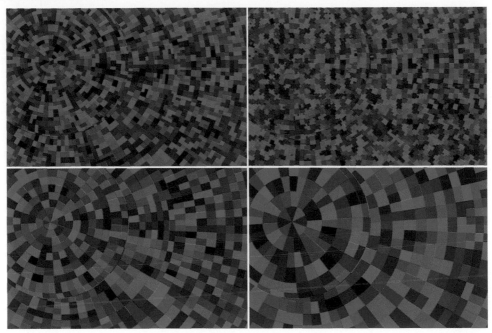

Figure 7.13 *Various sizes of micropolygon grids tiling the lid of a teapot*

The "eyesplits" frame-level **RIB** option is used to specify the splitting level or count. See Figure 7.14 for an example, where a cone that has displacement shading on it (to create the bumps) is shown at three different eyesplits levels 1, 2 and 3.

```
# level-3 eyesplits
Option "limits" "eyesplits" [3]
```

On the left is a level one split, meaning the object is split just once, and the piece that is kept is rendered. You can see in comparison to the middle image that the hole in the middle has sharp, angular protrusions, showing that at level one the splitting is only a crude approximation to a clean slice. The middle column is better due to an additional split at level two. Compare this with the right column that shows level three splitting, where there is no appreciable change in the silhouettes. In other words, the third level is an overkill, two levels are just fine for this situation. The bottom images show shaded views and the top ones, micropolygon grids. The shaded images mask the fact at level three many more grids than adequate are produced (this situation is comparable to a suboptimal grid size value), something that is clearly visible in the grid images.

If you encounter eyesplitting, be careful to specify the smallest adequate value for splitting. Values much larger than that can make RenderMan appear to freeze as it ends up creating a very large number of splits (e.g. try the displaced cone example with eyesplits of 10). Note that the "eyesplits" option will be eliminated starting with PRMan version 12.

The standard Reyes algorithm performs high-quality hidden surface elimination with good antialiasing and can correctly account for motion blur and transparency. All this is possible due to the use of an A-buffer which has an alliterated expansion of "adaptive, antialiasing, area-averaging accumulation buffer". It meticulously book-keeps subpixel micropolygon fragments to create a good result. If you have a scene which does not require these features, you can ask for a standard Z-buffer algorithm instead. The image quality (edge antialiasing) will be lower but the rendering will be faster. This choice of default versus Z-buffer hidden-surface algorithm is specified via the Hider command. Figure 7.15 shows four spheres rendered with the standard (called "hidden" in the Hider command) hider on the left and the Z-buffer ("zbuffer") one on the right. In the Z-buffer case the edges show lack of antialiasing but otherwise the images are comparable.

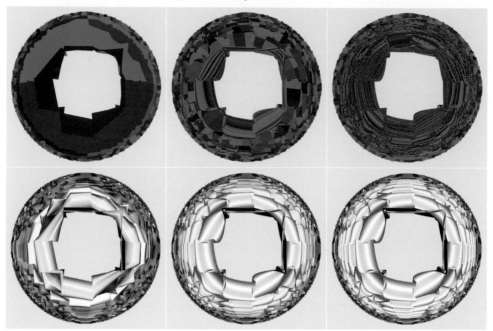

Figure 7.14 *Varying eyesplits*

"hidden" and "zbuffer" are the hiders that currently ship with PRMan (not counting the "photon" one used for global illumination). These two hiders are specified using the following RIB commands:

```
# standard hidden-surface elimination
Hider "hidden"
# simpler, Z-buffer
Hider "zbuffer"
```

Consult your renderer's documentation to see if the "hidden" hider might include implementation-specific options you can play with (e.g. in Section 7.2 we talked about turning jittering on/off in PRMan via the Hider command).

7.5 Miscellaneous controls

As you work more and more with RenderMan you are likely to encounter errors during rendering. A variety of things can cause errors – incorrect RIB syntax, correct syntax but illegal values, missing inputs such as shaders, textures or ReadArchive files, running out of resources such as memory and disk space, errors during the rendering process such as the eyesplits problem, etc.

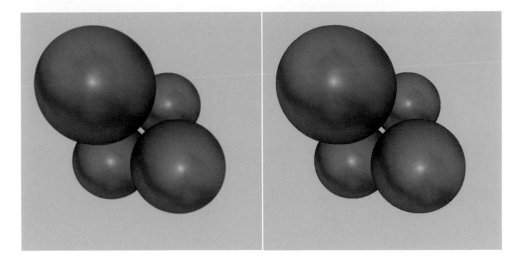

Figure 7.15 *Default vs. z-buffer hidden surface algorithms (hiders)*

RenderMan has an ErrorHandler command for specifying how you would like errors to be dealt with. It takes one of three arguments namely "ignore", "print" or "abort", whose meanings are self-explanatory. Note that "abort" causes RenderMan to abort only during severe errors. In other cases it behaves more like "print".

Here is an example to illustrate how error handling works. The leftmost image in Figure 7.16 shows the Gumbo elephant model properly rendered using these statements:

```
Surface "showPN" "fpx" 1 "fpy" 3 "fb" 12 "fr" 40 "fg" 5 "fny" 5
Patch "bicubic" "P" [10 2 0 10 2 0 14 2 0 14 2
# .. rest of the elephant model definition...
# ...
```

To create the middle image we hide or delete the showPN.slo shader file. At the top of the RIB file we include the following error handling directive and issue the render command:

```
ErrorHandler "ignore"
```

RenderMan silently renders the surface with its built-in headlight shader, ignoring the error that the actual shader is missing. Changing the error handling to

```
ErrorHandler "print"
```

and re-rendering produces the same grayscale image, but now a diagnostic message is printed out on the render window:

```
S01001 Cannot load shader "showPN". (WARNING)
```

Changing the error handling yet again, to

```
ErrorHandler "abort"
```

still generates the image (RenderMan does not abort) and produces the same S01001 warning message shown above. Next we put the shader back but deliberately remove the value for FOV:

```
# missing FOV angle!
Projection "perspective" "fov"
```

When the RIB is rendered we get the rightmost image in Figure 7.16 for two out of the three ErrorHandler choices. The "ignore" directive causes RenderMan to quietly render the image shown. The "print" option prints the following message and also produces the same render:

```
P79014 RIB syntax error (at line 11 in Elephant.rib, last token
OPERATOR(Transform)).
```

The "abort" choice too outputs the above error message but no output is created. Upon encountering the rather severe error, RenderMan prints the error message and simply exits.

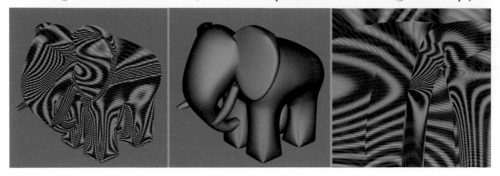

Figure 7.16 *Elephant: proper render, missing shader, missing FOV value*

If you like to know the details of how a frame is rendered, there is a statistics option that you can invoke:

```
Option "statistics" "endofframe" <output level>
```

Output level is a value that can be 1 or 2 or 3, depending on how much information you want.

Rendering the elephant model with Option "statistics" "endofframe" [1] produces output (after the frame is done rendering), that starts like this:

```
Rendering at 1024x1024 pixels, 2x2 samples
     "Elephant.tiff" (mode = rgb, type = framebuffer)
     Memory:          4.29 MB
     Real time:       00:15
     User time:       00:11
     Kernel time:     00:01
     Max resident mem: 13.05 MB
     Page faults: 44803, Peak pagefile usage: 43.54 MB, Peak paged
     pool usage:  0.04 MB
```

The statistics then go on to report memory breakdown in the form of a table.

Changing the reporting level to 2 includes in addition to the above, primitive count, grid count and shading information. Level 3 statistics adds to this extra texture information (not relevant in our elephant example) and more data on hidden surface elimination. Note that the information generated using level 1 should be adequate for a beginner.

8
Shading

In this chapter we talk about the look of things in a scene, achieved via small programs called shaders. The shading system in RenderMan is one of its best features. This chapter illustrates the diversity of looks that can be obtained using shaders.

8.1 Introduction

Coloring, lighting, shading and texturing are all terms used in 3D CG for talking about surface appearances. In the physical world, light interacts with a variety of materials in fascinating ways, leading to a rich visual diversity. From the translucency of a leaf against sunlight to the glint of a gold ornament, optical phenomena fills our environment. We handle an assortment of natural and human-made materials in our day-to-day lives, not paying special attention to how they interact with light. Likewise, we also encounter many types of light sources, ranging from sunlight and overhead lamps to car headlights and LED flashlights. Again, we take light for granted, for the most part not caring about how it illuminates objects. It is only under special circumstances that we specifically notice a material (e.g. when it is used to fashion sculptures) or light (e.g. when it is used in theatrical or cinematic settings) itself. Artists tend to see the world as an interplay of form, light and space. In rendering we are concerned about the interaction of form with light, and associated visual phenomena.

Every renderer offers facilities to simulate the richness of real-world surface/light interaction. The degree to which this can be achieved depends on the complexity of the renderer, and the extent to which it is under user control is a measure of the renderer's flexibility. RenderMan excels on both counts, offering superior image quality (which is borne out by the fact it is routinely used in movies to create photorealistic imagery) as well as a flexible, powerful and fun shading language with which users can write custom programs called shaders to impart the look of countless materials to their scene geometry.

What follows is a broad sampling of RenderMan shaders. This chapter is organized somewhat differently compared to the rest of the book. The emphasis here is on imagery (there are exactly 100 images in this chapter) which illustrate the range of possibilities offered by the shading system. While there is a subsection (8.4) on the shading language, this chapter is not a complete introduction to writing shaders. The rest of the chapter is more like a picture book, with comments that accompany the images presented. The RfB web pages will serve as a place for expanded, annotated versions of the material presented here. As usual, you will find everything necessary to recreate the images yourself, at the RfB site. Specifically, all the shaders discussed in this chapter are online. So if anything here interests you in these pages, feel free to download the relevant shader, study it, and modify it to suit your own needs.

In RenderMan, there are five different types of shaders. Surface shaders are attached to pieces of geometry, to impart surface appearances. You can think of surface shaders as the CG equivalents of materials. Displacement shaders do not really shade anything (using the word "shader" to denote them is a misnomer). What they do is to displace micropolygons, thereby altering geometry. Light source shaders simulate light emission and are therefore used to illuminate scene elements. Atmosphere shaders act on the volume that contains scene objects, imparting or altering object colors. Finally, imager shaders come into action after an image is rendered via the 3D pipeline, serving as a postprocessor.

Note that there is nothing special about the fact that RenderMan has these five shader types. Other renderers might have additional/alternate types. For example, Mental Ray also has contour, lens and other shaders in addition to the RenderMan shader types. What is important is that shader programmability exists in the first place. As you are about to see, that lets you create visual interest in your scenes. In comparison, less capable renderers only come with a few built-in shaders, severely limiting the imagery you can create with them.

Figure 8.1 shows all five types of shaders in a single image. The stellated polyhedral object has a wood surface shader and the floor, a marble one. The polyhedron is distorted (notice the bent edges) using a displacement shader. A spotlight shader illuminates the object and floor, while a smoke atmosphere shader dims the scene a bit by adding smoke into the spotlight beam (I am using Larry Gritz and Tony Apodaca's smoke shader presented in their *Advanced RenderMan* book). An imager shader fills with blue, the non-rendered regions on either side of the floor and wall surfaces.

Figure 8.1 *Sampler illustrating all five types of RenderMan shaders*

What is interesting is that without these shaders, the image will be all black. Every single pixel's color comes from the calculations carried out in the shaders. The conceptual underpinning of programmable shading is the notion of a shade tree, presented by Rob Cook during SIGGRAPH 1984. It is an elegant idea, which basically says that surface appearances can be built from the ground up using a hierarchy of primitive "look-building" blocks. This is a lot like how models can be constructed using geometry hierarchies, and complex motion can be composed using simpler motion constructs.

Figure 8.2 shows the shade tree for the common plastic surface shader. The appearance is idealized to be built up as a summation of flat, diffuse and shiny (specular) responses to light that falls on a plastic surface. We will discuss terms such as diffuse and specular later in section 8.5 but their meaning should be intuitively obvious to you. The figure also shows, on the top right, the RenderMan shading language program (known as the plastic shader) embodying the shade tree that is pictured. Do not worry about the shader code right now, it will hopefully become clear later. Just keep in mind that those few lines of code are what constitute "plastic" in RenderMan. If someone looks at the topmost teapot in Figure 8.2 and does not think that it looks like plastic, they have the choice of coming up with (writing) their own better version that replaces the one shown. So keep this fact in mind as you look at the rest of the images below. If you feel that something you see can be improved upon, go for it. In fact in all my examples for this chapter I chose simplicity and ease of presentation over complexity and completeness. My rationale is that if you understand the stripped-down versions, you can always add bells and whistles later.

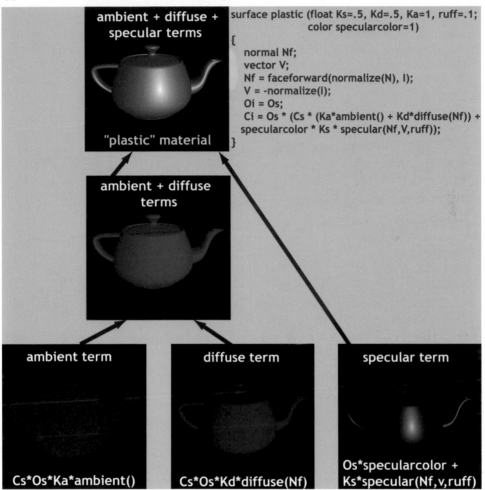

Figure 8.2 *A shade tree for the plastic shader*

The next two sections contain a few more examples of the five shader types, to ease you into the world of shaders. Following that (in section 8.4) is a brief introduction to the shading language. The five sections that follow after that (8. 5 through 8.9) contain a more in-depth look at each type of RenderMan shader. I had a lot of fun creating these shaders and using them to come up with the images, hope you too will derive joy out of learning how they function and eventually adapting them for your own use.

8.2 Using light shaders

This section and the next discuss shaders from a user's point of view as opposed to that of someone who would create (write) them. The premise is that you can still get a lot out of shaders if you learn how to take shaders written by others and use them in your own RIB scenes. You do not necessarily have to learn how to create them via programming. That being said, the full power of shaders can be at your fingertips if you do invest some time learning how to write them yourself. It is not that shaders are hard to program – they are not.

Using an existing shader in your RIB file is very easy. All you need is a compiled form of the shader, usually a small file on disk. Shaders are computer programs written in a text-based (human readable) language called the shading language, and then handed to another piece of software called the shader compiler. If your shader text file (referred to as "source code") is free of syntax (grammatical) errors, the shader compiler will create a new file from your source, for use by RenderMan. This file creation step is called compilation. In PRMan such compiled shader files end with a .slo file extension.

When you name a shader in your RIB file, PRMan will look for the corresponding .slo file when it renders your RIB. For instance to create the flat image on the top left of Figure 8.2, you would add this line at the top of your RIB file, somewhere right after WorldBegin:

```
LightSource "ambientlight" 1
```

The keyword LightSource signifies that you are specifying a light shader. "ambientlight" is the shader you are going to use, so you would need the compiled ambientlight.slo file available to the renderer if you are using PRMan. ambientlight.slo happens to come bundled with PRMan, so your own copy is not needed. The "1" denotes the light ID or light handle, which by the way can also be a string instead of a number (more on this later).

Figure 8.3 illustrates the four canonical lights that are part of RenderMan implementations. As mentioned, the top-left light is an ambient light, which imparts a flat, uniform look to surfaces. A scene lit only with ambientlight shaders will be devoid of any variation in light and shade. It is good for bringing up the overall illumination in a scene, since most surface shaders simply add the ambient light colors to the rest of shading calculations.

The top-right image shows a directional light source (called distantlight), where the light's actual location does not affect how brightly it illuminates a surface – only its orientation matters. The distantlight RIB call looks like this:

```
TransformBegin
Attribute "identifier" "string name" ["directionalLightShape1"]
Transform [-0.770091 0.231542 -0.594431 0 0.454474 0.853029 -0.256504
0 0.447675 -0.467685 -0.76214 0 -15.2184 7.90594 2.57382 1]
LightSource "distantlight" 1
TransformEnd
```

At the bottom left is a pointlight, an omnidirectional source. It shines equally brightly in all directions, and does dim surfaces as it moves away from them (therefore its location matters).

Finally at the bottom right is a spotlight, which sheds light only inside a cone centered at its location. It is directional (like distantlight) but also has an intensity (brightness) falloff (like pointlight).

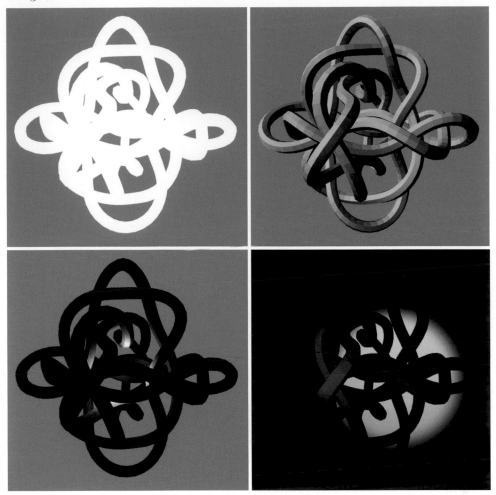

Figure 8.3 *The four basic light types*

Figure 8.4 illustrates the effect of light placement. The first three images show Gumbo lit by a single directional light from the top, bottom and front, respectively. Notice that each lighting choice imparts its own mood to the image. The fourth image shows uniform illumination, achieved with multiple directional light sources.

Just like scene composition, lighting is a vast topic. There are several good books you can read for in-depth information, some of which are *Magic of Light* by Jean Rosenthal, *Film Lighting* by Kris Malkiewicz and *Designing with Light* by J. Michael Gillette. In these books, you will find a wealth of knowledge related to controllable qualities of light such as color, angle, brightness, texture, hardness/softness and movement. Cinematography courses taught in film schools get into in-depth discussions about good ways to employ light as a design element (as more than just a source of illumination). Look online for Steve May's digital lighting course (currently taught by Matt Lewis, at The Ohio State University), and be sure to read Sharon Callahan's **SIGGRAPH** '96 excellent course notes on lighting for *Toy Story*. There is no substitute for hands-on experimentation however, so if you come across a lighting situation that catches your eye, try to recreate the look in your own scene files.

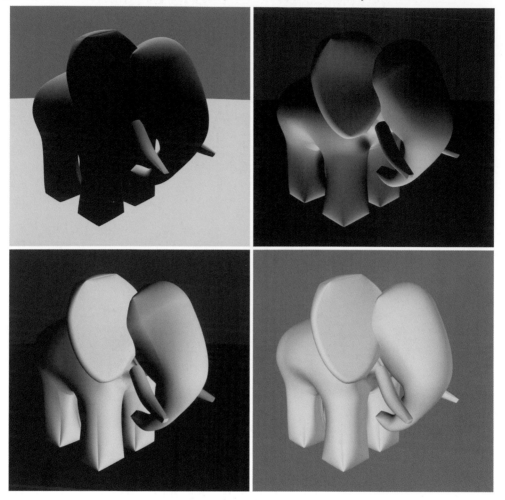

Figure 8.4 *Back, bottom, front and uniform lighting*

It is a fun exercise and a good habit to acquire, to guess the number and positions of light sources by looking at the specular highlights or shadows they create. Indoor atmospheres (art galleries, conference rooms, etc.) are often good places for this, as they tend to contain multiple lights. For example you can guess from the pair of highlights on each sphere in Figure 8.5 that there are (at least) a couple of lights placed overhead. Note that the highlights also show up in the reflections of the spheres on the blue plane.

Likewise, try to guess positions of light sources when you look at photographs, art and movies. Well designed images are the result of good composition as well as careful choices related to light types and placement. Learning to consciously become aware of this will help you light your own scenes better.

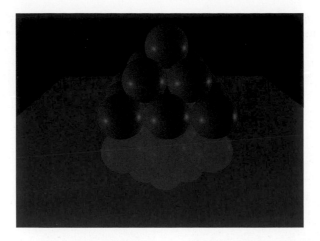

Figure 8.5 *Specular highlights are indicators of light positions*

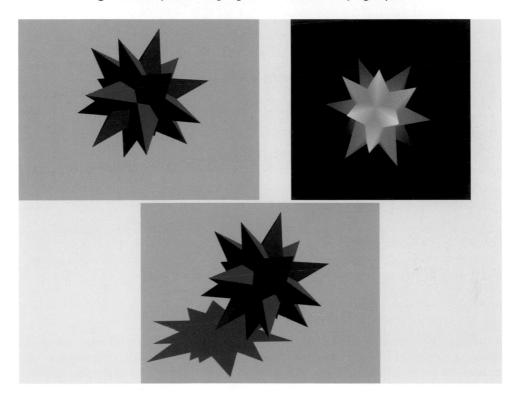

Figure 8.6 *Depth map-based shadow generation*

Figure 8.6 shows a common way to generate rendered shadows. In the real world, directional light sources shining on objects will produce shadows, there is no way to suppress them. But in CG rendering, one form of shadow generation is an additional, and if you like, an optional step. Figure 8.6 shows the idea. First a polyhedron on a plane is shown rendered, without shadows. Since the plane is featureless, you cannot even tell it is there. To add shadows, two additional steps are necessary. First, the camera is temporarily placed where the light is, and is oriented to lie along the light direction. This makes the camera see what the light illuminates. This image is rendered in the form of a grayscale depth map (referred to as a shadow map), pictured at the top right. For the actual shadow generation, this shadow map is consulted to see if the current shading point is visible to the light. If it is, that point is obviously not in shadow. Conversely, points not directly visible to the light are in shadow. Shadows offer strong cues in our visual perception, so we infer that the polyhedron is on a plane (not freely suspended in space), by looking at its shading in conjunction with the shadow-map-originated shadow.

Figure 8.7 *Depth map-based soft shadows*

Small point lights and strong sunlight both produce the kind of crisp shadow shown in Figure 8.6, but soft shadows are more common in everyday life, at least indoors. Figure 8.7 shows soft shadows created by our polyhedron. The softness in real-world soft shadows stems from the fact that indoor lights usually non-zero surface area and are not idealized point sources. It is as if the light emitting surface is equivalent to a collection of point sources, each of which creates its own sharp shadow. Scores of overlapping sharp shadows combine (average) to produce the soft edges.

Soft shadowing can be faked in our depth map process, by generating multiple shadow maps from a single sharp light source, by repositioning the light slightly differently each time. This is shown at the bottom of Figure 8.7, where the shadow maps look alike overall but contain subtle differences. To decide if a rendered point is in shadow, all the maps are queried to find out which ones saw the point in question and which did not. The responses are averaged to decided if that point is shadow or in light or in the region in between.

A different way to generate shadows is to use a form of rendering called ray tracing. The idea is to mimic the behavior of light in the real world, by following rays in the scene as they get reflected, refracted, transmitted or blocked by surfaces. Ray-traced reflections and shadows tend to be fairly realistic since the process emulates how light behaves physically. Figure 8.8 shows a ray tracing spotlight which casts shadows of the RfB surfaces on to the floor. No depth map is necessary if ray tracing is used.

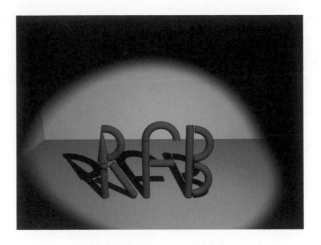

Figure 8.8 *Ray-traced shadows*

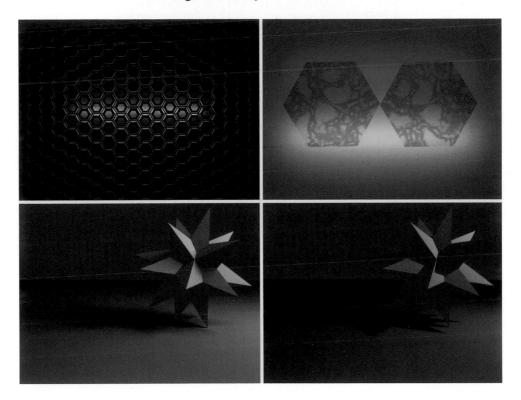

Figure 8.9 *Area light sources*

RenderMan supports the notion of area lights (in PRMan, pseudo area lights are supported, not true area lights). Light is made to appear to emanate from a surface, not a point. Figure 8.9 shows a linear, rectangular and sphere arealight source in the first three images, and a depth-mapped sharp shadow for comparison in the fourth (bottom right). In the top two images you can tell the shape of the light source by looking at the shape of the illuminated region. And in the third image, the off-screen sphere light creates a soft ground shadow.

Figure 8.10 *Negative spot light source ("dark bulb")*

CG lights also let us create illumination patterns that have no real-world equivalents. For instance in Figure 8.10, a negative spotlight is used to decrease, rather than increase, the brightness in the middle of a checkerboard. If a regular light source can be considered to banish darkness by shedding light, a CG darklight does the opposite by emitting darkness instead. All light shaders contain code that looks like this:

```
# calculate Cl, outgoing light color. Cl is a product of
# user-supplied light intensity and color and additional
# calculations performed in the light shader
Cl += intensity* lightcolor*.....
```

In other words, the light calculation done by the shader (represented by the .... above) is usually multiplied with the lightcolor attribute which the user might set in their RIB file, and by the intensity attribute which also comes from the user via the RIB file. In most shaders, no check is made to see if the intensity value that comes is a positive quantity. This means that you can turn almost any light shader into a darklight one simply by supplying a negative value (e.g. -1.5) for the light shader's intensity attribute:

```
# a 'bright' darklight!
LightSource "distantlight" 4 "intensity" -2
```

You can use such darklights to selectively reduce illumination in parts of your scenes. In other words, place your lights, illuminate, and if a region becomes overly bright, point a darklight at it to diminish the illumination. Doing so might be a lot easier than trying to position light sources to avoid illuminating a certain region in the first place.

As an aside, the images in Figure 8.10 depict a powerful illusion discovered by MIT's Ted Adelson, Professor of Vision Science. Counting from the top-left corner, the second square in the first row and the third square in the third (middle) row are actually of identical intensity, though the middle square seems lighter. Our minds lock on to the alternating dark and light pattern and find it hard to perceive that a "light" and "dark" square can be equally bright.

To help point out that the intensities are identical, a flat-gray constant colored annulus is shown floating on top of the checkerboard in the right image. The annulus covers the dark-looking square in the top row, and also the light-looking one in the center. Hopefully you can see that at both the squares in question, there is no brightness change between the annulus and the square. That should prove to you that the squares must be of equal brightness. Alternately you can render the images, examine the pixel values in an image viewer and see this for yourself.

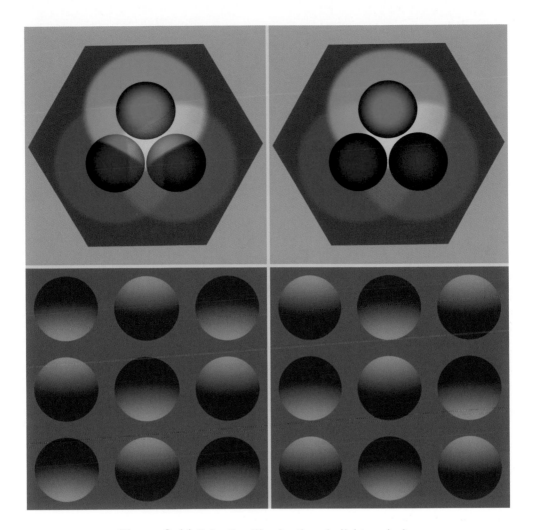

Figure 8.11 *Selective illumination via light exclusion*

Another useful, and non-physical aspect of CG lights is shown in Figure 8.11. At the top left, R, G and B spotlights are shown illuminating three spheres. Since the spheres are close together, the spotlight cones overlap, and as expected, so do the light beams. But in the top-right image, each spotlight selectively illuminates just its own object, ignoring ones nearby. This is achieved in RIB by turning lights on and off at various places in the RIB. For example the lights are first created using:

```
LightSource "spotlight_rts" "spotLightShape1" "coneangle" 0.75
"intensity" 1 "falloff" .25 "lightcolor" [1 0 0]
LightSource "spotlight_rts" "spotLightShape2" "coneangle" 0.75
"intensity" 1 "falloff" 0.25 "lightcolor" [0 1 0]
LightSource "spotlight_rts" "spotLightShape3" "coneangle" 0.75
"intensity" 1 "falloff" 0.25 "lightcolor" [0 0 1
```

By default, a light is on when it is first created, and stays on till it is turned off. To turn the last two off, the syntax is:

```
AttributeBegin
```

```
        Attribute "identifier" "name" ["|knot|knotShape"]
        ConcatTransform [0.75 0 1.29904 0 0 1.5 0 0 -1.29904 0 0.75 0
2.57 -0.825 1.545 1]
        Scale 1.2 1 1.2
        ShadingInterpolation "smooth"
                   # turn light#2 and light#3 off
        Illuminate "spotLightShape2" 0
        Illuminate "spotLightShape3" 0
        Color [1 1 1]
        Opacity [1 1 1]
        Surface "matte" "Ka" .4 "Kd" 1.1
        Sphere 1.5 -1.5 1.5 360
        AttributeEnd
```

Note that the turning off is limited to the AttributeBegin/End block we are in. After the AttributeEnd statement, the two lights are automatically turned back on by RenderMan. Selective illumination on a grid of 3x3 spheres is used to create the illusion (discovered by Vilayanur Ramachandran) at the bottom of Figure 8.11. The left figure shows four spheres that appear to come out of the plane (convex) and five that are concave. If the up/down light directions are reversed, the spheres appear to swap convexity and concavity as a result.

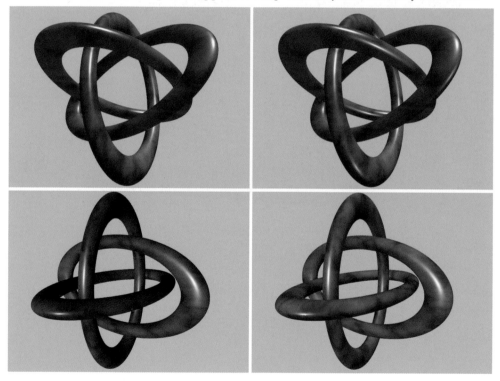

Figure 8.12 *Non-diffuse and non-specular lights*

Figure 8.12 shows yet another non-physical situation. At the top row, the two images are similar, except for an extra set of highlights in the right figure. In other words, a "non-diffuse" light illuminates the right figure, which creates only specular highlights on a surface without adding diffuse light to the surrounding areas. Such a light source is good for illuminating shiny surfaces (e.g. hair) to create extra highlights without brightening nearby regions. Likewise, the bottom pair of images show a non-specular light which only contributes diffuse light. How does this work? The gist is that in a **RIB** file, shaders can communicate with each other by passing bits of data from one to another. The light shader announces that it is non-diffuse (specular-only) source for example, and the marble surface shader correspondingly suppresses diffuse calculations for this light. As you can see such coupling between lights and shaders is very useful for creating specialized lighting situations.

In Figure 8.13, images (shown at the top right and bottom right) are used as illumination sources. In the top row, the rainbow image acts as an omnidirectional environment light source, where each light ray's direction is used to look up the ray's color in the image. The bottom row of Figure 8.14 illustrates a slideprojector light shader where an image (radial rainbow pattern in our case) is projected on to surfaces illuminated by the light.

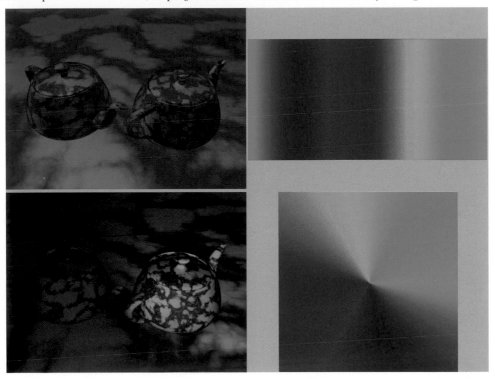

Figure 8.13 *Environment light sources (image-based illumination)*

8.3 Using other shaders

Having looked at some aspects of light shaders, we can now survey the other four shader types. As mentioned earlier, surface shaders simulate materials. Given an orange Spirograph surface and a light overhead, Figure 8.14 shows the application of three basic shaders to it. On the left, the "constant" shader colors the whole surface with a flat color, regardless of light position and camera orientation. The middle figure shows a matte shader where surfaces that face the light are brighter, and ones that fall away are darker. This is referred to as diffuse illumination. The last figure is shaded with a "plastic" shader which acts like a matte shader, with shiny highlights added. These highlights are called specular highlights, and are intended to be reflections of the light sources on the surfaces.

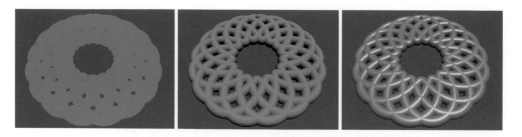

Figure 8.14 *Flat color, matte and plastic shaders*

Surface shaders usually modify a surface's inherent color, taking light sources into account. But where do the inherent colors (and opacities) come from? They are specified using the Color and Opacity RIB statements, and stand for the surface's actual, unmodified color and opacity. For instances the dice in Figure 8.15 have their colors and opacities specified as follows:

```
# left, pink die
# ...
Opacity [1 1 1]
Color [0.882352941176 0.0 0.527778833329]
...
# right, orange one
Opacity [0.294117647059 0.294117647059 0.294117647059]
Color [1 0.685247248604 0.0117647058824]
...
```

Figure 8.15 *Colors and opacities are inherent surface properties*

A surface can be shaded using one of many possible shaders, to simulate a particular look. Likewise, a single shader can be applied to a number of different surfaces. The top row in Figure 8.16 shows a South Indian "kolam" pattern. On the left it is shaded using a marble shader and on the right, with a brushed metal (LGBrushedmetal, by Larry Gritz). In the bottom row, the same spatter shader is used to simulate the look of spongeware (also called spatterware) on two different knot surfaces.

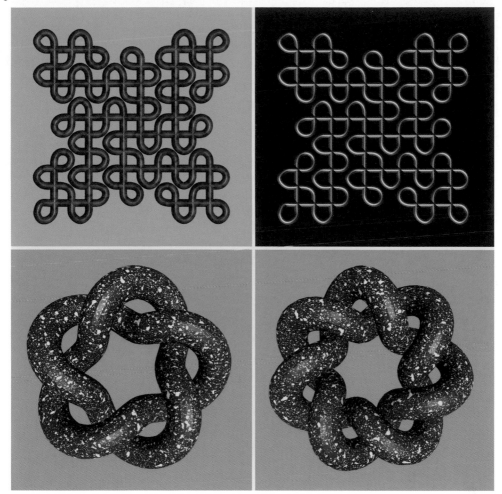

Figure 8.16 *Combining surfaces and materials*

Shaders are usually written to contain user-settable attributes, which are analogous to knobs and other controls on a piece of electronics. Just as users interact with the knobs to change the behavior of the device, so can they supply different values for a shader attribute to affect shading calculations.

In Figure 8.17, a wood shader is applied to a die. At the top left, the rings appear rather regular but at the bottom right, they appear warped. The only things that are different in the four images are the values for the shader attributes. The RIB statements are:

```
# wood shader invocation
# top left image: default values for the rings
Surface "wood" "Ka" .4 "Kd" 1.3
# ...
# bottom right image, more swirls
```

```
# Surface "wood" "Ka" .4 "Kd" 1.3 "grain" 8 "swirl" .75
# "swirlfreq" 1.6
```

Note that a surface shader can be invoked with just its name, as a minimum specification. Optionally, extra parameters can be supplied using the token/value pair notation as shown above and as discussed in Chapter 3 on RIB syntax. Notice too that the "Surface" RIB keyword is used to specify surface shaders in a RIB file. As you just saw, varying the value of a shader attribute results in the image being changed. This can form the basis for animations where in each frame the value of a given parameter (say, "grain" in the wood shader) can systematically be varied.

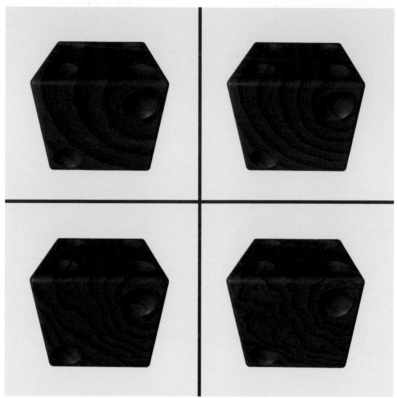

Figure 8.17 *User-controllable shader parameters*

Figure 8.18 shows the use of a home-grown anisotropic shader. In an anisotropic material, the color calculations are direction-dependent, so the surface appears to contain non-uniform colors that vary as a function of direction. By the way the shader used to create Figure 8.18 does not require any light sources in the scene. The entire coloring, including the highlights, is generated using calculations that mimic the effect of light/surface interactions – the anisotropy effect is simply faked.

The wood shader pictured above is an example of a "procedural" shader. A procedural shader is one where a pattern (which includes natural ones such as wood, stone, leather, marble and skin, as well as synthetic ones such as cloth weave, checkerboard, tiling) is synthesized using code. The alternative would be to use a photograph of the texture or patterns we want, in the form of a texture map (more on texturing later). The advantage of doing it procedurally is that endless variations of our pattern can be created just by altering the values of appropriate shader parameters.

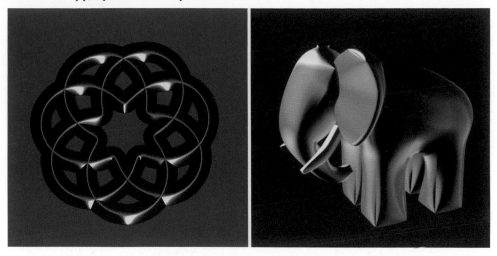

Figure 8.18 *A simple anisotropic (directionally non-uniform) shader*

Shaders are not always written to simulate surface appearances. Sometimes they are created to obtain diagnostics on their underlying surfaces, to serve as visual debugging (problem-solving) aids. For instance in Figure 8.19 below, the "wire" shader that ships with PRMan distribution is applied to the Gumbo and teapot surfaces, to expose underlying patch constructions in the form of wireframes.

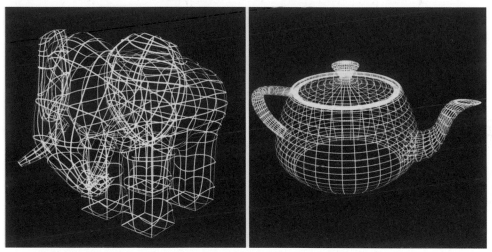

Figure 8.19 *A wire shader to visualize underlying surface construction*

In Figure 8.13, images were used as light sources. Here in Figure 8.20, they are used in a related fashion, where they serve as what are known as "environment maps". The idea behind environment mapping is as follows. If everything ever visible from a single point can be encoded in the form of an environment map (which is basically an image with some auxiliary data), that map can in turn be imagined to be pasted on to a large sphere, which encloses the point that generated the map in the first place. Now if some other object (teapot or Gumbo in our example) were to be placed at that point, the map can contribute colors to shade that object. In our example, the color on the teapot and Gumbo surfaces come solely from the environment map, as if the surfaces were perfectly shiny mirrors which totally reflect their environment. More commonly, a small amount of the colors from an environment map lookup are layered over an existing surface. This enhances realism by making the surface appear to be part of the environment.

RenderMan lets you create environment maps using the "txmake" command (see RfB online for usage examples). The idea is to first create a full panorama (e.g. using a camera and image stitching software) and use txmake to format it for RenderMan. The image mapped on to the teapot is indeed a panoramic one, but as the mapping on Gumbo shows, any photograph or image will do, it does not have to be a true panorama. The reflections still look rich, complex and credible as though a true panorama is what is being reflected.

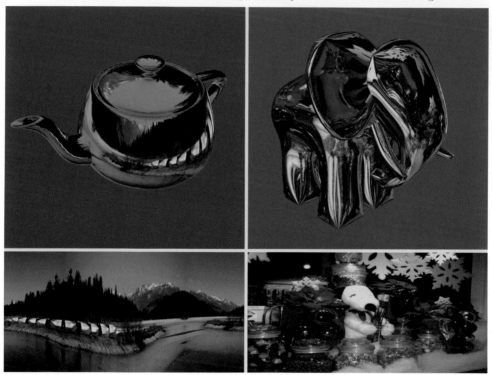

Figure 8.20 *A reflection shader that totally mirrors its environment*

Now we move on to examining the other three types of shaders (displacement, atmosphere and imager). A displacement shader is shown in Figure 8.21 where a "noise" pattern (more on noise in section 8.5) is used to alter micropolygon locations in 3D space. From creating roughness on water surfaces to wrinkles on skin, displacement generation is a very useful technique for adding detail to surfaces in the rendering stage. Note that the displacements actually alter surface positions, as if they had been created during surface modeling. But the point of course is that they are not. In other words displacement shaders offer a way to add modeling complexity (wrinkles, protrusions, roughness, periodic patterns etc.) at render time on to relatively smooth modeled surfaces. This offers the best of both worlds – the models themselves can be kept lightweight and simple and rarely need to be reworked, but the procedural shaders that add displacement to them can be tweaked to our heart's content until we get just the look we are after.

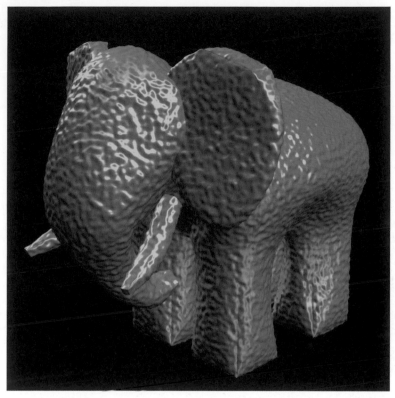

Figure 8.21 *A noise displacement shader*

Atmosphere shaders modify colors on surfaces, to simulate the effect the atmosphere might have, on the surfaces it contains. In Figure 8.22, a "fog" shader makes far-away surfaces fade into a dull gray color. Atmosphere shaders are also useful for creating smoke effects (such as in Figure 8.1) and for taking into account enclosed volumes (such as inside a skull) as well.

Figure 8.22 *A fog atmospheric shader*

Imager shaders offer a chance to perform some pixel-level image processing on the rendered pixels before they are written out to a file or displayed on the screen. A very useful imager shader is the "background" shader, which colors all the empty pixels with a user-defined value. In Figure 8.23, the gap between the faces is colored yellow. Without an imager background shader, the default RenderMan behavior is to output black pixels at the unrendered parts of an image, as shown in the right of Figure 8.23.

Figure 8.23 *An imager shader for filling non-rendered background pixels*

8.4 The RenderMan Shading Language (RSL)

RSL is a graphics programming language for writing RenderMan shaders. The basic idea is this. Type the following into a text editor and save the resulting file as learnRSL.sl. It is a skeleton source code (program) for a simple, do-nothing shader.

```
surface learnRSL()
{

}
```

Compile the file using the shader compiler that comes with your implementation of RenderMan. For example "shader.exe" is PRMan's shader compiler (on a Windows machine), and to compile our shader we would run this command:

```
shader.exe learnRSL.sl <Ret>
```

The shader compiler will generate a new file called learnRSL.slo, which is the compiled version of the small program you wrote. The .slo file is what will be used by RenderMan, not the .sl file you typed code into. If you bring up the .slo file in a text editor, it will not make much sense to you. The compact code it contains is meant for RenderMan.

After compiling, embed the name of the shader in a simple RIB file as follows:

```
Display "shaderexec.tiff" "tiff" "rgb"
Format 16 16 1
Projection "orthographic"
ShadingRate 100
WorldBegin
Translate 0 0 1
Surface "learnRSL"
Polygon "P" [0 0 0 1 0 0 1 1 0 0 1 0]
WorldEnd
```

When you render the above RIB, you will see a small 16x16 pixel window pop up with the rendered image, which would be all black. But the interesting thing for us is that

RenderMan ran (executed) your learnRSL shader. Shaders can be thought of as small RenderMan plugins. You need to embed their names in a RIB file and render that RIB in order to indirectly cause your shader to execute. You can continue using the RIB code and shader framework shown above, to learn the basics of RSL. Type code into the currently-empty learnRSL shader, compile, render the RIB, type more code, compile, render (run), and so on. For the first addition to your blank shader, try this:

```
surface learnRSL()
{
    float a=1.0, b=3.5;
    float c = a + b;
    print(c);
}
```

When you compile and run, you see the following printed on the shell window that contains the render command:

```
4 values:
    0:4.500000
    1:4.500000
    2:4.500000
    3:4.500000
```

Our shader consists of three lines (statements) which are executed in sequential fashion, as depicted on the left of Figure 8.24. float a=1.0 means that we are creating a named storage space called "a", to store and recall floating point (decimal) numbers. Such storage spaces are called variables, and programs make liberal use of them to store intermediate results, communicate with RenderMan, etc. So float a=1.0 refers to the creation of a floating point variable called "a", which will store the value 1.0 right after it is created. A variable will hold on to a value until it is made to hold another value at which point the older value is overwritten and discarded forever. After creating two variables "a" and "b" and initializing them with 1.0 and 3.5, we create a third variable called "c". "c" is not initialized with a hardcoded number like "a" and "b" were. Instead, it is initialized with a+b, which refers to the sum of the contents of "a" and "b". So variable "c" gets an initial value of 1+3.5=4.5. The print statement following the creation of "c" causes the shader to output the value of "c" so we can examine it. Note that the printing happens four times, not just once, because our shader is invoked at each corner of the single micropolygon that fills our render.

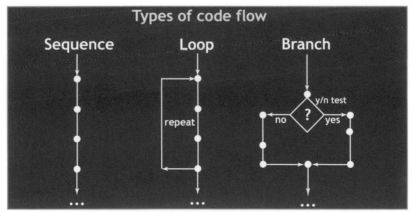

Figure 8.24 *Basic code execution flow types*

Similar to creating float variables, you can also create variables to hold a point, color, vector, normal or a string. A string is a collection of letters and numbers and is useful for example to store the name of a texture file:

string texnm = "House.tex";

texnm is our string value, and its initial value is the string House.tex. Try examining several shaders just to look for variable names and their types (float, point, vector, etc.). Sequential execution of program statements is one of three fundamental program flow types. As shown in Figure 8.24, the other two are looping and branching.

```
float i=0.0, sum=0.0;
for(i=0.0; i<11.0; i=i+1)
{
   sum = sum + i;
}
```

Looping is illustrated in the above code segment. Lines of code inside the "for" statement are looped, in other words, executed many times. How many times? We start with variable i containing 0, and keep looping as long as i is less than 11 (i<11.0). Each time after we loop, we increment i by 1 (i=i+1). So as the looping happens, i becomes 1,2 3,4... etc. i takes on 11, and when it becomes 12, the 'test' i<11 fails, and that is what terminates the looping.

```
if(sum < 5)
{
   Ci = color(1,0,0);
}
else
{
   Ci = color(0,0,1);
}
```

The above code snippet shows how branching is represented in RSL. The variable sum is examined to see the value it contains is less than 5 (sum<5). If yes, the variable Ci (which happens to be a variable that holds a color) is made to contain (is assigned) the color red. Otherwise, if sum is not less than 5, Ci is assigned blue instead. Note that these are the only two alternatives, since the question sum<5? can either be true or false.

The next concept to illustrate is that of a function (Figure 8.25). A simple definition of function is that it is a named piece of code which encapsulates useful computations.

```
float addNNum(float n)
{
   float i, sum=0;
   for(i=0;i<=n;i+=1)
   {
      sum += i;
   }
   return sum;
}

surface learnRSL()
{
   float sum = addNNum(200);
   printf("Sum of 200 numbers: %f\n",sum);
}
```

If you compile and run the above, you get the following (again, four times):

```
Sum of 200 numbers: 20100.000000
```

In the above, we create a variable called sum, and initialize it with addNum(200). addNum is a function, which takes a number as input and returns another number as output. From the name of the function and more importantly from the code for it, you can see that it adds 1+2+3+4+.... upto whatever limit we ask it to add up to. That limit is 200 in the above example (addNum(200)).

In our example the addNum function does all the work itself, but it could call (make use of) another function to do a part of its work, and so on. It is this kind of chaining of function invocations that is shown in Figure 8.25. RSL comes built in with a rich variety of functions that perform mathematical and geometric calculations, color conversions, string manipulations, lighting calculations and map access. Please see the Spec. and also your renderer's documentation to learn what is available. Functions are analogous to specialized, and consequently highly expressive, vocabulary in a natural language. If you are proficient with them, you can use them to express ideas concisely. The converse is also true – if you are not familiar with the list of pre-existing shader calls, you might be reinventing the wheel by coding up functionality already available.

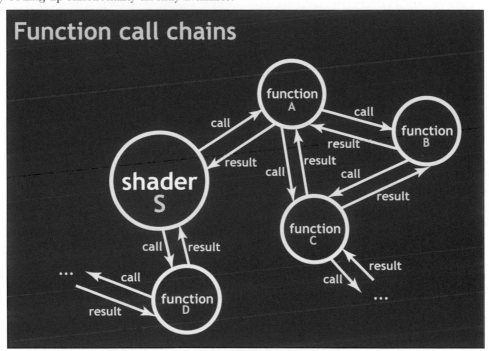

Figure 8.25 *Functions call other functions, forming a command chain*

When you are writing a shader, what kind of information about the currently shaded point is available for use? There are three sources of data, as shown in Figure 8.26. RenderMan uses pre-determined "global" variable names such as P, N, etc. to let you know the (x,y,z) of the point being shaded, its normal direction, and a host of other useful information. User settings for the knobs (parameters) in your shader is another source of data, and finally, variables you create in your shader are the third source. The goal of shader programming is to make use of these pieces of data to achieve something meaningful, e.g. to compute the color of the micropolygon vertex being shaded.

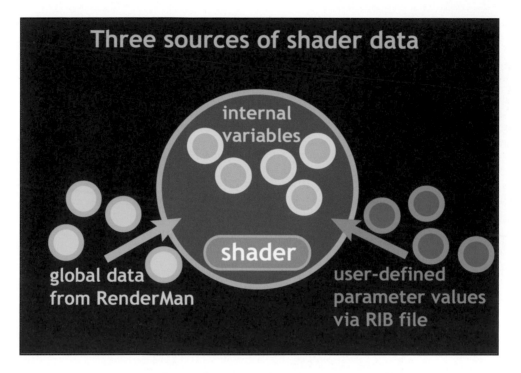

Figure 8.26 *Sources of data inside a shader*

I mentioned P and N as two examples of global variables using which RenderMan communicates valuable shading information to you, the shader writer. There are many more such "shader globals", and the list is somewhat different for each of the five shader types. Figure 8.27 shows the main ones for surface shaders. Please read the documentation to find out what information the variables provide. Note that some of those variables come into your shader expecting to be assigned a value by you (you would send data out of your shader back to RenderMan using such output variables). For instance in a surface shader, you are expected to calculate the current shading point's color and opacity and stuff them into global variables Ci and Oi respectively.

The shader writing philosophy can be summarized as follows. The point of shader calculations is to derive values for global variables such as Ci and Oi. Local variables and function calls are used to create expressions and intermediate results. Functions are powerful entities that do a lot of the intermediate calculations. They can be built into the shading language itself or be created by the shader writer.

Shader programming is a vast topic, with enough material to fill an entire book this size. The information presented above, while being enough to get you started, barely scratches the surface. I urge you examine literally dozens and dozens of shaders to see how they work. There is not much more to the RSL syntax than my quick introduction, but the magic is in the function calls. Please refer to the shading language documentation for the complete list of functions available, and practice writing small shaders which exercise them a few at a time. When you come across unfamiliar function calls in others' shaders, find out what the calls do. Also, if you do study a multitude of shaders, you will find certain programming patterns (idioms) repeated. For instance a line like this occurs in many surface shaders:

```
normal Nf = faceforward(normalize(N), I);
```

Globals N and I, which are the surface normal and gaze direction respectively, are used to compute a camera-facing normal via built-in functions normalize() and faceforward(). The result is stored in a new variable called Nf, for use in further calculations (e.g. the diffuse(Nf) function call will give you the diffuse color contribution for the point being shaded). If you understand the meaning of statements like this which repeatedly occur, you can quickly comprehend large chunks of shader code. The "Aha!" moment that occurs when you figure out what a block of code does is an enjoyable one, and I encourage you to seek out your own such moments.

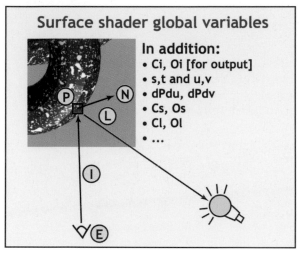

Figure 8.27 *Surface shading-related global ("magic") variables*

8.5 Surface shaders

Now that you know the basics of shader construction, we can examine a variety of shaders, to see what makes them work.

Surface shaders have only one purpose, and that is to calculate a value for the global variables Ci and Oi which are the current shading point's color and opacity respectively.

A useful exercise while learning shader writing is to synthesize patterns on surfaces. In Figure 8.28 are shown some simple patterns. At the top left is a grayscale ramp. One way to create it is as follows:

```
float ss = pow(s,gamma);
Ci *= color (ss,ss,ss);
```

The shaders are all applied to a flat rectangle that fills the image. The "s" global variable contains the texture coordinate in the horizontal direction, which increases from left to right as it goes from 0 to 1. So it can be turned into a grayscale value with the function call color(ss,ss,ss), where variable ss is derived from s by nonlinearly altering it using the power function pow().

The s and t texture coordinates (t is along the vertical direction) can likewise be used to create a checkerboard texture.

```
float    smod = mod(s * frequency, 1),
float    tmod = mod(t * frequency, 1);
```

```
color    dark = 0.5 * Cs;
if (smod < 0.5) {
    if (tmod < 0.5)
        Ci = lt;
    else
        Ci = dk;
} else {
    if (tmod < 0.5)
        Ci = dk;
    else
        Ci = lt;
}
```

mod(s*frequency,1) means that we are taking just the fractional part after s is multiplied with a checker frequency such as 15. As s and t vary across the surface, the fractional part is first less than 0.5, then becomes greater than 0.5, again becomes less than 0.5, and so on. A check is made for this in both s and t directions, and Ci is colored accordingly with one of two colors.

```
float d = sqrt((s-scenter)*(s-scenter) + (t-tcenter)*(t-tcenter));
d = sin(d*2*PI*freq);
d = 0.5*(d+1);
d = pow(d,gam);
Ci = color(d,d,d);
```

The code above shows how the concentric rings in the bottom right of Figure 8.28 are produced. At each (s,t), we find the distance to a user-supplied point (the image frame's midpoint, in our example). That distance d is fed to a sin() function which always returns a value between -1 and 1. Since color values only range from 0 to 1, the -1 to 1 range is compressed to a 0 to 1 range using d=0.5*(d+1). The result is passed through a pow() function and its output becomes the surface color. These three steps (feeding the result of a calculation to a sin() function, converting a value lying between -1 and 1 to a more usable value between 0 and 1 and using the pow() function to nonlinearly alter a value) are quite common shader "tricks". You can accumulate such a bag of tricks yourself by examining a variety of existing shaders. At first some of the usage might seem foreign, but after a while you will begin to see their usefulness. Eventually you will discover that a majority of shaders achieve their functionality simply by using a relatively small number of programming idioms over and over. In other words, small and simple calculations progressively contribute to the final result.

In Figure 8.29 are shown four shaders that turn incoming global values into colors, for visualization (usually diagnostics) purposes. At the top left is pictured a shader which turns the x, y and z components of the surface normal vector N into a color value. This is done as follows:

```
normal NN = normalize(N); // NN is a 'normalized normal'
vector posNorm = 0.5*(vector(1,1,1)+NN);
....
Cn = color "rgb" (comp(posNorm,0),comp(posNorm,1),comp(posNorm,2));
Oi = Os; // set outgoing opacity Oi to be surface opacity Os
# premultiply Ci with Oi
Ci = Cs*Oi*Cn;
```

N is first normalized, to make its x, y and z components lie between -1 and 1. Negative values are turned positive by adding vector (1,1,1) to the normalized normal (contained in variable NN), and a color Cn is constructed from the result. comp(posNorm,0) stands for the x component (0th component) of posNorm, likewise for the y and z components.

Note that color Cn is turned into outgoing color Ci using Ci = Cs*Oi*Cn. The calculated color Cn is multiplied with surface color Cs, and also with opacity Oi. Such multiplication of color Ci with opacity Oi is termed "premultiplication". If you request a four channel (RGBA) output, RenderMan will use Ci for RGB and Oi for the A (alpha) channel. So what the premultiplication does is to cause the alpha channel to be multiplied into the RGB channels, in the output image. This is done for the benefit of most compositing and post-production software which expect such premultiplied imagery.

Figure 8.28 *Simple pattern generation*

The other shaders show the distribution of (s,t) texture coordinates (top right image), the reflection vector (bottom left) and a measure of surface curvature (bottom right). Look at Thomas Burge's www.affine.org site for a more accurate curvature shader.

It is sometimes useful to visualize micropolygon grids and the micropolygons themselves, which is what the shader in Figure 8.30 does.

```
color Cgrid = randomgrid() ;
float mpc = 0.5+0.5*random();
Oi = Os;
Ci = Cs*Os*mpc*Cgrid;
```

randomgrid() is a built-in RSL function that returns a random color for each grid. To cause further variation for each micropolygon in a grid, the random() function is called, and its float output is used as a darkening factor to modulate the grid color. Note that the shading rate needs to be very coarse for the micropolygons to become visible.

Figure 8.29 *Diagnostic shaders that visualize global variables*

Figure 8.30 *Micropolygons and grids*

In Figure 8.31, the depth() built-in call is used to obtain the camera space depth at each shading point, and the result is turned into Ci. On the left, the depth is directly encoded as Ci to create a grayscale depth map. On the right, the depth is used to look up a result color from a list of colors:

```
color CD0=color(1,.01,0);
color CD1=color(1,.01,0);
color CD2=color(1,.17,0);
// ...
color CD10=color(0,0,1);
color CD11=color(0,0,1);

return color spline(z,
            CD0,CD1,
            CD2,
// ...
            CD9,
            CD10);
```

CD0 through CD11 are color variables, and the spline() function takes these color variables and a lookup float value (z in our case) and uses it to interpolate colors from the list to produce a smooth ramp color output.

The palette used is a special one, as its specific ordering of colors makes them fairly pop off the page. The experience is further enhanced through ChromaDepth™ glasses which contain a diffraction grating for one eye and a plain cellophane sheet for the other.

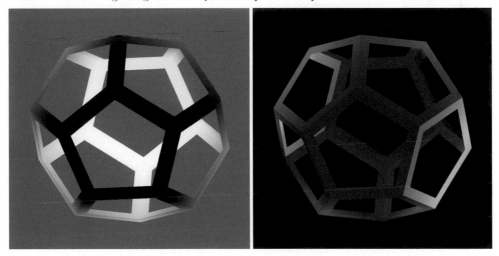

Figure 8.31 *z-depth and ChromaDepth™ shaders*

We have just seen examples of shaders that compute patterns and visualize rendering-related variables. But the main purpose of surface shaders is to compute the interaction between a surface and light sources that illuminate it. As we noted before, at each micropolygon grid vertex, an associated surface shader is invoked, with appropriate parameters. The shader is expected to make use of the incoming values to compute an appropriate color and opacity value for the micropolygon vertex. A common model used in such lighting calculations is illustrated in Figure 8.32. The last image shows a polyhedron lit with two light sources. An ambient light source adds overall uniform brightness, as shown in the top left. A directional light source provides a diffuse contribution (top right) and also a specular one (bottom left). The final color is a summation of ambient, diffuse and specular contributions from the lights. Note that the lights themselves are agnostic of the surfaces they illuminate. It is the shader code for the surface that decides which of these terms (ambient, diffuse, specular) to compute, and how much of each to include in the result. In fact I just decribed a simplified version of RenderMan's built-in plastic shader (see Figure 8.2 for source code).

The diffuse and specular terms deserve some more explanation. The diffuse color contribution is typically computed with a term such as $Kd*$diffuse(Nf). diffuse() is a built-in shader call that takes as input a normal vector (a direction), and examines a conical volume (known as the "illumination cone") centered at the shading point along the specified outfacing normal (like an umbrella turned upside down and held over your head), looking for directional lights inside the volume. For each light found, a facing ratio is evaluated, which is the dot product of the light direction and the surface normal. The closer the dot product is to 1.0, the more the light and the surface face each other and so greater the illumination. Likewise, if the light vector and surface normal are nearly perpendicular, the dot product is close to 0.0, and the light hardly contributes illumination to the surface at that point. Shine a flashlight head on towards a plastic ball, to see this for yourself. The part of the ball facing the light will appear brightest, and the illumination will drop off as the surface turns away from the light.This is what the dot product captures numerically. Note that the dot product between two normalized (length 1.0) vectors is an extremely useful quantity to compute in shaders. Depending on what the two participating vectors are, such a dot product result can be put to a variety of creative uses. The overall diffuse contribution is expressed as $Kd*$diffuse(Nf), where Kd is termed the diffuse coefficient and is a user-supplied factor which scales the color value calculated by the diffuse() function call.

Specular highlights are likewise captured by the specular() function, which takes not one but two vectors (and a roughness scattering factor) as inputs. The inputs are the viewing direction (eye to surface point) and surface normal. Again, an illumination cone is placed on the shaded point to look for lights within. When a light is found, it is examined to see if it shines along the view vector's mirror direction. The idea is that if the view vector and light direction are mirror-symmetrical about the surface normal, light will hit the surface, be reflected and enter the eye. Such a ray of light that comes towards the camera is termed a specular highlight. This however means that the highlight is just a small sharp point from a single light ray. Real materials have bigger highlights than that. To account for this, a roughness parameter is also input to specular() to expand the search for a mirror direction into a mirror cone instead. The color calculated by specular() is scaled using Ks, a user-supplied specular coefficient.

To round out the discussion of the plastic shader, note that $Ka*$ambient() is the ambient term which generates the flat image at the top left of Figure 8.32. As usual, user-supplied Ka (ambient coefficient) scales the color resulting from the built-in ambient() call which collects all ambient light shining on the surface.

While the overall plastic look can be derived in a single pass by setting appropriate values for Ka, Kd and Ks in the RIB file, it is often useful to obtain the ambient, diffuse and specular contributions as separate images by rendering the RIB file in three "passes", each time setting two of the three coefficients to 0. Using image editing software, the component images can be individually color-corrected, blurred etc. and then combined for the overall plastic look. This kind of editing flexibility is quite desirable in high-end visual effects work where these individual passes tend to get tweaked to obsessive perfection.

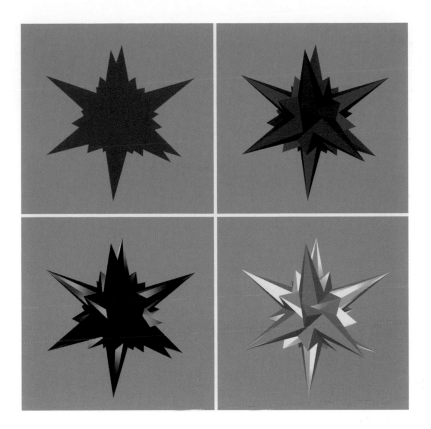

Figure 8.32 *Summation of ambient, diffuse and specular terms*

RenderMan's default shading mode is called Phong shading, and is illustrated in Figure 8.33. When colors are computed (by executing shaders) at the corners of a micropolygon, how should the four corner colors be used to shade the micropolygon surface? This question has at least three answers, as shown in the figure. The figure by the way contains four polygons which form part of a polymesh cylinder, and the shading rate is set to a high number to turn each polygon into a micropolygon. By turning off shading interpolation, we can get a flat, constant color per micropolygon, as shown on the left. This is referred to as flat shading, which has a faceted look. An improvement over flat shading is called Gouraud shading, which the middle image illustrates. Here, the four vertex colors are interpolated (smoothly mixed in) over the micropolygon surface. The resulting color variation gets us away from the faceted flat look, but some gradation is still visible. Note that shading interpolation needs to be set to "smooth" for this to work. Phong shading improves things further, by interpolating normal vectors (instead of colors) of the four corners, to compute new normals inside the micropolygons. These new normals are then used to calculate interior colors. Of the three shading types, Phong is the most expensive (calculation intensive) but offers the best results. As the images in Figure 8.33 indicate, you can still achieve Gouraud or flat shading by making appropriate modifications to your RIB files.

A lot of materials in the world react anisotropically to light, meaning that the interaction is direction dependent. For instance, almost all light that hits glass at a straight angle is able to get transmitted through, whereas light at grazing angles gets mostly reflected back. This is why edges of glass or even translucent plastic objects appear darker.

Figure 8.33 *Flat, Gouraud and Phong shading*

It is possible to write surface shaders that display anisotropic effects. Such shaders are longer (more code) than usual and sometimes tend to be heavier on the math side. The first image in Figure 8.34 shows a Spirograph surface that has a two-tone color, displaying what is known as the Fresnel effect. Fresnel surfaces display one color when viewed straight-on, and a related but different color at side angles. You can observe this effect on cars that have composite bodies and/or pearlescent paint coatings with embedded flecks. Adding even a subtle amount of such Fresnel-derived color variation to your surfaces will make them look that much more photoreal.

The hairs (NURBS curves) on the trefoil surface are rendered with a hair shader which you can get from Application Note #19 of the PRMan documentation. The anisotropy here is along the length of each hair, where the root is made to appear darker than the tip.

The third image shows anisotropic specular highlights. Normally, specular highlights have a round profile (remember the illuminance cone and the mirror cone within?). But in brushed metals, the streak marks from the brushing visually drag out highlights into non-circular shapes. Greg Ward (who is also the author of the famous Radiance radiosity renderer) came up with a modification to the standard specular calculations, to account for this anisotropy. The "kolam" surface shows such streaked highlights in each section of the surface.

The teapot image illustrates "glossy" highlights. Normally, a highlight has a bright center, with intensity falling off away from it. But the teapot shows flat highlights, reminiscent of lip gloss or a ceramic surface. The way it is achieved (the technique is due to Greg Ward and Larry Gritz) is this: the regular specular value is used as an input to a smoothstep() function which outputs a value within a narrower (clamped) intensity range, resulting in a flatter highlight.

The fifth image shows scattering of highlights, using noise. The idea is to use specular() to compute highlights, but feed it non-physical (perturbed) values for the surface normal and eye vector directions. The scattered highlights are reminiscent of hammered metal surfaces.

Finally, the trefoil knot image shows that highlights can be shaped into custom patterns such as starbursts. This kind of glint is achieved by choosing two orthogonal (perpendicular) directions to flare the highlight along. Du(P) and Dv(P) give the rate of change of P along u and v parametric directions respectively (how steeply the surface falls off when you take a unit step along u or v) and can be used as preferred directions along which to compute the cross pattern.

I mentioned Fresnel anisotropy, which is an edge effect, while discussing the two-tone Spirograph surface in Figure 8.34. This is illustrated further in Figure 8.35. The top two images show two different ways the effect can be computed. The image on the left is a quick, simple approximation to the Fresnel computation, and is derived using N.I, the dot product between the surface normal and view direction. At the silhouette edges of objects, the dot product is 0 and at straight incidences, the dot product is 1. We turn this dot product into a Fresnel factor (an intensity scaling term). The code to do this is as follows:

```
// fake-Fresnel-factor computation - once Kr is computed,
// you can use it for a variety of things: to fade out reflections
// towards edges, to brighten edges, to make edges more transparent,
// to use as a mixing factor for two-tone coloring etc.
vector Nf = faceforward (normalize(N), I);
vector V = normalize (I); // V opposes N
float Kr = 0.5*(1+normalize(Nf).V);
# the following pow() term is modeled after Christopher Schlick's
# approximation of the Fresnel calculation
Kr = pow(Kr,ior);
Kr = K1+(K2-K1)*pow(Kr,Kexp);
Ci = color(Kr,Kr,Kr);
```

The image on the top right of Figure 8.35 uses the built-in RSL fresnel() call, which takes vectors N and I (and other parameters) as input and computes a true Fresnel factor. Feel free to use either the real computation or the fake one, in your shaders. The real fresnel call is more accurate but the fake version also does pretty well. The call to the fresnel() function looks like this:

```
/////////////////////////////////////////////////////////
// Fresnel reflection.. Main input is ior, aux. ones
// are K1, K2 and Kexp for remapping Kr
/////////////////////////////////////////////////////////
float INDEX=ior;
vector Nf = faceforward (normalize(N), I);
vector V = normalize (I);
float Kr=0, Kt=0;
if(ior==0)INDEX=1;
fresnel (V, Nf, (V.Nf > 0)? INDEX:1/INDEX,Kr, Kt);
Kr = K1+(K2-K1)*pow(Kr,Kexp);
/////////////////////////////////////////////////////////
/////////////////////////////////////////////////////////
Ci = color(Kr,Kr,Kr);
```

The left image in the middle row of Figure 8.35 shows a closeup of the Spirograph surface where the Fresnel factor is directly expressed as Ci. The image is reminiscent of scanning electron micrography (SEM). On the right, a glow effect is achieved on Gumbo by using the Fresnel value to set opacity. Since edges have smaller (close to 0) Fresnel values, the opacities there are lower, making the surface lose its edges. This gives the appearance of a fuzzy glowing volume.

On the bottom left of Figure 8.35, the colorful Spirograph image is created by using the Fresnel factor as a lookup into a ramp of rainbow colors, using the spline() function. The bottom right image shows an edge matte, where the Fresnel value is used to brighten edges in relation to the interior. Such edge mattes are very useful in making CG surfaces integrate nicely into live action imagery. For instance you could render an edge matte for a character, blur it a bit in an image processing package and use the result to add a little rim light on to the character, using the dominant color from the background plate as the color for the rim light. That will make the character appear to receive the same light as nearby objects in the background.

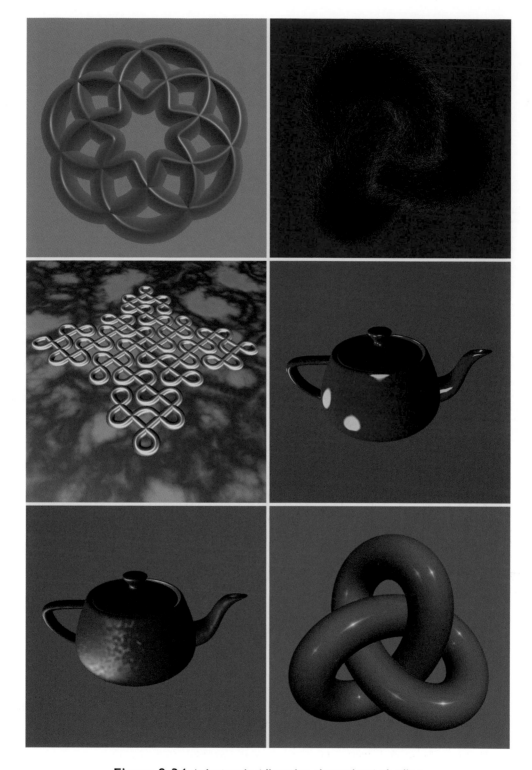

Figure 8.34 *Anisotropic (direction-dependent) shading*

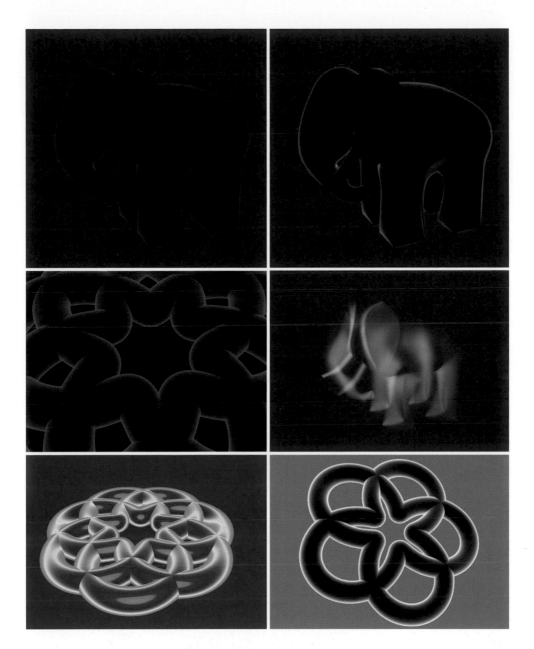

Figure 8.35 *Edge anisotropy*

Figure 8.36 illustrates noise. Noise is one of the most fundamental and useful building blocks for shader writing. Simply put, noise is a unique grayscale (0 to 1) value associated with every point in space. There is no correlation between adjacent samples. In other words, you cannot pick out visual patterns by scanning your eye across a line in any direction over a noise image. The left image in Figure 8.36 shows noise on a square, and on the right, noise is pictured over Gumbo. Obtaining a basic noise value could not be simpler:

```
float f = noise(P);
```

Each new value of P yields a different value for f, but a specific value for P always gives the same noise value. In that sense, noise is not time-dependent or "random".

noise() is a built-in RSL call whose input can be a float, point or a vector. There are several variations of the basic noise calculation, you can look them up in the literature if interested. As a simple example, signed noise (which varies between -1 and 1 instead of the usual range of 0 to 1) is defined as follows:

```
#define snoise(x)  (noise(x) * 2 - 1)
```

A good book to read about noise() and procedural graphics programming is Ebert et. al's *Texturing and Modeling*. The noise function was invented and popularized by Ken Perlin, who teaches at New York University (NYU). His web site contains historic material on noise as well as various presentations and experiments with noise patterns. Perlin's basic idea is to precompute noise values on the vertices of a lattice grid, and smoothly interpolate these values to produce a unique noise value for every unique point in space.

The problem with basic noise() is that it is too unpredictable, meaning that it is completely uncorrelated. Some structure would be nice to have, as it can help with pattern formation. Turbulence is the name given to one such way of obtaining structure, and this is shown in Figure 8.37. A, B, D and F are noise images, but at different spatial scales. In other words, A is obtained by turning "noise(P)" into a Ci value, while B results from computing "noise(2*P)" instead. The multiplier for P is called noise frequency. Higher the frequency, finer the noise.

Turbulence results from cumulatively adding noise with higher frequencies, on to a base noise image. Adding B to A gives C, our first-level turbulence image. C contains two frequencies, one from A and the other from B. To C we add D to get E, which is more turbulent than C, with three frequencies. You can see that the result is starting to develop a marble-like pattern. We do one more level of addition, combining noise image F with E. The result is G, our output turbulence image. Note that finer and finer copies of noise are accumulated by correspondingly darkening them as well. The darkening is accomplished using an amplitude scale factor, as in "ampl*noise(P*freq)". With successive additions, freq increases while ampl decreases. Turbulence shaders usually compute the turbulence values using a for() loop to sum over the noises at various frequencies and amplitudes.

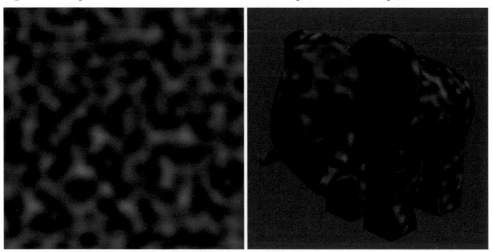

Figure 8.36 *Noise*

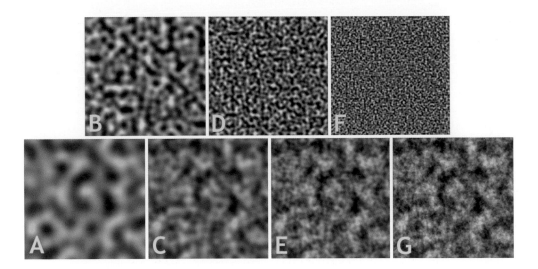

Figure 8.37 *Turbulence synthesis*

Figure 8.38 illustrates a sampling of noise and turbulence-based shaders. A chrome reflection, colorful glass (funkyglass shader by Larry Gritz) and wood shader are pictured in the top row, while stone, spatter and a blue marble (due to Darwyn Peachey) shader are in the bottom row.

You should attempt to become very familiar with the properties of noise and turbulence computations. They can be put to an astonishing variety of uses, for more than just marble, wood and other material computations. They can be used to alter positions, normals, directions and even color values. These additional possibilities are illustrated in many shaders throughout the rest of the chapter, keep an eye out for them.

Figure 8.38 *A sampling of noise/turbulence shaders*

A special form of turbulence computation leads to the synthesis of ridged multifractals, pictured in Figure 8.39. Ridge-like bright lines meander throughout, at various spatial scales. This form of fractal has been popularized by Ken Musgrave and is invaluable in synthesizing natural-looking terrains. You can look up "fractal Brownian motion" (fBM) for another form of turbulence.

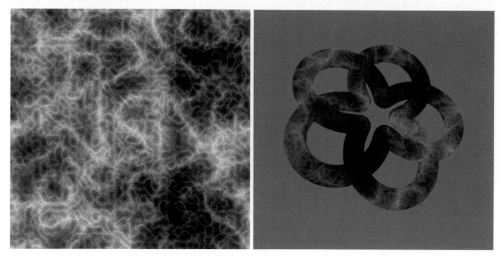

Figure 8.39 *Ridged multifractal*

Classic noise is continuous, smooth across all space. RSL's cellnoise() function on the other hand outputs discrete values. If space is pictured as a lattice of cellular volumes, everywhere inside a given cell the cellnoise() function returns the same value. The next cell over would have a different value throughout its own volume, and so on. At the top left in Figure 8.40, cellnoise is visualized over Gumbo by calculating a fixed point using cellnoise() inside each cell, and finding the distance from our shading point to that cellnoise "feature point". Basically the output of cellnoise() is used as a spatial offset to the cell's center, to obtain a feature point inside the cell. The feature point is thus an alternate representation of the cellnoise() value. Because it is a point, we can perform distance calculations between it and other points. Also, since this feature point can be anywhere inside a given cell and that location will vary between adjacent cells, we get a cell-to-cell variation in our distance computations. The image on the top right of Figure 8.40 shows Voronoi cells created using cellnoise(). Think of our current cell (which contains our shading point) as the center of a 3x3x3 Rubik's Cube, and our neighboring cells to be the surrounding cubes. We can examine the lattice of 26 (27-1) cells that surround our cell, compute a feature point on each neighbor, keep track of the closest of the 26 feature points and return that as the result of a Voronoi closest-cell function. The distance between this closest feature-point and our shading point is turned into a grayscale C_i value. Shading points that happen to be equidistant from adjacent feature points form the relatively bright outlines of Voronoi cells.

In the bottom left image, shading point P is first passed through the noise() function before being fed to the Voronoi closest-cell call. This results in dark uneven ring patterns across the surface. Finally in the bottom right one, the Voronoi distance (distance to the closest feature cell) is modulated via a sin() function which leads to concentric rings of alternating bright and dark intensities emanating from the feature points. As is evident, such small variations on the basic computations can produce interesting looks, often in unexpected ways.

As an aside, the cellnoise() function can be used as a random sequence generator, since feeding it values of 1, 2, 3, etc. will produce different outputs which would serve as random numbers.

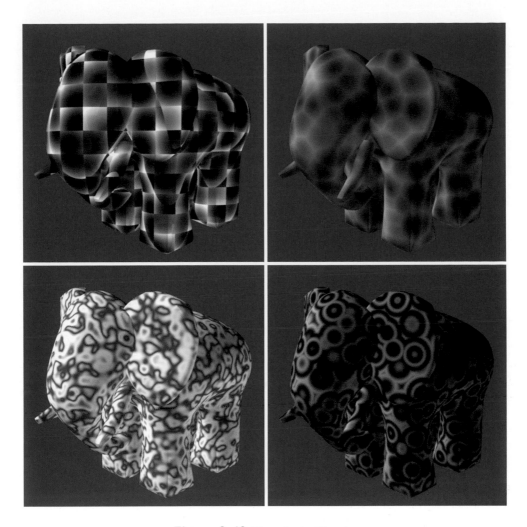

Figure 8.40 *Discrete (cell) noise*

Figure 8.41 illustrates the process of texture mapping, a fundamental operation common to all renderers. The essence of the technique is shown on the top left image. We are given a 2D image (a "texture map") and a surface in 3D and are asked to paste (decal) the image on to the surface. Since our surface is just a square in perspective, the obvious thing to do is to line up the image corners with the square corners and paste the image over. If the 3D surface has a single crease as shown on the top right, we can still line up the corners and paste.

But how does the lining up and pasting occur in rendering? Every texture map, regardless of its resolution or aspect ratio, is equivalent to a unit square with corner coordinates (0,0), (1,0), (1,1) and (0,1). A value of (0.5,0.5) always refers to the dead center of a texture map, and so on. Given the name of a texture map (which is a file on disk) and a pair of coordinates (such as (0.2,0.8)), RSL's texture() function call looks up the color at that texture coordinate (location) and returns the result. So for texture mapping to occur, every micropolygon vertex on our surface needs to contain a texture coordinate value, which will be used by texture() to look up a corresponding color towards Ci computation.

Note that texture map access is performed using the following texture() call:

```
color Ct = texture(tmap,s,t);// tmap is our texmap file on disk
```

The above call shows how to look up an RGB color triplet at a given texture coordinate pair (s,t). To look up just a single channel (R, G, B or A) instead, specify a channel number 0, 1, 2 or 3 respectively, after the map name:

```
float Cgr = texture(tmap[2],s,t);//[2] specifies green-channel lookup
```

In practice, texture coordinates are associated only with vertices or CVs, and are interpolated across surfaces spanned by these vertices/CVs. So how do we attach texture coordinates with vertices/CVs in the first place? There are several ways. One is to use a 3D paint program to directly paint texture coordinates over a surface. The resulting coordinates (which we will call (s,t) from now on, since that is how RenderMan refers to them) are used to look up an image texture during rendering. For a parametric patch such as a NURBS surface, the (s,t) values are derived from the parametric (u,v) values, so a unit NURBS patch, no matter how complex its 3D shape is, will automatically have (0,0), (1,0),(1,1) and (0,1) as the texture coordinates at its corners, making it easy to decal map a whole texture map over the complex surface (we imagine stretching the map to make its four corners coincide with the four patch corners, and patting down the map to lie on the surface). Texture coordinates can also be computed on the fly inside a shader just before a texture() lookup call, or existing (s,t) values can be modified via calculations before doing a lookup. This last notion of (s,t) modification is shown in the next five illustrations in Figure 8.41. The first image shows a star-shaped surface with (s,t) values on its 11 vertices (10 corners, 1 interior vertex) that cookie-cut a portion of the texture (the texture is repeated on all illustrations for side-by-side comparison). On the right, the (s,t) values are offset (translated) before looking up the texture, which makes the texture shift on the surface. The images in the third row illustrate scaling and rotation of (s,t) before texture lookup. You could combine several scale, translation and rotation operations to perform more complex lookups. In the bottom row, the image on the left shows the texture being repeated. This is done using the mod() function, as in:

```
ss = mod(s*s_repeat,1.0);
tt = mod(t*t_repeat,1.0);
```

By multiplying s and t with a repetition value (e.g. 5) and taking just the fractional part of the result, we create multiple 0 to 1 ranges from the single range coming in via (s,t). Each smaller 0 to 1 range brings in an entire copy of the texture, and that is what leads to repetition of texture.

Finally, the right image on the bottom row illustrates a very powerful idea. You can look up colors in more than one texture map using a given (s,t), and combine the result colors any way you want. Here we simply add the colors from the "Becky" and "ramp" textures. You can generalize this approach to perform a modification of (s,t), look up texture in a map, do another modification, look up texture in a different map (or even the same map), and so on. RenderMan places no restrictions on how many sets of texture coordinates you can manipulate or how many texture() calls you can make. This lets you create maps for a variety of surface characteristics, look up textures and modulate those characteristics. Color maps, opacity/transparency maps, dirt maps, light maps and specularity maps are some common map types. Any attribute that you can visualize over a surface can be turned into a map, and looked up in a shader with a texture() call. This is how you can breathe life into otherwise boring, dull surfaces – using maps, you can make sure that attributes such as color vary unevenly across a surface, making them appear realistic. Cold, clinically perfect surfaces (sometimes termed "too plasticky") as a rule do not integrate well with live action imagery.

Figure 8.41 *Texture mapping*

So how are texture maps different from raw images, and how do we create them? In PRMan, the "txmake" command line program is used to create texture maps from TIFF images. By convention, texture maps are named with a .tex or .tx extension. Look up the documentation on running txmake or its equivalent for your alternative RenderMan renderer.

What these texture creation programs do is to take the original R, G and B (similar processing occurs for alpha channel if one exists) channels from the input image, and create scaled-by-half copies of them, with attendant loss of detail. If we start out with an original image resolution with power-of-two values (e.g. 1024x1024 or 2048x512), the scaling down process will ultimately yield a version with just a single pixel in the horizontal and/or vertical dimension. E.g. a 256x256 TIFF image will yield scaled-down versions with pixel dimensions 128x128, 64x64, 32x32, 16x16, 8x8, 4x4, 2x2 and 1x1. Conceptually, the single pixel 1x1 image represents the zoomed out version of the original. The successive tiles of R, G, B channels can be stored in the clever "MIP-map" format invented by Lance Williams, a computer graphics pioneer. As shown in Figure 8.42, laying out R, G and B next to each other at a certain resolution will create a hole where a smaller set will fit, and so on.

Given an (s,t), the texture() call automagically accesses the appropriate pair of adjacent resolutions (e.g. the 128x128 one and the 64x64 one), looks up colors on both, and interpolates between the two. Which levels to access is determined by the area the looked-up texture will occupy on the image. Smaller the occupied area, smaller the tiles that are looked up. If you imagine laying each successive RGB image centered over the previous one, an image pyramid results with the smallest image at the top/apex.

Figure 8.42 *MIP map construction*

In addition to direct texture painting, assignment via parametric (u,v) and algorithmic generation/manipulation of (s,t), yet another technique is called projection texturing. There are several variations, and the most common ones are shown in Figure 8.43. The idea is to imagine that the texture map exists in stained-glass fashion over a simple geometric shape (cube, cylinder or sphere in our case) that surrounds the surface we would like to texture map. If the stained glass surface is illuminated from outside, the texture (or more appropriately, texture coordinates) will be projected on to our surface. At the top right is planar projection, where the image is projected "flat" over the teapot. The shape of the teapot is irrelevant. For a curvy object like the teapot this type of projection does not work well but it is ideal for projecting on to relatively flat surfaces such as a TV screen or a billboard. The cylindrical projection type is illustrated in the bottom right. You can see the texture curving around the sides of the teapot like it should, but on the lid the projection appears incorrect (since the projection surface is an open cylinder, it only projects correctly on to a nested cylindrical surface). Finally, spherical projection is shown in the bottom right. This looks better than the cylindrical version, but the lid still shows problems. This is because our texture map is a rectangle and is not meant to be wrapped around a sphere without causing distortions. The projection is only a approximate one. It is however possible to prewarp the texture image so it will project more accurately. The subject of map projections has been extensively studied by cartographers over centuries. You can look up resources on the web (e.g. the USGS site) if this topic appeals to you.

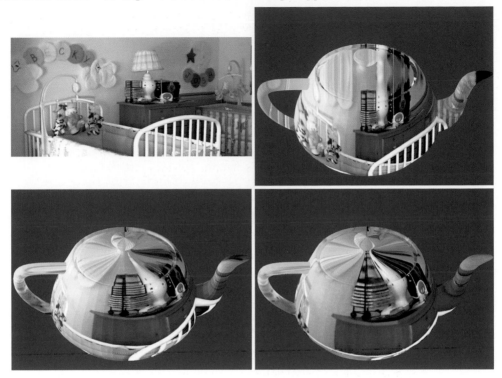

Figure 8.43 *Basic projection texture types*

Since you can look up colors (and opacities too) in a texture map using texture(), you can treat the shading system as a way to do image processing. Convert the images you want to process into textures, write shaders to do image processing and apply the shaders to an image-filling square or rectangle. Dedicated image programs such as Photoshop or GIMP excel at such image filters, but if you have an idea for a new filter and want to test it out quickly, writing a shader to do so is not a bad idea.

Figure 8.44 shows four examples of simple image manipulation. At the top left, original colors are replaced with duotone shading derived from two user-supplied colors. The original color is converted to an intensity (luminance) value between 0 to 1, which in turn is used as a blending factor for the duotone:

```
color Ct = color texture(txnm,ss,tt);
// approximation for NTSC luminance formula
float lum = 0.3*comp(Ct,0) + 0.6*comp(Ct,1) + 0.1*comp(Ct,2);
Ci = mix(col1, col2, lum);
```

The mix() function takes a pair of colors and an interpolation parameter, and returns the blended color.

At the top right, a blue matte is added to the image by checking if the shaded point lies outside a central circle. On the bottom left, the texture call is used twice: once to look up color at (s,t) and again, to look it up at (t,s). The two colors are averaged for the final result. This produces an image symmetrical about the left-leaning diagonal. Try looking up more colors, e.g. at (s,1-t), (1-t,1-s), etc. Averaging more of these colors will produce more mirror reflection axes in the output, reminiscent of a kaleidoscope (but with 90 and 45 degree symmetries instead of 60 and 120 degree ones). The image on the bottom left results from warping texture coordinates using the noise(0 function:

```
point PP = transform("shader",P);
 vector turb = ampl*snoise(PP*freq);
ss  =   s + comp(turb,0);
tt  =   t + comp(turb,1);
ss  =  clamp(ss,0,1);
tt  =  clamp(tt,0,1);
Ci  =  color texture(txnm,ss,tt);
```

ss and tt are obtained by adding noise-based offsets to s and t. Because doing so might result in ss and tt falling outside the 0 to 1 range, the clamp() function is used to truncate values to the 0 to 1 range.

Figure 8.44 *Texture map image-processing*

Similar to the texture() call is an environment() call, which takes the name of an environment map (a special form of texture map) as input and returns a color value resulting from the map lookup. But instead of (s,t) to index the map, it takes a normalized vector, in other words a direction, as the lookup input. The direction is internally converted to an equivalent (s,t) for texture lookup purposes. This process is called environment mapping, as it lets an image (map) be used as a wraparound environment for a scene. It is an elegant and powerful idea which lets you use external imagery (photographs, artwork or even other rendered images) to color and light surfaces in your scene. It is one of the best ways to integrate live action and CG, and is a staple in the world of visual effects. The T-1000 chrome character in *Terminator 2* is a good example of environment mapping.

There are two types of environment mapping, spherical and cubical. The spherical version is shown Figure 8.45 (the cubical case follows). We start with a 360-degree panoramic image, possibly acquired through a series of overlapping photos "stitched" together using panorama-manipulation software as shown at the top of the figure. If you cut such an image out and glued it end-to-end like a ring, the image would wrap around. It represents the full view around the axis about which the photos were taken. The strip-like image with a long aspect ratio is compressed lengthwise to an aspect ratio of 2:1, producing what is called an equirectangular panorama. The features in the image look tall and squished but the panorama still wraps around. This TIFF image is input to the txmake program with a "-envlatl" flag, if you are using PRMan. The resulting image is named with a .env extension, signifying that it is an environment map.

The .env map can be input to the environment() call, together with a lookup ray direction. RSL's reflect() call is used to obtain a reflection vector at each shading point, to use with the environment call:

```
Rray = reflect(-V,Nf);
if (envnm != "")
{

   Rray = vtransform ("shader", Rray);
   Cr = Kr * color environment(envnm,Rray);

}
```

The vtransform() call transforms the reflection vector into what is called "shader space". Just like geometric primitives can be enclosed in AttributeBegin/End or TransformBegin/End pairs, so can shader calls. Shader space refers to the cumulative transformation resulting from such a nesting, at the point in the RIB file where the shader is invoked. Doing operations in shader space gives you a way to rotate, scale and translate points, normals and vectors inside your shader, simply by adding transformation calls in your RIB files.

The right image in the middle row shows the result of performing environment lookup on sphere and a torus. Since the environment is totally reflected on the surfaces, it looks like they are made of thin glass and were placed in the middle of the environment, right at the place where the panorama images were snapped. Note the pinch points on the surfaces. These result from the fact our panorama image is not a fully spherical panorama, it is only a cylindrical one. The images did not capture all of the sky and all of the earth, so the texture stretches to compensate for the missing information in the map. Nevertheless it is still a good approximation. Indeed, any image (not even a cylindrical panorama) can be converted to a spherical environment map and used for reflections. This is shown in the bottom row of Figure 8.45.

Figure 8.45 *Spherical environment mapping*

Cubic mapping, which is the other type of environment mapping, is illustrated in Figure 8.46. The map used is a synthetic, made-up one but the idea is as follows. Imagine taking square aspect-ratio photos inside a room. Align yourself with the walls, stand in the middle and take a picture. This would be your +Z image. Turn right, take a photo, repeat this two more times to get images along the +X, -Z and -X directions. Face forward again (along +Z), look up, snap a +Y picture. Finally, look down and take a -Y picture. If you glued these six images on the inside of a cube, you should have a replica of the space you are in, inside the cube. Now any object inside the cube can have the environment reflected on it, by shooting a ray outward to collect the color at the point it hits.

With PRMan, the six component images are fed to txmake with a -envcube option, to create a cubical environment map.

After that the result can be used in an environment() call just like with the spherical case. You can view environment maps using the 'sho' command (or equivalent). Doing a "sho" on our cube map displays the image at the top left of Figure 8.46 without the X/Y/Z labels (which I added for illustration). In other programs the same six images are displayed using the "cross" format shown to the right. The bottom row shows the results of applying the cubical map to the sphere/torus combination and the Utah teapot. The sphere shows soccerball-like seams, which are artifacts resulting from the fact that mine is not a true cubical environment map. Nonetheless it does illustrate how the maps are looked up to be applied on to the sphere.

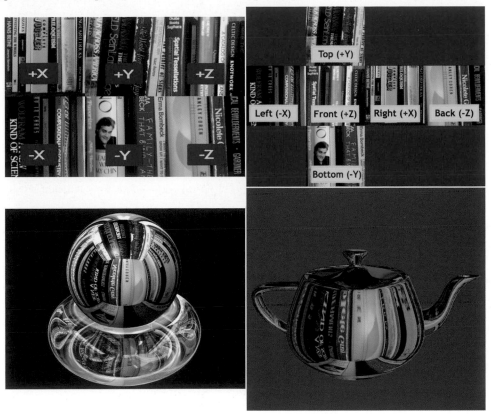

Figure 8.46 *Cubic environment mapping*

Paul Haeberli has another style of environment mapping, illustrated in Figure 8.47. Here, we need a 360 degree, all-immersive map encoded into a circular region inside a square image. The image on the very top-left shows the interior of Cafe Verona in Palo Alto, California, photographed with a hemispherical fisheye lens. Such a lens captures everything in front of it, including top and bottom. By facing the reverse direction, the other half of the view can be obtained to complete the full immersive view. But Paul chose to simply mirror the first image to use as the reverse image, as a quick hack. Such a pseudo-panoramic image can be seen in the middle row, left. Given this image, a shader's reflection rays can be mapped to look up points inside the circular area of the panorama. This is illustrated in the bottom left image. Another example is shown in the right column. Here, the starting point is not even half a panorama, it is just a regular image. But it can be warped using a RenderMan shader and rendered on to a hemisphere, to create the pseudo-panoramic image. From here on the texture can be looked up as usual.

In my environment map illustrations the texture is applied 100% on to surfaces, without taking surface color and surrounding lights into account. In practice you would treat the environment as just an additional layer, for subtle blending with existing materials.

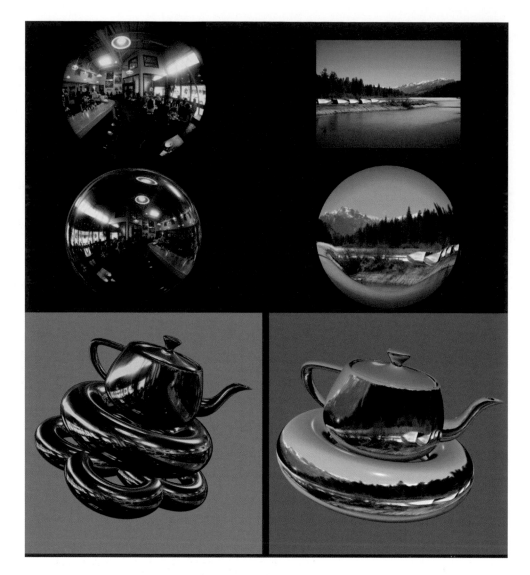

Figure 8.47 *Haeberli-style environment mapping*

Figure 8.48 illustrates simple cases of refraction and transmission. Refraction (top right) is achieved by using the RSL refract() call to compute a refraction vector at the current shading point, and turning it into (s,t) for texture access. It appears as if a glass paper weight is placed over a picture of orchids, where the paper weight acts as a magnifying glass. The thin glass look (maximum transmission in the interior, opaque at the edges) shown in the bottom row is achieved using a Fresnel factor to mix in a different color at the edges. Even though we have managed to portray what looks like glass, the shader calculations are not entirely physically-based. But for most purposes this is adequate, the rationale being that "if it looks right, then it is right".

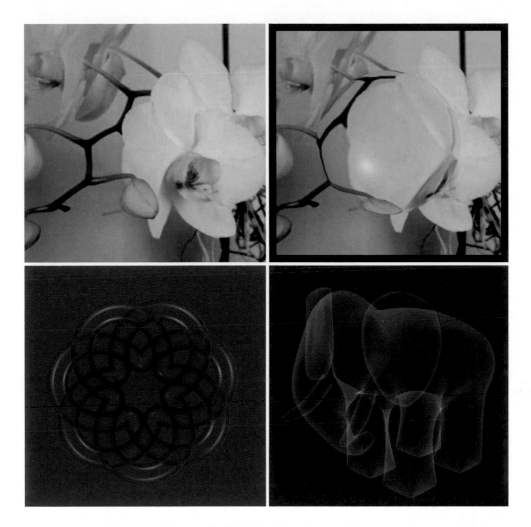

Figure 8.48 *Refraction, transmission*

Figure 8.49 shows some examples of expanding on the basic idea of the diffuse() call. The top row illustrates translucency (which is not the same as transparency). Translucent objects react to light "behind" them as well. The diffuse() call deals only with forward-facing normals, so if a thin cube with a marble texture shown at the top left of the figure contains a light source inside, the diffuse() call is unable to take that light into account. The result is that the surface looks opaque. Even if transparency is increased, the image on the right will not result. To obtain the translucent image on the right, we modify the standard shading definition to take into account a "Kd2*diffuse(-Nf)" term, where -Nf refers to the "back" of surfaces visible to us. So if there are lights behind the surface, diffuse(-Nf) will account for those as well, leading to translucency. Further, if the -Nf and the Nf side each have their own texture map, the result is more dramatic. In particular, the texture on the reverse seems to be visible right through the surface. Translucency is good for depicting thin surfaces such as parchment, fresh green leaves and even skin. *A Bugs Life* from Pixar has dramatic examples of this sort of effect.

In the second row, the diffuse(-Nf) idea is used to add a different undercolor to the Spirograph surface (right image). In the image on the left, it does not seem like the surface is sitting on the plane, whereas on the right, using the plane color to also shade the bottom of the Spirograph makes the two more integrated. It is a cheap version of color-diffusion (also called radiosity), a global illumination phenomenon which we will encounter in section 8.10.

A related notion is that of a double-sided surface. In the left image of the third row, a single flower texture map is used to shade both the outside (convex) and inside (concave) surfaces. What if we wanted the inner surface to have a different texture, as shown on the right? We can use the N.I dot product to decide if the surface we are looking at is a true outside surface (facing us) or the flip side of an outside surface (not facing us). If it is indeed the flip side, we can assign it a different texture as shown. Prof. Malcolm Kesson from Savannah College of Art and Design teaches an excellent RenderMan class, and in his online course notes discusses such a two-sided shader. The code for two-sided texturing looks like this:

```
surface dblsidedtex
(
   string txnmf="", txnmb="";
   float dbl=1;
)
{

   string txnm=txnmf; // front texture is the default one

   // If we are looking at a reverse side, switch to
   // 'back' texture
   if(N.I>0)
      txnm=txnmb;
   // now look up texture as usual..
   // note that texture(txnm) will look up RGB color
   // in the map name held in the txnm string variable, at
   // default texture coords (s,t). We don't
   // need to say texture(txnm,s,t), the (s,t) is
   // implicit
   Ci = texture(txnm);

}
```

The built-in diffuse() function call uses the L.N dot product (between light source direction and surface normal) to limit shading on the surface to the hemisphere containing the light source. This is adequate for most purposes, but what if we want the light to diffuse along the surface past the hemisphere boundary? We would have to write our own definition of a "wrapped-diffuse" function that does allow us to set our own shading limits. Such a shader is shown in the bottom row of Figure 8.49. On the left is a standard matte shader which uses the RSL diffuse() call, for reference. The middle image shows the use of the wrapped-diffuse call where the shading is expanded to include more of Gumbo, resulting in a uniformly illuminated, area-light look. Such diffusion wrapping past the hemisphere limit is sometimes helpful in matching CG lighting with live action images.

We can also go the other way and "unwrap" the light diffusion, thereby limiting shading to a small sliver on the surface. This is shown in the bottom right.

Rob Bredow from Sony ImageWorks discussed such a wrapped-diffuse shader, at the RenderMan course during SIGGRAPH 2002. You can find another version of the wrapped-diffuse model implemented by ZJ and Rudy Cortes, in the RenderMan Academy web pages.

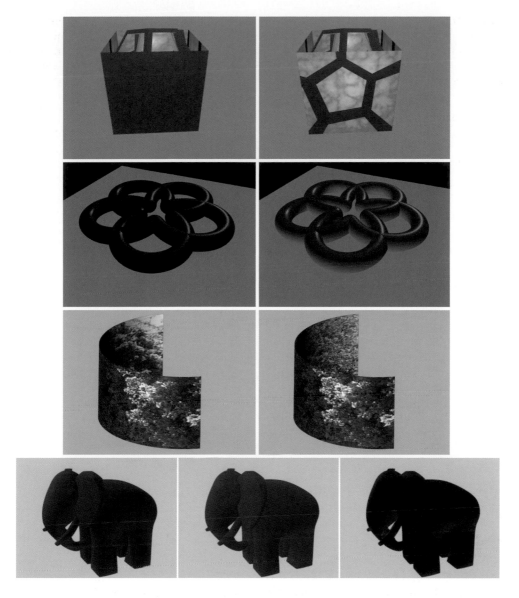

Figure 8.49 *Translucent, double-sided and wrapped-diffuse shading*

In Chapter 4 ("Geometric Primitives"), we talked about constructive solid geometry (CSG) in section 4.16. Since that chapter was about primitives and not shading, we did not investigate what would happen if CSG operations are carried out on surfaces that have different shaders on them. Figure 8.50 shows a "difference" operation, where a gray slab removes material from a gold colored Spirograph surface. You can see that the exposed surfaces inherit the slab's shader, not the Spirograph's. This is because the subtracting (cutting) object is the gray slab, and what we see as the exposed cutaway of the Spirograph surface is in reality a leftover section of the gray slab. You can use this fact to create animations of surfaces being cut open to reveal surfaces made of a different material compared to the exterior. Try doing a similar experiment with the intersection operator on these surfaces, to see what the shading on the intersection surface will look like.

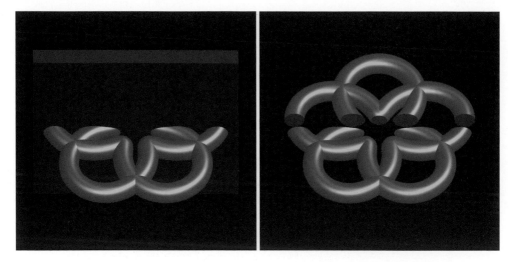

Figure 8.50 *CSG and shading*

Figure 8.51 shows a technique where the background ramp is constructed by using mix() to blend between a sky color and earth color. The interesting part here is how the interpolation value is derived. There is an image-filling rectangle which receives the ramp shading. If the rectangle happens to be a unit NURBS plane, we could just use the "s" or "t" texture coordinate as the blend parameter, knowing that it will go from 0 to 1 along the height. But what if the rectangular plane is really made up of a tiling of small rectangle polygons? There will be no unifying texture coordinate from top to bottom in that case. The solution is to convert the micropolygon position P, into what is called the NDC (Normalized Device Coordinate) space. Any point on any surface can be converted to NDC space as follows:

```
point PNDC = transform("NDC",P);
```

We start with incoming P, and end up with our own PNDC point variable that contains P expressed in NDC coordinates. Here is the good part – in NDC space, x coordinate always varies from 0 to 1 left to right, and y, from 0 to 1 top to bottom (the 0 to 1 range comes from the normalization). The z coordinate is always 0. So to get our blend factor, we simply do:

```
float blendfac = ycomp(PNDC);
```

The entire source code for the NDC ramp shader is as follows:

```
surface NDCramp(color ct=1;color cb=0;float gam=1.0;)
{
  point PP = transform("NDC",P);
  float y = ycomp(PP); // 0 to 1, top to bot.
  y = pow(y,gam);
  Ci = mix(ct,cb,y);
  Oi = 1;
}// NDCramp
```

NDC space can be used in advanced ways for creating maps for reuse, in multi-pass renders. Note that in our gradient ramp example, the background did not need to contain a camera facing, image-filling rectangle. It could be filled with nuts, bolts, Gumbos and teapots thrown together in heap so as to fully cover the image plane. Our ramp shader will still convert each P into a proper unified NDC value, and our ramp will still look just like the one in Figure 8.51.

Figure 8.51 *NDC gradient ramp*

I touched upon the notion of shading spaces earlier. When we say P or N or L or I etc. in a shader, in what coordinate system are those quantities expressed? They are in the "current" coordinate system, which could be one of world, object, shader, NDC or camera. Surprisingly the RI Spec. does not specify which, so it is implementation-dependent. If you want to make certain you are in a certain space, use the transform(), vtransform() and ntransform() calls to convert your quantities into known spaces like we did in our NDC ramp example above. Each space has uses and drawbacks, and which space you choose depends on the situation. Figure 8.52 shows a pair of identical shapes, expressed in object space (top row), world space (second row), camera space (third row) and shader space (bottom row). Look carefully at the marble shader patterns on the surfaces (it might be helpful to compare the locations of the white splotches).

In the top row, the marble pattern is computed in object space. This means that P, N, etc. are translated to the space the surfaces are defined in, regardless where they are in space now when being shaded. Because the surfaces contain identical geometric data, their object spaces are identical. So the marble patterns on them are identical as well. If you fill the scene with dozens of these surfaces, they will all appear to have been carved out of identical marble blocks, a situation that is not realistic. So next we try to compute the patterns in world space. In the left image the surfaces are away from the blue square torus. Each surface has its own pattern, which is good. But if an unseen hand grabs the surfaces and moves them closer to the torus (right image), you would see the marble patterns swirl across the surfaces as they move through space. Because the computations are in world space, where the surfaces are located determines the pattern. This might make for amusing animations but again, it does not reflect reality. If we compute in camera space, simply panning the camera (left versus right image, third row) will cause the textures to change. Again, this is probably not what we want. Finally, we use the shader space, which is the right thing to do. We can nest each object's Surface shader call in different transform or attribute blocks (e.g. one can contain a rotation about Z but not the other one). This gives us what we want: each object has its own texture, which does not change as the objects move or the camera moves. Except for special cases, try to do your shader calculations in "shader" space, as it provides the most flexibility.

Figure 8.52 *Shader spaces*

In Figure 8.53 are shown some colorful shaders. Again, these are good practice shaders for you to dissect and explore techniques and RSL calls. At the top left, NDC is used to compute hue values that are anchored at the image center. To its right, s and t are used with mod() to again create per-patch ramp colors. At the bottom left, expressions involving P, N, noise() and sin() are used to fill the surface with colorful patterns indicative of soap film. Finally, at the bottom right, the shader uses three illuminance loops in sequence, to gather light along three user-supplied illuminance cone axes. In our illustration each cone receives one colored light, and the shader combines the results into Ci. Note that you cannot obtain such an image using combinations of lights with just the matte() shader which has just one fixed illuminance() loop – the three custom loops in our shader are essential.

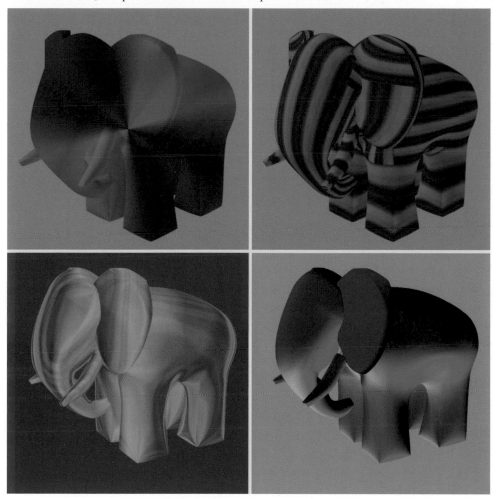

Figure 8.53 *Colorful shaders*

8.6 Displacement shaders

Displacement shaders let you alter the positions of micropolygons before they are shaded by surface shaders. In other words, the global variable P can be assigned a new value inside a displacement shader, unlike the case with the other shader types where P is a read-only variable which cannot be overwritten. Displacement shaders are specified in RIB files using the "Displacement" keyword. Also, whenever displacement shaders are specified, you also need to include an Attribute statement that declares the bounds of displacement, i.e. the maximum spatial displacement that will occur as a result of executing the shader. If you omit the Attribute statement, you are likely to get a flawed image containing partial displacements and holes.

In Figure 8.54, the sin() function is used to compute grooves along which to displace P. The top row images show displacements based on s or t texture coordinates. The bottom left image shows displacements along both s and t. In the bottom right image, the Pixar "sinknurl" shader that ships with PRMan produces the displacements shown.

The statement that produces displacements based on the "s" texture coordinate is shown below:

```
if(0==paramdir)  // displace based on 's'
{
    P += ampl*sin(sphase+s*freq*2*PI)*normalize(N);
}
```

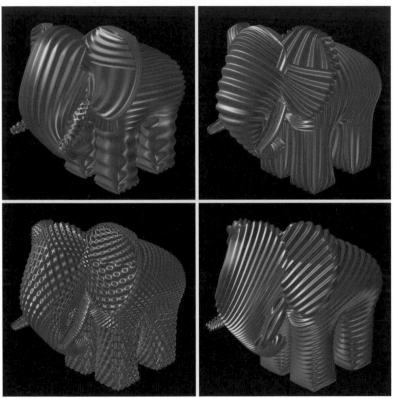

Figure 8.54 *Periodic displacements*

The noise() function can also be used to provide values for displacement, resulting in realistic displacements that mimic stucco, stone texture, etc. Figure 8.55 shows are pair of noise-based shaders. On the left, the output of noise() at the current shading point is used to displace it along the surface normal, creating a rough surface texture. On the right is shown the PRMan "cloth" displacement shader, which creates weave-like grooves by using s and t texture coordinates as inputs to the noise() function.

Figure 8.55 *Noise as displacement*

The ridged multifractal which we encountered in Figure 8.39 is a perfect choice for producing rock-like displacements, as shown in Figure 8.56. The surface is covered with small cellular displacements, with larger, lower frequency ridge lines producing chunkier protrusions.

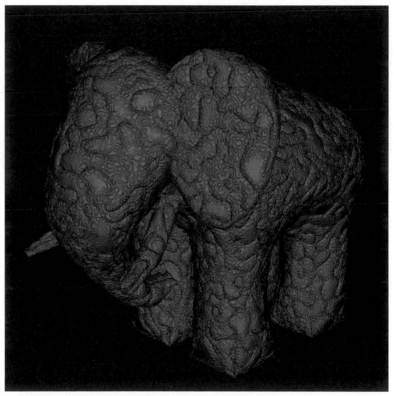

Figure 8.56 *Ridged multifractal displacement*

In Figure 8.57, the cellnoise() function or more specifically, the closest feature point Voronoi call is used to create cellular displacements that look like hammered metal, mud cracks and leather. The basic idea is to find the closest Voronoi feature point, and use the vector connecting the current point and feature point as the axis along which to displace.

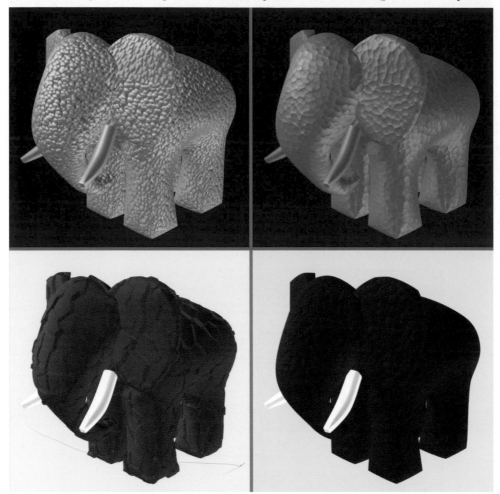

Figure 8.57 *Cellular displacement patterns*

Texture maps can also be used for displacements, where the looked-up color (or float) value can be used to derive the extent of displacement. In Figure 8.58, the right image in the top row shows a chip-carved wooden block generated from the z-depth image on the left. Without the displacement, we would simply have a smooth slab rendered with the wood surface shader. The chip-carving pattern is impressed into the surface by our displacement shader which looks up a grayscale value from the z-depth image using the (s,t) texture coordinates at the current shading point and uses the gray (intensity) value to displace micropolygons along the reverse of the surface normal. Likewise, in the bottom row, the Spirograph depth image is used to displace the sides of a cube. Note how the edges of the displaced surfaces catch the light. In this case the same texture map is used on all six cube faces to create displacements, but you can use a different map for each face if you like. Such image-based displacements might be a quick way to impart some relief textural detail to an otherwise dull/smooth surface.

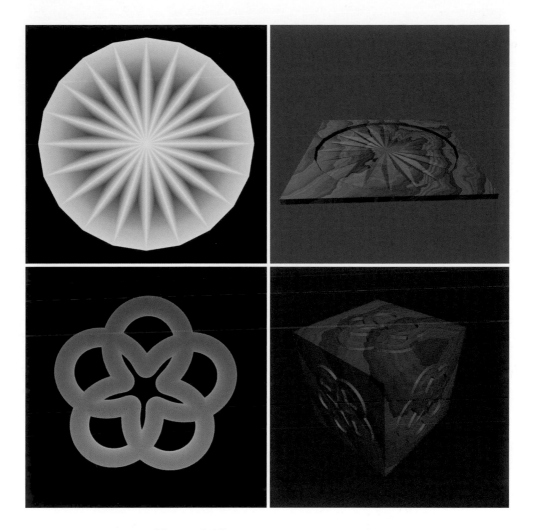

Figure 8.58 *Image-based displacements*

If an entire object is displaced to the left or right using camera space coordinates, a stereo pair results as pictured in Figure 8.59.

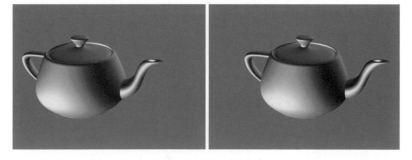

Figure 8.59 *Eye-space displacement to generate a stereo pair*

Figure 8.60 illustrates bump versus displacement mapping. As noted earlier, displacement mapping actually moves micropolygons in space. This means if you look at the silhouettes of a displacement object, you expect to see a change in the silhouette as a result of the displacement. For instance, on the top left of Figure 8.60, the Spirograph surface looks rough everywhere including silhouette edges. Contrast this with the image on the right, which also looks rough on first glance. But if you look at the silhouette, you can see that it is smooth, with no displacements at all. The rough look in the interior is produced by setting N to different values based on noise, in other words, by bumping N. Hence this technique is termed bump-mapping. If you frame your bump-mapped objects so as to hide their silhouettes, bump-mapping offers a faster, cheaper and better alternative to true displacement mapping.

At the bottom of Figure 8.60, the Penrose star shape again shows the difference between displacement mapping (left) and bump mapping (right). In the bump mapping version the normals are bumped, but the shader we are using visualizes grids and micropolygons without taking normals into account and shows that the micropolygons do not undergo any change during bump mapping.

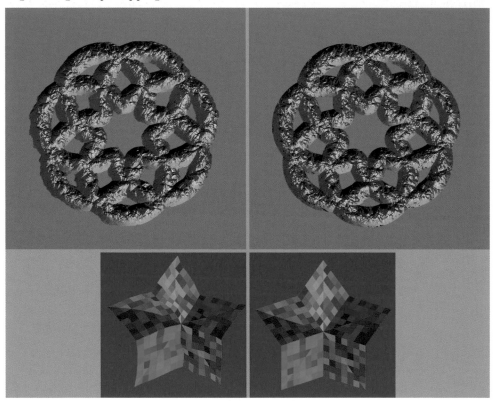

Figure 8.60 *Bump versus displacement*

8.7 Light shaders

Light source shaders allow you to create your own lights for illuminating objects in your scenes. The key global variable you would fill in a light shader is Cl, which is the light color.

In addition, for directional lights, you would also set L, the light direction vector. Note that inside a surface shader, the L vector points away from the surface and towards the light. But in a light shader, it is the opposite – L points away from the light towards the surface it illuminates.

The built-in spotlight shader that comes with **PRMan** has a fixed distance-based falloff of 2 in accordance with Lambert's illumination principle where the intensity falloff is proportional to square of the distance. So in your scene if you have a spotlight that is far away, you would have to crank up the intensity to hundreds or even thousands of units,, to compensate for the falloff. Or alternately, you could create your own spotlight with a user-specified falloff. This is shown in Figure 8.61, where the falloff parameter is gradually increased to fade out the light.

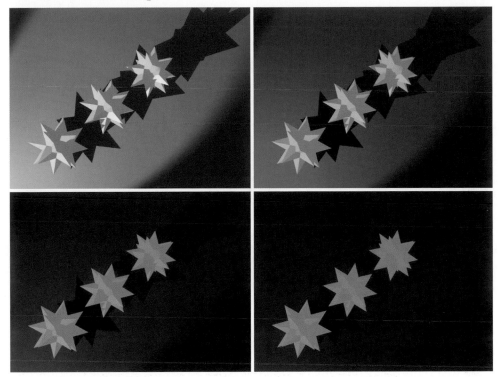

Figure 8.61 *User-defined intensity falloff*

Depth mapped shadow generation is revisited in Figure 8.62. The top-left image shows how a directional light (yellow arrows) is positioned relative to the surface. The bottom-left image is the depth map rendered from the light's point of view. Once this depth map is generated, it can be used inside a shadow-creating light shader as follows:

```
Cl *= 1 - shadow(shadowname, Ps, "samples", samples,
"swidth", width, "twidth", width);
```

The RSL shadow() call takes the name of the shadow (depth) map as input, and returns a float value that is proportional to how much the point Ps is in shadow. Note that inside a light shader, the global variable Ps denotes the currently shaded point. Points not in shadow will result in a 0.0 output from the shadow() call, so the code snippet shown above ensures that such points are shaded as-is while shadowed points do get darkened.

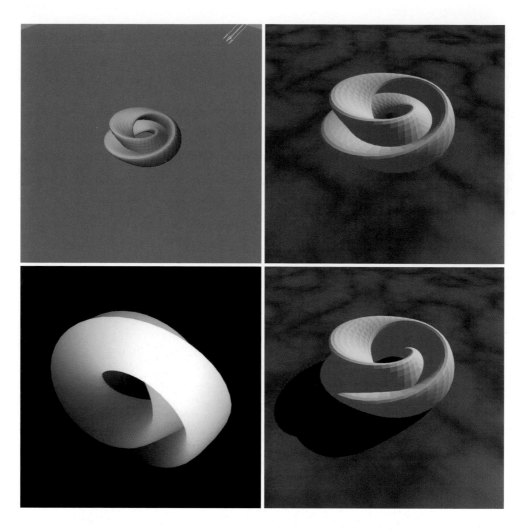

Figure 8.62 *Depth-mapped shadow*

A rectangular area light is shown in Figure 8.63. As noted before, area lights offer broad illumination zones, and this makes their shadows soft. Also, it is common to include an area light itself as a visible scene element. In contrast, ambient, spot, point and distant lights are not usually pictured in the rendered image – only their illumination is. You can create custom area lights by sampling any piece of geometry (e.g. a Spirograph) at uniform intervals over the surface and emitting light from each sampled point. By the way, true area lights via the "AreaLightSource" RIB command are not supported in PRMan. You can however achieve area light effects by sampling geometry as just mentioned and using the standard LightSource command to invoke your pseudo-arealight shader.

While a piece of geometry can only be shaded by a single surface shader (and be optionally displaced by a single displacement shader), it can be illuminated by multiple light source shaders. This is in keeping with the real world where a surface made of a certain material can be illuminated by any number of light sources. Note that a lot of shading functionality can be expressed either in a surface or light shader. When you do have that choice, opt to create a light shader, since it offers the possibility of being invoked multiple times (each with its own set of parameters) over a surface.

As an aside, it is instructive to think about when and how light shaders are invoked by RenderMan. Surely, all the light sources in a RIB file are not "on" in the physical sense, for the duration of the render. What really happens is that when a point is being shaded, its illumination cone in the surface shader (if the shader code contains the relevant code) is used to identify lights that potentially affect the shaded point. It is only those lights that are selectively invoked, to obtain light colors at the current point. Those light colors are then used by the surface shader to eventually come up with Ci and Oi as usual. In other words, it is as if all lights in a scene are always "off", and surface shaders turn on just the light(s) they need, obtain the data they want and then turn the light(s) off again.

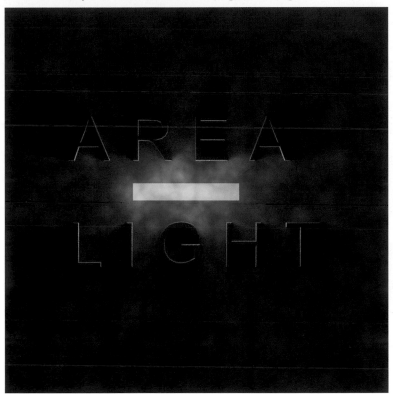

Figure 8.63 *Rectangular area light source*

Figure 8.64 shows a Phong light and rim light shader. On the left is the Phong light which only illuminates a narrow specular zone on a surface (in that aspect it is similar to the non-diffuse light shown in Figure 8.12). Likewise on the right is a rim light which only illuminates edges (silhouettes) of objects. Such custom lights are easy to write, and offer you precise control while you light your scene. By the way, custom light shaders are specified using the RIB LightSource command identical to how you would specify a built-in light. For instance the pair of Phong lights in Figure 8.64 are declared as follows:

```
LightSource "phonglt" 1 "from" [0 2.7 0] "to" [0 0 -1] "sharpness"
160 "intensity" .75
LightSource "phonglt" 2 "from" [10 2.7 0] "to" [0 0 -1] "sharpness"
100 "intensity" .8
```

Figure 8.64 *Phong and rim lights*

Figure 8.65 shows two instances of a rainbowlight shader applied to a set of polygonal tori. The shader works by taking the dot product of the light direction L with a user-supplied direction, multiplying the result with a hue frequency (also user-specified) and using a mod() function to turn the result into a hue value for the light along that direction L. In other words, this is a light where the emitted color varies as a function of direction. The mod() function ensures that the variation is periodic, thereby creating colorful fringes of illumination across surfaces. The hue frequency determines fringe spacing. Our example uses two rainbowlight sources that have different hue frequencies and orientations, creating overlapping sets of radial and concentric fringe patterns.

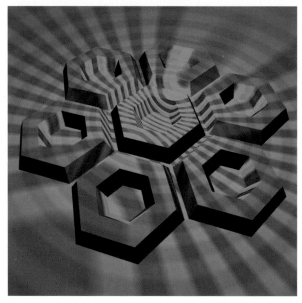

Figure 8.65 *Rainbow light*

Similarly Figure 8.66 features a different kind of fringe light shader, where it is the length of the light vector that is modulated to create the fringes. The RSL function length() returns the length of an input vector, so in our case the length of the light vector L at a given shading point is given by length(L).

Figure 8.66 *Fringe-emitting light source*

In Figure 8.67, a single vertical line through a texture map (at a "u" value specified by the user) is used as a ramp to look up colors, based on how the surface normal N is pointing. Upward pointing normals receive sky colors from the top of the ramp, while downfacing normals pick up earth colors from the bottom.

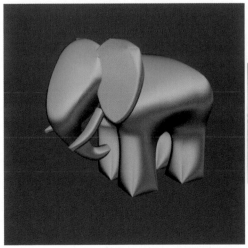

Figure 8.67 *Texture map as light source*

A completely arbitrary, non-physical light is illustrated in Figure 8.68. It uses the components of the normalized light vector L to calculate light color Cl. The x and y components of the vector are used to calculate terms (x*x-y*y) and (2*x*y) which serve as the red and green channels of the light color at the shading point. In addition, another term is obtained by taking the dot product of a user-defined direction and the shading point (a physically meaningless operation, but useful for pattern generation nevertheless). These three terms are fed to the sin() function to create fringes. The code fragment is as follows:

```
# (x*x-y*y) term
float real = pow(abs(x*x-y*y),gam1);
real = 0.5*(1+sin(f1*real));

# (2*x*y) term
float imgn = pow(abs(2*x*y),gam2);
imgn = 0.5*(1+sin(f2*imgn));

# dot-product term
float dotp = 0.5*(1 + uD.PP);
dotp = pow(dotp,gam3);
dotp= 0.5*(1+sin(f3*dotp));

# resulting light color derived from the three terms above
Cl = lightcolor*intensity* color(real,imgn,dotp);
```

It is interesting that we can use such made-up expressions in light shaders to create colorful emissions of light. Such specialty lights can be used at low intensities to liven up scenes, by breaking up regions of uniform illumination.

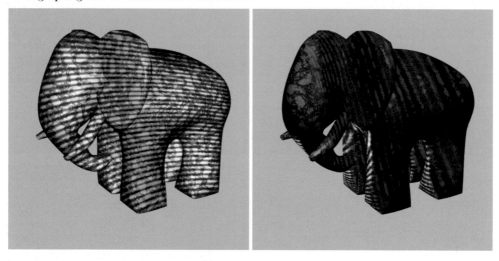

Figure 8.68 *A non-physical light*

Figure 8.69 illustrates four noise-based light sources. The figure on the top left shows a shader by Malcolm Kesson, which I call "kessonlt". It adds noise to the shading point and uses the result to derive a light direction for illumination:

```
# transform shading point Ps to "shader" space
point Pt = freq*transform("shader",Ps);
# add noise to the shading point, and use the result as
# a light direction
vector ldir = 2*noise(freq*Pt) - 1;
solar(ldir,coneangle) # emit light along the computed direction
{
    Cl = intensity * lightcolor;
}
```

At the top right, a noisy directional light shader derives light color by evaluating noise() for the quantity Ps+N (sum of the shading point and surface normal).

The bottom-left image illustrates a noisy pointlight shader where the light's intensity is modulated using noise() of the light vector L. Because we modulate intensity (brightness), the shader appears to emit light in the form of bright and dark splotches.

The shader on the bottom right (a "cellulite" shader) emits light in cellular patterns derived using cellnoise() and Voronoi calculations which were discussed earlier.

As the four examples in Figure 8.69 illustrate, you can create novel procedural light sources using noise() together with standard global variables such as Ps, N and L. Such specialized light shaders might serve as synthetic versions of cuckaloris (also called gobo) lights used in theater and film.

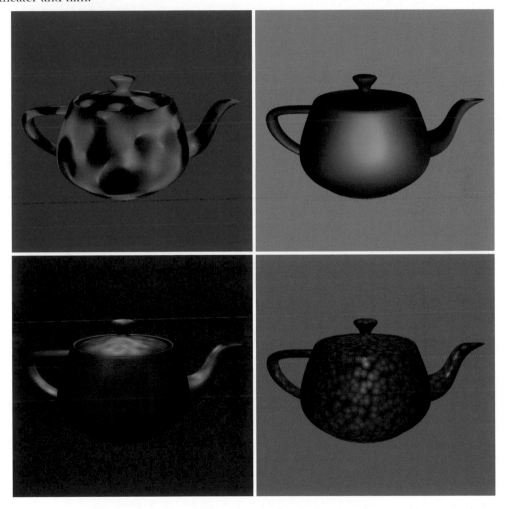

Figure 8.69 *Noise-based procedural lights*

Gobo/cuckaloris effects can also be achieved by using a texture map to project light through, analogous to a slide projector. Such a shader is shown in Figure 8.70.

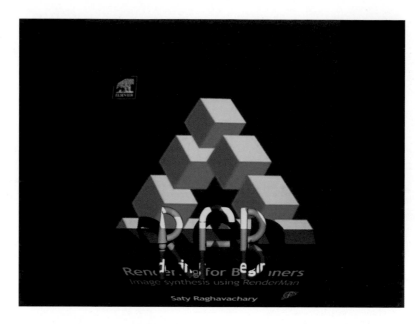

Figure 8.70 *Slide-projector light*

You will notice in many renders that the actual light source doing the light emission is itself not pictured in the scene, area lights being exceptions. If you do want to include a point light source (for example) in a scene, the simplest thing to do is to place a piece of geometry where the light is located, as shown in Figure 8.71. Here a light-enclosure surface shader is applied to the pair of cubes which serve as light source geometry. This shader creates a circular pattern on each face of the two cubes, to make it seem like they each enclose a light. Note that the result looks better than shading each cube with a single solid color.

Figure 8.71 *Light sources that are visible in the scene*

This section showcased a number of light shaders. As you can see, they are quite useful in setting up a variety of lighting conditions. To appreciate being able to write your own light source shaders, ask yourself how you might use just the four basic light types (ambient, point, spot and distant) to achieve the same lighting that the custom shaders provide – you would conclude that in many cases, this is simply not possible.

8.8 Volume shaders

Volume or atmosphere shaders allow for the participatory media (air, smoke, water, etc.) to influence the color and opacity of surfaces that are immersed in the media. Many examples of such "atmospheric phenomena" exist in the physical world, such as objects appearing dimmer due to fog, underwater hue shift, atmospheric perspective, etc. In RSL, atmosphere shaders typically use the eye vector I to alter surface variables Ci and Oi.

Figure 8.72 shows a fog shader whose code is as follows:

```
float d;
color wh = color(1,1,1);
d = pow(length(I)/maxdist, falloff);
d = 1 - exp(-d);
Ci = mix( Ci,bg,d);
Oi = mix( Oi,wh,d);
```

Here, length(I) is used to derive a mixing factor d to alter both Ci and Oi. As d increases, Ci is blended more with a fixed background color, while Oi is made more opaque by mixing with white.

Figure 8.72 *Heavy fog*

A depth cue shader is shown in Figure 8.73. Here, increasing distance is used to fade out opacity, making objects far more transparent than ones nearby. Depth cuing is a useful technique for applying to surfaces such as wireframes, where bunching up of data near the horizon (due to perspective) can be eased somewhat by fading out opacity.

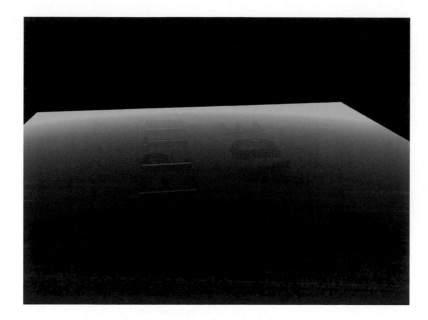

Figure 8.73 *Depth cueing*

An extreme example of atmospheric perspective is seen in Figure 8.74. Artists use the term to describe a phenomenon whereby distant objects lose color saturation and definition, while taking on a bluish gray hue. To simulate this accurately would require an advanced understanding of light scattering, but we can approximate it by using "length(I)" to mix in a farcolor value supplied by the user.

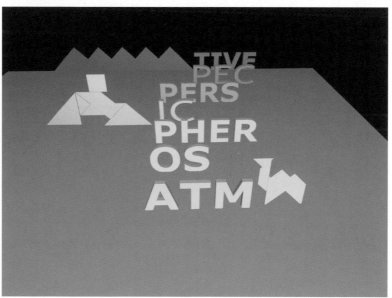

Figure 8.74 *Atmospheric perspective*

Likewise, underwater hue shift (Figure 8.75) can be achieved by using "length(I)" to first create a color that varies smoothly with depth, and then mixing that with existing Ci. The code is as follows:

```
d = length(I);
if(d<=mindist)
   c = fg;
else if(d>=maxdist)
   c = bg;
else
{
   d = (d-mindist)/(maxdist-mindist);
   d = pow(d,gam);
   # make c vary between fg and bg (colors) as a function of d
   c = mix(fg,bg,d);
}
Ci = inten*mix(Ci,c,mixf);
```

Figure 8.75 *Underwater atmosphere*

Figure 8.76 shows another atmosphere shader that shift hues by a user-supplied amount, based on depth:

```
color c = ctransform("rgb","hsv",Ci);
float h = comp(c,0); # obtain just the hue value
float d = length(I);
# the mod() function below creates hue fringes
h = mod(h+d*shift,1.0);
# use 'h' as the new hue value, but keep existing
# saturation and value as is
c = color "hsv" (h,comp(c,1),comp(c,2));
# mix the new fringe color with existing Ci
Ci = mix(Ci,c,mixf);
```

As you can see, these atmosphere shaders are just a few lines long but can effect a variety of changes in Ci. Note that in the above code, the RSL ctransform() call is used to convert Ci from its existing RGB to new HSV space, since we need to be in HSV color space to shift hues.

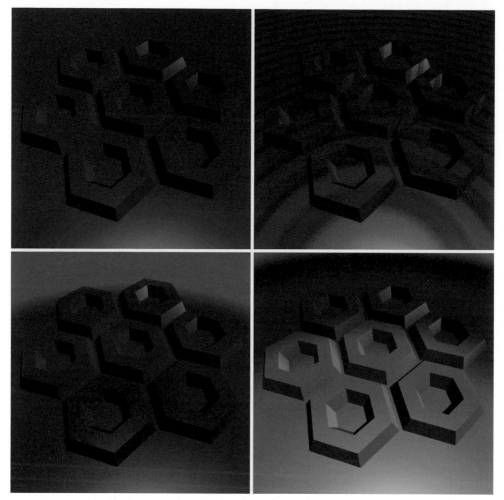

Figure 8.76 *Hue-shifting atmosphere shader*

Patchy fog is illustrated in Figure 8.77:

```
vector II = vtransform("shader",I);
float n = ampl*noise(freq*II);
d = pow(n/maxdist, falloff);
d = 1 - exp(-d);
```

Here, the I vector is used to derive a noise value which is then used to create the fog mixing factor.

Atmosphere shaders are specified using the Atmosphere RIB command. For instance the patchy fog in Figure 8.77 is generated using:

```
TransformBegin
Attribute "identifier" "string name" ["directionalLightShape2"]
```

```
Transform [-1 -9.1002e-017 -8.19466e-017 0 0 0.669167 -0.743112 0
1.22461e-016 -0.743112 -0.669167 0 0 0 0 1]
LightSource "distantlight" 3
TransformEnd
#### atmosphere shader invocation
Atmosphere "patchyfog" "color bg" [1 1 .95] "float falloff" [ 1.3]
"float maxdist" [ 8.000 ] "freq" .3 "ampl" 18
AttributeBegin
Attribute "identifier" "name" ["|pPlane1|pPlaneShape1"]
# .. geometry and surface shader specification
# ...
```

Figure 8.77 *Patchy (noise-based) fog*

8.9 Imager shaders

The last category of shaders supported by RenderMan is the imager shader. In an imager we are able to read and write Ci and Oi. Imager shaders are optional, and each scene can contain just one imager call. If an imager does happen to be present in a scene, it is invoked only after all the rest of the shading (using surface, displacement, light and atmosphere shaders) is completed. Imagers carry out their operations on a per-pixel basis. Conceptually, imager shaders are similar to Ken Perlin's "Pixel Stream Editor" (PSE) and pixel/fragment shaders supported by modern programmable graphics hardware.

In Figure 8.88, a "background" imager shader fills the non-rendered area with a user-supplied red color. Most images in this book make liberal use of the background imager shader, since I wanted to avoid filling the imagery with pure black backgrounds.

The source code for the background imager shader is as follows:

```
imager bg(color bgcol= color(0.5,0.5,0.5))
{
    Ci+=(1-Oi)*bgcol;
```

```
    Oi=1;
}// bg()
```

Imager shaders are specified in RIB using the Imager command, like this:

```
# ...
Format 900 900 1
Display "Imager_bg.tiff" "tiff" "rgb"
# the 'bg' imager shader - its only input is a color value
# to use for filling the background (non-rendered) pixels
Imager "bg" "color bgcol" [.69 .24 .11]
# ...
```

Figure 8.78 *Flat background imager shader*

A ramp background imager in Figure 8.79 makes the two rendered polyhedra appear to float in space. The ramp color varies from blue at the top to bluish-white at the bottom, simulating the appearance of sky. Note that the use of such vertical color ramps is a common trick in cel animation to create the illusion of stylized skies, ground planes and horizons.

The ramp imager shader uses the following code to calculate the ramp parameter:

```
option("Format",rez);
# curr_y is used as the mix factor for ramp generation
curr_y = ycomp(P)/ rez[1]; // 0 to 1, top to bottom
```

The option() call is used to retrieve the output image resolution (width, height), and the image height (which is contained in rez[1]) is used to derive a ramp mix factor. In an imager shader, P is global variable that contains the coordinate of the current pixel (which would be (0,0) in one corner and (xres-1, yres-1) in the diagonally opposite corner, where xres and yres are image resolution values).

Note that PRMan only supports the "background" imager shader. If you include any other imager call in a RIB file, it will be ignored by PRMan. So I used Scott Iverson's AIR

RenderMan implementation to generate Figure 8.79 which requires using the ramp imager. You can find AIR at www.sitexgraphics.com.

Figure 8.79 *Ramp imager*

A "bgfill" imager shader is a useful one for filling in non-rendered pixels with values from a texture map, thereby placing rendered objects in the context of the scene they might be in. In Figure 8.80, a tribar object is the only rendered element and is surrounded by pixel colors from a texture map filled in by the bgfill imager shader:

```
imager bgfill(
string txnm="";
float xres=1024.0;
float yres=1024.0;
)
{
    color bgcol = color(.5,.5,.5);
    float s,t;
    if(""!=txnm)
    {
        // note that we don't have to pass in (xres, yres)
        // ourselves through the shader arg.list - we can
        // query its value here inside the shader, using
        // option("Format",rez);
        s = xcomp(P)/xres;
        t = ycomp(P)/yres;
        bgcol = color texture(txnm,s,t);

    }
    Ci+=(1-Oi)*bgcol;
    Oi=1;


}// bgfill()
```

Figure 8.80 *Texture-filling imager*

To render Figure 8.80, I used Aqsis, a free RenderMan-compatible open-source implementation of REYES. If you are looking for a non-commercial alternative to PRMan, Aqsis is definitely the software to get.

8.10 Global illumination

Global illumination (GI) functions were first made available in PRMan version 11 which was introduced in the fall of 2002. PRMan has always been a powerful photoreal renderer, but with the availability of the new GI features, its capabilities have been significantly extended.

So what exactly is GI? In short, it is everything that the classic REYES algorithm cannot render. Since the current micropolygon being shaded has no knowledge of the environment it is in, there is no way to make the shading calculations take into account neighboring surfaces that might reflect/bleed colors or otherwise influence the results. Because of not being able to take a micropolygon's global environment into account, the rendered images, as photoreal as they might seem, will still appear to lack a certain amount of realism. GI is an umbrella term used to refer to a variety of everyday optical phenomena such as color bleeding, caustic pattern formation, ambient light occlusion, etc., all of which involve a broader range of mutual interactions between lights and surfaces. This is what makes them hard to fake with a renderer that only shades "blind", without taking surroundings into account. Look at Figure 8.81 which shows photographic examples of several of these phenomena. In the bathroom sink image, you can see color bleeding from the shiny purple ornament and green sponge on to the sink. The water in the bottle creates a caustic pattern on the paper underneath. There are reflections in the mirror and ornaments. The markers in the cups (top right image) exhibit color bleeding ("radiosity"). The photo on the bottom left again shows a transmission caustic, where the water in the glass acts like a lens to focus light right into the shadow region. The image on the bottom right shows sunlight from the window hitting a stainless steel faucet, creating wild patterns of reflection caustics on the wall.

Figure 8.81 *Real-life global illumination*

In everyday life you can observe many such phenomena involving light and surfaces. They are not unusual at all, indeed they are quite commonplace. But that does not mean that renderers have been able to calculate and render these effects right from the beginnings of CG. In fact many of these phenomena have proved intractable until recent times, partly because of the scarcity of good algorithms to compute them and partly due to the lack of raw computing horsepower. You could very easily stick an orange traffic cone on a piece of white cardboard to make the orange color bleed on to white, place your hand nearby to cast a shadow into the bled color and use your other hand to shine extra light into the shadow using a mirror. To set up a CG scene to render such a thing in real time is not trivial! In the physical world, light/surface interactions just happen, no digital computations are involved. But to be able to render them in CG is a different matter.

Within the past decade both computing speed and graphics research have been gaining up on GI issues, making impressive progress on both fronts. We are starting to see GI imagery in movies such as *Finding Nemo*, *Shrek2* and *Shark Tale*. The trend will only continue, as GI permits us to synthesize imagery that display a new level of photorealism.

In this section we will focus on six main aspects of GI . The first is ray tracing. The idea of ray tracing has been around since the early 1980s. A ray tracer (which is a form of renderer) sends out into the scene, a light ray from every pixel in what would ultimately be the rendered image. Each ray enters the scene, gets reflected, refracted, transmitted and attenuated by objects in the scene, and accumulates colors and opacities of surfaces encountered along the way. After a predetermined number of such "bounces", the ray stops traveling further, and the accumulated color and opacity become the originating pixel's color and opacity.

Note that the ray tracing described above is backwards compared to what happens in real life. In the physical world, light rays (trillions of photons) continuously leave a light source, illuminate objects and finally enter the eye (or imaging device) to create an image. But in classic ray tracing, it is as if light rays leave the eye, looking for surfaces to gather colors from. It is done this way and not in the "forward" physical sense, since with forward ray tracing there is no guarantee that rays leaving a light source in a scene will ultimately reach all the pixels in the rendered image in finite time so as not to leave holes (unfilled regions) in the image.

Conceptually ray tracing is a very simple idea which nevertheless produces extremely realistic imagery. In Figure 8.82, the ray-traced image on the left shows a shiny die placed on a checkerboard, inside a room with checkerboard walls. You can see both the checker pattern as well as the die's own ground shadow, being reflected back on to its surface. Such realistic reflections are hard to fake by just using image maps for texture lookup.

The right image in Figure 8.82 is a tribute to Turner Whitted, who helped popularize ray tracing with a classic 1980 paper titled "An Improved Illumination Model for Shaded Display". The image shows reflection, refraction and transmission as well as shadows on the checkerboard floor.

In RSL, the trace() function call takes a point and a direction, traces a single ray and returns a resulting color. PRMan makes GI functionality fairly easy to use in our shaders, via just a dozen or so carefully chosen calls that have been added to RSL. All the pre-GI function calls and tricks will still work, making the GI implementation fully backwards compatible. For the excellent way in which GI functionality has been added to PRMan, the software team at Pixar deserves great kudos.

Figure 8.82 *Ray-traced reflection, refraction*

Figure 8.83 shows a ray-traced stained glass effect. Here, a ray tracing pointlight picks up colors from a texture map in order to cast a colored shadow on the ground.

Figure 8.83 *Ray-traced transmission (stained glass effect)*

The second GI phenomenon of interest is radiosity, shown in Figure 8.84. The colors from the teapot bleed on to the floor below. The floor is colored using a shader which gathers light from the surroundings via an indirectdiffuse() GI call.

Figure 8.84 *Color bleeding ("radiosity")*

The top image in Figure 8.85 shows ambient occlusion, another GI phenomenon. If you look around you can spot dark corners and volumes practically everywhere, even in the middle of an environment with strong sunlight. Since light cannot bend in free space, it cannot reach nooks and crannies, underside of roofs, insides of drawers, etc. Ambient occlusion seeks to create imagery that correctly shows these occluded areas. In our example, the web-like surfaces prevent light from reaching deep inside. We are using the gather() illuminance construct inside a light shader to collect information about the surface, specifically, how much of the surface can be reached by direct rays.

In the bottom figure the occlusion factor is used to brighten affected regions instead of darken them. The result is that the object seems uniformly lit from underneath.

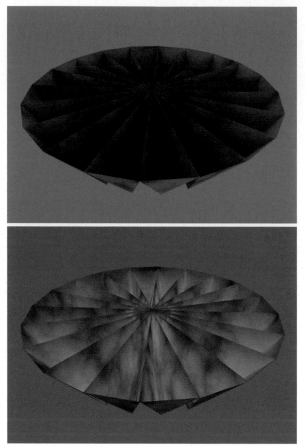

Figure 8.85 *Ambient occlusion and inverse*

The fourth GI phenomenon is subsurface scattering, shown in Figure 8.86. First studied by Pat Hanrahan and recently popularized by Henrik Wann Jensen, the idea is to create extra illumination on a porous/translucent surface (such as skin, marble or a block of ice) by allowing some light to enter the surface, bounce around a bit, collect illumination from the interior and then exit.

The top left image in Figure 8.86 is rendered without subsurface scattering. It has a rather dull and non-porous solid look. On the right is an image with a little subsurface scattering, where the light is able to penetrate just a little into the surface. You can already see the difference. The surface has a waxy sheen resulting from light entering the surface. On the bottom left image the light penetrates even more into the surface, imparting the surface with even more of a nice diffuse glow. At the bottom right is shown a fake subsurface effect, obtained using "length(L)" in a surface shader to brighten points on the surface closer to the light source. This simple hack does work extremely well in conveying a feeling of light penetration into the surface.

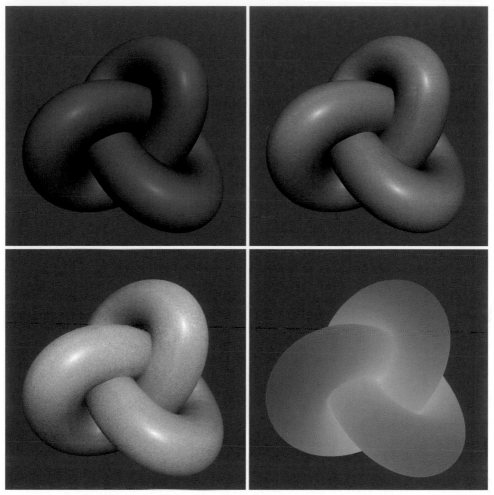

Figure 8.86 *Subsurface scattering*

Caustic patterns (our fifth GI category) are illustrated in Figure 8.87. The first image on the top left is actually fake caustics, and is an improvement on an idea originally due to Larry Gritz. His observation was that the core of a shadow region can be brightened instead of being darkened. Noise is added to break up the bright core and the result undergoes a threshold clamping to limit it to the core region. In addition to these, the rest of the gray shadow can be turned into a colored one to obtain the image shown.

The rest of the images in Figure 8.87 illustrate actual caustics calculations. On the top right is a transparent polyhedron, rendered without caustics for comparison. The second row shows reflection caustics. The polyhedron is imagined to be made of chrome, which reflects incident light out as a caustic, towards the side where the lightsource is. The bottom row shows a transmission caustic, where the surface is supposed to be made of glass and exhibits caustic patterns in the shadow region.

The two types of caustics are obtained in two passes. In the first pass, a photon map is generated (these are shown at the right in the second and third row) by filling the scene with photons and making them react to chrome or glass objects in the scene. This first pass is computed using the "photon" hider **RIB** call (instead of the usual "hidden" hider):

```
# use 4000000 photons to calculate the photon map
Hider "photon" "emit" 4000000
```

The resulting illumination is recorded as a photon map (a file on disk, viewable using PRMan's "ptviewer" helper program), which is looked up by a causticlight shader in the second pass to compute the actual caustics.

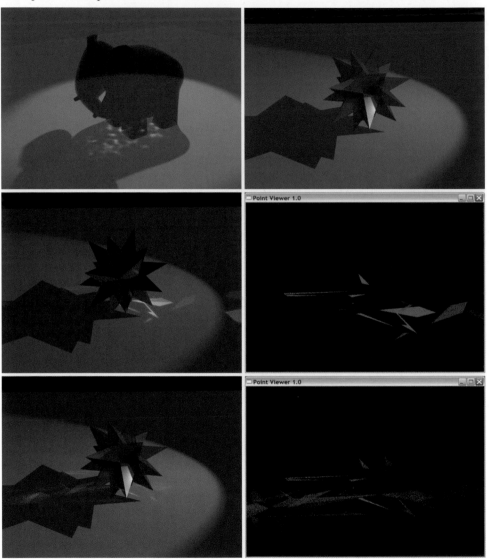

Figure 8.87 *Caustics*

The final GI category we will look at is image-based illumination, shown in Figure 8.88. We have seen prior examples where image maps have been used to look up the environment, ramp color, used as a slide projector source, etc. The difference here is that only diffuse lighting is contributed to by the image map. The idea again is to convert an image (top right in our figure) to an environment map and use it to look up color via an environment() call. The image needs to be heavily blurred (unlike the one shown here for illustration) before being turned into a map.

The map is then used in a GI light source to provide color. The light computes occlusion via the occlusion() RSL call, to create soft shadows and occluded regions. The occlusion factor is combined with color from the environment map, to compute outgoing light color Cl. The result is that surfaces can be illuminated with just an image-based light, and the light will color objects using colors in the texture. Surface shaders on the scene objects process light as usual (e.g. with a diffuse() call), not being aware that the "light" is really coming from an environment map. You can see in the image below that the environment map made from the books image correctly illuminates the surfaces. For instance the blue and red colors in the left of the map end up on the right of the trefoil surface.

There is much more to image-based lighting, and I refer you to Paul Debevec's excellent site (www.debevec.org) for information, theory, tutorials, sample images and free software.

Figure 8.88 *Image-based illumination*

8.11 Non-photoreal rendering

A lot of 3D CG focuses on photorealism, for good reason. It is gratifying to be able to synthesize imagery that fool the eye. For a lot of live action/CG integration, photorealism is indispensable.

But the fact is that when it comes to selecting a look or a rendered object, photorealism is just one of a myriad of choices. Artists have built up a formidable collection of rendering styles and techniques, and the goal in non-photoreal rendering (NPR) is to explore these techniques for use with CG, thereby expanding the possibilities for artistic representation using the medium of CG. RenderMan is powerful and flexible enough to encourage a variety of NPR exploration. Let us look at ten examples.

Figure 8.89 illustrates the illumination model proposed by Bruce and Amy Gooch, where surfaces that face a light source are shaded with a shift towards warm (red, yellow, orange) colors, while surfaces that face away are shaded with a bias towards cool (blue, purple) colors. Artists have used this warm/cool idea to make surfaces in a painting appear to advance or recede, and the Gooch model brings that notion to rendering.

The red surface shown on the top left does not have the Gooch model applied. On the right the colors have been mixed with blue and orange as per the Gooch model. The effect is exaggerated here for illustration, but in actuality you would cause just subtle shift in colors.

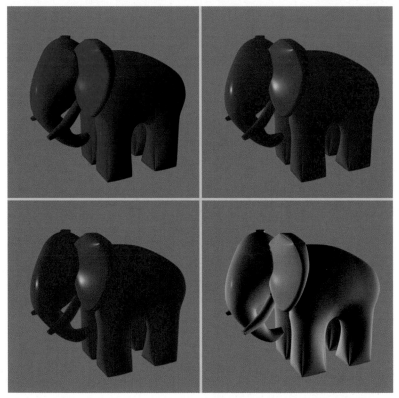

Figure 8.89 *Warm/cool contrast (Gooch illumination model)*

A variation on the Gooch model is shown at the bottom left, where the back surfaces also receive the warm color, sandwiching the cool color zone from either side. This tends to portray adjacent surfaces with a clearer separation. At the bottom right this sandwiching effect is applied on a compressed color range, creating a sepia tone look.

Figure 8.90 illustrates simple toon shading, where N.I is used to threshold shading into the three zones of shadow, midtone and highlight. In addition the silhouette edges are colored with a thick black line.

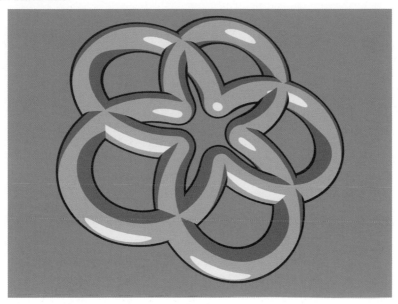

Figure 8.90 *Simple toon shading*

A pen and ink stipple effect and line squiggles are shown in Figure 8.91. The dot stippling is obtained by using a random number at each shading point to decide whether to put down a dot or not. The squiggly lines are the result of adding turbulence to the process.

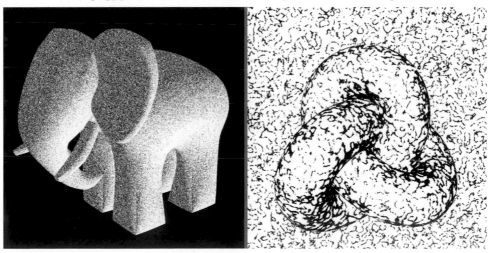

Figure 8.91 *Stippling with dots and squiggles*

A couple of displacement shaders are shown in Figure 8.92. Both use images for displacement. The pincushion shader displaces perpendicular to the plane, while the Vasarely shader displaces along the plane. While displacement shaders can operate on any type of geometry, it is most useful to apply pincushion displacements to a set of thin cylinders (pins) and the Vasarely one to a set of parallel curves (or thin cylinders). You can obtain novel deformations by pairing displacement shaders with custom geometry in this way.

Figure 8.92 *Pincushion and Vasarely shaders*

The next example in Figure 8.93 shows an idealized woodcut effect. Here the diffuse shading value at each point is used to either broaden or narrow a set of parallel stripes. As an exercise, try adding noise to the process to make the render seem more life-like. Our woodcut stripes are created using the following code snippet:

```
point PNDC = transform("NDC",P);
float ss = xcomp(PNDC);
float tt = ycomp(PNDC);
float stripewidth = 1.0/(nstripes);
float whichbin = tt/stripewidth;
```

```
float frac = mod(whichbin,1.0);
whichbin = whichbin - frac;
// diffuse
color d = Ka*ambient() + Kd*diffuse(faceforward(normalize(N),I));
float gray = 0.333*(comp(d,0) + comp(d,1) + comp(d,2));
gray = pow(gray,gamma);
// use whichbin, frac and gray to widen/narrow the light/dark
// stripes
// ...
```

"whichbin" is a variable which calculates whether the current shading point falls in a light band or dark. The "frac" variable is compared with the diffuse shading result in the "gray" variable to determine if the band we are in should be widened or narrowed.

Figure 8.94 illustrates the process of overprinting, using the woodblockprint shader written by Scott Johnston. In the first pass shown at the top left, the six spheres and the plane underneath are shaded with woodblockprint. The resulting rendered image is turned into a texture map to use in pass2 (top right) where the results from the second shading are printed over the first render, obscuring parts of it but not others, creating a rich, layered look. This process can be repeated however many times you want. During each pass the lights are repositioned a little differently to change the surface shading slightly.

How does each shading point know to combine its result with the corresponding point underneath? It is converted to NDC space, and the resulting (s,t) is used to look up texture in the old image to combine with the current one.

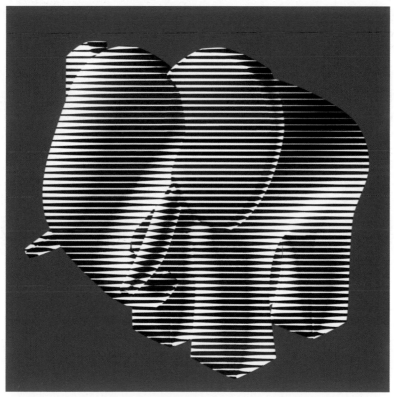

Figure 8.93 *Simple woodcut effect*

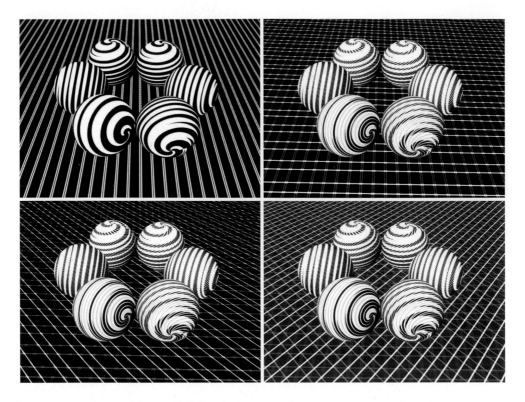

Figure 8.94 *Woodblock multipass overprinting*

Figure 8.95 shows another overprinting process based on a similar NDC idea, but this time we use long, thin, overlapping brushstrokes. The top left image shows that the image is initially covered with a dense set of sprites, which we will use as brushstrokes. Each sprite has an associated "strokeID" attribute, available inside our shader via the **RIB** file's custom attribute mechanism. The overall idea is to repeatedly overwrite parts of the existing image with new brushstrokes, creating a constantly evolving (never "finished" at any stage) set of renders. We can stop anytime our latest image looks pleasing to the eye. If we playback all the intermediate images as a sequence, we would see paint strokes animating across the surface in a rather haphazard fashion.

Here is how the image is continuously altered. In the first pass, each stroke looks up the color underneath it (via NDC coordinates) in the flower texture map, to yield the image on the top right. This first pass image is the same as the texture map itself, and no visible paint strokes have been generated yet.

In the next pass, the current rendered image is brought in as a texture, and the strokeID on each sprite is used to compute an offset before looking up texture. The offset causes each stroke to look up color not directly underneath itself, but in a nearby region instead. This causes the strokes to stagger, and the result is an image where the existence of the paint strokes is manifested as local shifts in texture. This new image layer is mixed with the incoming one and gets written out as the new image. The process can be repeated, to obtain progressively complex images. At any point you could retrace your steps by bringing in an older texture map from an earlier step, or occasionally even add in a foreign texture to incorporate that into the mix. You can obtain lively brushstroke animations by applying this process to an entire image sequence.

Figure 8.95 *Overprinted brushstrokes via texture mapping*

An image texture can be turned into a set of oversized halftone dots rather easily. The use of such a shader is illustrated in Figure 8.96. First the mod() function is used to group a set of neighboring shading points into a single square cell, and the texture map is evaluated at the midpoint of the cell. The luminance of the color resulting from the texture lookup is then used to decide the size of the halftone dot (filled circle) for that cell. If we are rendering dark halftone dots, a bright underlying luminance value will result in a small halftone dot. Alternately if our halftone dots are light, this should result in a large dot.

At the top left, the unaltered image is shown for reference. The top right image shows that the halftone dots can be created with just user-supplied colors. Alternately, we can incorporate some color from the underlying texture, as shown in the bottom left image.

An entire cell can be replaced with the single color at the cell center to obtain a mosaic image as shown in the bottom right image in Figure 8.96.

Figure 8.96 *Halftones and rectangular mosaic*

Noise can be used to add turbulence to hue, saturation and value components of a color, to obtain very colorful images such as the one in Figure 8.97. The surface does not need to contribute its Cs at all, all coloring can come from the procedural calculations.

Figure 8.98 shows how you can simulate paint strokes using Voronoi cells (via the cellnoise() function call) combined with texture lookup. The underlying geometry is a zoomed-in sphere. In the left image, the RIB call for the Voronoi shader does not have any transformations, so the textured Voronoi cells (our paint strokes) are uniform in size and scale. On the right however, non-uniform scaling is introduced as follows:

```
TransformBegin
Scale .95 .95  .324 # scale less in z compared to x and y
Surface "Vortex" "freq" 25 "jitter" 1. "Ka" 1 "Kd" 1.2 "txnm"
"BeckySq.tex" "mixf" 0.6 "mixf2" 1.0 "space" "shader"
TransformEnd
Sphere 2 -2 2 360
```

As a result the brush strokes are thinner and appear stretched over the sphere, producing a slightly different painting style. This is most evident at the edges of the image.

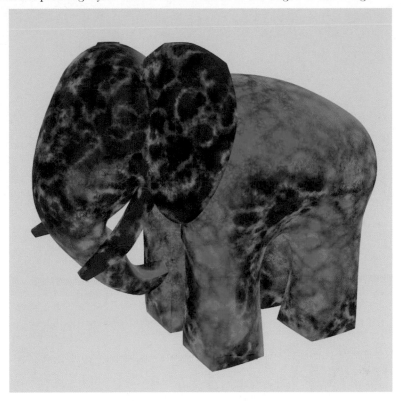

Figure 8.97 *Colorful HSV turbulence*

Figure 8.98 *Voronoi paint strokes using cellnoise*

Finally, Figure 8.99 shows a colorful abstract image obtained by bouncing a specular ray around, inside a closed sphere. This technique was first explored by Kevin G. Suffern.

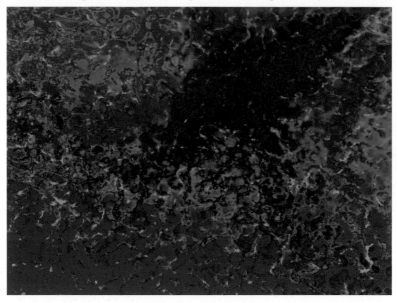

Figure 8.99 *Abstract art from ray tracing specular highlights*

8.12 Wrapup

This concludes our tour of shading facilities in RenderMan using the RSL. A lot of ideas were presented in this chapter, to inspire you to delve into shader writing. Take your time studying the shaders online at the RfB site. Modify them, create new ones by combining existing ones, add more parameters to the argument lists, etc. In short, have fun discovering what the shading language can do for you. Before you know it, you will find yourself creating your very own shaders.

Knowledge of elementary mathematics (proportions, interpolation, averaging), vector arithmetic and spatial concepts (distance, location, direction, length), trigonometric and logarithmic/exponential functions, equations from color theory etc. prove extremely useful in shader writing. If mathematics is not your cup of tea, try to at least brush up on the topics mentioned above. Without some mathematical knowledge of what shaders do, you might find yourself blindly copying and pasting code from others and getting frustrated at not being able to advance past that stage.

Drawing and painting skills are very useful for creating texture maps. In large graphics/animation studios employ texture painters whose sole responsibility is to create such maps. The advantage of painting textures as opposed to creating them procedurally is that painting is a more direct approach, and the maps can be precisely tailored to suit the vision of the art director and the scenes in which the textures will be used. Conversely, procedural textures do have the advantage that variations can be generated just by altering parameters that synthesize the patterns – no painting is involved.

It also helps to develop a keen awareness of lighting situations around you. Nature can provide you with examples and ideas for many things you might like to simulate with shaders. Develop an appreciation for things like long shadows during mornings and evenings, light shining through young green leaves, cloud patterns, dappled sunlight through a canopy of leaves, brightness of garden flowers in mid-day sunlight and reflections of the setting sun in bodies of water.

Human-made objects display a variety of visual phenomena as well. If you find yourself behind a gasolene tanker on the freeway, notice how the stainless steel tank exterior reflects a large portion of its environment. Heavily tinted windows on downtown office buildings strongly reflect other nearby buildings and also at times display warps in the reflections. The interaction of light with glass can only be described as magical. From art glass sculptures and stained glass windows to vases and chandeliers, decorative as well as functional uses of glass abound. Look for reflections, refractions, the Fresnel effect, colored transparent shadows and caustics when you are near glass objects. Walking through rows of parked cars on a sunny afternoon, you can observe Fresnel color shifts, strong specular highlights and cascades of reflection caustics from the rims on the wheels. Notice caustic patterns in your coffee cups and at the bottom of swimming pools. Objects containing fluorescent dyes offer studies in radiosity, and so on.

Even our living spaces provide ample sources of phenomena applicable to CG rendering. Look for ambient occlusion in practically every building and room you are in. If you are in a conference room, notice how the rows of overhead lights create specular highlights on the shiny table underneath. Concert halls and theaters are great places to observe how light is used as a creative design element to affect atmosphere and mood. The use of light emitting diodes (LEDs) in architectural lighting is a recent and growing trend, creating a soft look which you can duplicate in your RenderMan scenes using area lights.

These phenomena and lighting situations are always around us, and it is a matter of training the mind and eye to actively notice them. It does become an addictive habit, so try not to overdo it! In the words of my colleague Jim Leuper, "Life is not a shader".

If you do want to get into RenderMan-based lighting and shading in a serious way (to pursue it as a career), you would need to do your modeling and animation work in an animation package such as Maya or Houdini, and use their export facilities to output the RIB, shaders and maps needed for command line rendering through RenderMan. In these 3D programs you can manipulate shader parameters through GUIs, set RenderMan global values through property sheets, set up multiple rendering passes using visual controls, etc. In other words, you can work with RenderMan without doing any typing.

For instance, Figure 8.100 shows a Slim UI for the standard plastic shader, running inside Maya. With Slim you can visually connect shader blocks (called appearances) to create rich, complex shading networks. You can also bring existing .slo files on to the Slim palettes and apply them to your Maya objects.

Alternately, you can use standalone programs such as ShadeTree or ShaderMan to create shaders. Such programs offer a visual "connect the boxes" dataflow paradigm, again permitting you to hook up shader components using a GUI to end up with complex, non-trivial shaders. These programs output regular RSL code which you can examine, modify if necessary, compile and use the resulting .slo files in your scenes.

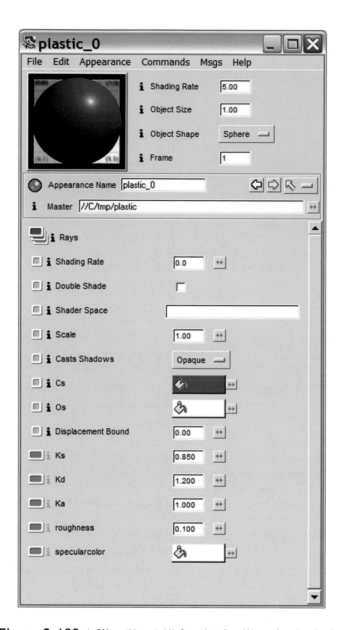

Figure 8.100 *A Slim (Maya) UI for the familiar plastic shader*

9
What's next?

Now that you are familiar with the basics of RenderMan, it is natural to wonder where to go next. This chapter will provide some directions for you to explore. Also, we take a look at possible developments for PRMan and the field of rendering in general.

9.1 Next steps for you

As you should know by now, RIB files that are used to create complex imagery often come from scenes set up in an animation package, translated into RIB via a built-in mechanism or a plugin. So a major next step for you is to learn how to set up your scenes in one of the animation programs that support rendering using RenderMan and use its RIB translator to generate and render RIB files. For instance, Maya's scenes can be translated by MTOR/Slim or MayaMan, both plugins to Maya. These translators also feature GUI-based shader construction mechanisms, making it easier for you to create complex RenderMan shaders by connecting blocks of pre-existing functionality, without manually writing code. The translators also make it easy to set up multi-pass rendering (e.g. for shadow mapping) and distribute your RIB files to a network of machines set up for rendering (a "render farm").

Alternately, if you would rather generate RIB files programmatically and have an interest and ability to write software, you could look at RIB bindings (constructs that produce RIB) available for languages such as C/C++, Java and Perl. The RfB page has links to several bindings currently available. You would find the use of bindings particularly convenient if you have models that describe the entities you would like to render (e.g. equations for physical phenomena, experimental data for molecular structures, formulae for curves, surfaces and other mathematical objects, etc.).

If you find shader writing enjoyable, you could focus on it by developing your programming skills further. It also helps to have an analytical bent, since the visual phenomena you would hope to translate to shaders are ultimately described by math equations. Also, if you would like to develop shaders to work with Maya and the MTOR plugin, it might be worthwhile to explore how to write the shaders in the ".slim" format (instead of PRMan's ".sl" format), since doing so lets you visually hook up your .slim shaders with building blocks that ship with MTOR/Slim (the shader interface will not let you do that with .sl shaders compiled into .slo). See the MTOR/Slim documentation for examples and how to get started with this. Shader writing is very specialized, and can lead to a fun and lucrative hobby/career.

Alternately, if you enjoy using texture maps to add realism to scenes, you could specialize in texture painting using programs such as Photoshop and then bringing the resulting images into RenderMan for use as maps. Also, if you have an eye for coloring and lighting (C&L) in general, there are excellent cinematography books that discuss lighting techniques which you can adapt for CG rendering.

Even though this is a book about RenderMan, I should mention that if you want to explore other photoreal renderers, you do have a variety from which to pick. Mental Ray is a leading competitor to RenderMan, and ships as a free plugin for Maya. Brazil and Arnold are two global illumination renderers that produce high quality output. Radiance by Greg Ward is another highly accurate global illumination renderer, available under an open source license. Please see the RfB web page for links to these and similar programs.

Figure 9.1 presents an alternate organization of materials in the book, based on the familiar "lights/camera/action" call. You could use such a grouping to discover a set of related topics you would like to pursue in more detail.

9.2 PRMan advances

As is the case with the past releases, the PRMan team at Pixar will no doubt continue to incorporate rendering advances into future releases of the product. This might take the form of new illumination techniques, shading language calls, geometric primitives, camera models, etc. Also, there is always room for continual improvement in terms of processor and memory usage and rendering optimizations through modifications to the Reyes algorithm itself.

Additional RenderMan implementations, bindings for more programming languages, translators for more animation packages, UI-driven shader generators are all desirable to bring more practitioners into the field and keep the RenderMan community growing. Then there is the tantalizing possibility of RenderMan running on commodity graphics hardware (see the following section), something which will revolutionize movie-making, electronic gaming and digital entertainment as a whole.

9.3 Future directions for rendering

3D graphics began with a quest to photorealistically render synthetic imagery. That quest has served us very well, leading up to systems such as RenderMan. But when it comes to visual representation, photorealism is simply just one of a myriad collection of styles. Over several centuries, artists throughout the world have evolved a fantastic diversity of media and styles, when it comes to capturing the essence of 3D on to 2D surfaces. "Non-photoreal rendering" (or NPR) is an umbrella term applied to CG research that devotes itself to graphics techniques and algorithms that render 3D scenes using these alternate styles of imagery. To date, a plethora of styles and media have been simulated, including pencil drawings, pen and ink, markers, pastels, wet watercolor, dry brush, oil painting, woodcuts, airbrush, cartoon rendering and others.

Craig Reynolds maintains a vast list of online NPR resources at www.red3d.com/cwr/npr. Also, Bruce Gooch has a collection of NPR links at www.cs.utah.edu/npr. Browse through these links to see for yourself the pace of innovation in this exciting field. Many of the techniques you would come across are suitable for implementation using RenderMan.

This line of research will continue, bringing more artistic styles into the fold and improving on existing ones. The bottom line is that NPR provides CG artists with ever-expanding flexibility in choosing how their 3D scenes will look. Combined with gaming and other interactive techniques, it will let end users explore 3D worlds made up in rich artistic styles, rivaling perhaps vivid dreams and hallucinations!

Introduction
- 3d pipeline
- REYES

Action
- geometric primitives
- level-of-detail
- procedurals
- FrameBegin, FrameEnd
- sidedness
- bounds
- grouping, nesting, transforms
- instancing
- reference geometry

Camera
- resolution
- display drivers
- secondary buffers
- matte channel
- pre-multiplication
- projection
- clipping planes
- depth of field
- motion blur
- exposure, gamma
- quantization
- quality/mem/speed tradeoffs
- spaces, coordinate systems

Lights
- light types
- turning lights on/off
- materials, shading
- color, opacity
- global illumination
- shadows
- maps: texture, environment, etc.

Script
- RIB structure
- RIB syntax
- entity files, 3d clip art
- include files
- RIB compression

Figure 9.1 *An alternate classification of topics in this book*

If diverging from photorealism is the focus of NPR, continuing research on global illumination (GI) techniques goes the opposite direction, paving the way for even more realism by capturing more optical and visual phenomena that are common in the real world and have not yet been renderable in a convincing away in a reasonable amount of time. There are also phenomena such as iridescence, phosphorescence, bioluminescence, fluorescence etc. for which convincing CG models do not exist yet. While it is possible to fake these using existing shaders in conjunction with image-processing and compositing techniques, true CG models for these would enable the realistic image synthesis of such phenomena under user control (e.g. in a game). In the real world, materials and light interact in very complex ways, at the chemical, molecular and atomic levels. There are no computations, the interactions just "happen". CG of course uses digital computations of light/surface interaction models to synthesize imagery resulting from such interactions. While the early models were sufficient to capture the rather simpler effects, ongoing research aims to capture more of what we commonly see in the real world. More sophisticated mathematical models of illumination combined with faster hardware are making it possible to achieve increasing realism in 3D imagery.

Another development currently underway in rendering (as I write this in 2004) is nothing short of a revolution in graphics. I am referring to programmable hardware shading. Graphics rendering hardware (OpenGL acceleration cards) on commodity personal computers have been steadily getting faster and cheaper over the past decade or so. Effort is now underway to define "high level shading languages" to permit the writing of shaders which will be directly executed on the rendering chips (known as Graphics Processing Units or GPUs) instead of being executed as software. Figure 9.2 shows how things stand right now. OpenGL (from the OpenGL Architecture Review Board) and DirectX (from Microsoft) are the two main lower level graphics interfaces supported by leading GPU vendors such as NVIDIA, ATI and 3Dlabs. If you have a computer with one of these graphics chips, you can learn to write shaders directly in OpenGL (specifically, OpenGL2) or DirectX but you would be dealing a lot with the raw details of the underlying hardware. Since it is more desirable to deal instead with familiar shader level constructs such as surface normals and light directions, higher level shader languages are being developed.

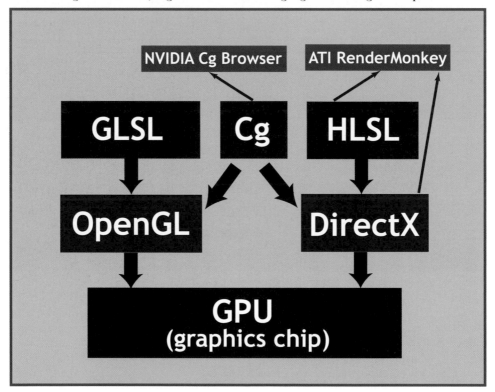

Figure 9.2 *Programmable hardware shading*

The idea is that shaders will be written using these more natural higher level constructs (in a language closely resembling the RenderMan shading language) and will subsequently be translated to lower level instructions that will be executed on the GPUs. You currently have a choice of three such higher level languages – Cg (from NVIDIA), HLSL (from Microsoft) or GLSL from the OpenGL consortium. The RfB page has links to more information on these. In addition, you can obtain the NVIDIA Cg Browser (Figure 9.3) or ATI's RenderMonkey interface (Figure 9.4) to browse through shader collections (written using Cg or HLSL respectively). If you did have a machine with one of these GPUs and played around with shaders that execute on them, you would be amazed at the interactivity – what might take seconds or even minutes to render in a software-only environment can be seen to run in real time, representing a speedup spanning several orders of magnitude! Such is the power of special purpose graphics hardware. Mirroring the trend in general purpose processors, it is safe to predict that GPUs will only continue to get faster, cheaper and better as time goes by.

If you are interested in programming for GPUs, obtain a suitably equipped computer, download the developer tools (free) from the vendor sites and start getting your feet wet. Currently you will have to hand-translate a RenderMan .sl shader, into, say, a Cg shader program. In the future we might see shader compilers that might automatically translate .sl or .slo files into Cg, HLSL, GLSL etc. When that happens your RenderMan shader-writing skills might be in more demand, since there will be a bigger market for them (see below).

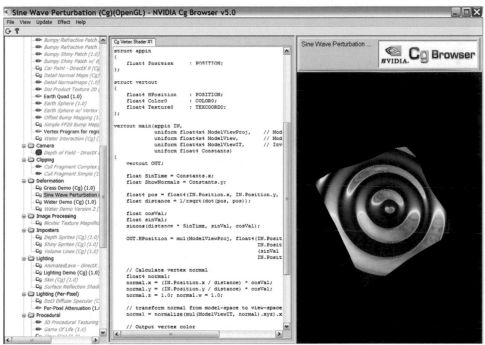

Figure 9.3 *NVIDIA Cg Browser interface*

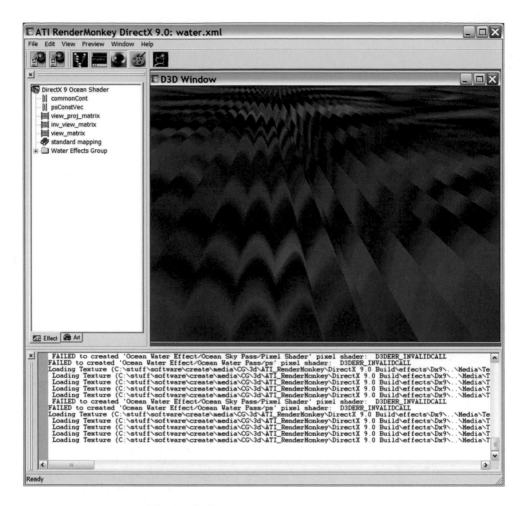

Figure 9.4 *ATI's RenderMonkey interface*

It is quite a feat to accelerate shading computations to make them run in real time, but the designers of these GPUs have an even bigger goal, and that is to marry photorealism with real-time rendering. This would become possible when entire sequences of RIB files (and not just the shaders they refer to) can be rendered at cinematic resolutions on hardware in real time. Arriving at this milestone will lead to dramatic advances in movie making and gaming and also give rise to other forms of entertainment not yet conceived.

Along these lines, NVIDIA's Digital Film Group (which includes Larry Gritz, some of his Exluna colleagues and other RenderMan experts) recently announced the availability of Gelato, a hardware-accelerated film quality final-frame renderer. Gelato is not another RenderMan implementation however – it is a brand new renderer developed from scratch by Larry and his colleagues. It even comes with its own shading language called the Gelato Shading Language (GSL) and can render RIB files via an open source plugin which reads RIB.

10
Resources

As you might imagine, there is plenty of material available on RenderMan since it has been around for a while. I will list the most pertinent ones below. If you look up enough of them you will find that the various sources contain references to each other, forming a nice "tangle" of links.

10.1 Books and papers

There are currently only four other books on RenderMan (Figure 10.1). If you are serious about learning more, try to purchase all of them.

Figure 10.1 *Other RenderMan-related books*

The RenderMan Companion by Steve Upstill ("RC" for short) is the first ever RenderMan book. It was first published in 1989, right after PRMan was made available to the public. There were no RIB translators to the few commercially available animation packages available at the time. The "C" language interface was the principal way to generate RIB files, so that is the focus of the first half of this book. While this interface can still be used to generate RIB (especially procedurally), it is not the predominant way anymore. The latter part of the book is about the Shading Language, and contains material that is still pertinent.

It contains good explanations of the various shader functions and also has a gallery of shaders with source code.

Texturing and Modeling by Ebert et. al. is the next book to consider. Now in its third edition, it is a multiple-author collection of topics about procedurally modeling, animating and rendering natural phenomena, textures and shapes. While the book is not about RenderMan per se, several of the authors use it (specifically the Shading Language) in their examples. You might even be able translate snippets of non-RSL code (from "C") into RSL yourself. In any case the book will serve as a useful reference when you are dealing with procedural techniques.

Advanced RenderMan by Tony Apodaca and Larry Gritz (with contributions from other authors) serves as a much-needed update of RenderMan information, since the "RC" book is somewhat dated and since the RenderMan specification has undergone changes (additions, mostly) over the last few years. It contains implementation details and advice on a variety of topics such as volume shaders, lighting techniques, non-photoreal rendering and subdivision surfaces. It is also a good source of information on shader anti-aliasing, a topic you will no doubt confront if you get into production quality shader creation.

Essential RenderMan Fast, Ian Stephenson's book, is an entry level one dealing with RIB files, "C" language API and the Shading Language. Most examples in the book will run on PRMan and also on "Angel", Ian's own RenderMan implementation which he makes available at his book site (see the RfB page for a link).

SIGGRAPH Proceedings are a rich source of rendering material, presented in the form of papers. Proceedings from recent years contain a wealth of knowledge on non-photoreal rendering, global illumination and hardware-accelerated shading, which are all current topics of intense research focus. While some of the papers are very mathematical and might be difficult to follow without sufficient training, even just reading the introductory sections and browsing through images should give you a feel for where things are headed. Two papers in particular that present PRMan's origins (both fairly easy to read) are "The Reyes Image Rendering Architecture" by Cook, Carpenter and Catmull (1987), and "A Language for Shading and Lighting Calculations" by Hanrahan and Lawson (1990).

10.2 Courses

RenderMan-related courses have been taught at SIGGRAPH in 1990, '92, '95, '98, '99 and 2001, '02 and '03. These are taught by leading professionals such as Tony Apodaca and Larry Gritz, and others in the CG industry who are intimately familiar with RenderMan and use it on a regular basis. The material for all these courses (except the one taught in 1990) is available as PDF files at the "RMR" site (see below). I highly recommend you download these. Collectively there are hundreds of pages of excellent information in those notes. The collection of course notes span all aspects of RenderMan. Many of the courses also feature case studies from actual productions that used RenderMan to generate cinematic imagery, so you gain those perspectives as well.

Some academic institutions offer RenderMan courses, and their class notes are often online. The Ohio State University, Purdue, Savannah College of Art and Design, University of Hong Kong and Gnomon School of Visual Effects are some such institutions. You can try to sign up for such a class if you happen to live near one of these places but at the least, you can check out the course material online, which often include galleries of student work.

10.3 Web sites

Even though I will be mentioning several sites below, the only web address (URL) you will encounter in this section is that of the RfB site, which I maintain at http://www.smartcg.com/tech/cg/books/RfB. Since addresses of sites and pages might change, I thought it would be best to maintain a current list online at the RfB site, which would function as a "link amplifier" (Figure 10.2) in addition to containing materials that accompany this book.

At the RfB site you will find all the materials (RIB files, shaders, maps, etc.) needed to reproduce the RenderMan imagery in this book. You will also find additional clarifications of material in the book (based on reader feedback) and an errata (corrections) section. There might also be an "extras" section with materials that did not make it to the book.

There are several excellent sites maintained by other individual users. The best of them ("mother lode", in gold miner parlance) is the "RenderMan Repository", or RMR for short. Maintained by Tal Lancaster, RMR features a comprehensive collection of links to SIGGRAPH and other course notes, sample RIB files, shaders (arranged by category), tools and utilities, converters, implementations, alternate language bindings and other peoples' sites. It also contains links to material presented at the "Stupid RAT Tricks" contest, held each year since 1999 during the RenderMan User Group meeting at SIGGRAPH. RMR is a site you must visit on a regular basis.

Katsu's Room (by Katsuaki Hiramitsu) is a site that contains unusual techniques with shaders to create things such as trees, lens flare, clouds and ocean water. RenderMania, a site maintained by Simon Bunker also contains links to shaders and tools, as does Deathfall. In addition, Deathfall is a CG community site that hosts individual users' pages containing valuable tutorials and shaders. The RenderMan Academy is another site (maintained by Rudy Cortes) which contains useful tutorials. The Affine Toolkit by Ted Burge is a nice collection of tools, shaders and RenderMan information. Steve May's RManNotes is an excellent resource devoted to systematic shader construction, and a file called "rmannotes.sl" that is part of RManNotes contains useful shader macros used in dozens of shaders you will encounter on the web.

In addition to users' pages, you will also find valuable information at vendor sites as well. For instance Pixar's site contains a timeline of RenderMan history, list of movies where RenderMan has been used, their classic shorts collection, the RenderMan Specification, etc.

Dot C Software (creators of the RenderDotC renderer) maintains a site which contains a wealth of links to RIB translators and several other RenderMan implementations. ART (makers of RenderDrive and PURE hardware RenderMan implementations) has a site which features an extensive gallery of images created using their products.

10.4 Forums

The web sites mentioned in the previous section present information in a passive way. This is fine, until you run into difficulties or simply have questions. Then you would turn to forums which let you post questions and receive responses (usually from experienced users, usually in short order). comp.graphics.rendering.renderman is one such forum (a Usenet newsgroup, to be more precise) that you should peruse on a regular basis. Its existence predates the Web, and features a helpful, active and knowledgeable user base. "highend3d" is another forum with a RenderMan board (for questions and discussions) and links to tools, shaders, etc. available for downloading. The Pixar site also has a forum (registration is required and is free) which is particularly friendly to beginners. A related resource is the "RenderMan FAQ" which used to be updated frequently by Larry Gritz. Unfortunately the last update was back in December 2002 but it still contains useful, relevant information.

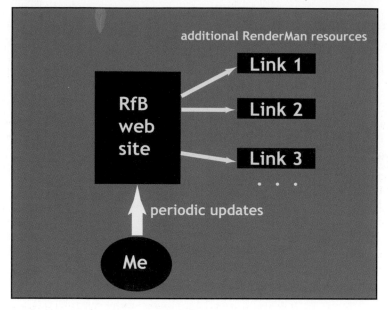

Figure 10.2 *The RfB site as a link "amplifier"*

10.5 Software documentation

In addition to the above, you will find useful material in the documentation that ships with your software. For instance, "RenderMan Artist Tools" (RAT) comes with an extensive set of documents including tutorials, shader reference, etc. Of all the documentation, the "Application Notes" need to be singled out for mention. These were hard to come by until just a few years ago, and now it is nice that they come bundled with the renderer. Be sure to read these notes carefully, as they contain very specific details on a variety of PRMan topics. The latest note (as of 2003) is #37, "Translucency and Subsurface Scattering". The RAT documentation also includes information on MTOR/Slim which is invaluable if you plan on rendering Maya scenes with PRMan.

10.6 Miscellaneous

The web is a vast source of knowledge and information about rendering. If you look up relevant terms in a search engine (Google is a current favorite) such as "RSL", "global illumination" etc., you will come across several links to these. Be sure to make the best of them. There is such an abundance of material out there from which to choose. In addition, experienced colleagues (if you work in a CG production environment) are always a good source of RenderMan-related knowledge. Finally, you can treat me as an additional resource and can send me email at **saty@smartcg.com** for help/information. Good luck with your RenderMan explorations!

Index

16 bits/channel, 231
2D, 1, 18
3D, 1, 18, 23
3D cursor, coordinate system as, 159, 191
3D graphics pipeline
    atmosphere, 14
    camera space, 16, 203, 313, 319
    clipping, 17
    culling, 18
    far clipping plane, 16
    FOV, 16, 204
    hidden surface elimination, 19, 37
    near clipping plane, 16
    perspective projection, 18
    raster (array of pixels), 20
    Reyes architecture, 33
    scanline z-buffer, 22
    shading step, 21
    stages, rendering pipeline, 15
    view volume (frustum), 16, 17
    viewpoint, 14
    virtual camera, 14, 201
    z-buffer, 20, 258
3D paint, 300
3D painting, 10
3Dlabs [*see also* CG vendors; custom rendering hardware], 358
8 bits/channel, 231

A Bug's Life [*see also* movies], 100, 309
A-buffer, 257
Adelson, Ted, 270
Advanced RenderMan [*see also* books], 262, 362
Affine Toolkit, The [*see also* RenderMan-related web sites], 287, 363
affine transformations [*see also* transformations], 200
AIR [*see also* RenderMan implementations], 30, 334
algorithms, rendering, *see* rendering algorithms
Alias [*see also* CG vendors], 23
aliasing, 244
alpha channel, 11, 226, 287
ambient light, 289
ambient occlusion [*see also* global illumination], 339, 340, 353
ambientlight [*see also* light shaders], 264
anaglyph stereo, 235
anamorphic squeeze, 222
anamorphic warp [*see also* Skew], 169
Angel [*see also* RenderMan implementations], 30, 362
animated shorts, Pixar's, 26, 27
animation, 5
animation sequence (RIB), 69
anisotropic shader, home-grown [*see also* surface shaders], 276
anisotropy, 291, 292, 294, 295
antialiasing, 226, 245, 258
antirotational symmetry, 166

aperture, 215
Apodaca, Tony [*see also* CG researchers], 362
Application Notes (RenderMan Artist Tools), 364
Aqsis [*see also* RenderMan implementations], 30, 336
arbitrary output variables (AOV), *see* auxiliary output buffers
architectural lighting, 353
area lights [*see also* light shaders], 269, 353
AreaLightSource [*see also* RIB commands], 322
Arnold (renderer), 355
ART [*see also* CG vendors], 31
Art and Science of Digital Compositing, The [*see also* books], 202
artistic representation [*see also* non photoreal rendering (NPR)], 12
aspect ratio, *see* frame aspect ratio (FAR)
ATI [*see also* CG vendors; custom rendering hardware], 31, 358
atmosphere [*see also* 3D graphics pipeline], 14
Atmosphere [*see also* RIB commands], 332
atmosphere shaders, *see* volume shaders
atmospheric perspective [*see also* volume shaders], 7, 330
atmospheric phenomena, 329
attribute block (RIB), 68
AttributeBegin [*see also* RIB commands], 68, 165
AttributeEnd [*see also* RIB commands], 68, 165
attributes, specifying in RIB, 64
auxiliary output buffers, 228, 229
axes, coordinate system, 157
axis transformations, *see* coordinate spaces

b-spline [*see also* spline curve types], 79
back face culling, *see* culling
background [*see also* imager shaders], 280, 333
Bagula, Roger, 153
Basis [*see also* RIB commands], 61, 80
basis matrices, 81, 108
Believe Inc. [*see also* CG vendors], 31
Believe Renderer [*see also* custom rendering hardware], 31
Bezier [*see also* spline curve types], 79
bgfill [*see also* imager shaders], 280
bicubic filter [*see also* pixel filters], 249
bicubic surface, 106, 111
bilinear patch, 106, 111
billboard textures, *see* sprites
Blinn, Jim [*see also* CG researchers], 133
blobbies (metaballs)
    ellipsoidal type, 136
    explanation, 133
    reference geometry for, 148
    segment type, 137
Blobby [*see also* RIB commands], 134, 240
block nesting, 161, 191
Block, Bruce, 210
Blue Moon Ray Tracer (BMRT) [*see*

also RenderMan implementations], 29
bluemarble [*see also* surface shaders], 297
books
    Advanced RenderMan, 262, 362
    Art and Science of Digital Compositing, The, 202
    Computational Geometry in C, 92
    Essential RenderMan Fast, 362
    Film Directing Shot by Shot, 210
    Five Cs of Cinematography, The, 210
    NURBS Book, The, 127
    RenderMan Companion, The, 29, 361
    Texturing and Modeling, 296, 362
    Tilings and Patterns, 94
    Virtual Lego, 182
    Visual Story, The, 210
Boolean (CSG) operations, 138, 141
bounding box view [*see also* rendering styles], 8
Bourke, Paul, 99
box filter [*see also* pixel filters], 247
branching ("if" .. "else"), shading language, 282
Brazil (renderer), 355
Bredow, Rob, 310
Brinkmann, Ron, 202
brushed metal [*see also* surface shaders], 275
brushstroke rendering [*see also* non photoreal rendering (NPR)], 348, 349
buckets, 37, 254, 255
built-in functions, shading language, 283
bump mapping [*see also* displacement mapping; mapping], 320
Bunker, Simon, 363
Burge, Thomas, 287, 363

"C" language interface, RIB, 29, 361
Callahan, Sharon, 266
camera coordinate system, *see* camera space
camera matching [*see also* live action/CG integration], 202, 209
camera move, what is a, 204
camera moves
    contrazoom (zolly), 209
    dolly, 5, 206
    Dutch Tilt, 205
    nodal pan, 234
    orbit, 207
    pan, 205
    slit-scan effect, 235
    swish pan, 206
    tilt pan, 206
    zap zoom, 205
    zoom, 204
camera space [*see also* 3D graphics pipeline; coordinate spaces], 16, 203, 313, 319
camera specification, 201
Carpenter, Loren [*see also* CG researchers], 25
Catmull, Ed [*see also* CG researchers], 25, 100, 109
Catmull-Rom filter [*see also* pixel filters], 247
Catmull-Rom spline [*see also* spline curve types], 79
catrib [*see also* PRMan software], 72

causticlight [*see also* light shaders], 342
caustics [*see also* global illumination], 336, 341, 342, 353
cell (discrete) noise, 298, 299
cellnoise() RSL function, 298
cellular displacements, 317, 318
CG, 1, 2, 23, 26
Cg (C for graphics), 359
Cg browser, 359
CG commercial software, 24
CG production companies, 23
CG researchers
  Apodaca, Tony, 362
  Blinn, Jim, 133
  Carpenter, Loren, 25
  Catmull, Ed, 25, 100, 109
  Clark, James, 23, 100
  Cook, Rob, 25, 262
  Debevec, Paul, 343
  Ebert, Dave, 296, 362
  Gooch, Bruce, 344, 356
  Gouraud, Henri, 9
  Gritz, Larry, 29, 30, 292, 341, 360, 362
  Haeberli, Paul, 307
  Hanrahan, Pat, 25, 340, 362
  Jensen, Henrik Wann, 340
  Johnston, Scott, 347
  Lawson, Jim, 25, 362
  Leech, Jon, 251
  Lewis, Matt, 265
  May, Steve, 265, 363
  Musgrave, Ken, 297
  Newell, Martin, 9, 108
  Perlin, Ken, 296, 333
  Phong, Bui Tui, 9
  Piegl and Tiller, 127
  Reynolds, Craig, 356
  Sequin, Carlo, 100
  Upstill, Steve, 29
  Ward, Greg, 292
  Whitted, Turner, 338
  Williams, Lance, 25, 301
CG vendors
  3Dlabs, 358
  Alias, 23
  ART, 31
  ATI, 31, 358
  Believe Inc., 31
  Evans and Sutherland, 23
  NVIDIA, 31, 358
  RenderMan Interface endorsers, 28
  Side Effects, 23
  Silicon Graphics, 23
  Softimage, 23
  TDI, 23
  Wavefront, 23
checkerboard illusion [*see also* optical illusions], 270
chrome reflection [*see also* surface shaders], 297
CinemaScope (widescreen format), 222
Clark, James [*see also* CG researchers], 23, 100
clipping [*see also* 3D graphics pipeline], 17
clipping planes, 217
ClippingPlane [*see also* RIB commands], 217
cloth [*see also* displacement shaders], 316
code execution, shading language, 281

Collins, Brent, 100
Color [*see also* RIB commands], 5, 61, 274
color bleeding [*see also* global illumination], 14, 310, 336
colorful shaders [*see also* surface shaders], 315
ColorSamples [*see also* RIB commands], 225
comments in RIB files, 60
compiler, shader, *see* shaders/shading, shader compiler
Computational Geometry in C [*see also* books], 92
computer graphics, *see* CG
ConcatTransform [*see also* RIB commands], 171, 187
concave polygon, 90
Cone [*see also* RIB commands], 129
conics (conic curves), 132
constant [*see also* surface shaders], 273
constructive solid geometry (CSG), 138, 311
containment, blocks for, 191
continuity across patches, 118
contrazoom (zolly) [*see also* camera moves], 209
control vertices, *see* CVs
convex polygon, 88
convex/concave illusion [*see also* optical illusions], 272
Cook, Rob [*see also* CG researchers], 25, 262
Coons patches, 143
coordinate spaces
  camera space, 16, 203, 313, 319
  current coordinate system, 313
  custom coordinate system, 198
  normalized device coordinate (NDC) space, 312, 315, 346, 347, 348
  object space, 14, 313
  shader space, 30, 313, 314
  world space, 15, 313
coordinate system, 157
coordinate system transformations, *see* coordinate spaces
CoordinateSystem [*see also* RIB commands], 198
CoordSysTransform [*see also* RIB commands], 198
Cortes, Rudy, 310, 363
Courtney, Tim, 182
CropWindow [*see also* RIB commands], 220
cross format, cubical environment map, 307
CSG operations
  difference, 138, 311
  intersection, 139, 311
  union, 139
cubic splines [*see also* spline curve types], 79
cubical environment map, 305, 306
cuckaloris (gobo), 327
culling [*see also* 3D graphics pipeline], 18
current coordinate system [*see also* coordinate spaces], 313
current transformation matrix (CTM), 188
curve (primitive), 76

Curve [*see also* RIB commands], 76
curve control, 76
curve tension, 76
custom area light [*see also* light shaders], 322
custom coordinate system [*see also* coordinate spaces], 198
custom rendering hardware
  3Dlabs, 358
  ATI, 31, 358
  Believe Renderer, 31
  Geometry Engine, 23
  hardware acceleration, 24, 360
  NVIDIA, 31, 358
  PlayStation, 23
  RenderDrive, 31
  Reyes Machine, 31
  RM-1, 31
  XBox, 23
cutout view [*see also* rendering styles], 11
CV multiplicity, 87
CVs, 76
Cylinder [*see also* RIB commands], 128
cylindrical panorama [*see also* panorama], 305
cylindrical projection [*see also* projection], 302

darklight [*see also* light shaders], 270
data sources for shaders, 283
de Casteljau curve subdivision, 82
Deathfall [*see also* RenderMan-related web sites], 363
Debevec, Paul [*see also* CG researchers], 343
Declare [*see also* RIB commands], 64
default camera, RenderMan's, 202
deformation blur, *see* motion blur, shape-change
DelayedReadArchive [*see also* RIB commands], 70, 145
depth cue [*see also* volume shaders], 329, 330
depth cueing [*see also* rendering styles], 7
depth map [*see also* maps], 228, 268, 289, 318, 321
depth of field, 215
depth-mapped shadows [*see also* shadows], 12, 321, 322
DepthOfField [*see also* RIB commands], 215
Detail [*see also* RIB commands], 250
DetailRange [*see also* RIB commands], 251
diagnostics, rendering, 260
diagnostics, shaders for, 277, 286, 288
dicing primitives, 64
Dickson, Stewart, 100
difference (CSG) operation [*see also* CSG operations], 138, 311
diffuse illumination, 273, 290
directional light, 264, 290
Disk [*see also* RIB commands], 133
Displacement [*see also* RIB commands], 316
displacement bounds, 316
displacement mapping [*see also* bump mapping; mapping], 13, 37, 320
displacement shaders
  cloth, 316

noise displacement, 278
periodic displacements, 316
pincushion effect, 346
realistic displacements, 13
ridged multifractal displacement, 317
sin() displacement, 316
sinknurl, 316
Vasarely shader, 346
woodcut effect, 346, 347
Display [*see also* RIB commands], 63, 224, 225
display driver, 225
distantlight [*see also* light shaders], 264
dithering, 232
dolly [*see also* camera moves], 5, 206
Doo and Sabin, 100
dot product, 290, 292, 293, 310, 324, 325
double-sided shading, 310, 311
Dutch Tilt [*see also* camera moves], 205

Ebert, Dave [*see also* CG researchers], 296, 362
edge matte [*see also* live action/CG integration], 293
edges, polygon, 15
Entity files (RIB), 60, 70
Entropy [*see also* RenderMan implementations], 30
environment map [*see also* live action/CG integration; maps], 277, 278, 305, 306, 343
environment mapping [*see also* mapping], 277, 306, 307, 308
environmental light [*see also* light shaders], 273
Eppstein, David, 94
Ercolano, Greg, 236
error handling in RIB, 259
ErrorHandler [*see also* RIB commands], 259
Essential RenderMan Fast [*see also* books], 362
Evans and Sutherland [*see also* CG vendors], 23
Exposure [*see also* RIB commands], 216, 232
exposure calculation, output stage, 232
extra data, attaching to primitives, 65
extrusion [*see also* modeling operations], 120
eye coordinate system, *see* camera space
eye space, *see* camera space
eyesplits (RIB option), 257
Eyesplits [*see also* RIB commands], 257

f-stop, 215
faces, polygon, 15
facing ratio, 290
faking shadows, 227
far clipping plane [*see also* 3D graphics pipeline; near clipping plane], 16
Ferguson, Helaman, 100
field of view, *see* FOV
file formats, 39
file, output to, 225
Film Directing Shot by Shot [*see also* books], 210
filtering, 36, 210, 247
Finding Nemo [*see also* movies], 27, 100, 337
Five Cs of Cinematography, The [*see

also books], 210
flat shading [*see also* Gouraud shading; Phong shading; rendering styles], 8, 9, 291
focus distance, 217
fog [*see also* volume shaders], 279, 329
Fong, Julian, 182
For The Birds, 27
Format [*see also* RIB commands], 61, 63, 219
FOV [*see also* 3D graphics pipeline], 16, 204
fractal Brownian motion (fBM), 298
fractional matte objects [*see also* matte objects], 231
frame aspect ratio (FAR), 219
frame block (RIB), 68
framebuffer, output to, 225
Fresnel approximation, 292
Fresnel effect, 292, 353
Fresnel factor, 308
fringe light shader [*see also* light shaders], 323
function calls, shading language, 282, 284
function chaining, shading language, 283
funkyglass (colorful glass) [*see also* surface shaders], 297

Gaussian filter [*see also* pixel filters], 247
Gelato (renderer), 360
GeneralPolygon [*see also* RIB commands], 91
geometric form, 73
GeometricApproximation [*see also* RIB commands], 252
Geometry Engine [*see also* custom rendering hardware], 23
Geri's Game, 100
GL, 23
global illumination
    ambient occlusion, 339, 340, 353
    caustics, 336, 341, 342, 353
    color bleeding, 14, 310, 336
    renderers, 356
    image-based illumination (IBI), 342, 343
    photographic examples, 336
    quest for realism, 357
    radiosity, 339, 353
    ray tracing, 338
    PRMan Release 11 (R11), 27, 336
    subsurface scattering, 340, 341
global variables, shading language, 283
glossy highlight, 292
glow [*see also* surface shaders], 293
GLSL [*see also* Cg; HLSL], 359
gobo (cuckaloris), 327
Gold, Christopher, 97
Gooch illumination model [*see also* non photoreal rendering (NPR)], 344
Gooch, Bruce [*see also* CG researchers], 344, 356
Gouraud shading [*see also* flat shading; Phong shading], 8, 240, 291
Gouraud, Henri [*see also* CG researchers], 9
GPU (Graphics Processing Unit), 358
graphics file formats
    .ma (Maya), 49
    .obj (Wavefront), 47

additional file formats, 52
    PBM, 40
    PostScript, 42
    SVG (Scalable Vector Graphics), 40
grid size, 34, 255
Gritz, Larry [*see also* CG researchers], 29, 30, 292, 341, 360, 362
Grunbaum and Shephard, 94
Gumbo, 109, 110

Haeberli, Paul [*see also* CG researchers], 307
hair [*see also* surface shaders], 292
halftone dots [*see also* non photoreal rendering (NPR)], 349, 350
handedness in coordinate systems, 150
Hanrahan, Pat [*see also* CG researchers], 25, 340, 362
hard/soft edged shadows [*see also* shadows], 13
hardware acceleration [*see also* custom rendering hardware], 24, 360
hardware shading, programmable, 358
Hargittai, Istvan and Magdolna, 174
headlight (RenderMan default) shader [*see also* surface shaders], 67
height (Pz) surface, 110, 115
Hermite [*see also* spline curve types], 79
hidden line [*see also* rendering styles], 7
hidden surface elimination [*see also* 3D graphics pipeline], 19, 37
Hider, 246, 258
high level shading languages [*see also* shaders/shading], 358
highend3d [*see also* RenderMan-related web sites], 363
highlight [*see also* specular reflection], 9, 10, 292
hints in RIB files, 60
Hiramitsu, Katsuaki, 363
HLSL [*see also* Cg; GLSL], 359
holes in polygons, 91
homogeneous coordinates, 85
hotspot, *see* specular reflection
hue shift shader [*see also* volume shaders], 331
hull (CV hull), 79
hyperbola, 77
Hyperboloid [*see also* RIB commands], 130

Identity [*see also* RIB commands], 187, 190
identity matrix, 190
illuminance cone, 290, 292, 315
Illuminate [*see also* RIB commands], 272
illumination sources, images as, 273
illumination, selective, 271
image file output, Display statement, 225
image processing using shaders, 303, 304
image resolution, 219
image synthesis, 201
image-based displacements, 318, 319
image-based illumination (IBI) [*see also* global illumination], 342, 343
image-based lighting (IBL), *see* image-based illumination (IBI)
Imager [*see also* RIB commands], 334

imager shaders
  background, 280, 333
  bgfill, 335, 336
  ramp, 334
inherent color of a surface, 274
instancing, 73, 146
interface, modeling/rendering [see also
  RenderMan; RI Specification], 27
intersection (CSG) operation [see also
  CSG operations], 139, 311
isometric projection [see also
  projection], 19, 208
isoparametric curve ("isoparm"), 123
Iverson, Scott, 30, 334

jaggies [see also aliasing; antialiasing],
  244
Jensen, Henrik Wann [see also CG
  researchers], 340
jittering of subpixel locations, 245
Jobs, Steve, 26
Johnston, Scott [see also CG
  researchers], 347

Katz, Steve, 210
Kesson, Malcolm, 310, 325
key (channel), see alpha channel
knots (knot sequences), 87, 123

Lambert's illumination law, 321
Lamont, Rick, 30
Lancaster, Tal, 363
Lawson, Jim [see also CG researchers],
  25, 362
Leech, Jon [see also CG researchers],
  251
left eye/right eye stereo [see also stereo
  pair], 235
lens imperfections, 14
letterboxing [see also pillarboxing], 219,
  220
Leuper, Jim, 353
level of detail (LOD), 249
Lewis, Matt [see also CG researchers],
  265
light enclosure [see also surface
  shaders], 328
light handle (ID), 264
light shaders
  ambientlight, 264
  area lights, 269, 353
  causticlight, 342
  cellulite, 327
  custom area light, 322
  darklight, 270
  distantlight, 264
  environmental light, 273
  fringe light shader, 323
  kessonlt, 326
  linear area light, 269
  noise-based lights, 325
  noisy directional light, 327
  noisy point light, 327
  non-diffuse light, 272
  non-specular light, 273
  non-physical light source, 325
  Phong light shader, 323
  pointlight, 264
  procedural light sources, 327
  pseudo area lights, 269
  rainbow light shader, 324
  rectangular area light, 269, 322

rim light shader, 323
slide projector light, 273, 327, 328
specialty lights, 325
sphere area light, 269
spotlight, 265, 321
spotlight, negative, 270
texture map as light source, 325
light shaders, invocation by RenderMan,
  323
light source, texture map as, 325
light/surface interaction, 358
lighting, 261, 265
lighting model, 289
lighting passes, 229
LightMan [see also Translators to RIB],
  31
lights/camera/action, 356
LightSource [see also RIB commands],
  62, 64, 264, 322
line segment, 77
linear area light [see also light shaders],
  269
linear transformations [see also
  transformations], 200
lit view [see also rendering styles], 10
lit, textured view [see also rendering
  styles], 10
live action/CG integration
  altering gamma, 234
  blending CG and CinemaScope, 222
  camera matching, 202, 209
  credible composite, 226
  edge matte, 293
  environment map, 277, 278, 305,
    343
  motion blur as visual cue, 214
  "plasticky", 300
  wrapped diffuse shader, 310, 311
lofting [see also modeling operations],
  119
lookat point, see focus distance
looping ('for'), shading language, 282
Lucas, George, 25
Lucasfilm, 25

MakeShadow [see also RIB
  commands], 227
Malkiewicz, Kris, 210
map projections, 302
map types, common, 300
mapping
  bump mapping, 320
  bump vs. displacement, 320
  displacement mapping, 13, 37, 320
  environment mapping, 277, 306,
    307, 308
  texture mapping, 10, 299, 301
maps
  depth map, 228, 268, 289, 321
  environment map, 277, 278, 305,
    343
  MIP map, 301, 302
  photon map, 342
  shadow map, 227, 268, 321
  texture map, 276, 300, 301
marble [see also surface shaders], 274,
  313
materials [see also surface shaders], 9,
  10
mathematical objects
  Borromean rings, 242
  Boy's surface, 99

colorfield stereogram, 228
Costa (minimal) surface, 165
Farey's circles, 175
golden rectangle, 164, 183, 188
Hilbert curve in 3D, 78
hinged tessellation, 178
impossible tribar, 335
kaleidoscope, 172, 198, 304
knot, 275
kolam, 274, 292
Mobius strip, 156
origami paper stack, 185
osculating (kissing) circles, 175
Pendulum Harmonograph, 136
Penrose star, 320
Penrose tessellation, 136
Penrose tiles, 93, 241
RepTile (Sphinx) puzzle, 189
spiral, 188
Spirograph, 216, 273, 292, 310, 311,
  318
spirolaterals, 180
Star of David, 164
stellated polyhedron, 262
tangram, 89, 193, 194
ternary Truchet tiling, 177, 178
tessellations (tiling patterns), 93, 184
tetrahedron puzzle, 181
trefoil knot, 83, 292
tritorus, 153
Truchet tiling, 177, 178
matrix, transformation, 171
Matte [see also RIB commands], 230
matte [see also surface shaders], 273
matte channel, see alpha channel
matte objects [see also fractional
  mattes], 230
MaxMan [see also Translators to RIB],
  31
May, Steve [see also CG researchers],
  265, 363
MayaMan [see also Translators to RIB],
  24, 31, 355
Mental Ray, 262, 355
mesh (polymesh), 94
metaballs (blobbies), 133, 148
micropolygon, 33, 34, 35, 38, 239, 261,
  278, 281, 287, 288, 289, 291, 315,
  320, 336
MIP map [see also maps], 301, 302
modeling operations
  extrusion, 120
  lofting, 119
  revolution, profile curve, 121
  skinning, 119
  sweep, 120
modeling/rendering interface [see also
  RenderMan; RI Specification], 27
modularity (RIB), 70
mosaic grid [see also non photoreal
  rendering (NPR)], 349, 350
motion block, 210
motion blur, 210
motion blur as visual cue [see also live
  action/CG integration], 214
motion blur, multi-segment, 212
motion blur, shape-change, 212
MotionBegin [see also RIB commands],
  210
MotionEnd [see also RIB commands],
  210
motionfactor approximation, 214

moviemaking, 201, 207
movies
    A Bug's Life, 100, 309
    alphabetical list of, 28
    Finding Nemo, 27, 100, 337
    Shark Tale, 27, 337
    Shrek 2, 337
    Star Trek II: Wrath of Khan, 26
    Terminator 2, 305
    Toy Story 2, 100
    Toy Story, 266
    Works, The, 25
    Young Sherlock Holmes, 26
MTOR [*see also* Translators to RIB],
    24, 31, 355, 364
multifractal, ridged, 297
multipass rendering, 312
multiperspective panorama [*see also*
    panorama], 237
multiple render targets (MRT), *see*
    auxiliary output buffers
multiplicity, CV, 87
Musgrave, Ken [*see also* CG
    researchers], 297

named coordinate system, *see* custom
    coordinate system
near clipping plane [*see also* 3D
    graphics pipeline; far clipping plane],
    16
nested hierarchies (RIB), 68, 193
nesting transformation blocks, 161, 191
Newell, Martin [*see also* CG
    researchers], 9, 108
nodal pan [*see also* camera moves], 234
noise, 278, 292, 295
noise as displacer, 316
noise displacement [*see also*
    displacement shaders], 278
noise, additional uses for, 297
noise, signed, 296
noise-based lights [*see also* light
    shaders], 325
non photoreal rendering (NPR)
    abstract imagery, 352
    artistic representation, 12
    brushstroke rendering, 348, 349
    Gooch illumination model, 344
    halftone dots, 349, 350
    mosaic grid, 349, 350
    overprinting, 347, 348, 349
    paint strokes, 350, 351
    pen and ink stippling, 345
    pincushion effect, 346
    RenderMan for, 344
    research focus, 24
    sepia tone look, 344
    squiggly lines, 345
    toon shading, 345
    turbulence, HSV, 350, 351
    Vasarely shader, 346
    woodblockprint, 347, 348
    woodcut effect, 346, 347
non-diffuse light [*see also* light shaders],
    272
non-specular light [*see also* light
    shaders], 273
non-square pixels, 222
nonlinear transformations
    (deformations) [*see also*
    transformations], 200
normalized device coordinate (NDC)

space [*see also* coordinate spaces],
    312, 315, 346, 347, 348
NPR, *see* non photoreal rendering
NuPatch [*see also* RIB commands], 87,
    106
NURBS Book, The [*see also* books],
    127
NURBS surface, 116
NVIDIA [*see also* CG vendors; custom
    rendering hardware], 31, 358
Nyquist frequency (limit), 246
Nyquist sampling theorem, 244

O'Rourke, Joseph, 92
object instancing, 146
object space [*see also* coordinate
    spaces], 14, 313
ObjectBegin [*see also* RIB commands],
    146
ObjectEnd [*see also* RIB commands],
    146
ObjectInstance [*see also* RIB
    commands], 146
occlusion culling, 37
occlusion() RSL function, 343
Opacity [*see also* RIB commands], 274
opacity channel, *see* alpha channel
OpenGL, 23, 53, 358
optical illusions
    checkerboard illusion, 270
    convex/concave illusion, 272
    impossible tri-bar, 335
optical phenomena, 261
Option commands in RIB, 63
orbit [*see also* camera moves], 207
Orientation [*see also* RIB commands],
    151
orientation of primitives, 151
origin, coordinate system, 157
orthographic projection [*see also*
    projection], 208
overprinting [*see also* non photoreal
    rendering (NPR)], 347, 348, 349

paint strokes [*see also* non photoreal
    rendering (NPR)], 350, 351
painterly rendering, *see* non photoreal
    rendering (NPR)
painting, texture, 352, 355
pan [*see also* camera moves], 205
panorama
    cylindrical, 305
    full, 234, 278
    multiperspective, 237
    pseudo, 307
    spherical, 305
Paraboloid [*see also* RIB commands],
    131
parameters, user-settable, 283
parametric coordinates (NURBS), 300
parser, RIB, 61
particle systems, 73
Patch [*see also* RIB commands], 61,
    106
patches, 105
PatchMesh [*see also* RIB commands],
    106, 112
patchy fog [*see also* volume shaders],
    332, 333
pattern synthesis, 285, 296
patterns, shader programming, 284, 286
Pederson, Con, 235

pen and ink stippling [*see also* non
    photoreal rendering (NPR)], 345
periodic displacements [*see also*
    displacement shaders], 316
Perlin, Ken [*see also* CG researchers],
    296, 333
persistence of vision, 5
perspective, 1, 75
Perspective [*see also* RIB commands],
    167
perspective projection [*see also* 3D
    graphics pipeline; projection], 18
perspective transformation [*see also*
    transformations], 167
phenomena, visual, 353, 357
Phong light shader [*see also* light
    shaders], 323
Phong shading [*see also* flat shading;
    Gouraud shading], 8, 291
Phong, Bui Tui [*see also* CG
    researchers], 9
photon hider [*see also* Hider], 342
photon map [*see also* maps], 342
photoreal [*see also* non photoreal
    rendering (NPR)], 14, 201, 355
photorealism, 28, 292, 336, 337, 356,
    360
pi, 43
Piegl and Tiller [*see also* CG
    researchers], 127
pillarboxing [*see also* letterboxing], 219,
    220
pincushion effect [*see also* displacement
    shaders; non photoreal rendering
    (NPR)], 346
Pixar, 23, 29, 338, 363
Pixar's animated shorts, 26, 27
Pixar's RenderMan, *see* PRMan
pixel aspect ratio (PAR), 219, 221
pixel filters
    bicubic filter, 249
    box filter, 247
    Catmull-Rom filter, 247
    Gaussian filter, 247
    triangle filter, 247
pixel/fragment shaders, 333
PixelFilter [*see also* RIB commands],
    247
PixelSamples [*see also* RIB commands],
    61, 64, 245
planar projection [*see also* projection],
    302
plastic [*see also* surface shaders], 262,
    263, 273, 290, 353, 354
"plasticky" [*see also* live action/CG
    integration], 300
PlayStation [*see also* custom rendering
    hardware], 23
point cloud [*see also* rendering styles], 6
point of view (POV), 201
point primitive, 73
pointlight [*see also* light shaders], 264
Points [*see also* RIB commands], 73
points-polygons notation, 94
PointsGeneralPolygons [*see also* RIB
    commands], 95
PointsPolygons [*see also* RIB
    commands], 95
polygon, 88
Polygon [*see also* RIB commands], 59,
    88
polygonal mesh (polymesh), 94

polylines, 76
polynomial curves, 85
posterization [*see also* toon style], 12
preamble, RIB, 66
premultiplication, 287
primitives, geometric, 32
PRMan [*see also* RenderMan], 14, 25, 27, 29, 32
PRMan software
    catrib, 72
    ptviewer, 342
    shader, 280
    sho, 67, 306
    txmake, 278, 301, 305, 306
Procedural [*see also* RIB commands], 143
procedural RIB generation, 143
procedural shading [*see also* shaders/shading], 11, 276, 277, 279
procedural techniques, 362
procedural texturing, 352
programmability in shaders, 262
programmable graphics hardware, 333
programmable hardware shading, 358
projection
    cylindrical, 302
    isometric, 19, 208
    orthographic, 208
    perspective, 18
    planar, 302
    spherical, 302
Projection [*see also* RIB commands], 63, 204, 215
projection texturing, 302
protocol, RIB, 29
pseudo area lights [*see also* light shaders], 269
ptviewer [*see also* PRMan software], 342
Pythagoras theorem, 168, 179

quadric surface, 127
quantization, output stage, 232
Quantize [*see also* RIB commands], 231
quest for realism [*see also* global illumination], 357

Radiance, 292, 356
radiosity [*see also* global illumination], 339, 353
rainbow light shader [*see also* light shaders], 324
Ramachandran, Vilayanur, 272
ramp imager [*see also* imager shaders], 334
ramp shader [*see also* surface shaders], 312
random sequence generator, 298
raster (array of pixels) [*see also* 3D graphics pipeline], 20
rational b-splines, 86
rational curves [*see also* spline curve types], 86
ray tracing [*see also* global illumination], 268, 338
ReadArchive [*see also* RIB commands], 70, 213
real time rendering, 24, 360
realistic image synthesis, 357
reconstruction, pixel, 243
rectangles, rendered images as, 218

rectangular area light [*see also* light shaders], 269, 322
reference frame, 157
reference geometry in RIB, 148
reflection caustic [*see also* global illumination, caustics], 336, 341
reflection transformation [*see also* transformations], 184
reflectional symmetry, 173
reflections, 14, 336, 338, 353
refraction, 308, 338, 353
RelativeDetail [*see also* RIB commands], 251
Release 11 (R11), PRMan [*see also* global illumination], 27, 336
render passes, 290
RenderDotC [*see also* RenderMan implementations], 30, 363
RenderDrive [*see also* custom rendering hardware], 31
renderers/rendering, 1, 2, 3, 5, 10, 11, 12, 14, 25, 28, 261, 338
rendering algorithms [*see also* global illumination], 5, 22, 23, 32
rendering pipeline, *see* 3D graphics pipeline
rendering styles [*see also* non photoreal rendering (NPR)]
    bounding box view, 8
    cutout view, 11
    depth cueing, 7
    flat shading, 8, 9, 291
    hidden line, 7
    lit view, 10
    lit, textured view, 10
    point cloud, 6
    smooth shading, 8
    toon style, 12
    wireframe, 6
    x-ray view, 9
rendering, tradeoffs in, 239
RenderMan
    academic institutions teaching, 362
    interface, modeling/rendering, 27
    meaning of, 27
    origins, 26
    Oscar awards, 26
    PRMan, 14, 25, 27, 29, 32
    reference implementation, 29
    Release 11 (R11), 27, 336
    shading language, 11, 261, 263, 264
    SIGGRAPH courses, 362
    User Group, 363
RenderMan Academy, The [*see also* RenderMan-related web sites], 363
RenderMan Companion, The [*see also* books], 29, 361
RenderMan implementations
    AIR, 30, 334
    Angel, 30, 362
    Aqsis, 30, 336
    Blue Moon Ray Tracer (BMRT), 29
    Entropy, 30
    Pixar's PRMan, 29
    RenderDotC, 30, 363
RenderMan Interface (RI)
    advanced capabilities, 30
    core capabilities, 30
    genesis, 28
    RenderMan Shading Language (RSL), 3, 280, 361
    structuring conventions (RIB), 70

RenderMan Interface Bytestream (RIB), *see* RIB
RenderMan Repository [*see also* RenderMan-related web sites], 363
RenderMan Shading Language (RSL) [*see also* RenderMan Interface (RI); shading language], 3, 280, 361
RenderMan-related web sites
    Affine Toolkit, The, 287, 363
    Deathfall, 363
    highend3d, 363
    RenderMan Academy, The, 363
    RenderMan Repository, 363
    RenderMania, 363
    RfB, 25, 27, 72, 203, 261, 278, 355, 356, 359, 362, 363
RenderMania [*see also* RenderMan-related web sites], 363
RenderMonkey, 359
representation, visual, 356
representational styles, *see* rendering styles
resolution, 219
ReverseOrientation [*see also* RIB commands], 151
revolution, profile curve [*see also* modeling operations], 121
Reyes [*see also* rendering algorithms], 25, 31, 32, 33, 215, 239, 336, 356
Reyes Machine [*see also* custom rendering hardware], 31
Reynolds, Craig [*see also* CG researchers], 356
RfB [*see also* RenderMan-related web sites], 25, 27, 72, 203, 261, 278, 355, 356, 359, 362, 363
rgb(a) channels, output specification, 225
RI Specification, 28, 29, 30, 32, 53, 60, 73, 283, 313, 363
RIB, 4, 5, 23, 27, 29, 31, 34, 53, 181
RIB bindings, 355
RIB commands
    AreaLightSource, 322
    Atmosphere, 332
    AttributeBegin, 68, 165
    AttributeEnd, 68, 165
    Basis, 61, 80
    Blobby, 134, 240
    ClippingPlane, 217
    Color, 5, 61, 274
    ColorSamples, 225
    ConcatTransform, 171, 187
    Cone, 129
    CoordinateSystem, 198
    CoordSysTransform, 198
    CropWindow, 220
    Curve, 76
    Cylinder, 128
    Declare, 64
    DelayedReadArchive, 70, 145
    DepthOfField, 215
    Detail, 250
    DetailRange, 251
    Disk, 133
    Displacement, 316
    Display, 63, 224, 225
    ErrorHandler, 259
    Exposure, 216, 232
    extensibility of, 64
    Eyesplits, 257
    Format, 61, 63, 219

GeneralPolygon, 91
GeometricApproximation, 252
Hyperboloid, 130
Identity, 187, 190
Illuminate, 272
Imager, 334
LightSource, 62, 64, 264, 322
MakeShadow, 227
Matte, 230
MotionBegin, 210
MotionEnd, 210
NuPatch, 87, 106
ObjectBegin, 146
ObjectEnd, 146
ObjectInstance, 146
Opacity, 274
Orientation, 151
Paraboloid, 131
Patch, 61, 106
PatchMesh, 106, 112
Perspective, 167
PixelFilter, 247
PixelSamples, 61, 64, 245
Points, 73
PointsGeneralPolygons, 95
PointsPolygons, 95
Polygon, 59, 88
Procedural, 143
Projection, 63, 204, 215
Quantize, 231
ReadArchive, 70, 213
RelativeDetail, 251
ReverseOrientation, 151
Rotate, 164
Scale, 161
ScreenWindow, 222
ShadingInterpolation, 240
ShadingRate, 34, 64, 240
Shutter, 210
Sides, 151
Skew, 168
SolidBegin, 139
SolidEnd, 139
Sphere, 127
SubdivisionMesh, 101, 253
Surface, 64, 69, 276
Torus, 129
Transform, 171, 187
TransformBegin, 68, 159
TransformEnd, 68, 159
Translate, 5, 158
TrimCurve, 125
WorldBegin, 66, 202
WorldEnd, 66
ridged multifractal, 297
ridged multifractal displacement [see
    also displacement shaders], 317
rigid-body transformations [see also
    transformations], 200
rim light shader [see also light shaders],
    323
RiO [see also Translators to RIB], 31
RM-1 [see also custom rendering
    hardware], 31
RManNotes, 363
Rotate [see also RIB commands], 164
rotation [see also transformations], 158,
    164
rotational symmetry, 173
ruled surface, 106

sampling, 35, 243

sampling rate (sampling frequency), 244
sampling, temporal, 210
Saty's email address, 364
Scale [see also RIB commands], 161
scaling [see also transformations], 158
scanline z-buffer [see also 3D graphics
    pipeline; renderers/rendering], 22
scene description, 4, 5, 14, 24, 201
screen, output to, 225
ScreenWindow [see also RIB
    commands], 222
selective illumination, 271, 272
semantic errors (RIB), 71
sepia tone look [see also non photoreal
    rendering (NPR)], 344
sequential execution, shading language,
    281
Sequin, Carlo [see also CG researchers],
    100
shade tree, 262
shader "tricks", 286
shader [see also PRMan software], 280
shader attributes, 275
shader blocks, 353
shader generators
    ShaderMan, 353
    ShadeTree, 32, 353
    Shrimp, 32
    Slim (Maya), 353, 354
    UI-driven, 356
shader globals, shading language, 284,
    285
shader space [see also coordinate
    spaces], 30, 313, 314
shader writing, ideas for, 352
shader writing, overall philosophy, 284
ShaderMan [see also shader generators],
    353
shaders/shading
    high level shading languages, 358
    procedural shading, 11, 277
    RenderMan plugins, 281
    RIB, in conjunction with, 31
    shader compiler, 264, 280, 359
    shading calculations, 10, 11, 34, 38
    shading language, 11, 261, 263, 264
shading frequency, see shading rate
shading interpolation, 291
shading language [see also RenderMan;
    shaders/shading], 11, 261, 263, 264
shading networks, 353
shading rate, 34, 239
shading, double-sided, 310, 311
ShadingInterpolation [see also RIB
    commands], 240
ShadingRate [see also RIB commands],
    34, 64, 240
shadow (output) driver, 227
shadow map [see also maps], 227, 268,
    321
shadow() RSL call, 321
shadows
    depth-mapped shadows, 12
    faking, 227
    hard/soft edged shadows, 13
shape synthesis, 156
Shark Tale [see also movies], 27, 337
sho [see also PRMan software], 67, 306
Shrek 2 [see also movies], 337
Shutter [see also RIB commands], 210
Side Effects [see also CG vendors], 23
sidedness of primitives, 151

Sides [see also RIB commands], 151
SIGGRAPH, 25, 262, 266, 310, 362,
    363
Silicon Graphics [see also CG vendors],
    23
sin() displacement [see also
    displacement shaders], 316
single-sided surfaces, 151
sinknurl [see also displacement
    shaders], 316
Skew [see also RIB commands], 168
skinning [see also modeling operations],
    119
slide projector light [see also light
    shaders], 273, 327, 328
Slim (Maya) [see also shader
    generators], 353, 354
slit-scan effect [see also camera moves],
    235
slo (compiled shader), 264
smooth shading [see also rendering
    styles], 8
soft shadows, 268, 343
Softimage [see also CG vendors], 23
SolidBegin [see also RIB commands],
    139
SolidEnd [see also RIB commands],
    139
space transformations, see coordinate
    spaces
spatter [see also surface shaders], 275,
    297
specular highlight, 273, 290, 353
Sphere [see also RIB commands], 127
sphere area light [see also light shaders],
    269
spherical environment map, 305
spherical panorama [see also
    panorama], 305
spherical projection [see also
    projection], 302
spline curve types
    b-spline, 79
    Bezier, 79
    Catmull-Rom spline, 79
    cubic splines, 79
    Hermite, 79
    rational curves, 86
spline curves, 76
spline patches, 105
splitting primitives, 32, 34
spotlight [see also light shaders], 265,
    270, 321
sprites, 73, 107, 237, 348
stages, rendering pipeline [see also 3D
    graphics pipeline], 15
stained glass [see also surface shaders],
    338, 339
stairstep artifacts, 244
Star Trek II: Wrath of Khan [see also
    movies], 26
statistics, rendering, 260
Stephenson, Ian, 226, 362
stereo pair [see also left eye/right eye
    stereo], 319
stochastic sampling, 245
stone [see also surface shaders], 297
storage formats (RIB), 71
structuring conventions (RIB) [see also
    RenderMan Interface (RI)], 70
subdivision features (creases, holes,
    corners), 103

subdivision surface, 100, 252
SubdivisionMesh [*see also* RIB commands], 101, 253
subpixel, 35, 245
subsurface scattering [*see also* global illumination], 340, 341
subwindow, 220
Suffern, Kevin G., 352
supersampling, 245
support (channel), *see* alpha channel
Surface [*see also* RIB commands], 64, 69, 276
surface detail, 278
surface shaders
  anisotropic shader, home-grown, 276
  bluemarble, 297
  brushed metal, 275
  chrome reflection, 297
  colorful shaders, 315
  constant, 273
  funkyglass (colorful glass), 297
  glow, 293
  hair, 292
  headlight (RenderMan default) shader, 67
  light enclosure, 328
  marble, 274, 313
  materials, 9, 10
  matte, 273
  plastic, 262, 263, 273, 290, 353, 354
  ramp shader, 312
  spatter, 275, 297
  stained glass, 338, 339
  stone, 297
  wire, 277
  wood, 275, 276, 297
  wrapped diffuse shader, 310, 311
sweep [*see also* modeling operations], 120
swish pan [*see also* camera moves], 206
symmetry
  antirotational, 166
  five-fold, 93
  reflectional, 173
  rotational, 173
syntax errors (RIB), 71
syntax, shading language, 284

TDI [*see also* CG vendors], 23
temporal sampling, 210
Terminator 2 [*see also* environment mapping; movies], 305
texture coordinate, 299, 300
texture map [*see also* maps], 276, 300, 301, 355
texture map as light source [*see also* light shaders], 325
texture mapping [*see also* mapping], 10, 299, 301
texture maps for displacement, 318, 319
texture painting, 352, 355
Texturing and Modeling [*see also* books], 296, 362
three-dimensional, *see* 3D
Tilings and Patterns [*see also* books], 94
tilt pan [*see also* camera moves], 206
Tin Toy, 27
token value pairs, 62, 276
toon rendering, 228, 229
toon shading [*see also* non photoreal rendering (NPR)], 345
toon style [*see also* rendering styles], 12

Torus [*see also* RIB commands], 129
Toy Story 2 [*see also* movies], 100
Toy Story [*see also* movies], 266
trace(), RSL function, 338
tradeoffs, rendering, 239
Transform [*see also* RIB commands], 171, 187
transform block (RIB), 68, 161
transformation commands, 74
transformation hierarchies, 161, 190
transformation matrix, 171
transformations
  affine, 200
  commutation of, 186
  linear, 200
  nonlinear (deformations), 200
  perspective, 167
  reflection, 184
  rigid-body, 200
  rotation, 158, 164
  scaling, 158
  skew, 168
  translation, 157
TransformBegin [*see also* RIB commands], 68, 159
TransformEnd [*see also* RIB commands], 68, 159
Translate [*see also* RIB commands], 5, 158
translation [*see also* transformations], 157
Translators to RIB
  from other formats, 32
  LightMan, 31
  MaxMan, 31
  MayaMan, 24, 31, 355
  MTOR, 24, 31, 355, 364
  RiO, 31
translucency, 309, 311
transmission caustic [*see also* global illumination, caustics], 341
transmission through glass, 308
transparency channel, *see* alpha channel
triangle filter [*see also* pixel filters], 247
trim curves (NURBS), 125, 130
TrimCurve [*see also* RIB commands], 125
truck camera move, *see* dolly
Trumbull, Doug, 235
turbulence, 296
turbulence, HSV [*see also* non photoreal rendering (NPR)], 350, 351
two-dimensional, *see* 2D
two-sided surfaces, 151
txmake [*see also* PRMan software], 278, 301, 305, 306

union (CSG) operation [*see also* CSG operations], 139
Upstill, Steve [*see also* CG researchers], 29
user-settable attributes, 275
Utah teapot, 108, 109

variables, shading language, 281
Vasarely shader [*see also* displacement shaders; non photoreal rendering (NPR)], 346
version number in RIB files, 61
vertices, polygon, 15
view volume (frustum) [*see also* 3D graphics pipeline], 16, 17

viewpoint [*see also* 3D graphics pipeline], 14
virtual camera [*see also* 3D graphics pipeline], 14, 201
Virtual Lego [*see also* books], 182
visual dataflow, shading as, 353
visual debugging, 277
visual effects, 25, 26, 202, 290
visual illusions, *see* optical illusions
visual phenomena, 353, 357
Visual Story, The [*see also* books], 210
volume shaders
  atmospheric perspective, 7, 330
  depth cue, 329, 330
  fog, 279, 329
  hue shift, 331
  patchy fog, 332, 333
Voronoi, 97, 298, 317, 327, 350, 351

Ward, Greg [*see also* CG researchers], 292
Wavefront [*see also* CG vendors], 23
Whitney, John, 235
Whitted, Turner [*see also* CG researchers], 338
Williams, Lance [*see also* CG researchers], 25, 301
wire [*see also* surface shaders], 277
wireframe [*see also* rendering styles], 6
wood [*see also* surface shaders], 275, 276, 297
woodblockprint [*see also* non photoreal rendering (NPR)], 347, 348
woodcut effect [*see also* displacement shaders; non photoreal rendering (NPR)], 346, 347
Works, The [*see also* movies], 25
world block (RIB), 68
world coordinate system, *see* world space
world space [*see also* coordinate spaces], 15, 313
WorldBegin [*see also* RIB commands], 66, 202
WorldEnd [*see also* RIB commands], 66
wrapped diffuse shader [*see also* live action/CG integration; surface shaders], 310, 311

x-ray view [*see also* rendering styles], 9
Xbox [*see also* custom rendering hardware], 23
XML, 41

yaw, pitch, roll, 205
Young Sherlock Holmes [*see also* movies], 26

z-buffer [*see also* 3D graphics pipeline], 20, 258
z-compositing, 228
z-depth image [*see also* depth map], 11, 12
zap zoom [*see also* camera moves], 205
zfile (output) driver, 227
ZJ, 310
zoom [*see also* camera moves], 204